W9-ANJ-550

Spectrum Guide to
PAKISTAN

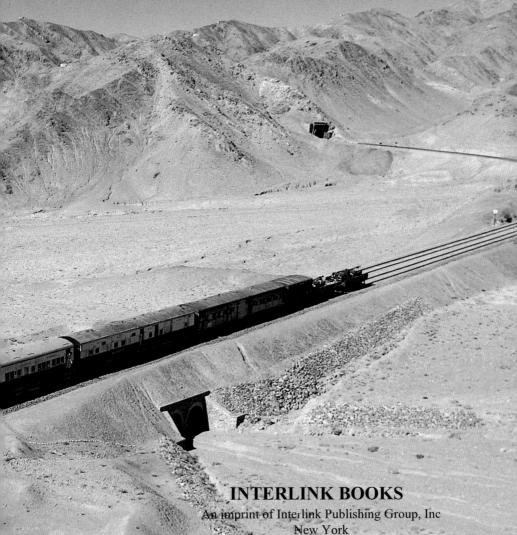

INTERLINK BOOKS

An imprint of Interlink Publishing Group, Inc

New York

Spectrum Guide to Pakistan

© 1998 Camerapix

First American edition published
in 1998 by

INTERLINK BOOKS
An imprint of
Interlink Publishing Group, Inc.
99 Seventh Avenue
Brooklyn, New York 11215
and
46 Crosby Street
Northampton, Massachusetts 01060

This book was designed and produced by
Camerapix Publishers International
PO Box 45048
Nairobi, Kenya

To order or request a catalog, please call
Interlink Publishing at 1-800-238-LINK

Website:www.interlinkbooks.com

Library of Congress Cataloging-in-
Publication Data

Spectrum guide to Pakistan/(compiled and
edited by Camerapix).— First American ed.
     p.   cm. — (Spectrum guides)
  Includes bibliographical references and
  index.
  ISBN 1-56656-240-6 (paperback)
  1. Pakistan—Guidebooks. I. Camerapix
Publishers International.
II. Series.
DS376.8.S67 1989b
915.49104´5—dc21   98-12460
                                          CIP

Printed in Hong Kong / China

The **Spectrum Guides** series provides a
comprehensive and detailed description of
each country it covers, together with all the
essential data that tourists, business visitors,
or potential investors are likely to require.

Spectrum Guides in print:
African Wildlife Safaris
Eritrea
Ethiopia
India
Jordan
Kenya
Maldives
Mauritius
Namibia
Nepal
Seychelles
South Africa
Sri Lanka
Tanzania
Uganda
United Arab Emirates
Zambia
Zimbabwe

Publisher and Chief Executive:
The Late Mohamed Amin
Editorial Director: The Late Brian Tetley
Art Director: Duncan Willetts
Project Director: Rukhsana Haq
Editors: Susan Williams and Jack Crowther
Co-ordinator: Nazma Rawji
Production Assistants: Kimberly Davis
and Ibrahim Saad
Photographic research: Abdul Rehman
Editorial Assistant: Rachel Musyimi
Design Consultant: Craig Dodd

Editorial Board

TABLE OF CONTENTS

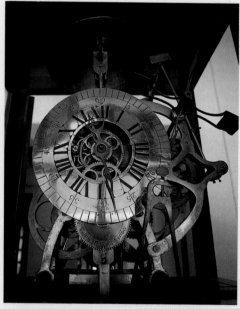

Half-title page: Mosaic in Thatta mosque. Title page: Steam train in the Kojak Pass.
Pages 8-9: Shishpar peak rising to 7,611 metres (24,972 feet). Pages 10-11: Lahore's Badshahi Mosque.

PAKISTAN

International Boundaries —·—·—·—
Provincial Boundaries —··—··—
District Boundaries ----------

Km. [ ] Km.
100 50 0 100 200

Miles [ ] Miles
50 25 0 50 100

A F G H A
A F G
PISHII
Pishin
QUETT
Quetta
30°N
Nushki
KALAT
CHAGAI
Kalat
B A L U o C H I
Kharan
KHARAN
Khuzdar
I R A N
Panjgur
KHUZDAR
PANJGUR
TURBAT
Turbat
Uthal
LASBELA
Gwadar
G W A D A R
25°N
KAR
Kae
A R A B I A N   S E A
Conical Orthomorphic Projection
65°E

12

HINDU KUSH

70°E

75°E

CHINA

80°E

GILGIT AGENCY
Rakaposhi
25,550 ft.

Hispar Glacier

Tirich Mir
25,260
CHITRAL

K2
28,250 ft.

Baltoro Glacier

Siachen Glacier

Chitral

Karakoram

FRONTIER NOT DEMARCATED

35°N

KOHISTAN

Gilgit

Nanga Parbat 26,660 ft.

Dir

Dir

SWAT

Dasu

JAMMU

BAJAUR
MALAKAND

Saidu

&

MOHMAND

Malakand

MANSEHRA

KASHMIR

PESHAWAR

MARDAN

Mansehra

Mardan

Abbottabad

ABBOTTABAD

KHYBER

Peshawar

ISLAMABAD

Islamabad

(DISPUTED TERRITORY)

N.W.F.P.

Parachinar

ADAMKHEL

Rawalpindi

Great Himalayas

KURRAM

Attock City

RAWALPINDI

KOHAT

ATTOCK

Miram Shah

AHMADZAI

Kohat

Jhelum

N.WAZIRISTAN

Bannu

Mianwali

JHELUM

Gujrat

BANNU

Gujrat

BHITTANI

SARGODHA

GUJRAT

Sialkot

SIALKOT

Wana

Sargodha

Gujranwala

S. WAZIRISTAN

DERA
ISMAIL KHAN

GUJRANWALA

Takht-i-
Sulaiman 11,100

Dera
Ismail Khan

JHANG

SHEKHUPURA

Shekhupura

Lahore

LARGHA SHIRANI

MIANWALI

LAHORE

Jhang

Faisalabad

KASUR

ZHOB

Zhob

FAISALABAD

Kasur

Zhob

PUNJAB

MUZAFFARGARH

Sahiwal

Loralai

Muzaffargarh

MULTAN

SAHIWAL

30°N

LORALAI

Dera
Ghazi Khan

Multan

VIHARI

Kohlu

Vihari

Bahawalnagar

DERA
GHAZI KHAN

BAHAWALNAGAR

KOHLU

Bahawalpur

Indus

BAHAWALPUR

Murad

RAHIMYAR KHAN

nali

Jacobabad

Rahimyar Khan

BAD

JACOBABAD

Thar Desert

NA

Sukkur

a

SUKKUR

ND

Khairpur

KHAIRPUR

WABSHAH

wwabshah

INDIA

Sanghar

SANGHAR

Hyderabad

Mirpur Khas

25°N

HYDERABAD

BADIN

THARPARKAR

Badin

RANN OF KUTCH

70°E

75°E

© Oxford University Press

13

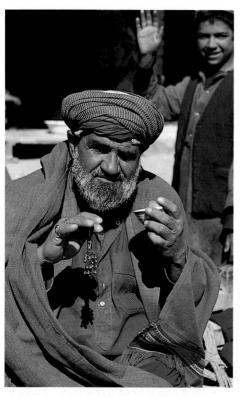

The Pakistan Experience

A Welcome

About 150 million years ago where Pakistan's mountains now jostle and grind there was a sea, its shores roamed by dinosaurs. As the molten core of the earth began to cool and form into rock it created immense pressures on the major continental plates — and so, century by century, the sea began to narrow as the Deccan plate of South India drifted closer to Asia.

Around thirty million years ago, where the soft sea bed gave no foundation, Asia began to slip south meeting the unyielding block of southern India.

Trapped between these two titanic forces the earth's crust buckled and folded over itself to form the greatest mountains on earth — the four mountain ranges of northern Pakistan.

Thus was the young nation of Pakistan born in ancient times, long before mankind evolved.

Pakistan's geophysical monuments — great mountains, rivers, and deserts — are as staggering in natural concept as its legacy of art and architecture is in human terms. Much of it was endowed during the two centuries the Great Mughals ruled India, but it also extends through time to the very dawn of civilization.

Though at first sight Pakistan appears to be all things Indian, the nation and its citizens are as different from the other as Ireland and the Irish from England and the English.

Yet, even close to half a century after people and country were given their own physical identity, a great many people around the world still think of Pakistan as an adjunct within India.

Closer acquaintance soon dispels the misunderstanding and brings its own reward. No illusory appendage of a hegemony of feudal princedoms and warring faiths, Pakistan swiftly reveals its own well-defined personality, shaped and moulded by a thousand years and more of adherence to the Islamic cause.

Even so, Christian, Hindu, Zoroastrian, pagan, and animist minorities prosper within this Muslim fold, their religious freedoms guaranteed by constitutional decree and Pakistan's inherent belief in individual, as well as national, liberty.

Both Muslim majority and secular minorities are inheritors of a land rich in beauty and natural resources. While these leave their own imprint on this nation of 103 million people and contribute to a measure of Pakistan's identity, they are also perhaps its one shared bond with India.

All seem ageless yet wherever you go, in this long and slender land that funnels up the north-western edge of the subcontinent, there's a pervasive and overwhelming aura of antiquity.

Two million years ago our first ancestors, pre-man and early man, made this area their home and slowly evolved ways of making stone tools and weapons and began hunting for food.

More recently, say 50,000 years ago, modern man, Homo sapiens, settled on the banks of rivers learning, in the passing of 40,000 or so years, to domesticate livestock and to sow and to reap.

Then, parallel to the great civilizations of the Egyptian Pharaohs and of Babylon in Mesopotamia, there developed equally great civilizations at Moenjodaro and Harappa on the Indus — cities of graceful brick, laid out on a grid system with drainage and other sophisticated elements of urban living.

And finally, about three-and-a-half millenniums ago, the first of the many armies of conquest that would seek to embrace the subcontinent and all its wealth within their empires, broke through the craggy, forbidding passes of the north-west mountains — Indo-Aryans carrying the seeds of the Hindu faith and philosophy.

They were followed by the devotees of peace and meditation of another great

Opposite top left: Pathan. Opposite top: Wandering Baluchi musician.
Opposite left: Sindhi girl. Opposite: Punjabi bride.

15

Above: Inlaid ivory portraits of the great Mughals on jewellery box in Lahore Museum.

philosophising faith that evolved out of the early Hindu vedics — the Buddhists, who imprinted themselves on the great Gandharan civilization of northern Pakistan, leaving a legacy of priceless art treasures including the sculpture of the Fasting Buddha now in Lahore Museum.

Three centuries before the birth of Christ came Alexander the Great who overran the Gandharan capital of Pushkalavati and visited Taxila but left no lasting trace.

Within the century Ashoka, a devotee of Buddha, had absorbed all of the Greek's conquests into his Mauryan empire. While his empire was shortlived, Ashoka's enduring achievement was the spread of Buddhism, which lasted through the Kushan era until it began to lose ground to Hinduism following the invasion of the Huns and the rise of new monarchies under Brahmin domination in the sixth century AD

Two centuries later, Muhammad bin Qasim carried the sword of Islam up the Indus to be followed, in the thirteenth century and in reverse direction, by Genghis Khan and his Mongolian hordes.

Of all these conquerors undoubtedly the greatest were the Mughals, of whom the first was Babur, a scion of Tamurlane and Genghis Khan. For more than 200 years they ruled the most glittering empire the world had ever known, only to be replaced in their decline and fall, by the British, the last who would subjugate the subcontinent.

And yet, ten million years after the common ancestors of mankind and the primates first roamed the open woodlands of the Punjab, some areas of Pakistan remain virtually as they were then — a grandeur of raw and untouched wildernesses that form some of the most dramatic landscapes on Planet Earth.

Now Pakistan invites not conquest but discovery. Welcome.

Travel Brief and Social Advisory

Some dos and don'ts to make
your visit more enjoyable.

No problem

The opening of the Karakoram Highway to foreign visitors in the mid-1980s has given birth to a rapidly expanding tourism industry in Pakistan. Now thousands of new visitors each year are discovering the dramatic landscapes of northern Pakistan in the Roof of The World where the road cuts through the ravines and gorges of the highest mountains on earth.

Before this, genuine tourists to Pakistan were few and far between — despite the many dramatic landscapes and historical centres throughout the rest of the country.

Some places in Pakistan are for the adventurous only. Others can be visited in style and comfort, even by the elderly or very young. Many parts of the country can now be reached with little difficulty. But the tourist needs to be prepared for some special conditions.

Be sensitive when travelling outside the major centres of Karachi, Lahore, Islamabad, and Peshawar, especially in those areas where tourism is still in its infancy.

Pakistan is a democracy and there are few, if any, restrictions on the well-behaved visitor — but you may find you need a permit to visit some areas.

Check with your travel agent and if you're visiting somewhere remote, be sure to let them, or friends and relatives, know where you're going and how long you intend to be away.

Getting Around

By road

There are few road maps on Pakistan, but the large-scale national and provincial maps by the Survey of Pakistan show main roads at least. Of these, the most useful are the contour maps on the scale of 1:1 million (ten kilometres to one centimetre or 15 miles to the inch). Be warned, however, that road grades are inaccurate.

Major city street maps are published by the Pakistan Tourism Development Corporation — PTDC.

Driving yourself is for the fatalistic — those who believe Allah decides all things. Few pay much attention to the traffic laws and it makes more sense to hire a driver and car. Remember the speed limit in built-up areas is fifty kilometres an hour (30 miles).

If you do decide to drive yourself, however, carry some tranquilizers to avoid sudden shortages of breath. You'll also need to develop the survival instinct of a rat up a drainpipe.

The real enemies are trucks, lorries, buses, minibuses — and darkness. The only allies are the rough shoulders of the road, evasive action — and daylight. So it's best to arrive wherever you're going before sundown.

With sudden sharp bends, roadworks, slow moving — and sometimes stationary — traffic without lights, driving on unfamiliar roads at night is akin to walking blindfold through a minefield. Then there are the hordes of *kamikaze* pedestrians and animals seeking early entry through the pearly gates.

Confusing signs

Signposts are usually in Urdu so most western visitors will have absolutely no idea which fork or turn to take. This is also compounded by the fact that when Pakistan went metric distances on some signposts were changed to kilometres but not on others.

And since these are given in Roman numerals and in Urdu it only adds to the confusion — as neither kilometric nor imperial signposts announce which scale is in use.

For a touch more Irish whimsy consider the fact that Pakistani drivers use the right indicator for two purposes: one to tell you it's clear to overtake, the other to show you that they intend to turn right.

Oncoming vehicles that flash their headlights mean the drivers think they have precedence — and not to get in their way. Don't. A final hazard, is the number of unannounced speedbumps which are often invisible, especially in deep shade.

The Pakistan equivalent of the autostrada, freeway, or motorway, is its National Highway

Above: PIA 737 at Skardu airport, sandwiched between the Himalaya and the Karakoram.

network on which you can assume, with reasonable safety, an average speed of between eighty and 100 kilometres an hour (50-60 miles).

Elsewhere, anticipate average speeds of under fifty kilometres (30 miles) an hour down to as little as twenty kilometres (12 miles) an hour on dirt roads and tracks.

Remember, in remote areas, especially the north, many of these tracks are only suitable for 4WD models, and then, unfortunately, only the short wheelbase jeep. Five hours in one of these may leave you feeling like you've just gone fifteen rounds with Mike Tyson.

Larger, more comfortable, 4WD vehicles — Range Rovers, Landrovers, and Land Cruisers —are often too wide and too long for many of the northern mountain tracks.

The cheapest form of road travel — and the most unpleasant — is by bus or minibus.

By Air

Till recently Pakistan International Airlines a public sector organization was the only national airline which had monopoly of air transport services in Pakistan, both for domestic and international routes. Now the government has involved the private sector in the development, improvement and functioning of air transport system in Pakistan with a view to ease the air traffic problem domestically and internationally. In private sector at present Shaheen Airlines, Aero Asia and Bhoja Airlines are operating successfully within their available resources.

Pakistan International Airlines (PIA) operates frequent scheduled daily flights in a fleet of modern aircraft to all major centres of the country with 747, DC-10, and Airbus working the direct flights between Karachi and Islamabad. On bus stop services between smaller centres, PIA uses 737 and Fokker Friendships.

Until the opening of the Karakoram Highway — KKH — air travel was the only practical way to reach the valleys in the north. And for those who cannot face the terrifying twelve-to-eighteen hour drive along the sheer face of the Indus gorge, it's still the only means.

But weather makes the service unpredictable. Clouds can cover the valleys and the peaks within minutes, leaving passengers at Islamabad or Peshawar airport to return, often day after day, until the weather clears.

Those stranded in inaccessible Skardu or Gilgit find the waiting even more frustrating, but one advantage is that hotel rooms can usually be extended because the next occupant is waiting at the other end.

Always confirm your return reservation at the PIA office as soon as you clear the airport.

By Rail

Pakistan Railways' extensive network of lines covers almost the entire country, except the mountainous north. Economic but slow, they offer a comfortable alternative to road transport. There are three classes — air-conditioned, first and second.

Visitors should think of nothing less than first class, and ideally opt for an air-conditioned coach, especially in sweltering summer. Better still, rent a Tourist Car, complete with dining and sitting room, which can be attached to any train.

You can park it in virtually any siding for as long as you wish. Travel in the grand style of the Raj, indeed.

Make your booking, both for seats and sleeping berths, well in advance. Bedding is provided on request. First class cabins are fitted with couchettes which must be reserved in advance, but bedding is unavailable. Take your oy/n food as well. There is plenty of water in all classes.

Special concessions are offered to tourists and well maintained Rest Houses are available as accomodation in many areas.

By Foot

Despite its many industries and swollen cities, Pakistan is still largely rural — and feudal. For many communities footpaths are the main links between the neighbouring communities.

You fan explore much of the countryside on foot but remember that these are often rough and stony and, even in winter, it can be very warm work. You need to carry plenty of liquids and food.

Don't over estimate your speed. Six kilometres (four miles) may take as long as two hours. Strong shoes are essential (See also In Brief for "Trekking advisory").

The people

Though less than three percent of Pakistan's population actually speak English, it seems that every one of its 130 million plus people invented the phrase "No Problem". Don't be reassured — it usually means you have a real and virtually insoluble problem.

But the constant use of this pharse also illustrates that wherever you go in this large and sprawling nation you can be sure of one certain aspect: Pakistanis want you to enjoy their country and their company.

While it can certainly be said that travel in Pakistan offers something for everyone, not all women will be overjoyed to see their sisters of the east clad in purdah — or themselves treated like curiosities from outer space.

The prime outcome of this curiosity — at least in the cities and larger towns — is a touch of what you might call "grapple and grope". Some Pakistani males are as adept at pinching and touching as the Lotharios (or should that be loatharians?) of Italy.

Unless you're in Karachi or the twin cities of Islamabad and Rawalpindi where some of the misses, if not the memsahibs, are decidedly modern in their outlook you'll rarely, if ever, see an unaccompanied woman.

In many cities and towns the local buses even have special sections for women only — as do some restaurants which you might fairly think would mar an evening out with the family.

So the golden rule for women is never travel alone in Pakistan. And never go off the beaten track by yourself. Even women-only groups can sometimes run into embarrassing situations.

Far better — find a reputable male escort or two. Failing that, carry a hefty stick and tie a suitably savage-looking dog to a lead. If you have children, however, they may be the most sensible protection of all: no woman with a child in tow is considered immoral.

That said, let it be clear — Ione women excepted — that Pakistanis are among the most hospitable and courteous people in the world. And, as is usual in the poorer nations, the poorer the person, the greater the hospitality.

Don't offend by refusal when you're asked to take tea or share a meal unless you're talking to one of the more sophisticated members of Pakistan society.

If it's a simple, non-glitzy village affair you'll discover that squatting, or sitting cross-legged, was originally invented in this country — perhaps because of a shortage of chairs or possibly because after practice it becomes increasingly more comfortable, which means that you can rest anywhere you choose.

If, however, you do eat seated in such fashion, tuck your legs under you. Showing the soles of feet or shoes is regarded as insulting.

Even more pertinent, avoid offering or giving anything, or indeed helping yourself, with the left hand. For reasons readily observable after a few days this organ of pretension is taboo, held to be unclean. So whenever you are in company the rule is use your right hand.

Children are a certain cinch wherever you go — Pakistanis love them and, as their birthrate demonstrates, can't live without them. Small kids will be fussed over, admired, and often sprayed with loving kisses.

As an added bonus to this delightful aspect of Pakistani society you will get no shy or diffident refusals from either men or children — though, here it comes again, always from the women — whenever you want to take their photograph.

Polaroid cameras are especially popular since the subjects can see the results before you move on. It's not vanity, just natural curiosity and an ingrained instinct for making you feel happy.

Clothes

Pakistanis and their neighbours, the Afghans, wear a unisex outfit known as the Shalwar Qamiz — a kind of voluminous, baggy pyjama suit that allows the body to remain cool and comfortable on the hottest day.

So when in Pakistan do as the Pakistanis do — keep your cool no matter how ridiculous you feel. The suits make sense as you'll find out if you try one.

For men, too, they give better protection against scrub and thorn than shorts. A sun hat also makes sense.

In the mountains, even in summer, make sure you carry some warm clothing for the cool and often chilly nights. In winter, warm clothing is also essential.

Some tour options

Thanks to the Karakoram Highway and the efforts of a travel company that began as a bus shuttle service between the twin cities of Rawalpindi and Islamabad in the mid-1960s. Tourism is spreading down from the northern mountains through the entire country.

For as Iqbal Walji, president of Travel Walji's in Islamabad, well knows, Pakistan potentially is one of the world's most exciting tourist destinations. "I've been spreading the message since we began operations," he says.

"This is a vast country with tremendous attractions. Leave alone the mountains, in Sind and Punjab we have two of the world's greatest deserts — the Thar and the Cholistan."

Camel safaris through these deserts with their ancient Mughal and Hindu forts are becoming increasingly popular.

And few cities in the world can boast the historic monuments that dominate 1,000-year-old Lahore. Then there's ancient Peshawar, gateway to the legendary Khyber Pass.

Such has been the success of Walji's campaign to put Pakistan on the tourist map that his organisation is now well-diversified with four divisions, eight offices in Pakistan's major tourist centres, as well as six active offices in Europe, America, and the Far East — and more than 400 staff experienced in all aspects of planning and executing tour itineraries.

The company at the moment handles almost fifty-five per cent of foreign tourists to Pakistan.

Its specialised Adventure Pakistan division handles the really exciting end of the business — boat rides down the Indus, jeep safaris through the old battlefields and mountains of the North-West frontier, camel treks through the deserts, and mountaineering expeditions to the far north.

Another division runs the country's largest car rental operation, Avis Rent-A-Car, while a sister company is an official IATA travel agency marketing — in reverse trend — individual and package tours to such exciting holiday destinations as Kenya, the Maldive Islands, China, Thailand, and Saudi Arabia.

Their latest itinerary is an interesting mix of adventure and culture, following the old route of caravans through the Central Asian region. It unveils the romance of the east. A combination of Pakistan and Central Asia States, it presents a unique driving experience through the historic cities of Tashkent, Samarkand, Bukhara, Urgench (Khira) and on to Pakistan, historic Lahore, modern Islamabad and traditional Peshawar through the beautiful north.

"We're all set for some exciting times ahead," says Mr. Walji.

Above: Adventure Pakistan jeep in the ruins of Maujgarh Fort in the Cholistan desert.

Laundry

First class hotels in major cities offer same day or twenty-four hour laundry and dry-cleaning services.

Alcohol

Intending visitors should note that prohibition prevails in Pakistan, perhaps the only country in the world where you need a licence to drink: an unusual souvenir for those who cherish such items.

If you like your beer or evening tot you won't find it easy. Only a few of the large, luxury hotels serve alcohol. For some reason, the Marriott Hotels, in Karachi and Islamabad, no longer provide this facility.

The answer-if you're prepared to go through the hassle-is to find the nearest prohibition office. Take your passport and apply for a drinking licence by declaring yourself a non-Muslim foreigner.

Kindly prohibition officials may well direct you to the local distributor in which case you will find the beer still costly but nothing like the hotel prices which were close to US$5 in 1993 for a half-litre lager bottle.

In Rawalpindi Flashman's Hotel also serves as a takeaway point for customers with the necessary licence.

The only known official bar in the country — where you can actually sit on a stool at a bar and chat to a Christian bar-man — is at the Pearl Continental, Peshawar.

Health

All intending visitors should have a thorough medical check before departing for Pakistan. You'll also need up-to-date inoculations against typhoid and cholera and, in particular, yellow fever if you are travelling from a region where this disease exists.

In addition, all visitors should take an anti-malarial prophylactic beginning two weeks before your arrival and for six weeks after your departure.

A gamma globulin injection provides some protection against hepatitis and it is well worth taking this precaution.

Photography

Sixty-minute and one-day processing of both colour and black and white film are readily available in all major centres.

It is forbidden to photograph military installations, airports, and bridges.

Above: Painted wagons make Pakistan's traffic the most colourful in the world.

When to go

The winter months — October to March — are ideal for visiting lowland Pakistan, from Karachi to Islamabad, although Islamabad and other northern cities do experience cold and snow. The areas around the capital are particularly delightful in March and April.

Ideally, the northern mountains should be visited between April and June or September-October.

Where to stay

Pakistan's main cities and provincial capitals — Karachi Quetta, Peshawar, Islamabad, Rawalpindi, Lahore, even Faisalabad — all have comfortable but expensive international class hotels.

Karachi Sheraton Hotel is conveniently 16 kilometres from the airport in the centre of the business district.

The spacious air conditioned rooms, beautifully furnished with thick pile carpet, colour television and in-house video, radio and taped music with big marbled bathroom, provide all comfort of a luxury hotel.

Equally attractive are the Sheraton Towers located on the 7th, 8th and 9th floor with separate lounge and reception area; Overlooking the pool side are independent split level units with duplex rooms, ideal for long staying guests, and smart rooms, luxurious bedrooms with all office amenities.

Karachi Sheraton, boasts a swimming pool, health club with sauna and jacuzzi, four restaurants, coffee shop and shopping plaza. Its modern design reflects the management's dynamic approach to customer service.

In all other major towns and regional centres there are a great many hotels which vary greatly in standards. Intending visitors should seek advice from travel agents on which is most suitable — or, if on the spot, carry out an investigation before checking in. See Listings for "Hotels".

Local authorities in many hill resorts run hotels especially for travellers and foreign tourists, but prices are expensive in relation to the standard provided. Swat, Gilgit, Hunza, and Gulmit, are the only valleys in the northern mountains with acceptable international standard hotels.

Alternative accommodation is available throughout the country in guest houses and rest houses belonging to various government agencies, many in the more inaccessible areas where there are no hotels at all.

The charges for the use of these are usually nominal. The standard of accommodation is good and in some the watchman doubles as cook. Booking these in advance, however, is a cumbersome process, exacerbated by Pakistan's endemic bureaucratic strangle hold. You need to identify — and then contact — the appropriate authority to make a reservation.

Even then, it's best to bear in mind that these rest houses are only available if they are not in use by VIPs or government officials. Visitors sometimes arrive to find that the rest house is already wholly or partly occupied by the last-minute arrival of some highlyplaced person, so be warned.

Standards also vary. For most, you should carry your own bedding, food, crockery, cutlery, and cooking utensils.

Cheaper but still reasonable accommodation is also available at youth hostels and YMCA hostels. The alternative is camping.

Camping

Camping may be possible in the gardens and open ground around rest houses and youth hostels if no room is available. In many areas of Pakistan there are designated campsites but these are not always properly maintained.

In some areas — such as Swat and Dir in the north — camping is expressly forbidden.

Sports and recreation

Despite the limited recreational facilities for the majority of its people, Pakistan is a sportsman's paradise — offering everything from the excitement of such popular sports as soccer, cricket, boxing, hockey, tennis, squash, horse riding, to the thrills of golf, polo, trekking, big game fishing, fly fishing, scuba diving and mountain climbing.

Swimming, yachting, windsurfing, big game fishing in the Arabian Sea, skin and scuba diving are all available at Karachi.

For fly fishing — and Pakistan trout is some of the gamest fish in the world — the mountain rivers cascading into valleys like Hunza, Gilgit, Kaghan, Swat, and Baltistan offer memorable challenges. Permits are easy to obtain and cost little. Hire a ghillie to lead you to the best lies but you'll need your own tackle.

Pakistan's plentiful wildlife and bird life has been diminished by over hunting and poaching and now hunting is totally prohibited. However, enterprising operators in the Punjab lay on splendid hunting safaris in which the trophy is one of the country's plentiful supply of wild pig.

Mountaineering in Pakistan is the most highly skilled and demanding in the world. Around fifty expeditions a year are given permission to attempt to climb some of the world's highest peaks. (See Listings for "mountain climbing" and "trekking" regulations).

National Anthem

The verses of the national anthem were written by a Pakistan poet, Abdul Asar Hafeez Jullundhri. The tune was composed by Ahmed G. Chagla.

Blessed be the sacred Land
Happy be the bounteous realm
Symbol of high resolve
Land of Pakistan
Blessed be thou citadel of faith.

The Order of this sacred land
As the might of the brotherhood of the people
May the nation, the country, and the State
Shine in glory everlasting
Blessed be the goal of our ambition.

This flag of the Crescent and Star
Leads the way to progress and perfection
Interpreter of our past glory, of our present,
Inspiration of ourfuture,
Symbol of Almighty's protection.

National flower

Jasmine was adopted as the floral symbol of Pakistan in 1954. Common to all parts of the country the flower can be found adorning houses in villages as well as growing in elegant gardens in the cities.

PART ONE: HISTORY, GEOGRAPHY AND PEOPLE

Opposite: Entrance to old Kot fort near Sukkur.   Above: Ancient Qur'an in Bahar script.

Land of the Pure

Plumes of cloud and spindrift, driven by the jet streams, trail misty pennants off the myriad high peaks of northern Pakistan that rise above 7,000 metres (23,000 feet). Here, in a tangle of ice-clad spires, the four greatest mountain ranges in the world collide in titanic tumult.

Where the tides of the Tethys Sea once ebbed and flowed, now the Pamir, Himalaya, Hindu Kush, and Karakoram mountains jostle each other for elbow room: tilting, sliding, slipping and grinding along the uncertain borders of Afghanistan, China, India, and Pakistan.

At the centre of this conflict, known as the Pamir Knot, each giant rises imperceptibly inch by inch every year in the constant shoulder to shoulder encounter.

Gaunt and massive, these mountains — to the north the Pamir, to the east the Karakoram, to the south the Himalaya, and to the west the Hindu Kush — form nature's most imposing barrier, known as ''The Roof of The World''.

From the Pamir Knot, the Himalaya curve more than 3,000 kilometres (1,900 miles) eastwards, like a giant scimitar, to the junction of Upper Assam with China and Burma. Since the beginning of recorded history, this immense wall, deterring would-be invaders, has served as a natural fortress.

To the north-west, however, where the scarp deflects off the buttress of the Hindu Kush and runs southwards, its composition changes. The range of arid mountains stretching to the shores of the Arabian Sea is riven with many passes.

Bounded on three sides by the land mass of the subcontinent, Pakistan's thousand-kilometre-long (621 miles) coastline runs from Iran, at the mouth of the Dasht River in the west, to the Indian border on the edge of Sir Creek in the east — made up of rocky headlands, pocket bays, lagoons, and wide alluvial plains that thrust inland, in some instances as deep as 130 kilometres (eighty-one miles).

For centuries the land was a part of India, that uncertain agglomeration of feudal princedoms, city states, oligarchies, and federations.

When the two sovereign nations of the subcontinent — India and Pakistan — were born in the partition of 1947, it was perhaps paradoxical that the Indus basin represented the heartland not of India but of Pakistan. Ironically, India's name, bestowed on it by the Persians and the Greeks, derived from the fertile breadbasket watered by that great river of civilization.

Though young in years, Pakistan's history began at the dawn of civilization in two places significant to the history of mankind, Moenjodaro and Harappa, which flourished

Above: Prehistoric ruins of Pakistan's oldest civilization at Mehr Gahr.

as advanced urban communities with well-planned drainage systems, brick houses and skilled handicrafts from around 3000 BC.

Now from an Independence population in 1947 of fewer than fifty million, Pakistan has developed into a dynamic nation of more than 100 million people, the world's ninth most populous, establishing a progressive society in which a better quality of life, including basic health, education, and job opportunities for all, is the most pressing commitment.

Rich in the variety of enterprise and skills which its peoples display, Pakistan is rich too in natural resources. Previously undeveloped mineral wealth beneath the barren surfaces of its deserts — coal, oil, gas, and marble — have been exploited since Independence to create new industries.

New technologies like nuclear power and research, vehicle and aircraft assembly, steel mills, cement, and electronics, have been grafted on to the more traditional infrastructures — textiles, farming, food processing, and shipping — which came into existence at Independence and just after.

Though Pakistan has thrice been at war with India, outnumbered in all but commitment and spirit, the pace of its development has rarely faltered. Despite the burden of its ever-increasing population, swollen by vast tides of refugees from the conflicts first in East Pakistan and then in Afghanistan, increasing standards of living and opportunity continue to reflect the wider spread and increasing diversity of the industrial dynamo that sustains the national economy.

A major catalyst for good in this progress has been the Pakistan Armed Forces through its many agencies devoted, not only to defence, but to national development and welfare.

Typical is the Karakoram Highway — that incredible ribbon of metalled road hewn out of the daunting cliffs and tunnelled through the sides of the stupendous mountains that form "the Roof of the World."

Diverse contrasts

Covering an area of more than 800,000 square kilometres (300,800 square miles) — bounded in the south by the Arabian Sea, by Iran and Afghanistan in the west, the Soviet Union to the north, China to the north-east, and India in the east — Pakistan is a land of scintillating contrasts and diverse subcultures.

Almost every form of environment known to mankind — from blazing desert to Polar ice, from rich forests to fertile plains, from great rivers and lakes to coastal lagoons —is found within its borders.

And it celebrates a colourful cultural diversity, bonded together in a common faith, which embraces many different lifestyles. There are the mountain people for instance — the Kohistanis, the pagan Kalash, the Hunzakut, the Pathan, and the Afridi of the North and North-West — displaying their hardy independent way of life, their courage and dignity an enduring thread that runs through the tapestry of national life.

Equally fascinating are the myriad tribes that make up the mostly pastoral nomadic communities of Baluchistan, the farming dynasties of the Punjab, and the fisherfolk, farmers, and nomads of the Sind.

They and the generations to come are possessors of a country rich in the beauty of its cultures and landscapes and its religious inspiration.

The broad ribbon which ties this tapestry together is the great swathe of the Indus River, its source far away in an icy lake in south-west Tibet. It cuts a dramatic passage through Jammu and Kashmir to Skardu, entering the Gilgit Valley well along its 3,100-kilometre (1,925-mile) journey to the Arabian Sea.

For the rest of this journey it runs through the middle of Pakistan, binding, rather than dividing, the two halves, to be swollen lower down by the waters of the four rivers — Jhelum, Chenab, Ravi, and Sutlej —that, with the Indus, give Punjab its name, the land of the Five Rivers.

Carrying nearly six billion cubic feet of silt during the three-month summer flood season, the Indus leaves behind each century enough debris to cover more than 2,000 square kilometres (772 square miles) to a depth of one metre.

As the Indus sustains the people of Pakistan physically, through the rich harvests that its waters nourish in the fertile fields of the Punjab and Sind, so Islam sustains them spiritually.

And despite a widespread level of comparative poverty, and three distinct suspensions of the democratic franchise, Pakistanis at all levels of society marked their first forty-two years of nationhood in 1989 with their basic freedoms intact and their Islamic ethos enriched and strengthened.

The Sword and The Fire

Written in blood and flames by the sword and the fire, if few nations can claim an ancient history as continuous — or as bloody and fiery as Pakistan's, fewer still can have been as extensively researched. Yet even so it poses an intriguing mystery. Who were the people who built the lost cities of Moenjodaro and Harappa — and what happened to them?

Almost 5,000 years ago, in what are now the country's Sind and Punjab Provinces, an unknown race established a nation state that was truly a great civilization — a community of artists, scientists, architects, and philosophers which flourished in cities that were remarkable examples of town planning at least 2,000 years ahead of their time.

Streets were laid out in a classic grid style with defined precincts for different sections of the population. They had underground sewage systems. Even on the second floors of their well-designed, neatly-built houses of burnt brick, there were flush toilets.

There are many more indications that these cities were built and developed by a sophisticated and innovative society, yet they fell into decay.

Eddies of dust and debris carried by the monsoons and heavy loads of silt left behind by the seasonal floods of the great river Indus buried their streets and malls.

Slowly, too, the plains on which the cities and towns were built sank. Within the span of a few short centuries it was as if Moenjodaro and Harappa and their kindred urban communities had never been. They lay beneath a deserted, fallow land — there to rest, undisturbed and undetected, for more than 3,000 years.

When the twentieth century began it was known that mankind had existed in Pakistan since the end of the last ice age, but all the evidence indicated that these human societies were extremely primitive — Neolithic followed by Stone Age man.

The prevailing archaeological assumption was that the development of sophisticated societies only began around the year 1500 BC when the first waves of Aryan invaders and

conquistadores broke through the Khyber Pass from Iran.

But in 1920, intrigued by local legends of a city of the dead, *Moenjodaro,* Sir John Marshall led an Indian Archaeological Survey team to a large grassy mound in north-western Sind and began to dig.

What they uncovered ranks as one of the greatest archaeological discoveries of all time. Within weeks, the evidence found in the ruins of Moenjodaro had turned on its head all conventional wisdom about the history of the yet-to-be-born nation of Pakistan.

The archaeologists had stumbled upon a true cradle of civilization — one that had flourished for 2,000 years. But what inspired its development and what brought about its extinction remains one of the great unfathomed mysteries of history.

Certainly by 1500 BC, the time of the first Aryan invasion, little, if anything, of this enigmatic federal state remained — and that little was only the last, decaying vestige of a civilization turned to squalor, the inevitable dark age that seems to succeed all major civilizations.

Aryan invasion

What is certain, however, is that in 1750 BC, the first invaders, the Aryans, crossed over into Pakistan from central Asia to write the first known and understood pages of Pakistan's fascinating history. Their invasion helped to shape events that took place more than 2,000 years later and still influences the destiny of two young nations, Pakistan and its neighbour, India.

They and their religion, interwoven with the spread of Buddhism, left a rich and priceless legacy of architecture, monuments, and scholarship.

In time, the alien language that these invaders from the Caucasus spoke became the *lingua franca* of the subcontinent. They also carried with them the seminal inspiration for one of the world's great religious forces. The language was Sanskrit and the religion evolved into Hinduism.

Their religious hymns, the *Rig-Veda,* the oldest surviving religious scripts in the world, tell of their conquest of north-western India, the land that is now Pakistan, and the name by

Opposite: Ruins of Mehr Gahr an 8,000-year-old settlement on Sind-Baluchistan border.

Above: Ashoka inscriptions from 2,500 BC at Shahbas Garha, NWFP.

which they called it — Sapta-Sindhu, meaning "Land of the Seven Rivers". One of the 1,208 Hindu vedas that exist from that era tells of victory won on the banks of the Ravi in Pakistan's Punjab Province.

Nomadic tribesmen — Aryans, a loose, collective term for people of many different origins — invaded the subcontinent in one of a series of incursions that took the peoples of the Caucasus into Persia, Turkey, and Greece and, not much later, Europe.

They fell into a settled existence. Though those tribesmen in the high plateaux and hills preserved much of their hereditary life style, in the fertile river valleys and lowlands they fused into a simple, rural feudal culture that absorbed the original inhabitants.

The Aryan arrival coincided with the Iron Age. The better weapons the new technology provided were concentrated in the hands of a few lords known as *Rajan,* royalty. With the help of the Aryan warrior classes, they consolidated their hold on the country and established powerful kingdoms across the land that they called Sindhu, later modified in Persian inscriptions to Hindu, softened in western accounts to Indu. Finally, in the first century AD, the Roman historian Pliny dubbed

it by the name that survives, Indus.

Of these kingdoms, perhaps the greatest was that of Gandhara with its twin capitals — Pushkalavati, now Charsadda in Pakistan's North-West Frontier Province, and Taxila, not far from Islamabad — ruled in the sixth century BC by the warrior king, Pukkusati. It became one of the most renowned Buddhist centres.

Another famous kingdom was established in southern Punjab, Sindhu-Sauvira, "Land of Heroes". And, in what is now central Punjab, the Madra tribe built a great capital known as Madrapura, which survives to this day as the golden city of Lahore.

For almost one thousand years the *Rajputs* developed their kingdoms and, as they did so, a well-defined class system began to emerge in the communities they ruled. Out of this arose the discriminatory social system of caste distinction.

In Sanskrit, *Arya* means nobleman and the Aryans became the high-born members of this new society, overlords of those they conquered. The Dravidians, who represented the low-born or serviles, were given the name *dasa,* meaning bond slave.

Caste system

Thus they established the caste order that still distinguishes the religious hierarchy of the Hindu — mankind's first organised system of apartheid — determining each Hindu's level and vocation in society from the time they are born until the moment they die.

The two senior levels of this hierarchy are composed of the Brahmins (priests, teachers, lawyers, and doctors) and the Kshatriyas (rulers, chiefs, soldiers, and administrators).

It was to these twice-born castes that the Aryans belonged. The dark-skinned Dravidians and the offspring of their miscegenation with the Aryans were condemned to the once-born Vaisya castes — farmers, traders, herdsmen, craftsmen, labourers, and domestic servants. The "untouchables", who disposed of the ordure, swept the floors, and cremated the Aryan dead, belonged to no caste. It was believed that even if the shadow of an untouchable were to fall on the high-born, ill-fortune might result.

Inaugurating an Age of Kingdoms, prelude to an Age of Empires, the Aryans fought a great tribal war on the Punjab plains around *Madrapura*, now remembered in Hindu mythology as the mahabharat (one of those involved in the conflict was the Bharat tribe).

These kingdoms grew wealthy and their treasures were many. They all invited plunder. In the wake of the Aryans, during the last millennium BC, other Caucasian tribes from Persia and Scythia, including the White Huns, came to see and conquer much of what was to become Pakistan.

Chief among these newcomers was the Persian emperor Cyrus. He founded the first great dynasty — his scions included Darius the First, Second, and Third — of the many which built empires in which India was the jewel in the crown.

In the sixth century BC, Cyrus the Great crossed the Khyber Pass and took possession of the land around Peshawar. Later his successor, Darius the First, extended the empire seizing all the major kingdoms of the Indus Valley and dividing them into four federal provinces — Gandhara, Makae (later Makran, now Baluchistan), Sattagudai (the Gomal Valley) and Hidus (now Sind and Punjab).

Commissioned by Darius the First, Scylax of Caryanda took a fleet down the Indus exacting tribute from the communities on its banks and demanding an annual levy for the royal treasury. Hidus alone paid 360 talents of gold, equivalent to more than £1.25 million a year in the currency values that existed in the first quarter of this century.

Images of tribute bearers, carrying burdens of treasure in bullock caravans, are carved on the walls of Darius's ancient palace in Persepolis.

Taxila

Taxila, standing at the axis of the imperial trade routes, was a principal beneficiary of Darius's expansion. Now it fell within the ambit of the Orient and royals, philosophers, and intellectuals flocked to its university for further education.

It was a period of great intellectual achievement. Kharoshthi, a new system of alphabetic writing from right to left, was one outcome. Another was the work of the grammarian Panini in perfecting the Sanskrit syntax. A new coinage, introduced by the Persians, was based on the Daric system of weighing gold and the local coinage, *karshapana*, was linked to this.

The Persians were able administrators as well as doughty fighters and, thus secure, peace and prosperity prevailed in the empire of Darius for many centuries. The political philosophies that governed the administration also left a lasting impression — one that influenced the founder of the next great dynasty that would rule over most of India, Chandragupta. He was educated in a Taxila seminary by the philosopher Kautilya, who undoubtedly influenced the creator of the Mauryan Empire with his analytical insight into the Achaemenian system of government.

Xerxes, another of Cyrus's descendants, also benefited from the Empire. One contingent of the great army that defeated the Greeks at Thermopylae was made up of soldiers from the Indus.

Herodotus recalls the presence of the "Hidus [who] wore cotton dresses and carried bows of cane, and arrows of cane with iron tips . . . under the command of Kharnazathres, son of Artabates. . . ."

He recorded the presence of other units from the same region, including the "Paktuans [who] wore cloaks of skin, and carried the bow of their country and the dagger". The Utians and Mukai (warriors from Baluchistan) and Paricanians who carried the same weapons were kith and kin. This contingent was under the command of Arsamenes, son of Darius, and served both as cavalry and infantry.

Darius the Third also called upon troops from his Indus Empire when he was defeated by Alexander the Great at Arbela in 330 BC. The contingent of Hidus, Bactrians, and Sogdians were led by Bessus, Darius's viceroy in Bactria.

Alexander the Great

Alexander's victory left the Daric Empire in disarray and created a political vacuum that was soon disputed by all manner of pretenders: Astes who ruled in Pushkalavati; Porus who dominated the Jhelum and the Chenab; and Ambhi who ruled Taxila.

Ambhi formed an alliance with Astes's opponent and brother, Sanjaya. Together they sought the support of Alexander, whose response was to put down these troublesome kingdoms and annexe the Daric empire to his own. It was as much a matter of pride as conquest.

The Macedonian stood on a military pinnacle without equal at that time. Marching out of his father's kingdom in 334 BC, he conquered all of Greece, Egypt, and Babylon within five years. He and his weary troops then spent a futile year attempting to bring to heel the always recalcitrant warriors of Afghanistan and Turkistan.

Now, having secured, if not a kingdom, at least the road to Peshawar, in 327 BC he founded the city of Alexandria and declared his intention to march into Pakistan. His troops, exhausted by eight years of fighting, almost mutinied.

They wanted to return home to enjoy the booty they had plundered. Alexander convinced them that honour demanded they must be seen to conquer the entire Persian Empire — and its easternmost boundary rested on the Indus River.

If they failed in this, he said, then they would have to acknowledge that the Persians were greater soldiers.

His new city lay in the shadow of a great range of mountains, the Hindu Kush, that march, step by step, out of the barren, brown hills of Afghanistan into Pakistan — the valleys between each of the ridges forming necklaces of green oases sustained by the grey snow-fed rivers that rush down their slopes.

After striding east through the Nawa Pass, bypassing the ancient town of Peshawar, the Macedonian King glanced to the north, where the gentle folds of the green foothills of the southern bastion of the Hindu Kush begin to rise up out of the plains. There was an allure, a promise about them, strong enough to divert him from his advance on the Punjab.

Dividing his 50,000-strong army, he turned northward with one half — leaving the other half to march on to Gandhara and besiege Pushkalavati. He crossed the Kabul River above its confluence with the Indus, somewhere around what is now Nowshera, the military town established two centuries ago by the British, and climbed the Malakand Pass that rises to almost 1,500 metres (5,000 feet).

Far below him lay a vivid tapestry of emerald rice paddies and terraced fruit orchards on the hillsides — ablaze with blossoms of white, pink, yellow, and red. Higher up, alpine meadowlands, filled with wild flowers, were caressed by a gentle breeze. Truly, as Pathan poet Khushal Khan Khattak wrote, it was a land "meant to give kings gladness".

Indeed, so much did it delight the King of Macedonia that he fought four major battles to make it part of his empire. The greatest of these was at Massaga, now Kat Kala, against the Assakenoi. Despite the war engines, mobile towers, and rock-hurling catapults that the Macedonian army had dragged through the rugged mountains, the Assakenian's 30,000 foot soldiers, 20,000 cavalry, and thirty elephant were locked in mortal combat with the 25,000 invaders for four bloody days before capitulating. Alexander himself was wounded.

According to the first-century historian, Curtius, the humiliated defenders despatched envoys to plead mercy from Alexander. When it was granted, the Queen of Massaga brought the Macedonian gifts and libations of wine in golden bowls.

Placing her baby son at Alexander's feet, the Queen was allowed to remain ruler. "Some have believed this indulgent treatment," wrote Curtius, "was accorded rather to the charms of her person than to pity for her misfortunes." At any rate, she later gave birth to another son, whom she named Alexander.

Battle for Bazira

Later, at what is now Barikot Hill also in Swat, Alexander waged a protracted struggle to capture the ancient town of Bazira. Unable to broach Bazira's walls, he left the town besieged and marched eastward along the River Swat to attack the town of Ora.

Alexander ordered one of his lieutenants,

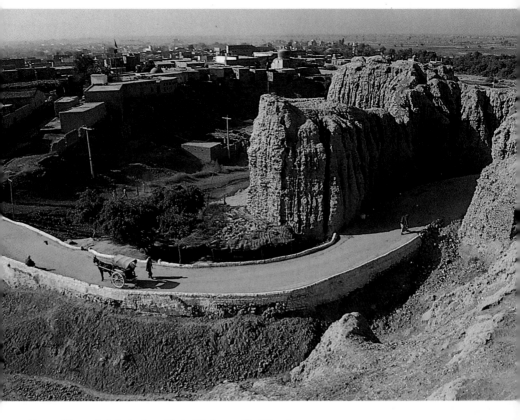

Above: Alexander's baked mud fort at Sehwan, Sind Province.

Koinos, to set up a garrison strong enough to deter the Bazirans from leaving the city to work their lands, and then to march on and rejoin his vanguard. But after Koinos established the garrison and left, the defenders streamed out to cut down the Macedonians and descend to the plain.

There they ran into the rearguard of Koinos's troops and quickly retreated. But before they reached the safety of Bazira's walls, more than 500 lay dead and seventy were taken prisoner. Soon after, on hearing of the fall of Ora, the disheartened inhabitants abandoned Bazira altogether — fleeing to the rocky peak of Mount Ilam which they called Aornos, to seek protection there among the divine spirits they worshipped.

Digging in among the big square blocks of rock that mark Ilam's peak, the Bazirans waited for the expected assault. It did not come at once. Ravines and gullies and fast-flowing streams hindered the advance of the Macedonian army, and its bulky and awkward war machines. Macedonian engineers took three days to build a ramp across a 500-metre-wide (1,600-feet) ravine. But then the infantry climbed the cliff face and the Bazirans fled, many falling to the sword.

The fighting was the fiercest the Macedonians had experienced in all their campaigns. By the time Alexander marched over the hills and reached the Indus near Hund, rejoining the other half of his army after their successful thirty-day siege of Pushkalavati, many months had passed. Now it was the spring of 326 BC and he decided to rest for a month before crossing the Indus to attack Taxila.

Lashing together hundreds of boats to make a pontoon bridge, he traversed the river and approached the ancient city. But Prince Ambhi, rather than see Taxila and his forces overwhelmed as at Pushkalavati, rode out to welcome Alexander. He had a proposition: he would recognise Alexander as ruler if the Greek would join forces with him against Pora, the Raja of Paurava.

Pora, recorded by the Greeks as Porus, had already sent an emissary to negotiate a treaty

33

with Alexander which gave the Macedonian and his armies safe passage in return for respecting the lives and property of Purava's citizens. But the talks failed. Indeed, the emissary was beheaded.

So Alexander readily accepted Ambhi's proposition and in early but heavy monsoon rains the combined forces made a forced march to an eastern tributary of the Indus, the Hydaspes (now the Jhelum) River where, on the opposite shore, Porus and an army of 35,000 infantry, 200 elephant, and 300 chariots awaited them. The odds were uneven, more than three-to-one, against Alexanders's 6,000 infantry and 4,000 cavalry.

Home advantage

In addition, Porus had the strategic advantage of fighting on his home ground with a river between him and Alexander's army. Also the Greek horses, which could sense the elephants, were clearly unsettled.

Yet, despite the sweltering heat of late June, as they pitched camps on opposite sides of the rivers south of Jhelum town for a face-off that lasted several days, Alexander was seemingly unworried.

Day after day, his men scouted up and down the banks of the river searching out a crossing until they finally discovered a shallow fording place about thirty-two kilometres (twenty miles) upstream.

It lay on the inside curve of a broad and long bend. On the opposite bank a sandy marsh, the Plain of Karri, stretched between the ford and the camp of Porus. When Alexander suddenly struck camp and moved upstream to cross, Porus was caught unawares. He had to march around the outside of the bend in the river, almost double the distance his enemy had to cover.

There followed one of the greatest battles ever fought by Alexander and his Greek followers. It continued for days with neither side seeking nor giving quarter until finally, weakened by loss of blood from an unstaunched wound, Porus fell from his elephant.

Taken before Alexander, Porus was asked what should be done with him. He replied majestically, "Treat me as a king". Ever a liberal victor, Alexander was filled with admiration. At once he offered Porus a senior place among the Greek officers and the

vanquished ruler accepted.

He then negotiated peace between Porus and Ambhi and, upon them swearing allegiance to his Alexandrian Empire, reinstated both as rulers of their respective kingdoms.

With this victory, the Greek turned his eyes covetously towards the treasures of the rich and princely states of India. But when he reached the Beas River, Alexander's advance came to an unexpected halt. His battle-weary troops refused to go farther. They had seen enough of war and treasure. All they now wanted was to return home.

Alexander, however, was unwilling to leave. If India could not be his, at least he would prove himself the equal of his great rival Darius and emulate everything that the Persian had achieved. Alexander ordered his men to follow the Indus River to the sea for their return home along the coast of Persia. In this manner, he could still take the land of Sind.

Indus march

Returning to the scene of his victory over Porus, he built a new city and set his men to building a vast inland fleet — 1,000 boats to sail down the Indus.

The battles that ensued were fierce and costly of life. Perhaps the fiercest was against the confederate army of Oxydrakai and Mallois (Malavas), outside the walls of Multan, where Alexander was wounded, almost fatally. Despite their rebellion, he was still a much-loved hero to his men and in retribution they spared neither man, woman nor child. All were put to the sword — in stark contrast to Alexander's usual policy of clemency and mercy.

In Punjab 3,000 Greek colonists, who had followed in Alexander's vanguard and settled there, heard rumours of his death and left for home. When Alexander recovered he marched to the mouth of the Indus, where part of his army joined the Greek fleet anchored in the harbour that was to become Karachi Port. Their reputation travelled before them. They met no opposition.

After they sailed home, Alexander gathered the remainder of his army and returned through the dusty deserts and mountains of Baluchistan. Food and water were scarce. Heat and adverse conditions took their toll. The ragged survivors of his once proud and all conquering battalions

Previous pages: Tomb of Jahangir — "Conqueror of the World" — Lahore.

limped into Babylon, sick and starving, early in 323 BC. There, worn out by his conquests, Alexander died of exhaustion in May of the same year, closing one of the greatest chapters thus far in the history of human warfare.

When word reached his generals, bitter infighting for power began. Seleucus Nicator found himself pitted against his rival, General Antigonis, and the armies of the two men fought many times for the treasures of Babylon, Persia, and Afghanistan. Nicator had intended to claim Alexander's legacy in Pakistan, but by the time he did it was too late; for when word of Alexander's death reached those distant provinces, the viceroys there rebelled.

Rise of Chandragupta

Unwittingly, Alexander had laid the ground for the first of the great Indian Empires when, offended by the outspokenness of a man of humble origins, Sandracottus (later Chandragupta), he had ordered his execution.

Chandragupta, however, escaped and when he slumped to the ground exhausted and slept, luck was with him once more. A full-grown lion that happened upon his recumbent form, instead of savaging him, simply licked away his sweat and then withdrew as Chandragupta slowly wakened.

The incident inspired the man to recruit a mob of renegades and set in motion an uprising that overthrew Pora and set Chandragupta upon the throne of Paurava.

He then set about expelling the Greek and Macedonian colonists and later turned east to capture Magadha. Thus Chandragupta established a new empire, which expanded during the next two decades as far as Bengal in the east, to Mysore in the south, and westward to the Hindu Kush.

By the time Nicator came to claim his Alexandrian legacy in 306-305 BC, Chandragupta's Empire was well-established. The Greek, despite his firm rule over a kingdom that stretched from Thrace (Greece) to Mesopotamia (Turkey) and the borders of the Magadhan Empire, was unable to overcome Chandragupta. But, his invasion rebuffed, friendships were established.

Chandragupta married a female member of Nicator's family and received the Greek ambassador, Megasthenes, at his new capital of Pataliputra, now Patna, on the banks of the Ganges in India's Bihar State.

Chandragupta, an unscrupulous tyrant who trusted nobody, feared so much for his life he never slept in the same room twice. He was constantly surrounded by a bodyguard of women warriors.

Yet he left a profound legacy. Among his greatest achievements was the building of the trunk road from Taxila to Pataliputra, a distance of 1,280 kilometres (795 miles) along which resthouses were built. He also inaugurated the world's first regular mail service — by pony. His combined armies were so powerful his empire was invincible. As well as becoming an intellectual capital, Taxila became a vast treasure house.

Chandragupta was succeeded by his son Bindusara, who ruled until 273 BC. In turn, he was succeeded by his son, Ashoka, who was the governor of Taxila. A mighty warrior, Ashoka — in a succession of bloody conquests — soon turned his inheritance into the Mauryan Empire, the greatest the world had ever seen.

Change of heart

As a young man, however, Ashoka was heavily influenced by the aura of meditation and spirituality that pervaded Taxila and, eventually, his bloody campaigns appalled him so much that he renounced violence and embraced the Buddhist philosophy, pre-eminently one of non-violence and concern for all living things.

Out of this change of heart arose the first conservation laws in the history of mankind, promulgated on pillars and rocks all across the subcontinent as Ashoka's edicts. Buddhism also became the first religion elevated to the status of an ordained Government faith, although Ashoka allowed freedom of worship.

The spread of Buddhism and the edicts were the enduring legacy of his reign. Two of Ashoka's pillars carved with his proclamations survive in Pakistan — at Shahbas Garha, near Mardan, and at Manshera.

But his empire did not survive his death in 231 BC. His principle of ruling by peace and love was out of key with the violent times and his army so weakened that, after his death, the empire was prey to one invader after another.

The Greek colonists who had settled Bactria established an independent Greek kingdom, incorporating the Indus Valley, in central Asia under an army led by Demetrius. They called it Gandhara. It reached its peak about 180 BC under Menander, who extended it to the Punjab and drew up a constitution creating a formal

Above: Bas relief carving on Gandharan tomb near Taxila.
Opposite: Fasting Buddha, Lahore Museum — one of the world's great artworks.

federal government of the conquered kingdoms.

Despite their ancestry, the Indo-Greeks were more Hindu than Greek, and Menander was a devout Buddhist. It was under his influence that the distinctive Gandhara art form, began to spread across the Buddhist world, eventually to leave a lasting glory.

Taxila grew in magnificence. It was modelled on Hellenistic lines of city planning. At its height, the city's bazaars were bursting with elephants, horses, and pedestrians, and the shops were choked with supplies of every conceivable form of goods.

This kingdom was not to last long, however. In the last century BC it was conquered by a Scythian army that reached the mouth of the Indus and captured Gujrat.

In the north, another invading force, the Parthians, set up court at Taxila, under Gondophares, where legend says that one of the visitors in AD 47 was the Christian missionary St. Thomas. He stayed only briefly, fleeing before the invading armies of the Kushans a year later.

He sailed down the Indus to India's Malabar Coast where he founded a church in AD 52. He died twenty years later when he moved to the east coast and was killed by Brahmins jealous of the number of his converts to Christianity.

The Kushans

Meanwhile, the Kushans were laying the foundations of the second of the great empires to be established in India. At its height, it extended from the Caspian Sea to the Bay of Bengal and from the Arabian Sea to the Ural Mountains. It endured for more than 500 years.

The Kushans, whose ancestral roots lay somewhere on the Chinese border, had a feeling for the grandeur of the old Persian empire and the glory of a great power. They took the imperial name of *Shao-nano-Shao* which survives today as *Shahanshah*. They established their empire and its capital at Purushapura (now Peshawar) late in the first century AD.

Under the second emperor, Wima Kadphises, there was such a strong reign of law and order that trade along the fabled Silk Route from China to the subcontinent flowed and burgeoned without threat or interruption.

His successor, Kanishka, earned fame as a conqueror and the love of his people as a patron of the arts, philanthropist, academic and religious missionary. He became the greatest of the Kushan rulers during his reign of forty-two years.

He, too, was a devout Buddhist. But, unwittingly, when he convened the fourth Buddhist council to reconcile differences, he actually opened the door to an alien form of Buddhism, the Mayahana school, which with its established priesthood and pantheon of gods was closer to Hinduism.

Among the many monuments he built is the Kanishka-Vihava at Peshawar, a Buddhist pilgrimage shrine for more than seven centuries. He also sent missionaries all across the subcontinent, Asia, and China, to build monasteries and carry the message of Gautama the Buddha. Gandhara became the second most important religious centre in the Buddhist world.

More importantly, the Kushan Empire was to go down in history as the Golden Age of the subcontinent — an era of unprecedented prosperity and peace, when towns and cities sprang up at an astonishing rate and trade between all the capitals of the known world, from Rome to Beijing, flourished.

Ironically, although these emperors were simple individuals rather than sophisticated, worldly characters, even today the art they inspired ranks among the world's most priceless.

Through their expanding contacts with the outside world, however, external influences crept in bringing about the eventual downfall of this great dynasty.

Unable to survive the erosion of its wealth and trade by the Sassanians of Persia, the Kushan empire fell when the White Huns, a people of obscure ancestry from the Caucasus, swept across the land and settled there, intermarrying with the well-established Aryans.

Sophisticated society

The Huns indiscriminately destroyed both Hindu and Buddhist temples — to such an extent, that in AD 528 the Hindu rajputs set aside their own wars and formed a federation to put down the invaders and their vengeful ruler, Mihiragula. His subsequent defeat led to the rise of the Gupta empire.

The old hegemony was replaced by a series of feudal princedoms under the domination of the Brahmin rajputs. The Chach dynasty took hold of Sind; other Hindu rulers created dominions in the north. Thus began the "golden era" of Hindu rule, a federation of small and princely states.

The complex and sophisticated urban societies of the Dravidians, the original inhabitants of the Indus Valley had virtually vanished by the time the nomadic Aryans invaded the region. Those settlements that did survive were destroyed.

In time, however, the Aryans also adapted to life in civic communities and changed their nomadic ways to settle as farmers. Although they in turn built cities, farming was the rock on which the economy prospered and the village remained the focus of social life.

This role was developed and organised during the Hindu period.

The village evolved to become the centre of a complex bureaucracy, a self-contained unit with its own local government.

Farmlands were organised as collectives and professionals and craftsmen (judges, bankers, traders, clerks, priests, potters, weavers, smiths, and carpenters) were employed by the community which paid them in kind with village produce.

The rulers of the kingdoms in which these small, tight-knit communities developed, guaranteed public security and arbitrated disputes, provided lawkeeping forces and promoted public works such as roads, canals, and bridges. It was perhaps the original bureaucracy.

It became a durable system, one that survived successive rulers and dynasties through seventeen centuries — from the second century AD up to the nineteenth century. Yet as each dynasty subjected the system to immense pressures, its flaws became evident.

The most overwhelming change that the system survived was the advent of Islam in the subcontinent.

Sword of Purity

Islam burst upon the world in the middle of the seventh century AD. Unlike the slow spread of Christianity, or the patient rise of Buddhism, in under a century it roared across the deserts of the Middle East, and westwards along the coasts of Africa and into Spain and even France, inspired by the religious fervour of Caliph al-Walid bin Abd al-Malik.

Zealous Islamic militants who had

Above: Remains of the first mosque built on the subcontinent at Mansura near Hyderabad.

overthrown the Sassanid dynasty in Persia carried it over the mountains into the deserts of Makran, now Baluchistan. But it did not gain a permanent foothold until early in the eighth century.

In 710 AD, the Caliph of Damascus's governor in Iraq and the East, al-Hajjaj bin Yusuf, commissioned one of his generals, Muhammad bin Qasim, to lead an expedition from Shiraz in southern Persia against Sind. He simultaneously organized an attack against the Chinese Empire and the Far East.

It was a time when what is now Pakistan was composed of a group of independent kingdoms — a Hindu king, Dahir, ruled Sind and Makran; Punjab was also a separate and powerful state ruled from Multan; and Kashmir had subordinated Taxila to the status of a vassal state.

The Sind capital was at Brahmanabad and the kingdom extended north as far as the present day town of Sukkur. Its principal port was Daibul which may have been Bhambore.

Sometime early in AD 711, Muhammad bin Qasim landed near Daibul with an army of 6,000 Syrian tribesmen — fierce and fanatical soldiers of the new faith — and besieged the port. When it fell, they destroyed its Buddhist

stupa, known as *dewal,* which gave the port its name, but in victory the general was magnanimous. Giving quarter to the conquered, he built the first mosque on the subcontinent and, to establish Islam permanently, he settled 4,000 Arab families in a new suburb of the town.

Then he marched inland into Sind to attack Niran, located not far from modern Hyderabad. Seeing his large army, swollen by 4,000 locally recruited mercenaries, the town priests surrendered Niran peacefully.

Bin Qasim went on to take Sadusan and then, like Alexander the Great, in the year 712 built a bridge of boats for his army to cross the Indus and meet the army of Dahir in a bloody confrontation near Rawar. During the battle the king was killed and his troops took to their heels in all directions never to reform.

Muhammad bin Qasim occupied Dahir's capital of Brahmanabad and reorganised his forces before marching north to claim Rur (near present-day Sukkur) and finally laying siege to Multan with its famous golden shrine to the sun god *Aditya.*

Al-Hajjaj had instructed bin Qasim that Multan was to be the final goal of the Muslim conquest, and for three full centuries it remained the northernmost point of the Islamic advance on the subcontinent.

Sind became a peripheral province of the all-powerful Caliphate founded in Damascus, and for the next three years, Muhammad bin Qasim set about laying the foundation stones of an Islamic state, establishing civic, social, and religious frameworks for society.

People of the Book

These were basically benign, reflecting the early Islamic virtue of tolerance, including freedom of worship. Buddhists and Hindus, Jews and Christians, even the Zoroastrians, were included among the "People of the Book" — a distinction that gave them protection under Islam.

Central authority from Iraq or Syria was imposed only distantly, but the faith was established and the Muslim community put down strong roots, reinforced by the arrival of fresh waves of Arab settlers.

Muhammad bin Qasim was not to govern long, however. He fell from favour and was killed when a new Caliph, Sulaiman, came to power in AD 715. Nonetheless, he left an ineradicable legacy.

Although, initially, the Muslims remained a tiny minority, Islam flourished for the next 300 years — at peace with other religions — until the eleventh century. It was then, during the Ghaznavid period, that the great expansion of the faith in the subcontinent was undertaken.

In AD 762, the Damascus Caliphate came under the control of a new dynasty, the Abbasids, based in Baghdad, Iraq. Nonetheless, the governors of Sind continued to remit their tribute (one annual tribute in the first half of the ninth century amounted to a million dirhams, equivalent to about £3.5 million in currency values in the second half of the 1980s).

Remote from central authority, Sind became a refuge for criminals, outlaws, rebels, and sectarians, who fled from the Gulf by sea. By the tenth century allegiance to the Caliphate was only nominal.

Each town appears to have had its own separate governor and the tributes ceased. Even so, Multan, which was vulnerable to the warlike rajput princes to the north, remained a bastion of the faith.

Ironically, a great deal of its wealth stemmed from the offerings the Hindu pilgrims brought to the shrine of the sun god. These the Muslim governors appropriated, passing on only a portion to the trustees of the idol.

The shrine also served to defend the town, for whenever Hindu potentates menaced the city walls, the governor-of-the-time threatened to destroy the sun god and the forces would withdraw.

New links were forged with other Islamic dynasties — the Persian caliphate of Buyid Amir and the Fatimid caliphs of Egypt and North Africa, who were great rivals of the Abbasid dynasty.

First Ismaili missions

During this century, the first Ismaili missions came to Sind from the Yemen. By the time Mahmud of Ghazni attacked Multan in the first decade of the eleventh century, the Ismailis were in a majority in that city and remained so, even after he deposed the local ruler, Abdul Fateh Dawood, in 1010.

While all this was going on, Islam was gaining ground in eastern Afghanistan and what is now Pakistan's North-West Frontier Province, following the rise of the Saffarid brothers, Yaqub and Amr bin Laith, at the end of the ninth century. Indeed, Sanskrit and Arabic inscriptions displayed in Peshawar Museum indicate that as early as AD 857 the word of Islam had already been heard in Waziristan. The inscriptions, some of the earliest found in the subcontinent, tell of a new mosque.

The real impetus for the spread of Islam throughout the subcontinent, however, came with the rise to power in AD 962 of a Turkish dynasty in Afghanistan and the succeeding Mongol dynasty.

The Ghaznavide era began when a Turkish officer of the Samanids, Alptagin, established a power base at Ghazni, close to modern Kabul. He was succeeded fourteen years later by an ex-slave, Abu Mansur Sabuktigin, who expanded the kingdom and fixed his eyes on the riches of India. Soon he was raiding across the Khyber Pass, easily turning aside any opposition raised in Mardan district by the Hindu rajput, Jayapal, who ruled from Lahore.

Eventually, Jayapal persuaded his fellow rajputs to form a confederacy to put down this nuisance. But when the two armies met on the plains of Peshawar in AD 991, it was a disaster for the confederates.

Sabuktigin, however, was more interested in plunder than conquest, and when his coffers were full, he retired to Ghazni to make a tally of his booty.

His son, Mahmud, who succeeded him on

his death in AD 997, was of like character. Each fall he set out on his father's war trail, marching ever deeper into Pakistan and India, as far as Aryavarta in the north and Gujarat in the west, before returning with his loot as the hot season began in spring.

It was Mahmud who, a decade after his father's victory, met another of Jayapal's armies and won a great victory. Such was Jayapal's shame that he immolated himself, setting fire to his own funeral bier.

His son and successor, Anandpal, vowed vengeance. Forming another confederation, he led the rajput armies against Mahmud's troops on the Peshawar plains in 1008. It was a tremendous battle.

Indeed, Anandpal was on the point of routing the Muslim army when a volley of fire-balls and arrows stampeded his elephant. Believing that he had deserted, his troops turned and ran and many were killed.

So brilliant were Mahmud's subsequent campaigns that the Abbasid Caliphate bestowed upon him the title of "Right Hand of the State and Protector of the Believers", *Yaminuddaulah Amirul Millat*. Before the end of his thirty-three year reign his authority extended from Iraq to the Ganges, and from Khwarazam to Kathiawar, while accounts of his military exploits brought him fame in far-distant countries.

This brilliant and audacious military commander was also an aesthetic and intellectual and he transformed Ghazni into a metropolitan centre without equal.

Embellished with fine architecture — mosques, gardens, and bridges — it had the most magnificent university campus in the east and the finest library any seat of learning had ever possessed. The most eminent scholars, poets, astronomers, scientists and philosophers came to the capital to meet, talk, and advance their knowledge.

Deeply devout, Mahmud relished his raiding expeditions, not only for the treasures they yielded, but for the opportunity they gave him to raze the heathen shrines and idols of the Hindus.

He left such a trail of destruction — shattered temples, fallen idols and slaughtered priests — in his wake that the enmity it provoked between Hindu and Muslim still smouldered nine centuries later.

He stripped untold wealth in jewels alone from the bodies of infidel captives and his booty, according to a contemporary account, "was beyond all bounds and calculations, including 500,000 Hindu slaves".

Shiva shrine desecrated

In the winter of 1023 Mahmud embarked on a major crusade, leading his army down the Indus to Multan, which surrendered without a fight, and on through Sind to the Arabian Sea.

Turning east along the coast to circle the Rann of Kutch, he came upon the unsuspecting city of Somnath, famous for its Shiva temple. Inside stood a three-metre-tall (10-feet) stone phallus, *lingam*, symbolising Shiva, the giver of life.

Surrounded by a circle of solid gold bells adorned with veils studded with precious stones, the image was tended by more than a thousand priests who bathed it each day with water carried from the sacred Ganges more than 1,600 kilometres (994 miles) from the city. So costly was the upkeep of the temple that taxes were levied on 10,000 villages in the region.

Mahmud was determined to destroy the temple and its idol. When his troops scaled the walls of the city, the Hindus sought refuge in the temple to pray for help but to no avail. After the righteous Mahmud had finished Somnath was bathed, not in the waters of the Ganges, but in blood: 50,000 citizens lay dead.

Even so, when he ordered the destruction of the sacred *lingam*, its attendants petitioned him to spare it in exchange for a heavy ransom. Mahmud remained adamant. The idol and the shrine were destroyed.

Mahmud also founded Lahore as it is known today, as the cultural and spiritual centre of Islam on the subcontinent, and as the administrative capital of Punjab, replacing Multan.

Determined to turn him back, the rajputs of northern India formed another confederation to fight his armies, but distrustful of one another they were easily defeated.

When Mahmud died his empire was overrun by Afghans from Ghor and his last supporters fled to seek sanctuary in Lahore.

Under Mohamed of Ghor, the Ghorids, who ruled for just over fifty years, pushed the frontiers of the Ghaznavide Empire still farther — well beyond the Jumna. If Ghorid rule was brief, it was also all-embracing and laid the foundation of Muslim domination throughout the subcontinent for the next five centuries.

Appointed Governor of Ghazni in 1173 by

his elder brother, Ghiyasuddin, Mohamed took the title of Shahabuddin and in 1175 conquered Multan. One year later he took Uchh and in 1186, after a decade of fighting, in a guileful, bloodless manoeuvre he took Lahore and wrested the control of Punjab, the final remnant of the Ghaznavide Empire, from the last ruler of the House of Ghaznavide, Khusrau Malik. He then murdered Malik and his family.

Nothing could deflect Shahabuddin from his purpose. In a tremendous battle at Tarain in 1193 he defeated the greatest of the rajputs, Prithvi Raj of Ajmer.

Slave Kings Dynasty

During the next decade Turkish slaves, appointed officers by his viceroy, Qutb-ud-din Ibak, demonstrated their loyalty and skills by claiming virtually all of India, Gwalior, Kalinjar, Kalpi, Badaun, Qannauj, Benares, Meerut, Bihar, and finally, Bengal, for the Ghorid Empire. This was the origin of the "Slave Kings" dynasty. Both the Ghaznavide and Ghorid dynasties, which originated in Central Asia, ruled their Empires from bases outside India.

To those who followed Shahabuddin, however, the Punjab plains promised a degree of wealth and comfort undreamed of in the hot, arid mountains of their Afghanistan homeland. When he was killed on his way back to Ghazni in 1206, they saw little point in returning with their plunder when this pleasant land of plenty was theirs to occupy.

Furthermore, their homelands were being swept by successive and cataclysmic Mongolian invasions, of which the principle instigator was Genghis Khan, who chose to go no farther than Peshawar, the eastern gateway to the Khyber Pass.

Shahabuddin had neither scions nor heirs, which left a triangular struggle in the "Slave Kings" Dynasty for the succession. Installed as Sultan of Lahore, Qutb-ud-din Ibak eventually outwitted his two rivals, Tajuddin Yildiz and Nasiruddin Quabacha, and ruled until he fell from his horse during a game of Chaugan, an early form of polo, in 1210 — and died.

His death sparked a war of succession, eventually won by Shamsuddin Iltamash, one of his former slaves, who immediately established his capital in Delhi.

The stage was thus set for the consolidation and expansion of the Muslim dominion of India. Hindus from all walks of life enrolled for Government service, enlisted in its armies and, exempt from fear, worked as tradesmen, craftsmen, and farmers. Their status as an allied people, zimmi, entitled them to protection. The Muslim rulers guaranteed Hindus complete security of life and property and freedom to worship as they wished.

Yet they failed to establish a political system stable and strong enough to withstand either internal or external threats. During the next 320 years, though Delhi and the provincial capitals remained under Muslim rule, there were to be five different dynasties and thirty-three kings.

The "Slave Dynasty" was succeeded by the Khaljis, an indifferent set of rulers but for the second in line, Alauddin Khalji, who embarked on an adventurous course of expansion in the south and succeeded in establishing a powerful monarchy.

Perhaps his major achievement was the revival of a moribund economy, the stabilisation of prices and the eradication of the endemic corruption that plagued the administration, replacing it with efficiency.

When the last of the Khaljis expired, their place was taken by the Malik Dynasty of Ghazi, founded by Tughlaq. His son, Muhammad bin Tughlaq, was so concerned to maintain power that he alienated both Hindu rajputs and Muslim military and spiritual autocracies.

He finally died in battle at Thatta in Sind. At least Tughlaq had some degree of determination unlike Feroz Shah, the vacillating wimp who succeeded him. He was so eager to appease each and every faction that the empire collapsed and, when he died, most of the outlying provinces declared their independence.

Tamurlane, the Earth Shaker

His successor had little or nothing to rule and thus Tamurlane, the Earth Shaker, progenitor of the Great Mughals to follow, found the subcontinent when he invaded India at the end of the fourteenth century.

No other invader took such a toll.

In 1398 he swept through Peshawar, Taxila, and the Punjab, to capture Lahore and Delhi. Embarking on a holy vendetta against the Hindu in which many of the victims were Muslims, he wrought terrible carnage. "Towers were built high with their heads," one contemporary account reported.

When he departed from Delhi, installing his emissary, Khizr Khan, to form the brief and forgettable Sayyed dynasty, the city was so ruined that it was said that no living thing, not even a single bird, was seen among its ruins for at least two months.

The Sayyeds were followed by the Lodhi Afghans who briefly re-established Muslim supremacy in Delhi, Bihar, and Punjab, and became patrons of learning and orthodox Islamic principles. But they were no match for Babur the Tiger, fifth scion of Tamurlane, who in 1526 marched into the subcontinent to establish what was to become the most glittering empire in the world.

The first of the Great Mughals had arrived.

Though fifth in line from Tamurlane and fourteenth in line from Genghis Khan, in the hierarchy of the Afghan invaders of Mongolian and Turkish descent, Babur was but a minor prince. Indeed, when he was eighteen he was dispossessed by an uncle of his inheritance — the equally minor province of Farghana, north of the Hindu Kush, in what is today the Soviet province of Tajikistan.

Thus ousted, he roamed central Asia with an army of mixed Mongolian and Turkish descent fighting with varying success for more significant possessions. But, even after he had twice won and lost Kabul, he never doubted his destiny.

He secured the city for a third and final time in 1504 and turned his eyes at once to India. But though he thrice raided into Pakistan to bring the recalcitrant Pathan hill tribes to heel in the matter of the tributes, he confessed in his diary that he never found a suitable opportunity.

The Mughal Empire

Nineteen years after he established himself in Kabul, however, at a time when the viceroy in Lahore, Daulat Khan, had antagonised the Lodhi dynasty, opportunity did present itself.

When Daulat Khan heard that Ibrahim, the Lodhi Sultan, was marching from Delhi to punish him, he invited Babur into Hindustan. The first of the Mughals needed no further bidding to turn his face eastwards. Aided by cannon and muskets never before seen in India, he took Bajaur on the Peshawar plains and then sent a messenger to Ibrahim Lodhi demanding that he cede the Punjab which, Babur informed him, was his by right.

The request was ignored. As Babur's march

Above: Miniature of Babur, first of the Great Mughals.

from Kabul took longer than Ibrahim's from Delhi, he arrived at Lahore to find the gates of the city locked and the emissary he had sent imprisoned. Daulat Khan was on the run and the Lodhi dynasty's army was already ranged against his seemingly inadequate forces.

Yet Babur defeated the much larger defence force "with great slaughter", razed the city bazaars and looted its many magnificent treasures. He then stormed south to Dipalpur to do the same there.

His rapid cavalry pincer movements and light field artillery left all who faced his army in disarray. During the next two years, he ranged all through the territory between Lahore and Kabul, and his inherent military genius won him mastery of the wide plateau under the Himalaya.

On 29 April 1526 he demonstrated his real genius as a field commander in the final battle for Delhi on the plains at Panipat, sixty-five kilometres (thirty-five miles) north of the city.

The sun was "spear high" as Babur's tiny force of 12,000 cavalry faced Ibrahim's 100,000 strong army of horsemen and foot soldiers, the largest in Asia and believed to be invincible. But it was led by disenchanted subordinates and Babur's military strategy and the disaffection of many of Ibrahim's generals ensured him a brilliant victory.

Above: Birthplace of Akbar the Great at Umarkot, Sind.

Ibrahim slain, his army slaughtered, Delhi was Babur's.

Although it was a great prize, he and his troops, mountain men all, loathed the capital and the heat.

Despite "Hindustan's riches of gold and silver", they thought only of the cool streams, leafy trees, and meadows of their alpine homeland. But in an eloquent speech this paradoxical soldier, who was both tyrant and poet, despot and intellectual, fond of alcohol and opium, persuaded his soldiers not to abandon their new conquest but to remain and seal its destiny.

He then marched to Agra where his first act was to order landscape artists to lay out a Persian garden —the first of the many beautiful Mughal gardens which are one of the dynasty's great legacies to the subcontinent.

During the year that followed Babur met much opposition from the rajputs determined to restore their dominance. But when, by sheer military genius, he defeated another army of monumental size, led by Rana Sangha,

Above: Rajput fort at Umarkot where Humayun was given sanctuary.

at Kanwaha, thirty-two kilometres (eighteen miles) west of Agra, he faced only one more major battle. This took place on the banks of the Ghagra two years later when he defeated an Afghan army to become master of India from the Indus to the borders of Bengal.

Babur dies saving his son

He was not to rule for long, however. Legend says that when his beloved son Humayun lay dying in September 1530, a seer told Babur that he would only recover if he gave away the one thing that he loved most.

Babur replied, "He loves me best" and prayed to take Humayun's illness upon himself. From that moment, Babur grew sick and his son began to recover. Three months later, in December 1530, aged forty-seven, Babur was dead. He was buried at Kabul.

Humayun had once been advised by his father never to act against his brothers, no matter how much they might deserve it. The son, who inherited his father's sensitivity — and his weakness for opium — found this advice only too congenial and suffered for it.

As soon as Humayun's younger brother, Mirza Kamran, governor of Kabul and Kandahar, heard of Babur's death he moved to Lahore to make his own bid for power.

However, Babur's viceroy, Mir Yunis Ali, was intractable and remained loyal to the genuine heir.

So Kamran resorted to a deceitful ruse. He sent an allegedly "denounced and expelled" nobleman to Lahore. Yunis Ali, quite taken in, gave the nobleman and his followers refuge. Within days the guests he had welcomed had locked him up and taken over the city.

In Agra, Humayun bowed to the *fait accompli* and made his younger brother ruler of the Punjab as well as Kabul and Kandahar — only to be rewarded, through the years, by Kamran's many acts of treachery. Always remembering his father's words, however, he invariably allowed Kamran to live to betray another day. But eventually Kamran exhausted even Humayun's magnanimity and trust. After one final betrayal, he put out Kamran's eyes and banished him to exile in Mecca, Saudi Arabia.

Although he masterminded the conquest of Gujrat, there were long periods of lost opportunities and neglected administration during Humayun's reign. Despite his many social gifts, this "fair and fatal king's" indecisiveness and self-indulgence were to cost him dear.

One such period of inertia followed

Humayun's conquest of Bengal, when he was cut off by monsoon floods. This gave his major opponent, the Afghan king, Sher Shah Khan, time to rebuild his armies and in 1540, in two subsequent battles with Sher Shah, he lost all that he and his father had won.

Humayun fled to what is now Pakistan where he spent fourteen frustrating and fruitless years, wandering from one small principality to another with an ever-dwindling band of loyal followers, including two of his brothers. It was a fateful retreat, for during this time he married fourteen-year-old Begum Hamida Banu, the daughter of one of his brother's spiritual advisers.

Soon after this wedding he was forced to retreat across the Thar desert at the height of the summer heat and he and his men nearly perished. They were saved by the kindness of the rajah of a small principality who gave them shelter, and after a while, leaving his pregnant wife behind, Humayun resumed his wanderings.

Akbar the Great

Some time later, on 20 October 1542, when he was camped in the Thar desert he received news that made him weep from both sorrow and joy: Begum Hamida had given birth to a son. His sorrow arose from the poverty that prevented him from giving presents to his followers as custom demanded; his joy at the birth of an heir who, he said, "will fill the world as this perfume fills my tent". The boy was Akbar.

Soon after this he headed for Kandahar where two of his brothers, including Kamran, were in control but confronted by their army he fled into Persia. The Shah promised him military support if Humayun would renounce the Sunni Islamic sect and convert to the Shia sect, making it the official religion of his dominions. Thus the Persians provided the army by which Humayun, in a second momentous battle at Panipat, regained the Mughal Empire from Sher Shah's successors.

For Humayun, however, this long-awaited victory was short-lived triumph. No sooner was he back within the walls of his Delhi fortress than, six months later — on his way to prayers, say some accounts; in an opium trance, say others — he slipped on a stone stairway and split open his skull.

Just before his death, perhaps with a prescient sense of impending doom, Humayun had appointed his thirteen-year-old son, Akbar, Governor of the Punjab. Humayun had entrusted the job of counsellor and guardian to a favourite and renowned general, Bairam Khan. When the accident happened the two were on their way to Lahore.

Worried lest contenders usurped Akbar's inheritance before messengers reached the boy and the general, Humayun's courtiers resorted to a subtle subterfuge. Each morning one of Humayun's servants donned the royal robes and appeared at the audience window to convince the people that the king was still alive.

The messengers found the two *en route* to Lahore at Kalanaur. They hurriedly returned to Delhi where, on 11 February 1556, Akbar was crowned before his uncles had chance to steal the throne. The coronation was the first they knew of Humayun's death.

Akbar was destined to become the greatest of all the Mughal emperors. He inherited few of his father's flaws and most of his ancestors' strengths.

In accordance with the late King's will, General Bairam Khan became Regent until Akbar reached the age of eighteen. During these five years the young boy king learned much from this able teacher and guide, both about rebellion and about handling men to ensure full control of his kingdom.

Akbar's Legacy

Akbar had formidable natural talents for the task of kingship. Despite his short stature, he was physically powerful, more so even than his legendary grandfather Babur. He was ruthless, too. He had one of his brothers thrown twice from the Delhi walls — the second time because he did not die the first.

Yet he was also staggeringly liberal — another of those paradoxical Mughals, endowed with a massive capacity for both slaughter and intellectual sensitivity, for conquest and aesthetic pursuits.

This had a profound effect on his personality: history shows that his life was an anguish of conflicting conscience. But nothing deterred him from his inevitable destiny. Within months of ascending the throne, he defeated (under General Bairam, again at Panipat) the rajput

Opposite: Kamran's pavilion, Lahore's oldest surviving Mughal monument.

Above: Karachi Museum miniature of Akbar the Great's Sikandra mausoleum.
Opposite: 17th-century painting of Akbar on an elephant.

confederacy that at one point recaptured Delhi from him.

He went on to enlarge the Mughal Empire until it stretched from the Bay of Bengal in the east to the Persian border in the west, embracing much of southern India and Sind, most of Baluchistan in the south, and the Himalaya to the north.

It was also typical of him that religious freedom prevailed throughout his empire, for he ever tried to reconcile the differences between Hinduism, Islam, Judaism, and other religions into one pure faith.

In 1575 he built a "house of worship," *Ibadat Khan*, at Fatehpur Sikri where each Thursday evening the foremost theologians in the empire met to discuss the conflicts between each religion and within the different sects of the Muslim faith.

These discussions, which lasted the night long, were frequently bitter and recriminatory. Opposing theologians often came to physical blows. On one occasion, Akbar himself was so incensed at the insults that an eminent Shiite mullah heaped on the companions of the Prophet that he had the mullah bound to the foot of an elephant and dragged through the streets until he died.

Otherwise, in an age of dogma he was remarkably liberal. "Formerly," he wrote, "I persecuted men in conformity with my faith and deemed it Islam. As I grew in knowledge, I was overwhelmed with shame. What constancy is to be expected from proselytes of compulsion [forced converts]? If men walk in the way of God's will, interference with them would be in itself reprehensible; if otherwise, they are under the malady of ignorance and deserve my compassion."

Perhaps Akbar's lasting achievement, even greater than the empire that he expanded and consolidated, was his creation of the most advanced administrative system of government of its age. For it was this, as much as anything, that helped to keep the Mughal Empire intact for another two centuries.

It was Akbar, too, who endowed Lahore with its lasting grandeur when, near the end of his reign, he made it his capital during what were arguably his court's fourteen most brilliant years.

Many of his buildings still stand, monuments to a society that drew the most distinguished scholars, writers, intellectuals, poets, artists, and musicians of the day. But in 1598 he re-established his court at Agra where, seven years later, he died to be buried in the shrine of his own Universal Religion at Sikandra.

For months before this his court was in terrible turmoil over the succession. One son was dead from drug addiction and another dying from the same cause. A third, Prince Salim, known for his indulgence in drugs, alcohol, and women, was so ambitious that more than once his father warned him against anticipating his accession.

He was the natural and logical choice. The only alternatives, Salim's own sons, Khusrow and Khurram, were too young. Thus, hours before he died, with great misgiving about the future of his empire, Akbar named Salim as his successor.

Conqueror of the World

The new Emperor, who took the title of Jahangir, "Conqueror of the World", was as contradictory as his sire. Absolutely ruthless and extraordinarily intellectual, similarly liberal in thought and tolerant in matters religious, he was also impressively impartial in the administration of justice.

Though he lacked his father's genius, he restrained his self-indulgence and became a shrewd, capable, and determined ruler, who enlarged the Empire through the addition of Kangra, and plagued the Hindu rajputs of southern India with continued aggression.

He is perhaps remembered best, however, for his fervid marriage to Nur Jahan, the daughter of a Persian nobleman in the service of Akbar whom Jahangir made his prime minister. Nur Jahan's brother, Asaf Khan, fathered Mumtaz Mahal, the woman whose beauty inspired Jahangir's son, Khurram, to commission the greatest of all the world's architectural masterpieces, the Taj Mahal.

Ironically, as Jahangir's health and reason failed in his last years, Nur Jahan grew determined to see her own worthless brother-in-law, Shahr Yar, succeed to the throne.

But although she virtually ran the Empire, Jahangir would not concede the succession. His eldest son Khusrow died mysteriously in 1621 after being imprisoned by his father following a coup attempt, which left Khurram to accede after Jahangir's death in 1628. Khurram took the name of Shah Jahan.

Again, here was another Mughal paradox who shared the Jekyll and Hyde personality of his predecessors and lacked none of the cruelty that ran in the Mughal blood. Indeed, the two pretenders to his throne, Shahr Yar and Dawar Bakhsh Bolaki, son of Khusrow

Top: Painting depicts splendour of the Mughal court.
Above: Miniature of Shah Jahan, the Architect King.

Above: Anarkali, the condemned lover — re-enacted in a Lahore playhouse.

and Shah Jahan's nephew were soon put to death along with various other male royal relatives and all those associated with them, in an orgy of domestic blood-letting. It was something none of his forbears had indulged in.

Once his throne was secure Khurram gave full play to the powerfully creative ruler inside him. Builder of the Taj Mahal, the Red Forts of Delhi and Agra, the greatest of all the Mughal gardens, Shalimar in Lahore, and a positive treasury of monuments both grand and beautiful, he bequeathed an architectural legacy, much of it surviving in both India and Pakistan, which marks the zenith of Mughal rule in the subcontinent.

In every respect he proved the most magnificent of Akbar's successors and his reign was something of a golden age. Never was the Mughal Empire more prosperous or secure.

Nor did he neglect the process of empirical expansion. He was handed Kandahar, a Persian possession, by its Governor in 1631, in return for heaping great honours upon the donor. He conquered all of southern India save the two Muslim kingdoms of Bijapur and Golkonda.

Taj Mahal

His crowning achievement, however, remains the Taj Mahal, which he dedicated to his wife Mumtaz Mahal who died in childbirth. So grief-stricken was he that he commissioned architects to design an immortal monument to her memory. How well he succeeded!

The broad concept of this unique memorial is attributable to Shah Jahan but those whose genius translated his ideas into such a perfect form have vanished unremembered.

Yet Shah Jahan's magnificent epoch ended badly.

As he aged, his powers declined and his three younger sons made no secret of their ambition to oust the Prince Regent, Darah Shikoh, his father's favourite.

Farthest from the seat of power though he may have been, it was the third son, Aurangzeb, who by his guile and military skills demonstrated his natural right to the Mughal throne.

In 1659, before the Taj Mahal was completed, Aurangzeb forced his father to surrender the Red Fort in Agra and there held him captive for the rest of his life, while his army won a decisive battle against the Prince Regent's forces on the Punjab plains.

His brother fled but was recaptured and assassinated, along with his son. When the Prince Regent's head was brought before Aurangzeb in Delhi to assure him his rival was truly dead, he wept.

"Let this shocking sight no more offend my eyes," he mourned. "Take his head and bury it in Humayun's tomb."

Meanwhile his father, although given every comfort, was condemned to live out his life gazing upon the monument he created to his greatest love as it emerged from the mists each morning across the river Jumna — destined to be dubbed the world's most beautiful work of architecture.

Last of the Great Mughals

Withdrawn, austere, and much feared, Aurangzeb left his own architectural monuments, among them Lahore's Badshahi Mosque, then the largest in the world. He also extended the Empire, slashing his way from Bombay to Kabul, and from the Himalayas to Cape Comorin.

Nonetheless, he was destined to be the last of the Great Mughals. His very severity brought about the Empire's inevitable decline. So fiercely did he impose the Islamic Sharia law upon the Hindu majority that rebellion was inevitable and, although it was ruthlessly suppressed, it was never thereafter wholly contained.

Though he ruled longer than any of his predecessors or heirs, dominating all events and overshadowing all other personalities of the age, he failed to secure the future of his own house. His death in 1707, at the age of eighty-nine, marked not only the end of his fifty-eight-year reign but also the end of the majesty and mystique of the Great Mughals.

He was succeeded by his son Bahadur Shah but the throne could not make the monarch. Five years after he took the throne, Bahadur Shah was dead and the empire was plunged into a series of wars of succession that hastened its end. In the 182 years from Babur's accession in 1525 there had been only six Mughal Emperors. In little more than half a century, ten more followed — almost all unmemorable — and although the Mughal line lingered on for another 150 years, its greatness was gone.

Another powerful factor in its demise was that of the Sikh Dynasty, based on the religion founded by Guru Nanak in Akbar the Great's time. This had sought the middle ground between Muslim and Hindu beliefs. It was a gentle faith, but when Aurangzeb attempted to wipe it from the face of the Punjab and beheaded Tegh Bahadur, its Ninth Guru, in December 1675, the dynasty turned militant.

Sikhs came into ascendancy in much of the old Mughal Empire, but never on a grand scale for there was already another, final, contender for the Indian Empire. It had come innocently disguised as a mercantile enterprise, but its eyes gleamed with greed for the Jewel in the Crown.

Imperial stage

Impressed by India's wealth as early as the sixteenth century, when the Mughal Empire was at its greatest, British business men were eager to exploit the opportunities for trade. In 1583 Queen Elizabeth 1 despatched the good ship *Tyger* to the subcontinent, entrusting to the captain a letter addressed to the King of Cambiaia.

The opulence and treasure of India was all too inviting for this small but ambitious island nation of six million people which had managed to impress its authority on a great deal of the known world.

Under Queen Elizabeth, soldiers and sailors of fortune had carried out grand conquests that gave Britain control of treasures in the Americas and elsewhere, but still its ambition was not sated.

Sixteen years after the *Tyger* sailed to India, the Queen granted the right to trade with the East to a group of entrepreneurs based in London. Their mandate also charged them to buy or seize, and thenceforth rule, whatever territories could be taken.

Nine years later — in 1608 — the first British ambassador to India, Sir Thomas Roe, presented his credentials at the court of Jahangir. He was greatly impressed by the wealth "of the most magnificent court in the Universe".

Six years after this, the East India Company opened its first office on the subcontinent, in Bombay. The Company did not implement its mandate to become conquerors. To rule, the directors felt, was an unnecessary expense. Instead, for fifty years, it enjoyed a unique monopoly, trading with moderation and due deference to Mughal rule, seeking concessions in Bengal in the east and on the Coromandel coast, through its representatives and Britain's diplomatic presence.

It was not until 1670, when the French, equally ambitious in matters of trade and

Opposite: Window in Shish Mahal, Lahore Fort.

empire, conquered and settled Madras, that this monopoly was broken.

During the next century, through the last great years of the Mughal empire and beyond, the two European powers came into open conflict on the subcontinent, culminating in Robert Clive's defeat of the Nawab of Dacca in 1757. Thereafter, the annexation of India into the British Empire began.

Aurangzeb's death fifty years earlier had left a vacuum in the subcontinent that was filled by war and bloodshed among different contenders.

Once again northern "Pakistan" became the route for conquerors who sought the wealth of India. In 1739, Nadir Shah, the Turk who had conquered Persia, launched an invasion and smashed the Mughal troops at Peshawar, continuing to cross the Indus at Attock. By the end of the year he held Lahore, cut a bloody wake through the Sikhs and went on to sack Delhi, before retiring to Kabul to count his booty.

Eight years later, Ahmed Shah Abdali Durrani had Nadir Shah assassinated. Seizing Kabul, from where he founded the first Afghanistan kingdom, he then proceeded to slash another trail of massacre through northern Pakistan to Lahore.

Durrani and his men on their march through Punjab slaughtered thousands of the Sikh faithful, desecrating the Golden Temple at Amritsar and defiling the ground with cow's blood. The survivors fled to the hills to regroup and recover.

When he tried to storm Delhi, however, Durrani was defeated by the Mughals and as he retreated the Sikhs came down from the hills with a vengeance and slaughtered every man they could catch. That many had also been the victims of the Afghan king made no difference. There was a new faith and a new sword on the subcontinent.

Beginning of the end

But in the eyes of most historians it was the 1715 concession by Emperor Farrukhsyar, granting the British extra-territorial rights in Bengal, the most prosperous province in the whole subcontinent, that was "to prove nothing less than the beginning of the end of the independence of India".

The Mughal Empire had already begun to disintegrate and it was the British battle for Calcutta in the east and the Sikh campaign in the north that rang its death knell.

The vacuum in the north enabled the Sikhs to build a strong nation in the Punjab which, undoubtedly, they would have expanded but for the British. Nonetheless, under the Singh dynasty they enjoyed a century of power in the north-west as the British slowly took possession of the rest of the subcontinent.

In their determination to crush the last of the Mughals and their supporters, the British ruthlessly subjugated the Muslims and encouraged the Hindus — a classic example of divide and rule strategy. Perhaps, if they had endeavoured to reconcile the differences between the two communities, the eventual division of the subcontinent might never have been necessary.

Meanwhile, under Ranjit Singh, the greatest warrior of his dynasty, the Sikhs expanded their kingdom until it extended from the mountains in the north to the Khyber Pass on the Afghan border in the west, south beyond Multan, and east virtually to the walls of Delhi.

Sind, which was controlled by the Mirs of Talpur, was broken into a confederation of small and princely states each ruled by a member of the Talpur family.

East India Company

The East India company which fronted Britain's imperial ambition made treaties with the Sikh and Talpur dynasties. The River Sutlej marked the boundary between British India and the Sikhs. Relationships between the British and the Sind rulers were markedly uneasy, however.

The defeat of the British army of occupation in Afghanistan under Lord Elphinstone precipitated a showdown between these two remaining independent kingdoms. The British armies were private forces of the East India Company, not of the British government. The Company had acquired a myth of invincibility which had persuaded its vassal Indian princes to acquiesce to British power rather than suffer defeat.

The Afghanistan humiliation made a show of British power necessary before the princes revolted. The unfortunate Mirs of Talpur were chosen to provide the set piece for this demonstration of military strength for two reasons: they were not considered strong enough to resist defeat; and Sind was an ideal base from which to launch a new invasion of Afghanistan.

So, despite the protests of James Outram, the British representative in Sind, Sir Charles

Napier led a British army to Miani where, on 7 February 1843, the Talpur armies were crushed in bloody battle and the exultant and ambitious Napier annexed Sind to the British Indian Empire.

Critics in Britain, increasingly bitter about the authoritarian and high-handed attitudes of the East India Company, described the events leading up to this battle and the actual battle itself as "the most disgraceful and unprincipled that has ever stained our empire in India". It was akin to a beaten bully going home to take it out on his wife.

All that remained free was the Punjab. But with the death of Ranjit Singh in 1839 and the state of anarchy that immediately prevailed, the end of the Sikh kingdom was inevitable.

In 1845, after a war in which fortune — and treachery in the Sikh ranks — favoured the British armies under Sir Hugh Gough, the Company took Punjab east of the Sutlej and also annexed Kashmir. Sir Arthur Hardinge, the Governor General, knew that the British troops could never hope to hold it and sold this enchanted valley kingdom to Gulab Singh, a rascal who had served in Ranjit Singh's army.

Despite the treachery of the Sikh leaders, the bravery that both armies displayed during this campaign was truly heroic. Sir Hugh was filled with praise for the valour of his Sikh enemies.

The rest of the Sikh kingdom, including Peshawar, became a puppet government of the British under Ranjit Singh's successors but there were deep intrigues and Lal Singh, the Sikh premier, was eventually tried for treachery and exiled.

Second Sikh War

The ultimate outcome was the second Sikh War. The British, again under Gough, now made a baronet, suffered two humiliating defeats at Ramnagar and Chilianwala before claiming a final, overwhelming victory at Gujrat, on 21 February 1848.

It gave the British the Indus — and an empire that stretched from the Bay of Bengal in the east to the Himalayan mountains in the north, embracing all the land in between, from the southern coast to the Bolan Pass in Baluchistan in the west, and to the Khyber Pass on the north-west frontier.

The symbolic jewel in the crown became a reality: the Koh-i-noor diamond that Ranjit Singh had worn in his headdress was added to the crown jewels of Westminster.

One final explosive confrontation remained — the Indian Mutiny of 1857, followed by one final piece of imperial expansion when, in 1901, Lord Curzon formed the North-West Frontier Province and established the garrison town of Quetta, beyond the Bolan Pass, as the capital of Baluchistan.

The major consequence of the Indian Mutiny for the Muslims of India was that it confirmed their estrangement from the mainstream of life.

The Mutiny began among the Indian soldiers, *sepoys*, of the British army in Bengal but swiftly spread across the subcontinent. It only failed because the Muslims and Hindus were unable to work together.

In the aftermath, the blame was set squarely on Muslim shoulders and the process of alienating them accelerated. Their cause was not helped by their strict religious injunctions.

While, as early as 1814, under the leadership and inspiration of Raja Ram Mohan Roy, Hindus began to exploit the benefits of western education and technology, the Muslims could not embrace any educational system that was not firmly rooted in the Qur'an and based on Islamic tradition.

When English became the official language in 1835 and an English education became the criteria for subordinate posts in public offices, the Muslims, fearing perdition if they satisfied these perfidious requirements, found themselves shut off from jobs in government, education and business. English law, often in conflict with Muslim traditions, was forced upon them. India's Islamic communities were in disarray while the Hindus prospered.

Sir Syed Ahmad Khan

Not until well into the second half of the century did a leader emerge who had the authority and personality to lead these disparate and isolated groups and begin to weld them together in the unity of the faith.

That man was Sir Syed Ahmad Khan who argued convincingly that, despite the injustices, the security, peace and tolerance of British rule in India merited the country the title of *Dar-ul-Islam*, the land of peace — not, as the religious leaders taught, *Dar-ul-Harb*, the land of war. He reconciled the differences between fundamentalist Islamic and Christian ideas by discovering their common Judaic heritage.

He suggested that because of this the Qur'an should be interpreted in the light of reason

and science, that the Muslims should take advantage of this era to learn all that they could from the West. His belief took firm expression in the establishment of the Anglo-Oriental College at Aligarh, later to become the Aligarh Muslim University.

Within a decade the Hindus, under a retired English civil servant, Allan Octavian Hume, who had retired to Simla, established the Indian National Congress which was to become the main instrument of the independence movement. Significantly, it also became the major obstacle to Muslim hopes and aspirations.

It was in 1905, when it was twenty years old, that Congress first considered India's constitutional future, tentatively suggesting isolated reforms and then, finally and boldly, stating self-government within the empire as its major goal.

One year later the Muslims, under Mohammed Iqbal, one of their most articulate leaders, founded the All-India Muslim League and political nationalism emerged to overshadow every other issue in India for the next forty years and to compound the irreconcilable differences that eventually led to the partition of the subcontinent as two separate nation states.

Ironically, the catalyst was Lord Curzon's partition of Bengal in 1905 that separated the predominantly Muslim east from the Hindu west — a move welcomed by the Muslims and denounced with ferocity by the Hindus. Indeed, so great was the outcry that six years later, in 1911, the division was cancelled. It had encompassed, however, the profile of the future East Pakistan, which endured until 1971 when it ceded to become Bangladesh.

Hindus Dominate Congress

Sir Syed Ahmad Khan was alarmed by the increasing power of the Hindu-dominated Congress and its relentless pressure for self-rule, for he knew that the minority Muslims would be dominated.

"Our two nations, the Mohammedan and Hindu, could not sit on the same throne and be equal in power," he said.

Attempts to reconcile the two politico-religious groups proved impossible. The basic tenet of the Islamic faith is that it is the one true faith: all others are heretic. Even if the Hindus had been willing to co-operate, and they were

not, the Muslims would have found it impossible.

Yet at one stage, the enlightened leader generally considered to be the founder of Pakistan, Mohamed Ali Jinnah, did seek conciliation with the Hindu.

Jinnah, a gifted lawyer born in Karachi who practised in Bombay, joined the League in 1913. He was seen as the "ambassador of Hindu-Muslim unity", but although he was close to Mahatma Gandhi they were never intimates, each distrusting the other, and the Hindu dominated Congress refused to take Jinnah's aspirations, shared by all moderate Muslims, seriously.

In the 1920s he became so disillusioned that he withdrew from politics and went to live in England, where he had studied law, intending never to return.

Congress's continued failure to recognise Muslim aspirations reached a crucial point in the 1930s. It was then that Sir Muhammad Iqbal, an idealistic poet, assumed a leadership role. His gifted literacy enabled him to articulate dreams of a Muslim homeland for the subcontinent's largest minority.

It was Iqbal who spoke of the shape of this nation at Allahabad in 1930 when he told delegates to the Muslim League: "Self-government within the British Empire or without the British Empire, the formation of a consolidated North-West Indian Muslim state, appears to me to be the final destiny of the Muslims, at least of North-West India."

He suggested that the Punjab, North-West Frontier Province, Sind and Baluchistan, should form the new nation-state.

At the same time the Cambridge visionary Chaudhuri Rahmat Ali gave it identity when he conceived the name of Pakistan — meaning "Land of the Pure" — as an acronym of P (for Punjab), A (for Afghans, or Pathans), K (for Kashmir), I (for Indus) and S (for Sind) with "stan", the Persian suffix meaning land or country.

The articulate Muslims now had a creed, an ideology, and a goal. What they lacked was a leader of power and charisma and so, in 1935, a delegation was despatched to London to persuade Jinnah to return to lead the now almost moribund Muslim League and guide it to the promised land.

Though the League had been weakened,

Opposite: Early morning sunrise bathes minarets of Badshahi Mosque, Lahore.

deadlines, the three-way division now forgotten, Sir Cyril Radcliffe was appointed to head the Commission that would divide India into two nations. The shape of this was announced on 3 June 1947 and was accepted unanimously, despite misgivings by Congress, League, and Sikhs alike.

Proportionately, the Sikhs had most to lose since the division sliced right through the middle of their Punjab homelands, cutting their communities in half.

Pakistan was more than vulnerable. "Only a miracle" wrote one observer, "could save the Pakistan Army from the fate which the enemies of the young nation were only too ready to forecast for it."

Indeed, on 24 April 1947, outlining the frailty of this new nation in a strategic appraisal for Lord Mountbatten, the last British Commander-in-Chief of India, Field Marshal Sir Claude Auchinleck, concluded that Pakistan was indefensible.

Fragile Child

By virtue of its geography, he said, West Pakistan formed "a long narrow stretch of country lying between the high tablelands and mountains of Baluchistan and Afghanistan and the plains of the eastern Punjab.

"The region being all length without breadth is basically difficult to defend . . . Whether attack should come from the West or the East there is a lack of depth so essential in modern war to success of any defensive plan.

"The average width of the region is about 300 miles [500 kilometres] only, except in the extreme south, while the distance from Karachi to Rawalpindi is about 700 miles [1,100 kilometres].

"If Kashmir is to be included in the region, the distance from Karachi to the Northern Frontier where it meets the Pamirs would be about 1100 miles [1800 kilometres]." Karachi was the only port and all communications converged in a bottleneck.

Pakistan was born, a fragile and undernourished child, some months later, amid apocalyptic bloodshed and hatred, on 14 August 1947. Mohamed Ali Jinnah, Quaid-i-Azam — "The Great Leader" — was appointed the new Governor-General of this nation within the British commonwealth of nations and Liaquat Ali Khan was its first prime minister.

It had no industrial infrastructure and little defence. Much of Pakistan's rightful share of the subcontinent's treasury — railway rolling stock, industrial assets, aircraft, and military equipment — divided by the British before they left, was denied it.

When the timetable for partition was decided, it was announced that India and Pakistan would have operational control of their own armed forces by that date and a committee was established to proportionally divide men, weapons, ammunition and supplies. The subcontinent's industrial and economic assets were also to be fairly allocated.

Division of "spoils"

The division of the British Indian Armed Forces seemed simple enough. Men and equipment had been listed and assigned to one force or the other. But there were critical imbalances in this paper division of the "spoils" of Empire.

Responsibility for moving ammunition, stores, equipment, and installations from one country to another was entrusted to a supreme command under Auchinleck, which was to last for ten years. In fact, it lasted just over three months. Auchinleck's establishment was wound up on 30 November 1947 on the undertaking of the Indian Defence Minister to accept full responsibility for delivering Pakistan's rightful assets.

The Indian treasury held four billion rupees at the time of Independence of which Pakistan was entitled to 750 million rupees. In the event, the country only received 200 million rupees.

The training establishments and combat units of the old Indian Army, the Royal Indian Navy and the Royal Indian Air Force were scattered throughout the subcontinent. Many units, with large numbers of Muslims, were in areas that were to remain in India. Most defence production facilities were in India, as were the bulk of the military stores.

Because of the disparity in the sizes of the two nations, Pakistan received fewer stores, supplies and facilities, and most of those allocated were never delivered.

On paper, at least, Pakistan received six armoured regiments to India's fourteen;

Opposite: Minar-e-Pakistan, Iqbal Park, Lahore.

eight artillery regiments to forty; and eight infantry regiments to twenty-one. It had been agreed that 150,000 men would be transferred to the fledgling army, along with 160,000 tons of ordnance stores, 60,000 tons of ammunition and approximately 1,700 vehicles.

Of the promised 160,000 tons of ordnance stores, no more than 2,500 tons had arrived by February 1948. More than a year later, Pakistan had received all it was to get — little more than 23,000 tons. Of 1,700 promised vehicles only seventy-four were ever delivered.

In Rawalpindi the new Pakistan GHQ was bereft of a single ledger, a single record, a single file, a single reference book; bereft, even, of a single sheet of paper.

But Muslim servicemen travelled from every corner of the subcontinent to participate in the nation's birth, many arriving months after the event.

In essence, Pakistan was a twin birth. West Pakistan with its teeming millions lay on one side of the subcontinent; East Pakistan on the other. The potential enemy, India, lay between with the capacity to strike on either side. The two Pakistans were the orphans of an international family with only the fires of their Islamic faith to warm and nourish them.

Pakistan's initial handicaps were exacerbated by the bloodshed that had taken place in the previous two years and which rose to an unparalleled and shocking climax immediately before, and in the long months after, Partition.

Although the Sikh religious leaders had endorsed the suggested lines of division, when the Radcliffe boundary award was announced, three days after Partition on 17 August 1947, the Sikhs, whose religious kingdom, farms, and businesses were now sliced down the middle, reacted violently.

Massacres

Within days a terrible massacre had begun which the 50,000 strong boundary force, stationed there to prevent just such an eventuality, was powerless to stop. Sikhs and Hindus fell on the Muslims remaining in the Indian Punjab while the Muslims across the border slaughtered the Sikhs and the Hindus left behind in Pakistan's Punjab. The treasured city of Lahore went up in flames.

Panic-stricken, the innocent and the weak on both sides — Hindu and Muslim — began to flee from each other's territory, harassed by

Sikh, Hindu, and Muslim, depending upon which faith they espoused and which gang caught them. Every atrocity imaginable was committed. Within days, long convoys were marching east and west seeking shelter in the other dominion.

Indeed, the exodus constituted the largest migration of mankind in the history of the world. At the end more than ten million people, including an estimated half a million dead, were involved.

Meanwhile in the Kashmiri capital Srinagar, in the tense moments before Partition, the country's eighty per cent Muslim majority voted on 19 July 1947, for accession to Pakistan.

But Maharajah Hari Singh, the Hindu monarch of this ancient kingdom, was reluctant to abandon his independence. Asking for the *status quo* to be maintained, on 15 August 1947 he entered a standstill agreement with the Pakistanis, under which the kingdom's posts and communications systems would be run by Pakistan personnel.

But now began an organized campaign of terror against the hapless Muslim Kashmiris: all firearms and weapons were confiscated and militant Hindu citizens given open licence to organize lynching parties. During the first days of Partition, thousands of Kashmir Muslims died.

Indian reversals

In response the Muslims began to organize themselves into a full army. The first sub-units were established in late September in Bagh, Rawalkot, Pallandri, Kotli, Mirpur, Bhimber, Gilgit Agency — governed by Kashmir but not an intrinsic part of the state — and Muzzafarabad. Quickly, these ill-clad, ill-armed soldiers seized Poonch, Muzzafarabad, Mirpur, and Gilgit.

On 22 October 1947, Hari Singh appealed to Nehru for Indian support. He was told it would be granted only if he ceded his authority and kingdom to India. With the Kashmiri freedom fighters at the doors of Srinagar, and along the banks of the Chenab River in the south, the Maharajah acquiesced.

Five days later, Indian forces moved in but the Kashmiris were undeterred. Establishing an Azad Kashmir Armed Forces headquarters in November, they raised sixteen regular infantry battalions and began to fight with dogged determination and inherent tactical skill.

One month later India protested to the United Nations Security Council. Throughout 1948 the fighting continued and, as the Indians suffered reversals, they mounted pressure on the Security Council to negotiate a ceasefire. It was ordered on 1 January 1949 with the promise of a plebiscite that was never held.

Ever since, the territory has been in dispute and the issue has continued to bedevil Indo-Pakistan relations.

By far the biggest tragedy to befall Pakistan in the first eighteen months of its existence, however, was the death of Jinnah in September 1948. There was no one to approach him, either in mental stature or ability to wield power wisely and well.

Unswervingly dedicated to the democratic ideal and the institutions which served it, he was a consummate constitutionalist at a time when Pakistan's own constitution was still being written.

Two years and one month later Liaquat Ali Khan was assassinated in Rawalpindi and the disintegration of government was complete. Under Jinnah's framework, executive power lay with the prime minister, but after the ensuing reshuffle, (Jinnah's successor, Khwaja Nazimuddin, became prime minister) the new Governor-General, Ghulam Muhammad, wanted to change the status quo.

He dismissed Nazimuddin in April 1953 and nominated Muhammad Ali Bogra, Ambassador to Washington, in his place. Bogra, however, was quick to realise that it was no sinecure and, when Ghulam Muhammad briefly left the capital (then Karachi) in September 1954, Parliament passed an act stripping the Governor-General of his overriding authority.

But Ghulam Muhammad outflanked his opposition, dissolving the Constituent Assembly a month later on the grounds that it had "lost the confidence of the people". He then proclaimed a state of emergency.

Since there was then no federal legislature, Ghulam Muhammad handpicked a new cabinet. Among its members was General Ayub Khan, Commander-in-Chief of the Armed Forces, who eventually became the first of Pakistan's military rulers.

The country was soon in disarray. After much infighting, on 23 March 1956 it changed its constitution from that of Dominion within the British Commonwealth to that of Republic within the Commonwealth. Pakistan only withdrew from the Commonwealth after the debacle of the 1971 war with India.

Two years later, in October 1958, the then Pakistan president, Iskander Mirza, abrogated the Constitution and declared the country under martial law — the first of the many martial law eras that have marked Pakistan's less-than-half-a-century history.

Ayub Khan

Within three weeks he himself was ousted by Ayub Khan whom he had appointed as the chief administrator of martial law. Corruption had become so endemic within the national and civic systems of administration that at first Ayub Khan was welcomed as a national hero by the people.

For the next four years Ayub Khan entrenched himself as president. Then in March 1962 he suspended martial law and proclaimed a new constitution that gave him wide-ranging executive powers, including the authority to override the elected Parliament.

Not surprisingly, as the 1964-65 elections demonstrated, his popularity waned, but the external threat from India continued to divert attention from him. Relations between the two countries still smouldered.

In 1965, India sent tentative expeditions into the barren Rann of Kutch to lay claim to this vast region of marsh and desert which belonged to Pakistan. Though it's difficult at times to establish who was in the right, there is little doubt that India was the most provocative of the two states. Despite many attempts to persuade India to withdraw peacefully, their forces continued to creep forward.

Pakistan believes it was left no option. In a surprise dawn attack, Pakistani troops, backed by artillery and tanks, forced the Indian Army to retreat, leaving behind armoury and tanks in large numbers. The British negotiated a ceasefire, but India's Prime Minister at that time, Lal Bahadur Shastri, vowed vengeance.

Face (community respect, standing in society) are all-important in the East and any humiliation or slight, whether justified or not, has to be countered.

Soon after the Rann of Kutch incident, Kashmiri freedom fighters — angered by seventeen years of Indian intransigence and procrastination over the plebiscite — raided across the ceasefire line to support fellow resistance fighters within India-held Kashmir.

India retaliated by attacking Pakistan defensive positions on the 1949 ceasefire line. Pakistan met the thrust with a counter-offensive on the night of 1 September 1965, crossing Jammu-Tawi and after capturing Akhnur, moving on to take Jaurian. By 5 September, Pakistan troops were poised within striking distance of Jammu itself.

Indo-Pakistan War

Incensed, at 0400 hours on 6 September 1965, India unleashed the full fury of its vastly superior forces with an all-out bombardment on the border between the two countries.

Eighteen years and three weeks after Partition, the long predicted full-scale war between the two nations had begun — without formal declaration.

Launching the offensive, India's General Chaudhri ordered his troops to march on Sialkot and then the ancient Mughal citadel of Lahore, jauntily inviting his officers to join him for drinks that evening in Lahore Gymkhana.

"With her twenty-one infantry and mountain divisions, one armoured division and one independent armoured brigade group — almost equal to a division — against Pakistan's seven divisions and an even larger margin of quantative superiority in the air," says one history of the war, "India felt that she could deliver a knock-out blow to Pakistan and finish off once and for all the Kashmir dispute which had been casting embarrassing shadows on her international image."

On paper it looked sublimely easy. Lahore was only twenty-two kilometres (thirteen miles) from the border and Sialkot, a major cantonment town, only ten kilometres (six miles) distant. The vital Lahore-Karachi road and rail arteries lay half an hour's tank ride from the Indian "jumping off" ground and the links to Rawalpindi, strategic headquarters, were just an hour's ride away.

India's front stretched along the entire 2,000-kilometre-long (1,242-mile) border — from Kargil in the north to Rajasthan in the south. With fewer than one-third of India's manpower or weaponry, Pakistan's situation looked bleak.

But General Chaudhri never kept his dinner date. Instead, thirty-six hours after he was to have toasted his victory in Lahore Gymkhana,

his Defence Minister Chavan told Parliament in Delhi that Indian troops on the Kasur sector had been withdrawn.

However, although initially the Indian forces were repulsed and the Pakistan Air Force achieved some major air victories, there can be little doubt that, in the long term, India would have overrun its weaker neighbour. So, seventeen days after the war began, Pakistan answered a United Nations call for a ceasefire.

Great Dictator

The Tashkent Declaration that Ayub Khan and the Indian Prime Minister signed in January 1966 was regarded by many Pakistanis as submission to India and the foreign minister, Zulfikar Ali Bhutto, resigned to form the popular Pakistan People's Party (PPP), determined to "defeat the great dictator with the power of the people". As a result, he and others were arrested.

Mass protests broke out. Ayub Khan's power, threatened also by the emergence of a strong independence movement under Mujib ur-Rahman in East Pakistan, steadily diminished. Unable to control the situation by force, he offered to talk.

Releasing a number of political prisoners, in March 1969 he held a round table conference in Rawalpindi — close to the new capital, Islamabad. The conference was a stalemate and Ayub Khan handed over power to General Muhammad Yahya Khan on 25 March. Once again Pakistan was under martial law.

The new leader paved the way for the restoration of democracy with the general elections of March 1970 but without success.

The political impasse between Mujib ur-Rahman's majority and Bhutto's minority party meant that Yahya Khan was unable to control the situation and in East Pakistan there was widespread resistance to the authority imposed from West Pakistan. The conflict escalated, reaching a climax with the prohibition of Mujib's Awami League and the arrest of its leaders on 25 March 1971.

Those that remained free fled with many of their supporters to India to form a government in exile. Inside the eastern wing of the country, the East Pakistani Rifles and other troops of Bengali origin rebelled and formed the secessionist movement named Mukti Bahini,

Opposite: Pipe major in a Pakistan infantry regiment.

which enlisted the support of the Indian forces.

Reprisals by the West Pakistan-appointed martial law administrators were frightening. On both sides, the scale of the massacres in East Pakistan were even greater than those of the Punjab in 1947.

In the meantime, the Indian Army poked, pushed, and prodded the East Pakistan defensive positrons along the border, while the Mukti Bahini sabotaged key installations inside the country and carried out other acts of terrorism and war.

Second Indo-Pakistan War

These intensified until finally the second full-scale war between India and Pakistan erupted on 3 December. Pakistan suffered humiliating reverses, culminating in the surrender of the Pakistani forces in East Pakistan on 16 December 1971. Forty-five thousand troops and an almost equal number of civilians of West Pakistan origin were taken prisoner and the Mukti Bahini proclaimed East Pakistan the sovereign state of Bangladesh.

Yahya Khan did not survive defeat. Four days after the surrender he was placed under house arrest and Zulfikar Ali Bhutto took over the government of (West) Pakistan.

Bhutto's reconstruction was impressive. He nationalized basic industries, banks, and insurance, began to democratize the civil service and initiated health and education reforms.

He was ousted in a 1977 *coup d'etat* by a virtually unknown army general, Muhammad Zia-ul-Haq, and was later tried for murder and hanged on 4 April 1979.

Once more Pakistan was under martial law — and remained so until 1985 when general electrons were held on a non-party basis with Zia-ul-Haq remaining President.

Three years later, in 1988, he dissolved Parliament and, after much procrastination, announced that there would be fresh elections in November that year but with restrictions.

In August, 1988, however, Zia was killed in a sabotaged military plane crash along with most of the country's military hierarchy.

But the interim President, Ghulam Ishaq Khan, assured the nation that the elections would go ahead on a full and unrestricted democratic franchise.

On 30 November 1988 in what might be regarded as an act of sweet attrition the Pakistan electorate voted Bhutto's former party, the Pakistan People's Party, under the leadership of his daughter Benazir, to an uneasy majority, defeating the opposition party of the Islamic Democratic Alliance, led by Nawaz Sharif.

Subsequently Benazir Bhutto assumed the Premiership of Pakistan — the first woman to govern an Islamic state.

In 1989, democracy, however uneasy, was also back in power in Pakistan.

The Benazir Government however, could not stay long and President Ghulam Ishaq Khan dissolved the National Assembly on 6 August 1990. In the October 1990 elections Islamic Jamhuri Ittehad under Nawaz Sharif swept the polls and the provinces. Nawaz Sharif's government could not complete its term because of its confrontation with the President.

On April 18, 1993 once again the President dissolved the Nawaz Sharif Government by exercising his constitutional powers under article 58(2)-b, an amendment made by General Zia-ul-Haq in order to control the elected government.

In a landmark decision, however, the Supreme Court of Pakistan on 26th May 1993 — restored the National Assembly and reinstated Prime Minister Nawaz Sharif along with his cabinet, holding that the action of 18 April 1993 was not within the ambit of power conferred on the President by the constitution.

In order to solve the political crisis, the entire political setup in the country was changed on 18th July 1993 as the National Assembly and all the provincial assemblies were dissolved and both President Ghulam Ishaq Khan and Prime Minister Nawaz Sharif quit their offices.

In the ensuing general elections in October 1993 the PPP emerged as the single largest party and Benazir Bhutto once again became the Prime Minister, remaining in power for more than two years.

Immediately after Benazir took the oath as Prime Minister, Mr. Leghari was elected president.

After Benazir Bhutto was ousted on 5th September 1996, Nawaz Sharif's PML won the subsequent elections and he became Prime Minister again on 17th February 1997. Following a legal tussle which threatened to provoke a constitutional crisis, Leghari resigned on 2nd December 1997. He was replaced as President by Rafiq Tarar, a retired Supreme Court Judge on 1st January 1998.

The People: A Colourful Tapestry Of Cultures

With more than ninety-seven per cent of the population Muslims, the people of Pakistan are culturally homogenous, united even more by the bond of the national language Urdu.

Nonetheless, the people form a diverse and colourful ethnic mosaic. The major languages spoken in Pakistan are Punjabi, Saraiki, Sindhi, Pashtu, Baluchi, Brahui, and Hindko.

Baluchistan

Ethnically, Baluchistan is pluralistic. The main groups, each with its own language and traditions, are the Baluch, the Brahui and the Pathans. There are also Sindhi and smaller groups of Meds, Jatts, Loris, and others of mixed origin. The ethnic origin of the Baluch remains obscure.

Baluchi ethnologists and historians like to fancy that the origin of the indigenous tribes goes back 4,500 years to the biblical Nimrod and to the Syrian God, Baal, or Balu, and his followers, the "Baluchis".

Certainly, the oldest communities did migrate from Syria through south Persia and into Baluchistan between the thirteenth and fourteenth centuries. Baluchistan sagas record the name of Heleb (Aleppo).

Despite the fact that they speak an Indo-Aryan language, many Baluchis believe they are descended from Semitic stock. They do look distinctively Semitic or Arabic and many tribal names are identical to those of Arabic tribes.

The scholarly view that they are probably the Chaldean descendants of the Belus dynasty of Babylonia — 2100 BC — finds support in the universal Baluch tradition which locates their original homeland in Aleppo in Syria.

The historical march of the Baluch from Babylonia to Baluchistan took more than two millenniums.

Iran became their second homeland, where for more than a 1,000 years they first inhabited the northern parts in ancient Medea and the Caspian region, and later the south-eastern regions of Seistan and Kirman.

They were in the armies of Iran under both the Achaemenian and the Sassanian emperors, and also acted as a buffer between the Iranians and the Turks. Firdausi in his *Shah Nama* pays tribute to their martial valour.

With the Scythian conquest of south-eastern Iran in 100 BC, the first Baluch people appear to have migrated eastward into the present area of Baluchistan and Sind.

The bulk of the present Brahui-speaking stocks and the Sindhi Saraiki-speaking Jatts were the pioneers of this first big migration into Baluchistan and adjoining provinces of Pakistan.

Realizing the growing power of the Baluchi, the last of the Sassanian rulers turned against them and, according to Firdausi, Nausherwan — AD 531-578 — tried to exterminate them.

During the seventh century AD, these Baluch were early converts to Islam and remained fortified in the Kirman and Seistan regions until the middle of the tenth century.

After encounters with the strong armies of two kings, the Buwaihid Azad-ud-Daulah and the Ghaznavid Sultan Mahmud, the eleventh century saw the second Baluch migration eastward. Marris, Kurds, Dodais, and others formed part of this migration.

The third migration, mainly from the present Iranian Baluchistan, took place by the turn of the fourteenth century. Among the migrants were Rind and Lashar peoples who subjugated the state of Kalat and moved onwards separately; the Rinds, following the northern Bolan route, founded the state of Sibi with its capital at Fatehpur, and the Lashar moving eastward established their state of Gandava.

Here they fought the Rind-Lashar War for thirty years, circa 1490-1520, which sapped their energies, brought in the Arghuns from Kandahar, and dispersed the bulk of the Baluch communities into Sind Punjab.

Ameer Chakar Rind, a great warrior — and lover — established Baluchi hegemony in the sixteenth century, welding the main Baluchi tribes into one community, through noble deeds and words.

After their encounters with mighty emperors, the people of Baluchistan survived in isolation at the cost of development, wrapped in a web of feudalism that has constricted and restrained their social advance.

The original role of the chiefs was to provide protection and guidance but they became extortionate overlords. The region in which they live was given the name Baluchistan in the fifteenth century.

Most tribes lived in what one fifteenth-

Above: Children of the Hunza Valley, northern Pakistan.

majority of the Baluch population living in the neighbouring provinces of Sind and Punjab.

Traditionally, life in this province has changed slowly.

Tent-camps, an essential feature of nomadism, are gradually being affected by the inexorable process of urbanization. The camps are usually small, ranging from a single to about a dozen households. Each family owns a black tent of goat hair or sheep wool called *gidan,* or of dwarf-palm called *kirri* or *kul.* The traditional name for the camp, in eastern Baluchi, is *halk,* or community.

Wrestling, horse racing, religious feasts, *melas* (fairs), and marriage feasts are the main recreational and ceremonial functions in Baluchistan.

In the *Makran* region, the seasonal harvest of the date palms called *hamen,* is an occasion for rejoicing and reunion of friends and relatives who return home for the harvest.

North-West Frontier Province

Perhaps the best known of all the Pakistan ethnic groups are the **Pathans** — that race of fearless and fearsome warriors of the North-West Frontier whose code of honour, *Pukhtunwali,* is based on three principles: revenge, hospitality, and refuge; (*badal, melmastia, nanwata*). This also embraces the virtues of equality, respect, loyalty, pride, bravery, *purdah* (women's exclusion), the pursuit of romantic encounters, Islam, and selfless love for a friend.

The essence of this code is honour. "I despise the man who does not guide his life by honour," wrote the great Pathan poet Khushhal Khan Khatak, "the very word 'honour' drives me mad."

The *Pukhtunwali* code is nowhere written down or formalized but every Pathan knows what is required of him.

The total Pathan population is estimated at between fifteen and seventeen million, of whom about nine or ten million live in Pakistan and the remainder in Afghanistan.

The main institution of Pathan society, and the only institution for the arbitration of honour feuds, is the *jirga,* an assembly of elders which meets to resolve local issues.

Jirgas may have as few as five members or as many as sixty. Only exceptionally, if for example a dispute between two major tribes is involved, will a larger *jirga* be called.

James Spain, a diplomat and writer, has

century poet called the "mountain fortress". Baluchistan's poet laureate later defined the alliance between the Baluchistan people and nature . . . "mountains were the forts of the Baluch, high peaks their comrades, hills their army, trackless furrows their friends, spring water their drink, leaves of the dwarf-palm their cup, thorny bushes their bed, and stony ground their pillow".

The 750-kilometre-long (470-mile) coastline is dotted with settlements of fishermen, a mixed ethnic stock of the ancient Meds, and the early settlers in this region.

In the nineteenth century, the British, who were more concerned with the maintenance of their authority than with social progress, confirmed the powers and privileges of these overlords.

Both epic poetry and the abundant tradition of folk song have shaped the songs and music of Baluchistan. Though Baluchi is spoken over extensive area in Baluchistan, the bulk of the present Baluch population is bilingual, and sometimes trilingual.

Baluchi and Brahui remain their mother tongues in the interior, while Sindhi and Saraiki have been adopted as mother tongues by the

Above: Dance troupe of the pagan Kalash tribe, Chitral Valley.

described the *jirga* as "the closest thing to Athenian democracy that has existed since the original." *Jirga* decisions are taken by consensus rather than by a majority and the *jirga* does not normally determine guilt nor inflict punishment, but rather aims to achieve a settlement that will satisfy all parties.

The point to remember is that Pathan custom, unlike Western law, is much more concerned with the satisfaction of the aggrieved than with the punishment of the aggressor.

First and foremost, he must be ready to revenge any insult or any harm done to him, to his family or his clan. This obligation is called *badal* and is nicely summed up in a local proverb: "He is not a Pathan who does not give a blow for a pinch."

In *Generosity and Jealousy*, Charles Lindholm notes that the vital matters of revenge and warfare dominate life in Swat — even inside the family.

Husband and wife, it seems, are locked in a continuous struggle for power. Husbands seek to subdue their wives and, failing that, to humiliate them, perhaps by taking a second wife. The wife responds by fighting and sometimes using magic spells against her rivals. Some resort to poisoning their husbands.

Men, notes Lindholm, are allowed — "and encouraged" — to beat their wives regularly. Only if bones are broken may she run away and even then tradition says she must return. Kith and kin of a shameful or shameless wife can take their own revenge by shooting her. In this instance it is doubtful if anyone will wish to quarrel with Lindholm's observation that "married life in Swat is fraught with tensions".

But, ever-friendly to strangers, hospitable to the point of what seems certifiable insanity, and incapable of speaking a lie, there's something magnificent about Pathan men.

Disdainful of wheedling and toadying, Pathans do not make good traders. To shame troublesome customers they prefer to give them what they want. Not, indeed, as Lindholm observes, a profitable way to run a store.

A favourite proverb to a favourite son says, "The eye of the dove is lovely, my son, but the sky is made for the hawk. So cover your dove-like eyes and grow claws."

The second pillar of Pukhtunwali is *melmastia,* hospitality to guests. Any traveller through Pakistan's tribal belt, once invited in by a Pathan, will be given a generous welcome and quickly made to feel at home.

Even the richest and proudest *Malik,* or

Above: Sindhi snake charmers, Hawke's Bay, near Karachi.

traditional elder, will personally serve his guests tea and biscuits or sometimes a full-scale meal — no matter what their social status.

Every *Malik* has his own guest-house where visitors are offered rest, food and shelter. Each Pathan village also has at least one communal guest-house, possibly two or three, to enable it to extend hospitality to travellers.

The final facet of *melmastia,* which has always been much harder for Westerners to fathom, is the right of sanctuary which every true Pathan is required to afford to anyone who requests it — even common criminals fleeing from the law.

Other duties of the *jirga* include making decisions concerning community property — for example, the location of a mosque, or the conveyance of the wishes of the clan to other clans and outsiders.

The *jirga* has few sanctions at its disposal to enforce its will. Nevertheless, to all intents and purposes, the word of the *jirga* is the only law the Pathans have or are prepared to accept.

Though their physical features vary from place to place, all Pathans speak one or the other of the two dialects of Pashtu, a language belonging to the Indo-European family.

Although they are essentially a people of the countryside and the mountains, they adapted remarkably well to urban life. **Peshawar,** only a few kilometres from the **Khyber Pass,** is, in its own way, as much an expression of Pathan society as the smallest village high up in a remote hill pass.

They use neither racial nor linguistic characteristics to distinguish themselves as a separate people. They say that a Pathan can be recognized by his adherence to *Pukhtunwali;* if he acts in accordance with the code then he is a Pathan and if he does not, then he is not a Pathan.

All Pathans belong to one of the three great branches of the race. Each branch, the Sarbani, the Bitanni (with Ghilzai as its descendant) and the Ghurghushti, traces its descent from a son of their common ancestor, Qais, whose exact date and identity are unknown.

Each branch has dozens of tribes: to name only a few of the best-known, the Shinwari and the Yusufzai are Sarbani; the great semi-nomad sects of Sulaiman Khel and Aka Khel are Ghilzai; and the Afridi and Wazir are Ghurghushti. All these tribes have kinsfolk who live in Afghanistan.

The Yusufzai, perhaps the largest, oldest,

Above: Boys harvesting grain in Hunza Valley.

and most sophisticated, live both in the mountains of **Dir** and **Swat** and in the fertile plains of **Mardan district** in the North-West Frontier Province — NWFP — which is a "settled district".

The Mohmands have two distinct sections. One, the Kuz (Lower) Mohmands, vigorous, land-hungry farmers, live in and around the settled districts north of the **Kabul River.**

The Bar (Hill) Mohmands occupy a separate tribal agency in a patch of barren, inaccessible hills near the **Durand Line.** Their *khans, maliks,* and *mullahs* have more influence than those of the more individualistic Yusufzai.

The Afridi are archetypal Pathans, having collected a whole catalogue of contradictory adjectives from those who have studied them — brave, cautious, honourable, treacherous, cruel, gallant, superstitious, courteous, suspicious, and proud.

Pleasant-looking men, light-skinned, often with blue eyes, they are as a rule slim and graceful. A Semitic cast of features and a partiality for full beards, added to the dignity with which the older men wear their flowing garments and light blue turban cloths, convey an impression of an assembly of Old Testament prophets. Their heartland centres on the Khyber

and **Dara Passes.**

The Turis of the **Kurram Valley** are Shia rather than Sunni Muslims. They have definite well-developed social, religious, and legal frameworks, with various *khels* following four different families of *sayyids* who have long dwelt among them.

Of the hill tribes, the Wazir and the Mahsuds, though often at war with each other, dominate the southern tribal territory.

In contrast to their northern neighbours, the Wazir and Mahsuds speak the soft Pushto of the south and dress largely in black and darker colours.

Their population has been increasing rapidly in recent years and many, especially Mahsuds, have left their home territories to join the military and to work at road and building construction in other parts of Pakistan.

Many hills tribes have members living in the plains of NWFP. Some tribes and groups, however, dwell exclusively in the NWFP. Their tribal structure has broken down somewhat but they maintain their Pathan heritage and customs.

The Daudzai, Muhammadzai, and Khalils constitute the hard-working yeomanry of the **Peshawar Valley.** The Bannuchis who occupy

Bannu City and the area around it are very active economically. The bazaars are clearing houses for goods from all over the Frontier. Their fields and orchards provide much of the food for the people of the nearby hills.

The Khattaks, whose lands run along the east bank of the Indus from above **Attock** to just north of **Kalabagh,** historically have come closer to being a nation than any of the other tribes.

Since the thirteenth century, the whole tribe has been led more or less consistently by one chief, and the equality which each man claimed did not lead to the semi-anarchy that often prevailed within and among the other tribes. In Khushhal Khan Khatak — ADl6l3-89 — they had a great warrior, statesman, and poet, whose achievements compared well with the other great Muslim and Indian leaders of his time.

There are, of course, other fascinating and important groups which are not properly Pathan, some functional, some racial: e.g., *sayyids* and *mians,* Gujars, and Awans, Peshawaris (as mixed and cosmopolitan a city population as any in the world), Mongols, and Qizilbash.

In the far north live the Kohistanis — "People of the Mountains" — with many different dialects and racial groups, the result of a mingling over the centuries of Mongol, Chinese, Iranian, Turkish, and Pathan blood with that of the original invaders of the subcontinent.

Some, such as the ruling family of **Hunza** and the Kafirs of **Chitral,** claim direct descent from Alexander's Greeks. To varying degrees, all these other people have come under the influence of the dominant Pathan society and culture.

Now the traditions are changing. Tribes are inter-marrying with other tribes and with non-Pathans. For women, the veil is much less ubiquitous than twenty years ago.

Urdu and English are common in areas where not long ago communication was exclusively in Pashtu. More and more Pathans are finding their way from tribal territory into the Province and from both into other parts of Pakistan. Even so, in such deep-rooted societies change is slow.

Nowhere is this more evident than among the pagan **Kalash,** a non-Islamic community living in the isolated valleys of **Chitral** whose faith is founded on animism. They survive as a twentieth-century anachronism in Islamic

Pakistan and have become a powerful magnet, not just for ethnologists and anthropologists, but also for the tourists lured by their colourful festivals, cultures, and traditions.

Kalash simply means black and describes the predominant colour of their clothing. Thought by many to be descendants of Alexander the Great's cohorts who stayed and settled in these parts, certainly a number of the Kalash feature fair hair, blue eyes, and are taller than their Chitrali contemporaries.

The Kalash have no recorded history and their genealogy is lost in the mists of time, but it is known that they met the hordes of Tamurlane, the earth shaker, in 1398, and those of the Mughal Emperor, Babur, in 1507.

Lost in a limbo of antiquity though they may be, the Kalash, however, are far from primitive. Their traditions and culture were seriously researched late last century by Surgeon Major Robertson, the hero of the siege of Chitral, who later became the British Political Agent in Gilgit.

Robertson visited the Kalash valleys in 1889 and 1891 and his study, *The Kafirs of the Hindu Kush,* remains a classic. It is still the best ethnological study of these people who worship a pantheon of strange gods — each a guardian of every eventuality — presided over by Imra, the supreme creator. This ancient religion is a mixture of animism and nature worship, characterized by rituals invoking fire, idol, and ancestor worship.

Two Kalash divinities command special veneration — Mahandeo, the virile warrior guardian god of crops, birds, and hunting, and Jestak, a female goddess who watches over the home and pregnancy, birth, children, love, and marriage.

Passionately fond of music and dance, the Kalash celebrate birth, marriage, and death with three different dances. They also mark the changing seasons of the year with a spring festival, harvest festival in mid-summer, a grape and walnut festival in October, and a New Year festival. The dates vary each year but the dancing, singing, drinking, and feasting is a tireless celebration of the joy of life which culminates in the sacrificial slaughter of goats on their smoke-blackened fire altars.

Significantly, the Kalash do not bury their dead. They are left in wooden coffins above the ground to disintegrate under the onslaught of rain, wind, sun, and snow.

Many coffins are ornately engraved and

Above: Hindu girls of Sind.

Above: Sindhi beauty.

the wealthier Kalash also carve wooden effigies to stand beside them. It implies no lack of reverence or love — rather a wish to keep the dead within the community.

Punjab

Punjabis take pride in their lineage. There is among Punjabis a native pride, a consciousness of human dignity, a sense of loyalty, a steadiness of purpose, a spirit of hardiness, which makes them good soldiers, good farmers, good workers, and good friends.

Their open-heartedness and hospitality to new ideas perhaps springs from an innate sense of equality, of a feeling of brotherhood among them.

This independence has its obverse, adding to the Punjabi character a strain of marked individualism. And yet, this is a simplification, because the Punjabi psyche is also nurtured on a complex value system, as emerges so vividly in the folk legends incorporated in the great metrical romances of *Heer-Ranjha* and *Sassi-Punnu*.

Punjab stock comprises five identifiable social groups. The Sayyids, with their collaterals the Quraishis, all named after their particular ancestor, were prominent scholars and religious leaders.

They were made Qazis, Muftis and heads of endowed seminaries. The Turks, Mughals, and Afghans formed the military and administrative sections. The Rajputs and their collaterals the Jatts comprised the yeomanry. The neo-Muslims kept their own castes or were called Shaikh Qanungo or Khwajas (corrupted to Khojas), confined mostly to the commercial classes.

In the smaller towns there is usually a separate *mohalla* (precinct) for most trades. There is likely to be a Mohalla Qazis (that is, of *qazia* or judges), a Mohalla Muftian, a Mohalla Hamdanian (that is of Hamdani one of potters), another of butchers, others of weavers, tanners, coppersmiths, blacksmiths, artisans, and so on.

Such segregation, though a legacy of the old guild system, betokens a stable social order and is not necessarily a sign of rigid differences of social levels, or inherited snobbery or inferiority on any side.

Sind

Before the emergence of the Indus Civilization the aboriginal inhabitants of Sind were probably hunters, and fisherfolk in transition towards pastoralism, with a little rudimentary subsistence agriculture.

The Mohannas of the **Manchar Lake,** fisherfolk who live for the most part in their boats, may be direct descendants of the lake-dwellers that existed at the dawn of the Indus Civilization.

Another class of Sindhi, whose way of life seems to have continued virtually unchanged since primaeval days, are the Jatts of the Indus delta country, who subsist almost entirely on the milk of their she-camels.

Most Sindhi Muslims belong either to the indigenous stock or are of Arab or Baluch origin. Those who tend to classify themselves as Sammat, by race descended from the Samma, Rajput, Lakha, Lohana, and Jatt inhabitants of the country at the time of its conquest by Muhammad bin Qasim.

Those remote forbears were predominantly Buddhist in religion, with a minority of Brahmin Hindus and Jains. The conversion to Islam of the great majority of their descendants was probably a continuous process during the succeeding eleven centuries of rule by Muslim dynasties.

For the most part, the Muslim peasants of Sind live in thousands of hamlets and isolated huts scattered all over the region, chosen for their arable or pastoral potential.

Houses are a single or two-roomed hut, of baked mud and thatch clustered, sometimes, round the high walls which enclose the mansion of a large land-owner.

Sind's villages and towns are conglomerations of flat-roofed houses where artisan workshops accommodate handloom weavers, potters, blacksmiths, and others.

To a large extent, Sind's cultural life was shaped by its comparative isolation from the rest of the subcontinent. As a result, it developed its own, exclusive artistic tradition. Arts and crafts, music and literature, games and sports have retained their original flavour. Sind is rich in exquisite pottery, variegated glazed tiles, lacquer-work, leather and straw products, needlework, quilts, embroidery, hand print making and textile design.

Melas (fairs) and *malakharas* (wrestling festivals) are popular, and falconry, horse and camel breeding, and racing are characteristic pastimes.

Jammu And Kashmir

Latter writers like G. T. Vigne, Francis Younghusband, and Walter Lawrence in the nineteenth century were so struck by the individuality of Jammu and Kashmir that they focused on the special ethnic characteristic of its people.

Vigne called them the Neapolitans of the East, Lawrence found pronounced Semitic features in them.

Even that most perceptive observer, al-Biruni — AD973-1048 — who accompanied the unsuccessful expedition of Mahmud of Ghazni to Kashmir in 1021 noted that the Kashmiri did "not allow any Hindu to enter" their lands.

And there still exists a mistaken belief by some that they are one of the lost tribes of Israel.

The origin of the name, Kashmir, is obscure. All that is certain from a continuous chain of documents started more than 2,300 years ago is that of all the regional societies of South Asia, Kashmir can claim the oldest settled continuity.

Antiquity apart, Kashmir also has the distinction of being the only place in the region that has a recorded history that goes back beyond the advent of Islam.

Originally composed by the Kashmiri Pandit Kalhana in 1148, *Rajatarangini* is a narrative in Sanskrit verse of Kashmir's ruling dynasties from the earliest period, supplemented by later authors (notably Jonaraja in the early fifteenth century) and updated after the Mughal Conquest in 1586.

Minorities

Religious minorities form only three per cent of Pakistan's population; but their contribution in business, education, medicine, and the arts is much greater.

Not only have the minorities been able freely to follow their professions and trades but encouraged to contest the specially created and reserved seats for them in the legislative assemblies of the nation. A Federal Minister for Minority Affairs safeguards their interest.

Christians, the biggest minority group, have made their homes in most parts of the country. Churches of virtually every denomination embellish the architectural horizon of most Pakistan cities.

Although Pakistani Christians have not restricted their attention to any one area of activity, they have made, and continue to make, outstanding contributions in health, education, railways, and the police. Many hold

Above: Dervish dancer, Lahore.

Above: Sindhi peasant.

senior positions in civil and defence services.

The Hindus of Pakistan, generally settled in Sind, celebrate their holy days with all their traditional colour. In the larger cities (particularly Karachi) the Hindu acumen for business comes into full play. Members of this community are extremely active in commerce.

Most of the Ahmadis, a relatively recent religious community, are of Punjab origin. The sect came into existence at the end of the last century when the preaching of Mirza Ghulam Ahmad attracted a large number of followers.

Ahmadis are also known as Qadianis since the belief originated in the town of Qadian in East Punjab. Though divided into the Qadiani and Lahori groups, they are well-organized and take part in virtually every field of economic activity.

The Parsis (or Zoroastrians), an extremely small minority concentrated in the larger cities of Pakistan, are almost exclusively engaged in business. Some of the foremost hotel and shipping magnates of Pakistan are Parsis and richer members of this community are well known for their philanthropic activities.

Buddhists are few but the cultural impact made by their ancestors has enriched the heritage of Pakistan. Ancient Buddhist temples, schools, and cities dot the archaeological map of Pakistan.

There are also many important Sikh temples and shrines in Pakistan which are looked after by the Government. The most notable among these is Nankana Sahib, the birthplace of Guru Nanak, the founder of the Sikh religion.

The Land: A Many Splendoured Country

Pakistan's varied and many-splendoured landscapes, divided into five major regions — the high northern mountains, the low western mountains, the **Potwar uplands,** the **Baluchistan** plateau, the **Punjab** and **Sind** plains — ring with magic names like the **Himalaya** and the **Karakoram,** the **Khyber Pass** and **Hunza.**

The mountains of Pakistan are linked with what in olden days was perhaps the most perilous trade route on earth.

And the other great mountain ranges, scarcely less daunting, the **Hindu Kush, Little Pamirs,** and the fiefdom of **Baltistan,** have also been a constant lure to the hardy explorer and adventurer.

Fabled Shangrila — **Hunza** — the kingdom of Lost Horizon on the Silk Route in the country's far north has long been admired for its magnificent setting, a slender narrow valley enclosed by some of the greatest mountains on earth, and the longevity of its citizens.

Valleys farther south, such as **Swat** and **Chitral,** are equally legendary and beautiful. No less renowned are the five great rivers that combine to form the lower **Indus,** and the great fertile lowlands that surround them.

And is there a boy or man anywhere who has not heard of the Khyber Pass, though few will be able to recall its contemporary to the south, the **Bolan Pass,** and fewer still will have heard of remote Baluchistan with its barren mountain ranges and wild **Makran** coastland?

There can be few countries where the geography has left such a decisive stamp on both the shape of history and the character of the people.

A vast and sometimes seemingly endless country, Pakistan comprises four provinces — Baluchistan, **North-West Frontier,** Punjab, and Sind. The respective capitals are **Quetta, Peshawar, Lahore,** and **Karachi.**

Ranging from the lofty mountains of the north, through dissected plateaux, to the dead-level plains of the south, Pakistan offers sharp contrasts of landscape and terrain.

Mountain and plateaux form about three-fifths of the total land area, the remainder forming an alluvial plain shaped by the Indus and its tributaries.

Lying north of the Tropic of Cancer, between latitudes 24°N and 37°N, Pakistan has a continental-type climate with extreme variations of temperature, modified in different regions by the rainfall and the amount of irrigation and afforestation or deforestation.

Areas close to the snow-covered mountains are characterized by a comparatively cold climate, those along the coast are influenced by the sea monsoons, and the rest of the land is generally dry — with thick dust storms and thunderstorms occasionally bringing brief release from the excessive heat of summer.

Stretching across the northernmost extremities, from east to west, a series of high mountain ranges, known as the Roof of The World, separates Pakistan from China, Russia, and Afghanistan. These are the Himalaya, Karakoram, and Hindu Kush mountains.

With thirty-three peaks higher than 7,315 metres (24,000 feet), and some above 7,925 metres (26,000 feet), the highest peak, K2 at 8,610 metres (28,250 feet), is exceeded only by Everest.

The region abounds in vast glaciers, sparkling lakes, and lush green valleys, particularly the southern slopes which receive heavy rainfall and are cloaked with forests of deodar, pine, poplar, and willow trees.

The Himalaya run from north-west to south-east for some 320 kilometres (200 miles), converging in the Karakoram and Pamir ranges above **Skardu.** The Karakoram and its offshoots, run roughly north-south. With the Pamirs, these spurs form the western borderland of Pakistan.

Beyond the Karakoram lies the Chinese province of Sinkiang. Across the Hindu Kush, in the farmost north-west, the Pamir border the narrow panhandle of Afghanistan that divides Pakistan from the Soviet Union.

The outer ranges include the **Pir Panjal** in **Hazara** which are rich in animal fossils.

Dominating the west, the Hindu Kush send off a number of spurs towards Chitral, Dir, and Swat. The highest point **Tirich Mir,** at 7,690 metres (25,223 feet), is surrounded by the perpetual snow and ice of its sister peaks.

The Hindu Kush outliers range south, ever decreasing in height, to **Mohmand** and the **Malakand hills** where they touch between 1,500 and 1,800 metres (5,000-6,000 feet). These mountains cover a large portion of the NWFP. South of the river Kabul spreads the 3,200-

metre-high (10,000-feet) **Koh-e-Sofed** range with the Sulaiman Mountains, south of the **Gomal River,** running almost 500 kilometres (300 miles) from the north to south, **Takht-e-Sulaiman** at 3,443 metres (11,295 feet) being its highest peak.

The **Marri** and **Bugti Hills** mark the southernmost extremity of the Sulaimans and the low **Kirthar** range the western boundary of the great plains of Sind.

These western mountains have a number of passes of special geographical and historical interest including the Khyber, the largest and most renowned, connecting Kabul in Afghanistan with the fertile Vale of Peshawar in the NWFP.

The **Tochi Pass** connects Ghazni in Afghanistan with **Bannu** in Pakistan and the Gomal Pass provides a route from Afghanistan to **Dera Ismail Khan.** The Bolan Pass connects the Sind plain with **Quetta** in Baluchistan and ultimately with Afghanistan through Chaman.

Baluchistan Plateau

Another dominant feature of Pakistan's landscapes is the extensive Baluchistan plateau at an altitude of around 600 metres (2,000 feet). But the province is full of contrasts ranging from gaunt and barren mountains to hillgirt basin plains.

Well outside the influence of the monsoons, Baluchistan receives scanty and irregular rainfall — about ten millimetres (four inches) a year while the temperature is extremely high in summer and low in winter. Owing to the continuous drought there is little vegetation.

In the north-east, ringed by mountains, lies the Zhob-Loralai Basin, larger than the **Quetta plateau** which is similarly enclosed by dramatic mountains.

In central and southern Baluchistan, enclosing the Sarawan region, mountains running north-south flank narrow valleys with a vast wilderness of mountains in the south.

The backbone of Baluchistan is formed by the **Central Brahui** range running from the north-east to the south-west while the north-western region of the province is a low-lying desert plateau with a number of salt beds and dry lakes. There are also large areas of mudflats on the extensive **Makran** coastline.

The **Kalat plateau,** at between 2,260 and 2,500 metres (7,000-8,000 feet) above sea level, in the centre of Baluchistan, is the most important of the individual plateaux.

In Punjab, the **Potwar plateau,** at an altitude of between 360 and 580 metres (1,200-1,900 feet), lies at the southern base of the Himalayan and Pir Panjal foothills, flanked in the west by the Indus, in the east by the **river Jhelum,** and the Salt Range in the south.

These are typical arid lands with undulating, denuded, and broken terrain. Agriculture is almost entirely dependent on the rainfall of between thirty-eight and fifty centimetres (15-20 inches) a year, and on the small irrigation dams built in the catchment areas of the streams.

Generally scrubby agricultural land dissected by deep ravines, it slopes from north-east to south-west and the **Soan river. The Salt Range** is geologically outstanding — its southern face is a continuous sequence of rocks from the Cambrian to the Pleistocene.

The gift of the Indus and its five eastern tributaries — Jhelum, **Chenab, Ravi, Sutlej,** and **Beas** — is the Punjab plain which stretches from the foot of the Potwar Plateau to **Mithankot,** where the Sulaiman Range meets the Indus.

Some twenty-five million years ago, during the Late Tertiary period, a series of violent volcanic eruptions shook the area where the Himalaya now stand.

At the time of their formation, a great rift valley — almost 2,000 kilometres (1,250 miles) long — lay along their southern edge where the Potwar plateau now stands.

In places, the floor of this valley was possibly 21,350 metres (70,000 feet) below the highest peaks. In successive epochs, gigantic rivers and innumerable streams rushing down from the mountains began to fill the valley with alluvium.

The Indus and Ganges plains is the same rift valley that once served as a gulf between the Himalaya and the main subcontinental peninsula.

The upper Indus plain, including Punjab, comprises a number of river valleys formed by the Indus and its major tributaries.

Flat and featureless, the plain slopes gently southward descending seventeen centimetres to the kilometre (one foot to each mile). Running south, south-west to the Arabian Sea over an

Opposite: Tractor and trailer on KKH beneath Passu glacier.

area of 518,000 square kilometres (200,000 square miles), the Indus plain is divided into upper and lower sections.

The only break in this alluvial monotony is small group of broken hills 300-500 metres (1,000-1,600 feet) high near **Sangla** and **Kirana** which straddle the Chenab.

The entire plain is extensively irrigated by a network of canals which has been greatly expanded and improved by the construction of link-canals, dams, and barrages and the Indus Waters Treaty with India.

The Sind plain

The lower Indus plain, including Sind, is dominated by a single river, the Indus. The Punjab plain and the Sind plain are connected by a narrow strip of plain south of the **Rahimyar Khan** district, known as the **Indus Corridor.**

The desert areas of the Indus plain include the steppes of the Sind **Sagar Doab,** between the Indus and Chenab rivers, **Nara,** or **Rajasthan,** in Khaipur, Sind, and the **Thar** desert in Sind's **Tharparker** district.

The Sind plain covers almost the whole of Sind province, stretching from the Punjab plain to the Arabian Sea. Through this vast tract the Indus, swollen by the waters of its five tributaries, meanders majestically, again giving life to an area of scant rainfall.

Like the Punjab plain, Sind is composed of an immense fertile valley to the west of the Indus and huge expanses of desert to the east. The many natural and manmade lakes attract thousands of migratory birds from Central Asia during the winter season. Further south, the desolate mudflats and swamp wastelands of the Indus Delta begin.

The Indus: River of History and Giver of Life

To the ancient Hindus the Indus flowed from the mouth of a lion, *Sinh-ka-bab*. They described the river in Sanskrit as the *Sindus*. The Greeks called it *Sinthus*, the Romans *Sindus*, the Chinese *Sintow* and the Persians *Abisindh*. It was Pliny who first called it *Indus* — and the name stuck.

In turn the *Indus* gave its name to India, and through accidents of navigation, to Indonesia and the West Indies, to the Red Indians and now to the world's largest, single water development programme.

The entire basin covers an area of about 901,320 square kilometres (348,000 square miles) of which 528 360 square kilometres (204,000 square miles) lie in Pakistan.

Rising in western Tibet, the Indus at first runs across a high plateau at the start of its 3,180-kilometre-long (1,980-mile) journey, then drops rapidly. Gathering momentum, it cuts its way north-west between the Karakoram and the Himalaya in the Roof of the World.

In Kashmir it crosses the United Nations ceasefire line and enters Pakistan in Baltistan. The first town on the upper Indus, Skardu, at 2,288 metres (7,500 feet) above sea level, stands on a bluff near the junction of the Indus and one of its great right-bank tributaries, the *Shigar.*

Below Skardu, the Karakoram and Himalaya close in and the Indus becomes a deep, relentless, dark-grey torrent, hurling itself through ravines of naked rock.

In a brief widening of its valley, the clear, jade-green **Gilgit river** foams down to meet it from the Hindu Kush. Standing across the Indus, these mountains force the river southwest where the **Astor** joins it from the east.

Thus reinforced, it now twists and swirls along a trough between the Hindu Kush to the west, and the huge rampart of **Nanga Parbat** to the east.

All along these upper reaches, narrow alluvial fans spill down occasional cracks in the mountain rock and sometimes, in the high mountains, a glacier slides across a tributary river holding it back to form a lake.

When the ice-dam breaks, it releases a great tidal wave reaching high up the cliffs in the Indus gorge, sweeping all before it. When the implacable river eventually forces its way through, the destruction downstream is catastrophic.

At last, just above a village called **Tarbela,** where the Indus breaks free of the Hindu Kush, one of the largest dams in the world has been built to hold and control water for irrigation and generate electricity.

For a short breathing-space the river runs wide and shallow from Tarbela across the Potwar Plateau. Then, at **Attock,** under the walls of the fort that Akbar built in 1586, the Indus gathers itself together again to force yet another mountain obstacle in its path, the Salt range.

Above: Fishermen on Kheenjar Lake, Sind.   Overleaf: Lake Satpara, near Skardu.

But this is the last. At **Kalabagh,** still 1,600 kilometres (1,000) miles) from its source, with roughly the same distance still to cover to the sea, the Indus emerges on the plains of Punjab.

Here at Kalabagh a big dam has been proposed. After some preliminary work, the work on the dam has not progressed. From the beginning this dam has become a controversial project between provinces.

Dramatic width

The second half of the river's course is as dramatic as the first, but in a different way. Instead of being narrowly confined within walls of mountains, the Indus spreads itself. Its bed is soon so wide that from one bank the other is invisible.

In summer, when the snow and ice melt in the north, the great river, spumey and grey, fills its bed to the brim. In winter, when the river is low, islands and sandbanks surface, and the clear water flows in a maze of channels at the bottom of sloping mudbanks.

When the river slows as it must, it drops the silt it has carried through the upper gorges, and its bed gradually rises. In heavy flood — perhaps a glacier dam is breached, or the monsoon arrives before the end of the summer snowmelt — it may charge out of its bed and cut a new channel across the plains.

Only one or two relatively unimportant tributaries flow into the Indus from the western mountains near Afghanistan at the beginning of its journey across the plains.

But halfway to the sea the Indus is joined by the greatest of all its tributaries from the east — the **Panjnad, Jhelum, Chenab, Ravi, Beas,** and **Sutlej.** Each has travelled a different path from the Himalaya, uniting only some eighty kilometres (50 miles) before they meet the Indus.

Below the twin towns of **Hyderabad** and **Kotri,** the Indus runs south to a delta of tamarisks, scrub, and saltwater rushes where the great river spreads out in dozens of shallow, meandering creeks and ditches.

Sixteen kilometres (10 miles) beyond the coast the Arabian Sea is discoloured by the silt of the Indus, and beneath its waters a deep canyon marks the channel of the river. The Indus, cutting through great mountains, driving across enormous sands, carves a last gorge in the sea bed.

PART TWO:
PLACES AND TRAVEL

Above: K2, the world's second highest mountain at 8,610 metres (28,250 feet) high.

The North: Mountains, Rivers, and People

Throughout northern Pakistan, each day's travel brings fresh revelations and the magic of incomparable vistas — breathtaking discoveries of snowy mountain crests, dynamic and colourful cultures, rare wildlife, jade lakes and rippling streams, dancing waterfalls, and pine-cloaked hills ablaze in summer with glorious alpine flowers.

Bounded in the west by Afghanistan, separated from Russia in the north-west by a narrow neck of land nowhere wider than fifty kilometres (30 miles), with China to the north, and Indian-held Kashmir to the east, northern Pakistan, tumultuous and magnificent, draws the breath of all who fall under its spell.

In its perpendicular wildernesses, treacherous and forbidding, few living things find sanctuary. Not surprisingly, therefore, fewer than one per cent of the world's ninth most populous nation, roughly one million people, live in the 140,000 square kilometres (57,000 square miles) of Pakistan's northern areas.

Above: Landmark monument Skardu town.

The region consists of the old **Gilgit** and **Baltistan** agencies; the former fiefdoms of **Hunza** and **Nagar,** now divided into three administrative districts; the **Swat** and **Chitral** valleys and the green hills above the **Grand Trunk Road** between **Peshawar** and **Rawalpindi.**

In these lost and hidden valleys a proud, hardy people till their precious soil and live far beyond the span of most mortals.

This glittering mosaic of human cultures contains many different ethnic groups and tribes, some the descendants of Genghis Khan and Tamurlane, some of Mongol, Aryan, and Turanian stock all homogenized by their shared Islamic faith but for one exception, the pagan Kalash of Chitral.

Hidden within their girdles of ice-encrusted peaks, these valley states have changed little over the years. Alone in their mountain fastnesses, cut off for centuries from any real contact with the outside world, these communities have maintained and enriched their traditions, uncorrupted by so-called civilizing influences.

Lost Horizon

And yet where nature is harshest it is also kindest. In the chasmic gorges beneath these mountains and their glaciers, flow rivers wild and wonderful that nourish tiny hamlets and villages like Hunza, the fabled *Shangri-la* from the pages of James Hilton's *Lost Horizon.*

The verdant, gentler hills of the **Pir Panjal,** including the incomparable **Kaghan Valley;** the moulded contours of the lower valleys of the Hindu Kush, like Swat and Chitral, the Himalayan valleys of Astor and Skardu — all perfectly counterpose the harsh, forbidding grandeur of the Karakoram and Pamirs.

Fed by the snowmelt and monsoon run-offs, great rivers like the Jhelum and the Indus are born in these mountains and gather momentum to bestow their bounty downstream on a land brought to fecund life by the spring and summer sun.

Winter is long and summer brief in The Roof of the World among the gable cliffs, ice cornices, vaulted pillars, sliding glaciers, and rock buttresses, chipped and carved into strange and eerie sculptures by the cutting edge of the sub-zero blasts.

Only in late May or early June do the snow-clad passes open, some to close again in September. Constantly on the move, pitted with deadly unseen crevasses hundreds of metres deep, the glaciers add the finishing touch to the most dramatic, if desolate, landscape in the world.

G.T. Vigne was the first to bring back an account of this, one of the world's greatest glacial systems, at a time when geographers were sceptical (as they were about ice on the Equator) that any glaciers could exist in a warmer latitude than those of the European Alps.

Colonel H. H. Godwin-Austen, after whom one of the glaciers is named, added graphic insight into the system through his sketches and observations.

Through blizzard, frost, and storm the surveyors moved forward, victim of altitude sickness, frostbite, and snow-blindness. At times lightning set their hair ablaze.

They had to hump heavy equipment, including forty-five-kilo (100-lb) theodolites, over mountains and across raging rivers — from one high point to another. Setting up a "trig" station in the most forbidding places, the surveyor then computed the angles between one base line, his station and a third point.

So accurate were these measurements that a series carried over hundreds of kilometres erred by no more than a fraction of a centimetre for each base kilometre.

Sometimes at altitudes of 4,570 metres (15,000 feet) or more, they had to dig down through several metres of snow to find a stable, level base on which to build a stone pillar for the theodolite.

Godwin-Austen's success rested not on his scientific skills alone. He was also a magnificent mountaineer. He had to be. Year after year, he broke the world's altitude record — from 5,973 metres (19,600 feet) to 6,065 metres (19,900 feet); from 6,278 metres (20,600 feet) to 6,400 metres (21,000 feet), at which height he built a "trig" station; until finally he stood at 6,827 metres (22,300 feet). Four of his stations were the world's highest for more than sixty years.

His descriptions of the glaciers and mountains were stirring. The endless, anguished creaking of rock and ice in mortal combat, moaning as if in agony — a noise sometimes drowned in the tearing, screaming, thundering frenzy of an avalanche — creates one of the most distinct phenomena of life in the Karakoram.

The extremes of temperature are the most severe in the world. In summer, rocks become

Above: Shangri-la hotel resort, Lake Kachura, near Skardu.

so hot that they blister the skin. In the long winter, it is the coldest inhabited place on earth.

The fact that people can live at altitudes of 3,658 metres (12,000 feet) or more, and survive the cutting edge of winds that blast against mountain peak and funnel furiously through passes and ravines, gives fresh scale to concepts of human endurance and hardihood.

Such a tangled knot of mighty peaks also gives new scale to human perspectives. The clasp of mountains that decorates the world's midriff is unique.

A "Silk Route" through these desolate mountain fastnesses existed long ago. Unmindful of the hazards, for more than 2,000 years traders and mule trains carried silk, tea, and porcelain from China over this tortuous route via the Khunjerab Pass to the subcontinent, to barter for gold, ivory, jewels, and spices.

Until 1891 the only fair weather footpath to Gilgit from Kashmir in the south was over the hazardous 4,175-metre-high (13,700-feet) **Burzil Pass,** across the **Deosai Plains** and through the Astor Valley to **Bunji.** The journey took about a month.

Covered with deep snow and ice for more than half the year, the desolate Deosai Plains above the pass stretch for more than nineteen kilometres (12 miles).

In 1892 another route was opened through the Kaghan Valley and across the 4,170-metre-high (13,685-feet) **Babusar Pass.** But both could only be used for three months of the year before the snows fell again. Many have been trapped and frozen to death.

These districts were finally opened up by the **Karakoram Highway,** which in the course of its 883-kilometre-long (548-mile) journey from **Thakot** rises, through the Himalaya and the Karakoram Mountains, to more than 4,570 metres (15,000 feet) and is one of the great engineering marvels of the world.

Getting there

Check with the relevant authorities — the Frontier Works Organisation (FWO), or police in Rawalpindi — before leaving to find out if the road is open. March-April and July-August are the worst months for landslides.

It takes between ten and eleven hours to cover the 594 kilometres (371 miles) from Islamabad to Gilgit, but allow more time for picnics, photography, and possible landslides.

Sightseeing

The Karakoram Highway starts officially at Thakot but **Havelian** in Hazara serves as railhead.

Launched under a 1966 Sino-Pak agreement, it took twelve long, perilous years to complete as it carved its way through the greatest mountain ranges in the world.

The seven-metre-wide (23-feet) highway involved twenty-three million cubic metres (30 million cubic yards) of earth works and rock cuts and consumed 812 tonnes (800 tons) of explosives, 81,284 tonnes (80,000 tons) of cement and 35,562 tonnes (35,000 tons) of coal. A further 81,284 tonnes (80,000 tons) of fuel and lubricants were used by the thousand trucks which maintained a constant shuttle, shipping supplies, men, and equipment up and down its length.

Eighty-five bridges and many tunnels mark the course of the highway. These permanent bridges were preceded by Bailey bridges which swiftly spanned the gorges and the rushing waters to keep supplies, and progress on the road, moving.

Today, it is a two-lane highway capable, it is said, of taking two tanks abreast, with as many as 1,708 culverts.

But for almost every kilometre (half-a-mile) gouged out of this unrelenting mountain domain, a man died — most through simple human error. Thirty died when their truck driver briefly lost concentration and drove straight over the edge of the road.

At Gilgit, the **Chinese Bridge** is distinguished by the lions carved on its structure, representing the Chinese God who keeps all safe in a storm.

Above the bridge stands a tranquil cemetery, shaded by trees, where the Chinese workers killed while building the highway — those the lion failed — lie in eternal peace. It is surrounded by the mountains, including the 7,787-metre-high (25,550 feet) Rakaposhi, which they fought and conquered but which finally claimed their revenge.

Landslides are frequent and one perennial problem is the movement of the **Passu** and **Batura Glaciers** beyond **Hunza,** which lie above the highway. The Batura flows for an astonishing seventy kilometres (44 miles).

But since it opened the highway has only once been closed for longer than a day — when Batura Glacier crashed down on it and the debris took three days to clear.

Azad Kashmir: United People, Divided Nation

Azad Kashmir, "Free Kashmir", in Pakistan is divided geographically into two zones — the hills and mountains of the north and west, and the valleys and plains of the south and east. Kashmir itself is divided between two nations by the Indian occupation of Jammu Kashmir.

Covering an area of 13,297 square kilometres (5,130 square miles), Azad Kashmir has a subtropical highland climate with an annual rainfall of 150 centimetres (59 inches). With a population approaching 3.5 million, there are about 260 persons to every square kilometre.

Formally known as Azad Jammu and Kashmir — AJ&K — Azad Kashmir is a nation within a nation. It has its own parliament with a President as the head of state and a Prime Minister as the chief government executive.

The Legislative Assembly is composed of representatives democratically elected by universal franchise. It is the assembly which elects the President, while the Prime Minister is the leader of the majority party.

For administrative purposes Azad Kashmir is divided into four districts — **Muzaffarabad, Punch, Kotli,** and **Mirpur.** The capital city is **Muzaffarabad** in **Mirpur district.**

Tourist resorts are being developed in many districts but movement is restricted along its eastern boundaries, notably because they form the ceasefire "line of control" with Indian-held Kashmir.

At no place are foreign visitors allowed within sixteen kilometres (ten miles) of the "line of control". Nor are they allowed into the Neelum or Leepa valleys, areas of outstanding natural beauty.

Drained by three rivers — the **Jhelum, Neelum,** and **Punch** — whose courses flow through stunning scenic valleys, Azad Kashmir stretches from the Punjab plains through the Himalayan foothills to the Pir Panjal mountains rising more than 6,000 metres (20,000 feet) above sea level in the north.

Previous pages: 6,000-metre-high (19,700 feet) Mitre Peak, Concordia.

Getting there

Muzaffarabad, is two hours drive from **Abbottabad.** You take the right fork just before **Manshera,** pass through **Garhi** Habibullah to Lohar Gali, with its panoramic views of the Jhelum valley and Muzaffarabad, and then descend to the capital.

There is also a summer route up the Jhelum Valley from **Murree** to Muzaffarabad.

Southern Azad Kashmir — Punch District, Kotli and **Mirpur** — can be reached from **Islamabad** via **Lehtar, Kahuta,** or **Mangla Dam.**

Petrol

Premium grade petrol is obtainable only in Mirpur. Regular and diesel fuel are available only at Muzaffarabad, **Bagh, Rawalkot, Hajira** and Kotli with any certainty.

When to go

Late March to early May and September to November are the ideal seasons in which to visit Azad Kashmir, avoiding extreme cold and heat.

Where to Stay

Government guest house, Muzaffarabad. Assembly Hostel, Chatter Domel, Muzaffarabad. PWD rest houses at Chikar, Chenari, Dhirkot, Bagh, Rawalkot, and Palandri. Inquire at PWD office, Muzaffarabad. Forest tourist huts and rest houses at Chikar, Loon Bagla, Dungian, Dhirkot, Shardi, and Kel. Inquire at the office of the Deputy Director Tourism, Forestry Department, Muzaffarabad.

You can also camp in Azad Kashmir, although there are no recognised campsites. See Listings for "Hotels".

Sightseeing

Muzaffarabad is notable for the sixteenth-century **Red Fort** that the Chukk rulers of the area built on a promontory overlooking the Neelum river between 1549 and 1552 as a defence against the Mughals. Centuries later, the Sikhs used it as an army camp but it was then abandoned.

The city's main **bazaar** is noted for its walnut carvings and Kashmiri shawls. Above the Secretariat stands 2,900-metrehigh (9,565 feet) Pir Chinasi.

The road north from Muzaffarabad passes the Red Fort, then crosses the Neelum river to climb upstream for sixteen kilometres (ten

Above: Alpine beauty of Azad Kashmir

miles) through a narrow gorge to Ghori, where it crosses over the Neelum again.

To the left, before the bridge, there's a trail that leads over the 3,890-metre-high (12,744 feet) **Makra mountain** to **Shogran in** the Kaghan valley.

From Ghori it's another six kilometres (three-and-a-half miles) to **Patika** where you can take a dirt trail over a timber suspension bridge to the high peaks that form the watershed of the Kaghan and Neelum valleys.

The main road along the Neelum Valley from Patika is a dizzying drive through a narrow gorge 250 metres (800 feet) above the river to **Panjgran,** where the valley bellies out beneath the **Kafir Khan** foothills.

Finally, beneath the conical peak of 3,500metre-high (11,336 feet) **Mali,** the road reaches the bridge at **Noseri,** forty-two kilometres (26 miles) from Muzaffarabad — as far as the non-Pakistani visitor may travel.

Yet ahead lies the most beautiful and unspoilt stretch of the Neelum valley, rival to the best of Kaghan and Swat. Here abouts the three-storey timber houses, with their steeply pitched roofs, are reminiscent of the alpine chalets of Switzerland.

Far up the Neelum Valley, some 160 kilometres (100 miles) from Muzaffarabad, above the village of **Kel,** directly to the north on the trail to Chilas, there are stunning views of Nanga Parbat.

Another scenic route, along the upper **Jhelum valley,** follows the old road from Muzaffarabad, beneath the **Domel bridge,** where green and fertile terraced grain fields and rice paddies line the valley slopes, to **Srinagar.**

Just ten kilometres (six miles) from Muzaffarabad there's a small lake formed by an avalanche where you can hire boats for fishing; and beyond that, another fifteen kilometres (nine miles) you come to **Garhi Dopatta,** where you cross a suspension bridge to take the trail that climbs into the Kafir Khan foothills.

Beyond Garhi Dopatta, high above the river and right for two-and-a-half kilometres (one-and-a-half miles), stands Saran close to the pleasant hill station of Chikar, set at 1,700 metres (5,600 feet).

With two comfortable rest houses, it's an ideal base for many splendid walks — one in particular along the ridge that runs behind the main rest house.

From Chikar, a jeep track leads on for

Left: Celebration at traditional wedding reception.

eighteen kilometres (11 miles) through **Loon Bagla** to **Dungian,** where there's another rest house and many more fine alpine walks with views of the Himalaya to the north and Indian-held Kashmir to the east.

Incredible Panoramas

One hour's drive from Loon Bagla is **Soudhan Gali,** at a height of 2,200 metres (7,200 feet) where you can follow a ridge trail through pine forests to **Ganga Chota,** one of the peaks of the Pir Panjal range with incredible panoramas over Murree to the west, the mountains around the Vale of Kashmir to the east, the Himalaya of the Neelum valley to the north, and Punch district to the south.

Following the main road up the Jhelum valley, the next village after Saran is **Hattian,** where a track across the river leads on to **Reshian** and over a 2,750-metre-high (9,000 feet) pass through the Kafir Khan foothills into the Leepa valley.

Soon after Hattian the road arrives at Chenari and then **Chakothi,** which marks the beginning of the Jhelum gorge leading to the Vale of Kashmir and the forbidden "line of control".

Another region of Azad Kashmir that offers splendid scenery, idyllic walks, and magnificent forests is Punch District, which can be reached by taking the Dhirkot road out of the Jhelum valley, past the sanatorium at **Chamenkot.**

The road dips down across a nullah to **Arja** and then continues straight on up the **Mahl valley** to **Bagh.** Along the Mahlwani Kas road, north from Bagh, is Soudhan Gali. You can also explore the valley upstream to **Dulli** and the **Haji Pir Pass.**

If, however, you turn right at Arja across the Mahl river, you'll climb slowly to **Rawalkot.** Here you can pass through the bazaar and drive thirteen kilometres (eight miles) along the Hajira road to **Kai Gala** bazaar, where there's a jeep track north to **Toli Pir** with its splendid forest walks and views of the Mahl valley and the Pir Panjal mountains.

South of Kai Gala is **Banjosa,** another hill resort with a luxurious rest house and many fine alpine walks offering panoramic vistas of the Pir Panjal and Indian-held Kashmir.

Though pleasant in springtime, Azad Kashmir's Kotli and Mirpur districts have little to offer in the way of scenery or excitement, with the exception of **Mangla Dam** on the Jhelum, in Mirpur district. Second only in size to Tarbela, it was a tremendous feat of civil engineering that created a vast reservoir many tens of kilometres long. Easily reached from the Grand Trunk Road at **Dina,** the dam is suitable for both boating and fishing.

Murree and The Galis: An Alpine Wonderland

Close to **Islamabad,** in the foothills of the Pir Panjal, cool in summer, crisp in winter, the **Murree Hills** at an altitude of around 2,300 metres (7,500 feet) offer some of Pakistan's most delightful alpine scenery.

In the middle of the last century the British raj turned it into a hill station and left their own brand of Anglo-Saxon nostalgia indelibly imposed on the local architecture and nomenclature.

They founded this new hill station on the meadows of Mussiari (or Mussidi) village, conveniently close to their military headquarters at **Rawalpindi.** The local word for high place, *Marhi,* was Anglicised to **Murree.**

It was the summer headquarters of the Punjab government until 1876 when it was transferred to Simla. Nonetheless, when the road from Murree through Muzaffarabad to Kashmir was completed, it continued to grow in importance. As elsewhere, when far from home, the British built a typical English resort complete with a **mall** for promenading and ceremonial parades, parks, churches and schools.

Today, the hills are a cool holiday retreat for citizens of Islamabad and Rawalpindi during the sweltering heat of summer. If there's anything at all of Empire left to savour, it's the slightly mildewed nostalgia of the old colonialists that arises from Murree's faded and dilapidated tin-roofed bungalows with names like **Primrose Cottage** or **Woodland Walk** — and what survives of the resort's quaint old **tea rooms.**

Getting there

You can travel a good metalled road from Islamabad or Rawalpindi through the hills to Murree town in about one hour.

Even in the 1880s, today's sixty-minute drive took little more than six hours by horse-drawn Victoria. These halted roughly every twenty-one kilometres (13 miles) or so at dak bungalows for passengers to rest and the horses to be changed.

When to go

Any time of the year is fine but summer is best, for in winter the hills are often covered in snow, although the road is rarely, if ever, blocked.

Where to Stay

The Pearl Continental Resort and Conference Hotel provides the best in conference and banquet facilities as well as all the luxuries associated with five-star accommodation. Cecil Hotel, The Mall; quaintly nostalgic of a Jewel in the Crown without that certain sparkle but all the dowdy elegance. Brightland Hotel; cheaper and it shows. View Forth Hotel; last of the Big Four.

There is also the Golf Hotel at Bhurban, an eight kilometre (five mile) drive from The Mall. However, usually all five hotels are booked up months in advance of the May-September peak season.

Another alternative are the many rest houses owned by various government departments. You could ask the PTDC, Rawalpindi, but latecomers are usually disappointed. See Listings for "Hotels".

Sightseeing

From **Zero Point** in **Islamabad,** the **Murree Road** crosses a flyover in a north-easterly direction and about fifteen kilometres (nine miles) out comes to a check point; after which, like most things in northern Pakistan, it abandons any pretence to the horizontal and climbs upward, gently at first, then more vertically, into cool, thick pine forest.

With landslides in summer and snow in winter, there's a slightly vicarious feel of the Karakoram Highway about it. Less entertaining are the endless convoys of horse- and camel-drawn traffic and pedestrians, which continuously slow you down, especially in the many little hamlets and villages.

If you've found this all too irksome by the time you reach **Tret** you can, if you have a driver, abandon your vehicle — and the idea of Murree — and start back on foot along the hills to Islamabad, a delightful if somewhat strenuous walk.

If you continue, however, forty kilometres (25 miles) out of Islamabad, you arrive at **Ghora Gali** with, to the right, its **Forest Lodge,** a cluster of well-kept time-serving rest houses owned by the Forestry Department. Even if you don't stay overnight, the shady gardens make an ideal picnic spot. From the village there's a road, to the left, that takes you to **Haripur** or the **Taxila valley.**

Above: Street scene in Murree Town.

Outside **Ghora Gali** there's a **toll gate** where you pay five rupees. On the hillside above the toll barrier, some **stone ruins** may cause waves of nostalgia in the breasts of those non-Muslims who find Pakistan's prohibition laws more than a little repressive.

No ancient archaeological site is this, but all that's left of the old **Murree Brewery**, destroyed in the tumult of non-alcoholic Independence in 1947. The Brewery, also a distiller of some savage rums and whiskies, re-established itself in Rawalpindi.

Three kilometres (two miles) beyond the forlorn brewhouse, the road climbs a ridge to **Ghora Gali College**. It was originally one of four Lawrence Colleges established for the children of British soldiers serving in the subcontinent. It stands above the lower end of what passes in Murree for The Mall. From the capital all this should take roughly an hour's driving.

On along The Mall to, nostalgia again, **Sunny Bank,** and right into the centre of **Murree**. Depending on the season you may have to complete The Mall part of the route on foot.

In summer it's closed to all cars except those residents with a permit — the dubious benefit of which is that, so heavy is the pedestrian congestion, the cars take longer than the walkers to reach their destination.

The local authority possibly employs an Irish traffic planner, since the one-way road system flows in one direction one week and vice-versa the next. Despite this, the accident ratio remains surprisingly low.

The **Post Office** at the north end of The Mall thus serves as something of a beacon in a sea of confusion and is a good place from which to launch your foot exploration down The Mall and the parallel, lower level **Bazaar.**

A late afternoon or early evening promenade and soiree along The Mall seems to be the townsfolk's main social recreation. If you prefer you can undertake this on horse or donkey back.

The **Murree Club** near the Post Office is where the Pakistan Constituent Assembly was held in 1955 and if you take a walk to **Kashmir Point** you'll discover the holiday homes of many embassies.

Once is enough

Not surprisingly one visit to Murree's town centre is enough for most people. Thereafter

Above: Dried fruit and nuts kiosk in Murree bazaar.

they seek out the sylvan delights of **Bhurban** or the resorts known as the **Galis.**

From Sunny Bank travel straight on to the first T-junction. Then turn left for the Galis or right for **Jhikka Gali, Gharial,** and Bhurban. Rarity among rarities, there's a signpost in English so there should be no confusion.

When you reach Jhikka Gali below **Kashmir Point** turn left for Bhurban, which is six kilometres (four miles) away on a long ridge that descends northwards to the Jhelum river.

The Pearl Continental Resort and Conference Hotel, Bhurban, situated in the Murree hills, is the first of its kind in Pakistan. Here you can experience five-star comfort including a game of golf, horse-back riding, or simply exploring the beautiful pine forests.

The comfortable **Golf Hotel** is notable for its splendid panoramas and the nearby nine-hole golf course, which is ideal for walking and picnicking. Many of the tees give stunning perspectives of hills, forests, and on some clear, fine days, monumental **Nanga Parbat,** the world's sixth-highest mountain.

For a small fee, the sociable club committee allows visitors to park their cars at the club house and has even provided a children's playground complete with swings and slides.

Subject to the state of the roads, which depends as much on the kindness of nature as local authority concern, from Bhurban you can continue to **Kohala** and **Muzaffarabad.** A longer alternative to Kohala is to go straight on at Jhikka Gali, circling beneath the pine-crested ridge where **Upper** and **Lower Topa** are situated, uncrowded and with fine camp sites.

Kohala itself is the gateway to Azad Kashmir and ninety-three kilometres (58 miles) from Islamabad. At this point, you can cross the Jhelum and either bore yourself rigid driving upstream to Muzaffarabad or turn right for **Arja** and the **Mahl river,** and from there pass over **Dalkot bridge** to **Lehtar** and **Islamabad.**

The Galis — from a word that in the local vernacular means "lane" — are a collection of fashionable hill resorts in the highlands between **Murree** and **Abbottabad.**

Most fall within **Hazara** district and on a clear day offer magnificent views of the Pir Panjal range in Indian-held Kashmir and Nanga Parbat in the north-east.

From Sunny Bank turn left at the T-junction for **Barian** and **Nathiagali** thirty-four kilometres (21 miles) away. The narrow road follows the high contours of the ridges rather than the dark floors of the precipitous valleys and is not for the vertiginous. There are sheer drops into the valleys below.

There's also the risk that your car, like people, might succumb to altitude sickness and just fold up on you. Most of the road is between 2,000 and 2,500 metres (7,000-8,000 feet) above sea level. Unless the beast is tuned up for high-altitude work, or turbo charged, it soon stalls.

Low-octane petrol helps as does a touch of rally driving — constantly revving to avoid stalling. If it doesn't work, you may sit there for an hour or two while the engine cools before you can restart. Luckily between December and April you run less risk of this happening as the road is usually closed.

At Barian you cross the boundary between the Punjab Province and the NWFP. If you're travelling in the reverse direction, there's a **toll booth** which perhaps illustrates the difference in the level of philanthropy between the two provincial administrations. On to **Sawar Gali** and **Khaira Gali,** eleven kilometres (seven miles) from the turn-off.

It was one of the typical, small British military cantonments, built all over these hills with an eye as much to rest and relaxation as training.

Now it's something of a ghost town. Most of the houses are empty and deserted. But the flat **parade-ground** makes a good picnic spot for those with young children or imagination enough to hear the ghostly tramp of marching as soldiers of the British raj prepared to do more battle for the Jewel in the Crown.

Even those lacking imagination, will find their pulses quicken when they view the Jhelum valley and the Pir Panjal range beyond.

Next of interest is **Changla Gali,** at 2,600 metres (8,400 feet) the highest point on the road with good picnic spots and splendid forest walks.

After this is an English sign marked **Khanispur/Ayubia** and right for **Ayubia National Park.** Named after former military dictator General Ayub Khan, the Park has a skilift that takes you to the crest of the hill which, unfortunately, is overflowing with touts, soft-drink vendors, and souvenir stalls.

If you don't intend to spend lunch at this spot — and the hotels don't inspire healthy appetites — choose your time well. The **skilift**

closes down for what can often be an extended lunch hour.

From Khanispur the main road passes through hills extensively developed with terraces and on to **Dunga Gali,** close to one of the highest summits in the Galis, **Mukshpuri.**

Not long after this you arrive at nostalgia personified, **Nathiagali,** complete with wooden **Anglican church,** English bungalows, even a **municipal park** topped by the neo-classic lines of the **Governor's house.** There is no sign, however, of English town planning. Nathiagali's road system is as bewildering and contrary as that of Murree, but mercifully much smaller and not so developed.

Where to Stay

Pines Hotel; somewhat pricey but worth it for the views and the exquisite if small garden. New Greens; again somewhat pricey but worth it for its elegant, timbered architecture, fine garden, and splendid views. Valley View; economic and good value still with splendid horizons.

But remember the same applies to advance booking, if not more so, as in Murree — and you must confirm in writing.

There are also rest houses, some exceedingly comfortable. See Listings for "Hotels".

Sightseeing

Many make Nathiagali their base for walks through the forests, but you can also trek or ride for about eight kilometres (five miles) along the water pipeline from the **Pines Hotel** via **Dunga Gali** to **Ayubia.**

A longer trek from the hotel takes you through a lovely meadow to the summit of 2,800-metre-high (9,243 feet) **Mukshpuri,** or along a track from the **Governor's house** to the crest of 2,960-metre-high (9,700 feet) **Miranjani,** a walk of about two hours.

Many continue, both walking and riding, from this summit to **Thandiani,** staying overnight at a Forestry rest house.

The road journey from Murree to Nathiagali takes an hour. It is another hour to climb from Nathiagali to **Abbottabad,** down steep but beautiful valleys to where the river rushes through a precipitous gorge.

There's a turn right to Thandiani thirty kilometres (19 miles) from Nathiagali.

Hazara: Fair Valleys and Rugged Mountains

The only part of the North-West Frontier Province that lies east of the Indus, **Hazara** covers some 10,000 square kilometres (3,800 square miles).

The **Margalla Hills,** the south-western foothills of the lovely Pir Panjal mountains, mark the southernmost boundary of a region of northern Pakistan which surely claims more beautiful and dramatic landscapes — both natural and manmade — than any comparable area.

The Pir Panjal and the Jhelum river delineate the region's eastern boundary and divide it from Azad Kashmir. The buttress of the Hindu Kush is its western flank and the Himalaya, where they lace into the Pamir Knot, form its northern perimeter.

Through this flows the Indus to be joined way downstream by the Jhelum. For much of its journey through Hazara, the Indus and its valley form the district's western boundary, dividing it from Swat. At Tarbela, sixty-five kilometres (40 miles) north-west of Islamabad, where the Indus emerges from its last gorge, a dam has transformed the area.

It's mighty flow stemmed, the Indus has bellied out to create one of the subcontinent's greatest lakes — several hundred square kilometres in area and more than 140 metres (450 feet) deep.

Villages and farms were inundated by the rising waters and, where once cattle grazed and cereals were sown and reaped, now the harvest is fish. From its muddy shores, thousands ply the lake waters. This glistening lake, with its green and pleasant landscape, gives grace to mankind's conceit.

Looking as if it has lain there since the Indus first sprang free of its mountain prison, it stretches northwards along the feet of Hazara's Black Mountains for almost 100 kilometres (60 miles).

A century and a half ago, at Sazin on Hazara's northern border with the Gilgit Agency, Nanga Parbat stirred in its long slumber and sent down a landslide, trapping the Indus floods behind a massive rampart of mountain rubble.

A lake almost as large as the one now at Tarbela — extending more than eighty kilometres (50 miles) to the town of Gilgit —

was formed behind this barrier. But a year later in June 1841, when Nanga Parbat shuddered again in its sleep, the dam was breached.

Gathering momentum and height, a gigantic tidal wave bore down through the narrow gorges for more than 160 kilometres (100 miles) until it spread out at Tarbela to race across the plains in a force so powerful it engulfed four towns and twenty villages, drowning many thousands and flooding the land around for thousands of square kilometres.

Getting there

Three roads lead from the Grand Trunk Road, the Imperial Highway that joins Lahore, Islamabad, and Peshawar into Hazara, all meeting at **Haripur** in the **Dor valley.** The smoothest is the one that turns right just beyond **Hasan Abdal,** forty-eight kilometres (30 miles) from **Islamabad,** cutting through the flat and fertile farmlands for thirty-three kilometres (21 miles) to Haripur.

There's a more difficult, but infinitely more scenic, route just north of the **Margalla Pass,** which travels through the Taxila valley crossing the **Khanpur Dam** and the **Harro** river.

The road bears left after the dam at the floor of a steep valley, through heavily eroded countryside, and enters Haripur from the east.

The third and most popular choice turns right in Taxila town just before the **Wah bypass,** where a sign in English says, "Welcome University College of Engineering", and goes on through **Sarai Khola,** past a heavy engineering complex, some other industries, and a cement factory.

Just past a rail crossing nine kilometres (six miles) after the turn-off, there's a tall, well-preserved Buddhist shrine, the **Bhallar** *stupa,* which has been sliced through the middle and has a retaining wall on the severed side.

The road twists and turns through many gullies to join the **Hasan Abdal** road two kilometres (one mile) before Haripur.

On the main Hasan Abdal-Haripur road, there's a left turn twenty-five kilometres (16 miles) after leaving the Imperial Highway, down a new road that leads over the Gandghar hills to **Sirkot** and **Tarbela Dam.**

Where to Stay

Springfield Hotel, The Mall, Abbottabad; Hotel Sarban, The Mall, Abbottabad.

There are forestry rest houses at Thandiani, Daddar, and Kundrun. Inquire at the Divisional Forest Office, Abbottabad.

There are PWD rest houses at Thandiani and Shakul. Inquire at the PWD, Abbottabad. See Listings for "Hotels".

Sightseeing

Haripur, eighty-one kilometres (51 miles) from Islamabad via the Hasan Abdal road, is named after Hari Singh, the most trusted and famous of Ranjit Singh's generals, sent to Haripur in the early 1820s to quell Hazara and "inflict severe chastisement" on its lawless tribes and communities.

Later, after the Sikh War of 1846, an Englishman, James Abbott, one of Sir Henry Lawrence's "young men", was despatched as an "adviser" to the Sikhs. During the second Sikh War, he took refuge with the Mishwanis. Abbott asked them to stand by his side and led them to the Margalla Pass to block the retreat of the Singh armies.

Abbott is best remembered in local folklore leading prayers in the town **mosque**, dressed in the long robes of Islam, wearing a long, white beard. Herbert Edwardes, his successor, founded **Abbottabad,** the town that bears his name, and Haripur became of secondary importance.

Famous for its fruit orchards, Haripur is still a bustling little town. It lies in the middle of a lush, fertile valley, well irrigated by the **Dor river** coming down from Nathiagali.

About one kilometre (half-a-mile) before you reach Haripur on the main Hasan Abdal-Abbottabad road there's a left turn, to **Tarbela,** which runs for nine kilometres (six miles) to the shores of the lake where many fishing boats are moored and the remains of old villages, evacuated when the valley was flooded, are visible.

Midway between Haripur and Nathiagali, about twenty kilometres (13 miles) stands **Havelian,** railhead for the **Karakoram Highway.**

The road bypasses Havelian over a bridge across the Dor river and climbs fifteen kilometres (nine miles) through brown and barren hills, over **Salhad Pass,** to **Abbottabad.**

At Abbottabad, 121 kilometres (76 miles) from Islamabad, where the highway runs through the town like an arrow for many kilometres, it touches only 1,300 metres (4,000 feet) above sea level, a height which made the town a popular hot season hill retreat for India's British rulers.

The 1980s have seen Abbottabad develop both as a military town and tourist centre. Almost everywhere you go in this town, situated at the southern end of the great bowl of the **Rash plains,** you meet the descendants of the Mughal armies — their twentieth-century training reflecting the proud martial heritage of their ancestors.

Pakistan's elite officer cadet training academy at **Kakul** stands on the hills to the north-east. For more than a century, the town has also been the headquarters of the famous Frontier Force Regiment, universally known as the "Piffers". Another famous regiment of the subcontinent, the Baluch, is also based there.

Former President Ayub Khan had his summer retreat in Abbottabad. **Frontier House,** his old residence on a ridge overlooking the Rash plains, has an incongruous **Chinese pagoda** in the garden.

Grand days

Abbottabad's old European suburb echoes the grand days of Empire. Climb up the hill through the bustling bazaar to the crest and there you will find the old **Anglican** church and **cemetery** surrounded by pine-shaded villas, bungalows, and the mandatory **colonial club.**

Though in need of repair, the church is still in occasional use. Borrow the key from the **vicarage** and walk inside. The stuff of Kipling springs to life. Plaques, recording the lives and deaths of British officers and men far from home, recall the days of death and glory on the North-West Frontier.

From Abbottabad, one-and-a-half kilometres (one mile) past the roundabout on the lower road, there's a road east to Nathiagali and Murree. It is the most direct approach to the finest of the Gali Hills and takes just one hour to reach **Thandiani.**

Another pleasant excursion from Abbottabad is towards **Sherwan,** a village on a 1,500-metre-high (5,000-feet) ridge in the **Tanawal** area west of Abbottabad, which is approached through the cantonment and up the hill to Frontier House, now a government guest house.

There's a left turn, just before the guest house gates, down through a fertile, wooded valley, and up the other side side to Sherwan.

Twenty-four kilometres (15 miles) north of Abbottabad, in the centre of a verdant bowl of farmland, emerald green in spring against the distant backdrop of snowclad mountains and nostalgically mellow in the fall, as the leaves turn to gold and russet, lies **Manshera,** capital of the district to which it gives its name.

The Karakoram Highway veers west of the town and cuts through three rocks on either side of the road. Although eroded and weathered through more than than 2,000 years, the faint outlines of the **inscriptions** carved on them in Kharoshthoti, the local Gandharan script, can still be made out, if dimly.

In that far distant past, the great Mauryan Emperor Ashoka paused here in his travels at this crossroads of two major trade routes from Kashmir and China, to inscribe edicts that have stood testament to time and the vagaries of man and weather.

Echoing the Buddha's edict to "embrace all living things as a mother cares for her son, her only son", his Fifth Pillar Proclamation gave protection to bats, monkeys, rhinoceroses, porcupines, tree squirrels, and the forests in which they lived.

The edicts remain in two places in Pakistan —here at Manshera and at **Shahbaz Garha** on the Peshawar plains.

These priceless legacies of so long ago have been covered by roofing to protect their ancient wisdom as a future heritage and form the focal theme of a public **park** built in 1988.

To the north-west of the road is **Bareri Hill,** looking unimpressive from here but from any other aspect dominating the **Pakhli plain.** The hill, named after one of the gods in the Hindu mythological pantheon, was sacred to the Hindus and an important place of pilgrimage. The path to the summit of Bareri starts from just below the rocks on the south side of the road.

North-west lie the beautiful **Black Mountains** and, at **Oghi,** there's a fort commemorating the frustration of British troops in their attempt to subdue the hill people who played hit-and-run from their mountain strongholds.

To the north-east, hidden in a forested, cup-shaped valley beneath the snows of 5,405-metre-high (16,219 feet) **Bhogarmang,** twenty-five kilometres (16 miles) from Manshera, another road leads off the Karakoram Highway, right, along the frothing waters of the **Siran river,** to the hill-town of Daddar, famous as a health resort for tuberculosis patients.

Beyond Daddar the road climbs sharply for twenty-eight kilometres (18 miles) through pine forests to a track which is the start of an enjoyable, easy three-day trek through **Bhogarmang** valley to Nadi and **Sharan** and down into the Kaghan valley at Paras (See "Kaghan: matchless pearl of the Himalaya").

Back on the Karakoram Highway, rugged scenery beckons the adventurer forward, through rocky gorge and between china clay cliffs, over circles of fertile valleys with panoramas of the **Black Mountains** westward, to **Batgram** and beyond.

Soon the road reaches the **Nandhiar watershed** and the rest house at **Shakul,** which stands on a bluff overlooking the plain, where the road veers north-west and sinks slowly down through terraced fields and avenues of poplar trees to the **Indus Valley.**

Near **Thakot,** beneath the slopes of **Pir Sar** above the river's western banks, you'll get your first glimpse of its raging torrent.

For many years Pir Sar was believed to be Aornos, the mountain peak that echoes in the history of Alexander the Great, and one notice-board by the road proclaims it as such. But Alexander and his armies never travelled this far.

A splendid **suspension bridge at Thakot** is the official start of the **Karakoram Highway.** As you cross, its twin towers at either side fittingly crowned, a sign welcomes travellers to the KKH.

Just beyond the bridge, above the river rapids, a **monument** commemorates the memory of those who died building the KKH.

Twenty-eight kilometres (18 miles) from Thakot, **Besham** boasts a **Kohistan Development Board — KDB — rest house.** Turn right one kilometre (half-a-mile) before the village and down a track marked by a cluster of blue KDB signs —none saying "rest house". It stands on the banks of the Indus and, well-equipped, makes a pleasant overnight stop.

Where to Stay

There are Kohistan Development Board — KDB — rest houses at Besham, Pattan, and Kayal. Inquire at the KDB, Kakul Road, Abbottabad.

Land of the outlaw

Beyond Besham you reach the boundary of

the recently formed **Kohistan district,** until the advent of the KKH possibly the most remote and backward region of Pakistan.

Covering an area of roughly 9,000 square kilometres (3,574 square miles), Kohistan is one of the highest regions in the world. It consists almost entirely of dauntingly rugged mountains, many above 4,750 metres (15,000 feet) high, that sandwich tiny, fertile valleys laced together only by a few rough trails.

It's at Besham that the old Silk Route veered westward, over the **Shangla Pass** with its magnificent panoramas and vistas, to cross into **Swat.**

One of the few settlements on this section of the highway is **Dubair,** notable for the **bazaar** that lines the road and the fine-boned, aquiline faces of the rifle-toting Kohistani tribesmen.

Because of the highway, one of Kohistan's many beautiful valleys, **Chowa Dara,** is easily accessible. Some thirty-five kilometres (22 miles) beyond Besham, this green and forested fifteen-kilometre-long (nine-mile) valley stands above a small reservoir perched atop a hill.

Soon after, you catch your first view of the steep-sided **Patan Valley,** a six-hour drive from Islamabad, with the **Pals Valley** cutting deep into Kohistan on the other side of the river.

Once a chain of volcanic islands in the Tethys Sea, floating on a small oceanic geological raft, Kohistan is the nut in the centre of the colliding continents — trapped and inexorably crushed between the two great continental plates and carried relentlessly northward at the reckless speed, geologically speaking, of about five centimetres (two inches) a year.

In December 1974 unstoppable India met immovable Asia. **Patan Town** and the valley were virtually obliterated. In the years since 1974, Patan has been much rebuilt and little remains to indicate the immensity of the disaster which struck this small community.

Take the turn right down a steep hill opposite the inscribed memorial to those who died building the Karakoram Highway and drive through the **bazaar,** a journey of about three kilometres (two miles), to the **KDB rest house,** fairly basic accommodation which offers splendid views over the Indus. The words on the memorial read:

"Sometime in the future when others will ply the KKH little will they realize the amount of sweat, courage, dedication, endurance and human sacrifice that has gone into the making of this road. But as you drive along, tarry a little to say a short prayer for those silent brave men of the Pakistan Army who gave their lives to realize a dream, now known as the Karakoram Highway. We pioneered the mighty Karakoram and carved a road with blood."

There's a glacier hanging above the head of the Pals valley, which you can see from the KKH six kilometres (four miles) after you leave Patan, heading northwards.

There's a more comfortable **rest house** and even finer scenery ten kilometres (six miles) beyond Patan at **Kayal,** across a small bridge, past some shops and left up a rocky track for 200 metres (218 yards) to where it stands.

It's near the entrance to the scenic **Kayal Valley,** left turn before the bridge — a good walk of about nine kilometres (six miles).

It's another twenty-seven kilometres (17 miles) along the KKH, tucked in behind the constant convoys of heavy-laden, gaily-coloured trucks, hauling their loads to Gilgit and beyond, perhaps even to Kashgar in China, to **Kamila** where the KKH crosses to the east bank of the Indus and cuts beneath the cliff 366 metres (1,200 feet) above the river, the most hazardous section. On average at least one vehicle a month plunges down the sheer cliff to the river.

The damage caused by mud and rock falls and earth movements is also greater than on any other sector — and members of the Pakistan Army's Frontier Works Organisation still lay down their lives in the struggle to maintain the highway and keep it open.

Just before **Sazin,** fifty-eight kilometres (36 miles) beyond Kamila, the mountains fall away from the road and the gorge widens out into a sandy valley.

The highway then continues climbing up towards the Roof of the World, around the massive base of **Nanga Parbat,** through gorges strewn with pebbles and gravel, to **Chilas** sixty-eight kilometres (42 miles) further on, perhaps the place where a century and a half ago the avalanche from Nanga Parbat blocked the Indus to form the great lake that stretched almost to Gilgit.

Overleaf: Watchtower, left, guards Malakand Pass, gateway to Swat.

Swat: The Valley of Kings

If one place can claim to encompass all the changes, both cultural and violent, that characterize the history of Pakistan it must be Swat Valley. And yet, until the 1970s, Swat was a living anachronism, a land locked in limbo — timeless, unchanging, and undisturbed.

Swat Valley, part of the North-West Frontier Province, stretches from the Malakand Pass above the Peshawar Plains, through the foothills of the Hindu Kush, to the easternmost extent of the high peaks of this stupendous mountain range.

Most of the people are Pathan. These fine-featured, olive-skinned folk, who look strikingly alike with their black hair and brown eyes are essentially rural folk — and everywhere men and women work the rich black soil of the paddies and grain fields.

Irrigation canals crisscross the land. Huge water buffalo with swept-back horns wallow in ponds and pools. By the roadside frequent tea houses offer refreshing cups of sweet, milky tea ladled out of huge, black-stained kettles. Columns of smoke eddy from the crude, stonewalled houses of the villages through a hole in the roof.

Despite the supreme beauty of this vale that the Pathan poet Khushal Khan Khattak said was meant "to give kings gladness", life is often harsh.

In summer temperatures often exceed 38°C (100°F) and there are frequent droughts and freak storms. In an area where only fifteen per cent of the land is arable this makes farming unpredictable.

The valley's human history extends from the first **Stone Age** settlements, through the Aryan invasion of 1700 BC, to the Hindu and Muslim eras of the subcontinent, and all the events since.

Swat is a veritable treasure trove of antiquity. The past is so contiguous to the present that some communities have been using the same graveyards for more than 3,000 years.

The Hindus and the Buddhists left a rich and priceless legacy of architecture, monuments, and scholarship in this verdant valley.

Swat's long history of Hindu civilization is commemorated everywhere by rock carvings and ancient forts. One of the 1,208 Hindu vedics from the *Rig Veda* tells of the Suvastu, now the Swat river. Buddhist *stupas*, monasteries, and rock carvings abound.

For the best part of 5,000 years — give or take only the last two decades — Swat was a feudal princedom. Its last ruler, deposed peacefully in a 1969 agreement with the Pakistan Government, was known by the curious title of Wali (curious, no doubt, because in full "the Wali of Swat" has a ring of inspired comedy about it).

His nineteenth-century predecessor was known by the even more curious title of Akhund. It inspired Edward Lear, the Victorian inventor of the limerick, to pen this verse.

Who why, or which, or what,
Is the Akond of Swat?
Is he tall or short, or dark or fair?
Does he sit on a stool or a sofa or chair, or squat,
The Akond of Swat?

Getting there

You can take either the thirty-minute flight from Islamabad or one of the three roads that link the Swat capital of **Saidu Sharif** to the outside world, all *passable*, and the word means only that, in saloon cars.

You can drive along the Karakoram Highway as far as Besham and then turn west over the **Shangla Pass** to **Khwazakhela** which takes at least ten hours in the driest conditions; or via **Shahbaz Garha** across the **Ambela Pass** to Buner and thence across the **Karakar Pass** which will take at least five hours; or you can take the main route from **Mardan** over the **Malakand Pass** which takes between three and five hours.

Petrol

There are petrol stations at **Saidu Sharif** and **Mingora**. If you are travelling farther north the last petrol pump is at **Bahrain**.

When to go

Spring and fall are pre-eminently the best seasons in Swat: the valleys are a riot of pastel blossoms or contrasting shades of russet; temperatures are ideal, the weather predictable. In winter, it's cold and the northern end of Swat, arguably its most lovely reaches, snowbound and inaccessible. In summer the heat is intolerable and the monsoons unbearable. You'll be denied the panoramas and vistas that, apart from the antiquities, are

Above: Traditional Swat Valley ferry — a wicker frame on inflated oxhides.

the main reason for visiting Swat.

Where to stay

There are many hotels in Swat Valley in the major resorts. In Saidu Sharif, Frontier House, Marghazar Palace Hotel, and Swat Serena. And in Mingora, Abaseen Hotel, Holiday Hotel.

In Bahrain, Asbhar Hotel, and Decent Hotel. And in Madyan, Mountain View Hotel, Nisar Hotel, PTDC Motel, book through PTDC, telephone Rawalpindi.

There are many more of varying standards — see Listings for "Hotels".

Sightseeing

From **Mardan** you drive to the 1,500-metre-high (5,000-feet) Malakand Pass which begins at **Daragai,** the road twisting and turning in an endless series of steep hairpin bends. Where it crests the summit there's a breathtaking view of the southern reaches of this magic valley.

The pass is guarded by **Malakand Fort,** famous for its nineteenth-century garrison of 1,000 Sikh infantry which, in 1897, defied an army of 10,000 Pathan zealots under the command of the so-called Mad Mullah, killing

almost 4,000 of them. It was said to be the greatest pitched battle ever fought by British forces in the North-West Frontier.

The town of **Bat Khela,** where the Swat leaves its tunnel under the hills and spreads out over a series of shallow weirs, marks the start of the descent into Swat.

The first bridge over the river leads into **Chakdara,** an ancient bazaar that once waxed rich on the passing trade of the great silk route between China and central Asia which cut through its main street.

Chakdara is rich in its treasures of the Buddhist era. All around the area are Buddhist ruins — monasteries and shrines. Many of the world-renowned Gandharan sculptures in **Chakdara Museum,** two kilometres (one mile) out of town on the Dir Road, were recovered from these ruins.

On nearby **Damkot Hill** stand the neatly excavated ruins of a large eighth-century **Hindu fort** razed by Mahmud of Ghazni, first of the Islamic conquerors, in the tenth century.

The hill's first occupants were the Aryan invaders and after they abandoned it monks of a first-century AD Buddhist community re-settled it.

In the sixteenth century Akbar built a

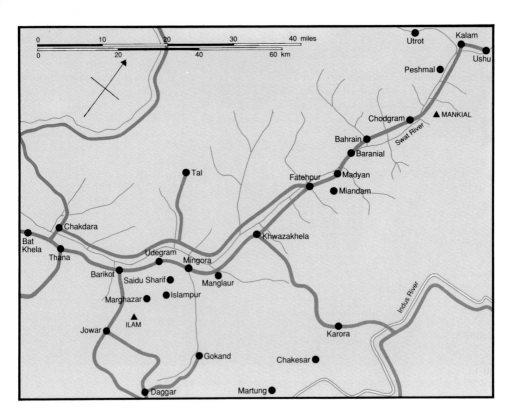

massive fort at its foot to guard the vital trade route between Kabul and Agra. Three centuries later, in 1896, the British built another on top of its ruins.

All that now remains on the summit is **Churchill's Picket,** a small observation post, where in 1897 Winston Churchill, a war correspondent for the London *Daily Telegraph,* was in the thick of a fierce battle against the feared and indomitable Pathan tribesmen.

At its western base lies a pile of boulders carved with Buddhist figures including Padmani, the lotus bearer Bodhisattva. The Buddhists built a *stupa* — a dome-shaped mound representing the way to *nirvana* — and monastery on top of Damkot's 1,200-metre-high (3,900-feet) summit and their community survived more than 400 years before it was overrun by the Hindu rajputs.

The gateway town into the valley proper is **Landakai,** some twelve kilometres (seven miles) beyond Chakdara, where visitors to Swat must register their presence at the police **checkpost.**

Close to Landakai, is **Nimogram valley** unique for its three *stupas* devoted to Buddha the Teacher, *Dharma,* the Buddhist doctrine,

and *Sangha,* the Buddhist order.

There are several votive *stupas,* too. Nimogram is also noted for some superb sculptures, unearthed during excavations and now housed in the Swat museum in the capital of Saidu Sharif.

On the main road, near the turn to Nimogram, you'll see the flat mound of **Barikot Hill,** scene of Alexander the Great's protracted struggle to capture the ancient town of Bazira.

Bazira's eighth-century Hindu rulers built a **fort** on the ruins of which one wall, rising fifteen metres (50 feet) high, still stands. The rest of the hill crest is under the plough, but the view of the verdant plains below against the backdrop of 2,810-metre-high (9,222-feet) **Mount Ilam,** its sacred peak encircled by clouds, justifies the climb.

Ilam, long the home of the local gods, inspired the religious mythology of Buddhist, Hindu, and Muslim. The Tibetans called it Mount Ilo and the Chinese traveller, Hsuan Tsang, who climbed the mountain in AD 630, identified it as Mount Hilo, the place where the Buddha, in a previous incarnation, sacrificed half his life to hear a few words of revelation.

The mystics who embraced his doctrine

found haven in Swat from the persecution of the marauding Aryans and named the valley *Udyana* — the garden.

Later, the Hindus carved the name Rama, one of Vishnu's incarnations, on the rocky summit. Before partition thousands of Hindu pilgrims trekked up the steep slopes to pay homage each year, passing on the way the now-abandoned summer home of the first Wali of Swat, at **Sufaid Mahal.**

The road to 1,300-metre-high (4,384-feet) **Karakar Pass** leads south from Barikot into the lovely **Buner Valley** where, in 1586, Akbar the Great suffered a rare defeat and lost most of his 8,000-strong army.

It's on this road, at **Gumbat,** that you can explore the ruins of one of the best preserved Buddhist **shrines** in Swat, a central cell encircled by a processional corridor surmounted by a fifteen-metre-high (50-feet) dome. Several small nearby *stupas* have become grassy mounds.

Golden days

Three kilometres (two miles) beyond Barikot on the main road is **Shingerdar,** a massive golden-domed *stupa,* painted with many figures and symbols, that's now a crumbling ruin.

The frieze at its base is made up of a series of delicate carvings depicting the Buddha's life. This *stupa* represents the apogee of Swat's Buddhist cultures in the third and fourth centuries.

On some nearby rocks there's the vague outline of an elephant which shows, according to local legend, that the rock is the metamorphosis of a white elephant despatched to this spot when the *stupa* was under construction with sacred relics of Buddha to be sealed inside.

When the job was done it fell dead and turned to stone (it's said, however, that the elephant's virtue was rewarded in its next incarnation when it was born a human being; though it must be arguable whether this represents reward or punishment).

About one-and-a-half kilometres (one mile) beyond the *stupa,* hewn out of the cliff face adjacent to the main road, is a large, much battered relief of Buddha.

Piles of stones at its base testify to the strength of an old belief that there was great merit to be won in the hereafter by hurling a rock at the image each time you pass; though any self-respecting Buddhist would consider such an act sacrilegious.

Left of this is a natural grotto containing the *bas-relief* of a bearded figure, wearing a halo, clad in the traditional costume of Swat's Kushan rulers — long coat over Cossack trousers and boots. The pedestal on which this stands is supported by lions and smaller images.

Six kilometres (four miles) beyond all this, at **Gogdara,** 100 metres (320 feet) or so off the main road, sadly defaced by modern graffiti that in no way match the originals, stands a cliff carved with images that go back 3,000 years and more: stylized oxen, ibex, dogs, horses, leopard, other animals, and warriors in the two-wheel chariots on which the Aryans rode into Swat about 1,700 BC.

Higher up the cliff is a sixth-century AD Buddhist relief, and 100 metres beyond, the same artists etched the brooding figure of Bodhisattva, the Padmani lotus bearer, and his attendants.

Close by is **Udegram,** developed out of a walled and castled predecessor, founded around 1,000 BC that flourished until the fourteenth century AD.

Its extensive, triangular ruins and eighth-century **Hindu fort** cover twenty different periods. Although identifying the main area as a bazaar and most of the ruins as shops, the Italian team that excavated the site in the 1950s, left most exhibits *in situ*, and unlabelled, perhaps understandably so.

Extending almost one kilometre (3,000 feet) along the ridge that divides the lower Swat Valley from the upper valley, the walls of the old town enclose a **spring** that served as the town's water supply.

It was channelled along a series of canals to storage tanks at the base of the six-metre-wide (20-feet) staircase that leads up to the citadel, its massive buttresses built from unmortared slate.

A grove of trees below the citadel marks the shrine of **Khushal Khan Baba**, one of Mahmud of Gazni's men who fell on the spot while leading the siege of the fortress, held by Raja Gira, the last Hindu ruler.

Six kilometres (four miles) beyond Udegram you arrive in **Mingora**, a bustling 2,000-year-old "metropolis" with **golf course**, hotels, and **airport.**

It's been a thriving trade centre throughout its history and its colourful **bazaar** offers a vivid mixture of hand-crafted silver jewellery, semi-precious stones, and cloths.

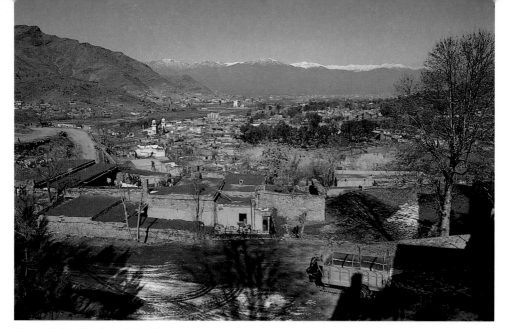

Above: Saidu Sharif, capital of Swat.

It's twin "city" is **Saidu Sharif,** the Swat capital, and seat of the feudal overlords who ruled the valley from the mid-nineteenth century.

Royal murder

When the founder of the last dynasty died in 1877 — you can see his **tomb** close to the **old palace** now a tourist hotel — Swat was plunged into forty years of internecine strife until his grandson, Miangul Wadud, sought British help and assumed the succession, pronouncing himself the Wali of Swat and murdering his two cousins thus wiping out any possible patrilineal challenge.

Wadud ruled as the Wali until 1949, when he abdicated in favour of his son, Miangul Jehanzeb. The new Wali built the capital's modern palace because his official guest house was unable to accommodate all his visitors. Set in flowered gardens, it is now a hotel, one of the capital's major buildings.

Another fine building houses **Swat Museum** and its renowned collection of Gandharan sculptures. There's also an exciting **folk history** section and exhibitions of local wood carvings, embroidery, and tribal jewellery.

The museum is about one kilometre (half-a-mile) from what was one of the world's most important Buddhist shrines, **Butkara.** Enough has defied the ages to testify to its original grandeur.

The original central *stupa* was built around the second century BC by the Mauryan Emperor Ashoka. Subsequently it was enlarged at least five times, each time by building a new *stupa* on top of the existing one, together with more than 215 votive *stupas.*

Built of soapstone, gilded and painted in bright colours, decorated with elaborate Gandharan statues, and encircled by a pathway set with green, yellow, and blue inlays, the main *stupa* is said to hold the ashes of Buddha.

Through the ages it was frequently damaged by floods and earthquakes and lovingly restored. Each new layer of plaster added to the *stupa* was painted with garlands, lotuses, and images of Buddha. Some still survive although broken in many places.

An Italian archaeological team had a field day in this area in the 1950s, uncovering not only Butkara's treasury of art and religious artefacts but discovering several other rich archaeological sites.

At a place called **Butkara II,** and at **Loebanr** and **Matelai,** around 500 Aryan **graves** dating from 1700 BC have been uncovered.

And across the Swat river, on the road from Mingora to the airport and golf course the Italians also excavated the ruins of an ancient Aryan town, **Aligrama,** dating from 1000 BC.

The road north out of Mingora follows a spur that falls sheer into the river. Roughly sixteen kilometres (ten miles) beyond Mingora, at **Jehanabad,** on a rock wall set in the hillside, there's a massive and ancient four-metre-high (14-feet) **carving** of the Buddha at the spot where it's said that he preached a sermon so moving that a stone *stupa* emerged on the place where he stood. The image is carved on this boulder.

Roughly another sixteen kilometres (ten miles) beyond this place is **Khwazakhela,** a thriving trading centre specialising in cloths, fabrics, and jewellery.

It must also be one of the world's original counterfeit centres. Master craftsmen forge ancient coins on request and, almost as instantaneously, produce fake masterpieces of old wood carvings shaped from the valley's newly-felled timber. No ordinary buyer, and few experts, can detect the false from the real.

Just as you enter the town there's a road east that traverses the glorious **Shangla Pass** to Besham and the Indus Valley.

As the rivers, fed by the snow melt and the monsoons, boil and bubble through narrow gorges along their rocky beds children fish waist-deep in the shallows with conical-shaped hand nets fastened on an oval frame of wicker and metal. Rafts are fashioned from driftwood and withies made buoyant with inflated ox stomachs and bladders.

Some distance out of **Khwazakhela,** roughly fifty-six kilometres (34 miles) from Saidu Sharif, is **Miandam,** considered to be the loveliest side valley in Swat.

The well-maintained road climbs about ten kilometres (six miles), through verdant terraced fields to the village perched at 1,800 metres (6,000 feet) at the top of the valley — cool and refreshing even in hot summer. It's well established as a resort with hotels serving the trekkers who come to enjoy the walking on the mountains that rise above the town.

Continuing along the main road north you soon reach the bazaar town of **Madyan,** another lodestone of the counterfeiter's art. Here the fakes are not just coins and carvings, but stone and stucco replicas of priceless Gandharan statues so faithful to the originals that many experts have been fooled.

The needlewomen also produce stunningly colourful and exquisitely made shawls, a craft that has continued through two millenniums — vivid reds, greens, blues, and yellows on black. They were mentioned more than a thousand years ago in a Sanskrit Buddhist text.

Another ten kilometres (six miles) up the valley is **Bahrain,** yet another treasure house of local arts and crafts. Superbly-carved doors, balconies, and windows, and two beautiful **carved timber mosques,** built after the decline of Buddhism and Hinduism, testify to centuries of practice.

The country beyond Bahrain is mountainous, the road constantly crossing the river from one bank to another, twisting and winding through the forest clad mountains, until at one section it emerges on a flat spur that curves around the bottom flank of 3,754-metre-high (12,320-feet) **Mount Mankial** at **Kolaloi** — providing a magnificent view of the ice-capped peak above.

Forty kilometres (25 miles) from Bahrain, at **Kalam,** it enters an ancient lake bed, now the rich and fertile **Utrot Valley,** beneath the magnificent heights of 6,256-metre-high (20,528-feet) **Mount Falaksir.**

At the start of the valley, the great fork of rock and water where the raging streams of the Utrot and the **Ushu** sweep through the pine forests to merge as the Swat, has been developed into an alpine tourist resort, including chalet-style **motel.**

The valley extends westward and in its upper reaches, 2,224 metres (7,300 feet) above sea level, stands the village of the same name. This maze of forest and trout streams is the delight of alpinists, trekkers, and fly fishermen.

Some head on north-east up the **Ushu Valley** where the jeep track rides for twenty-eight kilometres (17 miles) through dale, glen, and forest to **Lake Mahodand,** "The Lake of Fishes", rated by many the most beautiful trail in the whole of the subcontinent.

There's a rest house at **Ushu village,** eight kilometres (five miles) into the valley, and at **Matiltan.** There's also the **Gabral Valley** which has rest houses, too, like Utrot and Ushu.

Tougher souls, backpackers, the fit and the hardy, the foolish and the sublime, can go further — crossing heights of 3,650 metres (12,000 feet) or more — over the daunting and often impassable **Kachikani Pass** and then eastward to **Laspur** and the **Shandur Pass** to **Gilgit,** or west to **Masuj** and **Chitral** (see this section, "Trekking").

That the rewards are worth the effort is not in doubt. But most will find it easier to retrace their steps down the Swat Valley to Chakdara and take the road from there to Chitral.

Chitral: Silver-Frosted Mountains, Rivers Wild

Guarded from time immemorial by the daunting heights of the 3,208-metre-high (10,528-feet) **Lowari Pass** in the south and the massive buttresses of the **Hindu Kush** to the west, north, and east, the only entrances to **Chitral** until recently were those high and difficult passes, many of them closed for all but the brief summer months.

In whichever direction you gaze, mountains dominate the horizon. More than 320 kilometres long (200 miles), 1,500 metres (5,000 feet) high, Chitral is separated from the **Soviet Union** by the narrow **Wakhan corridor,** and from **China** by the **Hunza region.** The valley is drained by the **Masuj River** and its tributaries and is encircled by peaks of splendour.

These rise from 5,400 metres (17,750 feet) to the highest of the Hindu Kush peaks, 7,080-metre-high (25,290-feet) **Tirich Mir,** which appeared to Colonel William Lockhart, one of the first Europeans to explore this region in the last century, as "a mass of frosted silver".

After Independence, Chitral's administration became the responsibility of the federal Government in 1950, but in 1969 the area was absorbed into Pakistan's North-West Frontier Province.

In the 1980s all visitors were required to register their presence with the police — as much good housekeeping and concern for Chitral's guests as bureaucracy at work. There are many remote and inaccessible side valleys in Chitral in which it is easy to get lost. On many trails, particularly in summer, avalanches and rock slides pose a perennial hazard.

The capital, swollen by tides of Afghan refugees, boasts a long and dusty **bazaar** thronged with people and stalls offering local cloth, carpets, stones, jewellery, and the flat hats, distinguished by their rolled-up brims, that all Chitralis wear.

In 1895 Surgeon Major Robertson and 400 men were held under siege for forty-eight days at the **fort** by a combined force of the Dir and Chitral rulers.

Eventually, Colonel James Kelly led 250 men from Gilgit through the **Shandur Pass** to relieve the fortress. They covered more than 500 gruelling kilometres (311 miles) in the depth of winter. Thereafter, the British maintained a permanent garrison in Chitral Fort.

Getting there

There are scheduled flights from Peshawar to Chitral but they are dependent on the weather. The flight provides spectacular panoramas of the foothills and mountains of the Hindu Kush.

Confirm your return tickets as soon as you arrive. The airport is ten minutes drive from the town.

You can drive to Chitral by road via the **Malakand Pass,** Dir, and the **Lowari Pass,** but at 3,200 metres (10,500 feet) it is often blocked by snow during winter and is only open from May to October. Note also that most of the road is only suitable for 4WD vehicles.

Engineers of the Pakistan Army's parastatal civil engineering unit, the Frontier Works Organization, have started one of the most stupendous feats of road construction in the world — boring an eighty-two-kilometre-long (51-mile) tunnel beneath the Lowari Pass which, when finished, will open up the marvels of Chitral all the year round.

Petrol

Available in Drosh and Chitral only.

When to go

The valley is at its loveliest in April, when it's a riot of fruit blossoms, and in October, when the leaves turn to russet. But in winter it is deep in snow. You'll need warm clothes for evenings at any time of the year. Monsoons in July-August cause poor visibility, affect flight schedules and close roads.

Where to Stay

Mountain Inn, Chitral Town; close to the polo ground in a pretty garden and an excellent demonstration of the virtues of Pakistani home cooking. Tirich Mir View Hotel, Chitral Town; all that its name implies with the added bonus of wake up calls without request from the next door mosque — in time to see the the sun's first rays strike this magnificent peak. PTDC Motel, Chitral Town.

Opposite: Chitral Fort scene of an epic siege in the last century.

There are rest houses at Dir, Droshi, Madaklasht, Carete, Ayun, Birir, Bumburet, and Garam Chasma. Inquire at the Deputy Commissioner's office, Chitral. There are also some small but basic hotels in the Kalash valleys and other places. See Listings for "Hotels".

Permissions

You need permits to visit the three **Kafir Kalash valleys** of Birir, **Bumburet,** and **Rambur,** from the Deputy Commissioner, Chitral. You also need a second permit if you wish to see the **Kalash folk dancers.**

The visitor's permit is free; the dancing permit expensive. You pay the headman of the village who arranges the dancing.

Sightseeing

The 226-kilometre (141-mile) road journey from **Chakdara** in the lower **Swat Valley** to Chitral takes about eight hours. The road is surfaced as far as Dir and rough thereafter.

Just beyond Chakdara on the Dir road, there's a first-century **monastery,** nestling in a small valley at **Chat Pat,** that was buried in a landslide. It contained a treasury of Gandhara art — sophisticated metal sculptures carved by Bactrian artists imported from north Afghanistan by the Kushans. They are, however, inferior to the original Bactrian carvings and those by artists of local origin.

Some little distance away, at **Andan Dheri,** also on the Dir Road, an immense number of similar treasures — more than 500 along with many coins of the Kushan period — were discovered during excavations of what was probably the most important Buddhist centre in the region.

The *stupas* and the monastery which once stood here are said to mark the spot where, during one of India's great famines, Buddha, in an incarnation as Indra, transformed himself into a giant dead snake and allowed himself to be eaten by the starving. As it was cut, each piece of flesh miraculously renewed itself, thus saving the hungry and the sick.

The *stupa* beside the monastery stood twenty-four metres (80-feet) high. Built in the late first century, the main *stupa,* fourteen votive *stupas,* and the monastery were in use until the seventh century. Now much of the site is under the plough.

A few kilometres south-west of Andan Dheri, guarded at its narrowest point by the ruins of the massive eighth-century Hindu bastion of Kat Kala — "Fort of the Pass" — is the lovely **Talash Valley,** lined with unexcavated *stupas* and monasteries.

Yet Kat Kala is best remembered as the possible location of Massaga, scene of an epic battle between Alexander's 25,000 troops and the Assakenians (see "The Sword and the Fire," Part One).

Some forty kilometres (25 miles) beyond Kat Kala is **Balambat,** one of the oldest human settlements in the north, and possibly in the world — in continuous occupation by Aryans, Buddhists, Hindus, and Muslims, since 1500 BC.

Archaeologists have uncovered the ruins of houses built 2,500 years ago and the altars of fire worshippers, whose pagan rites are echoed even today by the burning of juniper on fire stands by pagan witches.

Some eighty-five kilometres (53 miles) from Chakdara you reach Dir where the road turns into a gravel and dirt track. Then there is another seventy-four kilometres (46 miles) of rough going to the Lowari Pass and down through a series of seemingly endless hairpin bends to **Drosh,** where the **service station** supplies low-grade petrol only.

There's also a small, basic **rest house** which you can book in advance through the Deputy Commissioner at Chitral and a small hotel, the **Drosh View.**

It's forty-two kilometres (26 miles) on to Chitral, often on precipitous ledges carved out of the gorge above the river.

Most houses are built of mud, but the walls of **Chitral Fort,** laid out amid the chequered green fields on the banks of the **Chitral River,** are built of sturdy stone.

Though the stonework is crumbling, the fort that was once the home of the old Mehtars, the rulers of the valley, serves now as the **police headquarters.** The setting is enhanced by the graceful lines of the **suspension bridge** that spans the river.

A century ago a seven-kilometre-long (4.4-mile) **racecourse** was carved out of a piece of flat, stony ground dominated by a mound of earth which the Mehtar used as his regal

Above: Kalash children, Chitral Valley.

grandstand.

It was in Chitral and other reaches of this northern fastness that British cavalry officers and horsemen discovered the sport of **polo** and exported it to the rest of the world.

Cruder, more vigorous, and certainly far more dangerous than its Anglicized version, the sport has been played for centuries. Each year thousands travel to Chitral to enjoy the town's three rugged polo tournaments held during Chitral's spring festival, and again in June and August.

Many enthusiasts believe the game derives from the Afghan sport of "pulling the goat", *buzkashi*, which is also played at the Chitral tournaments.

The aim is for the riders to snatch a dead goat and gallop around the field maintaining possession before dropping it in a circle in the centre of the pitch. In time gone by, celebrating the martial heritage of the Afghan Pukhtuns, there was no goat — just a living enemy, or his head.

Perched on a 2,750-metre-high (9,000 feet) plateau above the capital is the now unoccupied **summer palace** of the Mehtars of Chitral.

Woodcutters stride up to this height easily in about ninety minutes — less than half the time it takes the uninitiated to stumble and slip over the glacial moraine that bars the way.

The palace is a nostalgic evocation of the grand days of the feudal kings, an era when Chitral's fast-declining wildlife, particularly ibex and deer, was abundant. Inside, the trophies still cling to the wall alongside faded sepia photographs of the rajas who shot them.

Set amid green fields and colourful orchards, the palace provides a fine vantage point for the magnificent panorama of the valley against the dramatic centrefold of the Hindu Kush, majestic Tirich Mir.

Chitral folklore believes the peak is guarded by a ring of giant frogs, boguzai, and an inner ring of fairies disguised as seductive maidens, who meet the climber with bowls of milk or blood. Those who sip the blood, the legend runs, are never seen again.

Garam Chasma, where the **sulphur springs** are reputed to have healing powers for skin diseases, gout, rheumatism, and headaches, forty-five kilometres (28 miles) north-west of Chitral, makes a delightful day excursion, through deep narrow gorges and small valleys.

But most will set their sights on the Kalash valleys of **Bumburet, Rambur,** and **Birir,** in

Chitral's far north where, their history shrouded in mystery and legend, Pakistan's only pagan community, the 3,000 non-Muslim people of the Kafir Kalash known as the Black Infidels, live.

The easiest way to visit the valleys is by jeep, which your hotel or the PTDC can arrange. Alternatively, a taxi-jeep service operates between Chitral and Bumburet from a base near the **Mountain Inn.**

Twisting road

Bumburet, the largest of the three valleys, is also the most tourist orientated. The road to Bumburet twists and winds as it climbs the rumpled, barren mountain slopes to pass over into the valley at 2,750 metres (9,000 feet).

The two-and-a-half-hour drive takes you through the **checkpoint** and **toll station** at **Ayun,** after which the road branches right over the mountain and down to the valley, crossing a bridge on the valley floor and turning left into Bumburet. The village boasts three hotels, including the **Taj Mahal,** which is modest by any standards.

It's a gentle three-hour walk, or ninety-minute jeep drive, from Bumburet, the central Kalash valley, to Rambur, taking a right turn over the bridge on the valley floor.

Rambur has one basic inn with simple food and bedding. It's the only Kalash-owned inn in the three valleys. There's also a **rest house.**

From Chitral the easiest valley to approach is Birir, ninety minutes drive through Ayun, but it's a hard slog from Bumburet over a 2,400-metre-high (8,000-feet) mountain.

Dotted around these valleys are about twenty of the picturesque Kalash villages, their compact, rectangular, but windowless two-storey houses made of layers of timber, stone, and unbaked brick, many set into the side of the cliffs and hills.

The cracks in each strata of the building are filled with pebbles. The design has evolved over the centuries to withstand the frequent 'quakes and earth tremors that wrack this meeting place of the continents.

There are some holy places in the Kalash Valley forbidden to their often strikingly beautiful and unveiled women who, over their elaborately braided plaits, wear distinctive black headdresses decorated with cowrie shells and buttons and crowned with dyed feathers (see "The People," Part One).

Wherever you go in Chitral beauty and adventure await the wanderer. Here the hardy and experienced begin their treks through the high passes of the Hindu Kush, which form one side of the narrow Afghan panhandle that divides Russia from Pakistan.

Along the **Rich Valley** you trail over vertiginous tracks that often appear to plunge, terrifyingly, straight down the vertical cliff face, until you come to the 4,260-metre-high (13,980-feet) **Shah Jinali Pass.** The ascent to the spectacular summit is usually deep in snow.

You can then follow the trails along and beneath the ridgebacks of these daunting mountains to 4,500-metre-high (15,000-feet) **Darkot Pass** — the route taken by Chinese invaders more than 1,000 years ago — down into Gilgit and the riven tangled heart of the area's spectacular ravines and peaks.

Other treks include a relaxed expedition through the lovely pine forests from Drosh to **Madaklasht,** east of Chitral, and to **Koghozi:** or you can trek into the foothills of Tirich Mir or Swat valley. Ask the PTDC or one of the trekking agencies for advice.

Fishing

Chitral's mountain streams teem with trout stocked by hatcheries at Chitral and Bumburet. The **Lutkho river,** flowing from **Garam Chasma,** is said to provide the finest sport. The fly fishing season runs from April-September.

Permits are obtainable from the Fisheries Department, Chitral. Carry your own tackle.

Kaghan Valley: Matchless Pearl of the Himalaya

More than 160 kilometres (100 miles) long, the **Kaghan Valley** traces the course of the **River Kunhar** from a height of around 1,000 metres (3,000 feet) in the south to the 4,150-metre-high (13,600-feet) **Babusar Pass** in the north — once the only road to Gilgit and the Roof of the World. From there the trail leads on to **Chilas.**

Great forests roll down its steeply sloping walls, and glistening jade lakes, interspersed with meadows, lie like jewelled clasps in its floor beneath the shadows of the mountain ridges above.

Late spring, midsummer, and fall are the most attractive seasons in which to enjoy the Kaghan Valley's delights. Completely unspoilt and peaceful, there is no industry except forestry and no great population.

In most places the valley is extremely narrow with relatively rare views of the higher mountains. There are only two or three points where you can climb up to the higher levels and the summer grazing plateaux.

Getting there

Just before **Manshera** on the **Karakoram Highway,** there's a right fork along an old road that the Mughals followed to their beloved Vale of Kashmir.

From Manshera, turn right at the T-junction at the other side of the bridge and climb to the **Batrasi rest house** on the crest of a pleasant pine-forested ridge, about thirty minutes drive from Manshera.

The other side plunges down to the Kunhar river and leads — past a right turn for **Muzaffarabad** in Azad Kashmir — to **Balakot,** threshold of what many believe is arguably the most beautiful of all Pakistan's northern vistas.

There's a **PTDC motel** in the town where you can leave your own vehicle and arrange to hire a 4WD vehicle, but check that the tyres are in good shape. Hire rates for cars with drivers are expensive but it does mean that you can get out and walk when the track becomes too narrow and the drop too sheer — leaving the driver to negotiate the dangerous sections.

Petrol

The last reliable petrol is in **Abbottabad.** The two petrol pumps in Balakot are often closed — or out of gas.

When to go

The best time to visit Kaghan is May-June and September-October. **Naran** and **Shogran** are accessible from April to October, but the autumn nights are extremely cold. The only good time to attempt the **Babusar Pass** is August when the glaciers have melted but remember that it's also at this time, after the July monsoons, that the valley roads are at their worst.

Where to Stay

Park Hotel, Balakot. PTDC Cottage Hotels, Balakot and Naran. Inquire at PTDC Abbottabad. There are PWD rest houses at Batrasi, Naran, and Battakundi. Inquire at the PWD office, Manshera. There are forestry guest houses and rest houses at Shogran and Sharan. Inquire at the Conservator of Forests office for Hazara, Abbottabad, or Divisional Forest Office, Kaghan Division, Balakot.

There are some small basic hotels in Naran and other villages in the valley and a PTDC campsite in Naran. See Listings for "Hotels".

Sightseeing

There's little to see in dry and dusty **Balakot,** locale of a fierce nineteenth-century battle between the forces of a Muslim warrior, Ahmed Shah Brewli and Ranjit Singh's armies. Killed in 1831, his green-tiled mausoleum stands on the banks of Kunhar.

The main road out of Balakot, a left fork from the town centre over a bridge, is asphalt for forty-six kilometres (26 miles) to **Mahandri** but often hit by landslides and subsidence.

Twenty-four kilometres (15 miles) from the town, high on a precipitous eastern shoulder of Kaghan, stands the town of **Kaka.**

From here a trail, right, leads along a muddy and rutted lumber track through dense forest to emerge on one of the loveliest plateaux to overlook the valley — 2,363-metre-high (7,750-feet) **Shogran,** a fine place to spend a weekend,

Opposite: Alpine wonderland in upper Kaghan Valley.

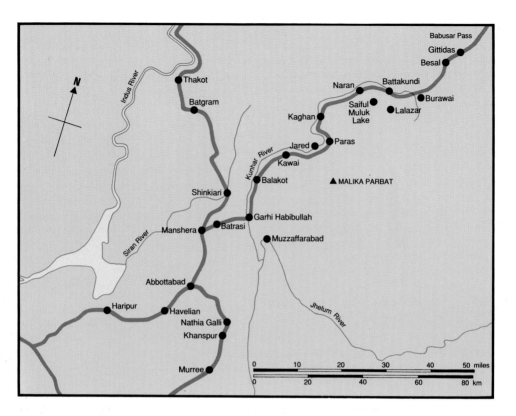

either in one of the rest houses or camping in the meadows.

There's a delightful walk of about two-and-a-half hours along one of the logging tracks to another Forestry Department rest house at 2,700 metres (8,750 feet), through shady forests filled with birds and flowers. From here trekkers can also climb over the hill to the **Neelum Valley** at **Ghori.**

Stirring in the fitful May breeze, flowers bend and nod in the green meadows beneath 3,884-metre-high (12,744-feet) **Makra;** while to the north, the towering mass of 5,289-metre-high (17,356-feet) **Malika Parbat** thrusts its ice spires into the sky.

Nearby, its other cohort, **Musa-ka-Musalla** — the "prayer mat of Moses" — bows its head in deference to the largest of the valley's peaks.

These meadows, and those above, are the summer pastures of the nomadic Gujar pastoralists. Independent and hardy, the Gujar women wear vivid, gaily-coloured dresses that reflect the pastel brilliance of the wild flower meadows.

From Shogran the road runs alongside the river to **Paras,** where there's a bridge to the side valley of **Sharan,** sixteen kilometres (ten miles) away. Little known and rarely visited, it contains one of Pakistan's most precious indigenous hardwood forests, rich in the abundance of its bird life, with tranquil walks that lead to idyllic views at the edge of escarpments and ridges.

At the bottom of the valley there's a comfortable **Forestry rest house,** a base for the many delightful walks to be enjoyed in the valley. You can also trek over the ridges to **Nadi** and down to **Daddar** in the **Siran valley.**

The next village along the Kaghan valley is **Shinu,** where you can visit the **trout hatchery,** and beyond that, forty kilometres (25 miles) from Balakot, is **Jared** and a government-operated Kaghan **handicrafts shop.**

West of Shogran, on the opposite plateau, another forty-five kilometres (28 miles) up the valley, **Naran** offers little in the way of natural beauty but is a major winter sports and fishing centre. It is also the turnoff point for the gem of gems in this treasury of natural jewels, **Saiful Muluk,** at the head of an eastern side valley ten kilometres (six miles) from Naran.

Floating limpid on the startlingly blue

waters of the one-kilometre-long (half-a-mile) lake is the mirror image of **Malika Parbat** at whose base — at 3,200 metres (10,500 feet) — at lies. It takes about three hours to walk to it.

Frozen over in winter, in late spring the lake's surface, reflecting its ring of ice-encrusted guardian peaks, is dotted with tiny islands of ice. In April and May the meadows on the lake shores become a riot of colourful wild flowers.

Lie here in the balm of a hazy summer day, amid the quiet and the hum of insects at work, and ponder the lake's name — taken from Prince Saiful Muluk, who fell in love with a lake nymph. So enamoured of her was he that one day he snatched away her clothing to gaze upon her beauty. To save her modesty, the nymph promised to wed the prince.

As they rode away into the sunset to live happily ever after, the nymph's demon lover was so incensed that he flooded the whole of the Kaghan Valley.

According to local folklore, fairies, demons, and nymphs still live in the waters of Saiful Muluk, revelling at night on its grassy shores. Woe to those who encounter these mythical folk.

From Naran, the valley extends another eighty kilometres (50 miles) to the top of the Babusar Pass, climbing through the mountain pastures to the treeless slopes around the village of **Besal**. The road is so neglected that even for the most adventurous it's a hair-raising journey.

Few indeed attempt it, but many do travel as far as Besal to gaze upon the font of the **Kunhar** — the one-kilometre-wide (half-a-mile) jade lake that so delighted whimsical Irish writer Dervia Murphy when she cycled from Ireland to India over the Babusar Pass.

Chilas: City of the Moon

Along the **Karakoram Highway** from **Sazin** to **Chilas** the land is bleak and arid, the soil leached by the fierce summer sun and the dry, cold winter, eroded by the constant gales that funnel down into this bowl, replenished by great deposits of flood silt from the Indus.

Yet, remarkably, all the way from the midway stage between **Patan** and Chilas, **Dassu,** to Chilas great stands of hewn, four-square timber crowd the roadside every ten or twenty kilometres (six-12 miles) — plucked from the lush, high-altitude forests of the invisible peaks above and hefted down the precipitous slopes with excruciating labour.

Chilas, the traditional crossing place of the Indus and for thousands of years a crossroads of trade, pilgrimage, and history, has been a stopping place for travellers for thousands of years — and the rocks and cliffs around Chilas testify to the centuries of traffic that passed this way.

Getting there

Just beyond a **checkpoint** there's a right turnoff the Highway to **Chilas town,** a good choice for an overnight stop after about nine hours driving from Islamabad. The road through old Chilas is a badly maintained 4WD track up to the **Babusar Pass**.

When to go

Spring, summer, and Autumn — the KKH is only open between April and October.

Where to stay

The Shangrila Motel, Chilas; outlandish comfort in an outlandish spot, but costly. Another hotel was also about to open when this guide was being compiled.

There is also a Frontier Works Organization — FWO — rest house. Inquire at the FWO, Rawalpindi. See Listings for "Hotels".

Sightseeing

Travellers of old rested in the chaotic, boulder-strewn landscape that surrounds this fifth-century "City of the Moon", *Somanagar*, where they inscribed the scattered rocks and cliffs with images and hieroglyphics that gave thanks for a safe journey, served to ward off evil, and comforted those who would follow in their perilous footsteps.

By the check point there's a 4WD track that leads down to the river and the first carvings appear on a rock to left after about one kilometre (half-a-mile).

These stylized images of animals, like the ibex and horses, festivals and riotous drinking parties, slave caravans and worshippers, royal couples and ploughmen, Buddhist *stupas* and religious symbols, form one of the great treasuries of upper Indus art.

The carvings and images and primitive tools from an earlier era cover an epoch that continued for more than 5,000 years.

There are more, nearer the river, on an isolated rocky hillock, depicting whole scenes — drinking parties, a ruler with captives, a horse festival, different types of *stupas* with worshippers, a ploughman and a royal couple.

Just one kilometre (half-a-mile) along the Highway from the barrier, on the hill to the east, there is a **rock** inscribed with fifth-century AD Gupta script that announces this was the entrance to *Somanagar.*

As it heads north from Chilas the Karakoram Highway skirts the base of **Nanga Parbat,** the "Naked Mountain", so called because some of its slopes are so steep they are bare of either snow or vegetation, and its topmost ridges form the outline of a woman.

For sheer size Nanga Parbat is almost without equal — not a single peak, in fact, but an entire massif culminating in an ice summit 8,125 metres (26,660 feet) high.

The rumpled flanks of its subservient attendants climb up out of the Indus Valley and there, beyond the blue-grey whaleback ridges, ringed by a halo cloud, rises its long ridge. Of all the great mountains at the Roof of the World, it is the most frequently visible.

Unequalled for scale, so is it for hostility. Apart from Everest and Annapurna in the south-east of the Himalaya, it has claimed the lives of more climbers than any other — close to fifty at the last count.

It was first conquered in 1953 by an Austro-German expedition. The world's greatest mountaineer, Reinhold Messner, made the first solo ascent in 1979.

In the world league of the fourteen peaks higher than 8,000 metres (26,250 feet), Nanga Parbat and K2 are considered the two most difficult. The climate all around the mountain — in the **Astor Valley** and others — reflects its natural savagery.

It's seen at its best about fifty kilometres (30 miles) from Chilas, where the highway crosses the Indus again and turns north, where you are far enough away to view it in all its incredible vastness.

All along the Indus between Chilas and Bunji the valley is a moonscape of barren, remnant glaciers and jagged peaks above which, wherever you turn, broods the great juggernaut of Nanga Parbat.

It was in the vale of Bunji in 1840, that Nanga Parbat sent down the landslide that dammed the Indus which was broached the next year by another tremor, causing the catastrophic flood that swept over the Peshawar Plains.

The name Bunji signifies the figure fifty in local vernacular and was bestowed on the vale because fifty villages were overwhelmed by the lake that backed up behind the natural dam within the space of six months. Now all is desert.

Seventy-four kilometres (46 miles) from Chilas, at **Jaglot,** you can see the old **Gilgit-Srinagar road,** leading off to the right, down a steep hill and across a suspension bridge.

It passed through Bunji and Astor before traversing the **Burzil Pass,** and then either the **Rajdiangan Pass** or the **Kamri Pass** into the Vale of Kashmir. The main supply route for the British garrison at Gilgit, it was called "the dreary road of slavery".

Five kilometres (three miles) beyond the bridge the Highway runs through a small hamlet, **Jaglot Farm,** where, down below, the bright, clear waters of the **Gilgit river** join the dark grey ribbon of the Indus. The Highway then follows the course of first the Gilgit and then the **Hunza river.**

Two kilometres (one mile) north-west of the confluence, the Highway crosses a steel bridge and forty-three kilometres (27 miles) further on meets the confluence of the Gilgit and Hunza rivers.

The Highway bypasses Gilgit town, forking right over the Gilgit river and going on to Hunza — but another two-lane highway leads the ten kilometres (six miles) straight to Gilgit.

Northern Delights

The snowclad peaks and narrow valleys of the **Northern Areas** lie amidst the towering mountains of the Himalaya and the Karakoram Range. Within a ninety-kilometre-radius (56-mile) of Gilgit, there are more than nineteen peaks which rise above 7,620 metres (25,000 feet), while **K2,** second-highest peak in the world after Mount Everest, stands in **Baltistan** — its summit reaching 8,610 metres (28,250 feet).

The region also boasts some of the world's greatest glaciers, sparkling lakes, and green valleys.

Pakistan's Northern Areas cover 72,496 square kilometres (27,984 square miles) with a population of about 850,000 an average of eleven people to each square kilometre.

Divided into three administrative districts — **Gilgit, Diamir,** and Baltistan (with twelve sub-divisions) — each under a Deputy Commissioner the region is administered by a Commissioner appointed by the Ministry of Kashmir Affairs and Northern Areas.

Gilgit: A Mountain Metropolis

Maharajahs or Mirs no longer rule over the once-upon-a-time kingdom of **Gilgit** which, though long a strategic centre that dominated 2,000 years of trade along the Silk Route, has little recorded history.

Before the advent of Buddhism, its pagan inhabitants were fire worshippers; then Hindu before the advent of Islam. It was invaded and subjugated around AD 750 by a Chinese force of 10,000.

These also occupied Baltistan before being ejected in turn by the Tibetans. Their reign, too, was brief, commemorated by five lines of ancient script in the Proto Sarada alphabet that give the history of the Tibetan kings who ruled at that time. The inscriptions were found near three ancient *stupas* excavated in 1934.

By the nineteenth century, when the Silk Route had fallen into disuse, the Muslim valley came under the suzerainty of the Hindu Maharajahs of Kashmir. Briefly, in 1877, the British established a power base in the town, but with too small an attachment for defence it was overwhelmed four years later.

Then, in 1889, in the name of Queen Victoria, Colonel Algernon Durand was posted to take command of the area, the most isolated outpost of the British Empire, forming a paramilitary police force, the Gilgit Scouts.

After the excitement of the drive or flight, Gilgit comes as something of a disappointment. It's dusty and dirty — sprawled for kilometres along one main street, reminiscent of a Wild West frontier town, with little of architectural or historical interest, except for the **Commissioner's House** and offices in a suburb above the town.

Set in a delightful garden, the ivy-covered colonial house with its high ceilings and tall, slender windows is the place where the former Hindu Dogra — ruler of Gilgit — surrendered when the district declared its independence from Indian-held Kashmir.

Few towns in the world can boast such a scenic backdrop, set in a ferdle bowl beneath the spectacle of Rakaposhi's snow-capped peaks at one end of the wide valley, and Mount Duboni at the other, with countless and possibly nameless other peaks between.

The mountainsides are barren-grey, capped with snow, but in the valley the colours vary with the seasons. In autumn they are at their most magnificent, as the leaves of the fruit and nut trees turn red and yellow against the cloudless sky.

Getting there

Daily services from Islamabad International Airport to Gilgit and Skardu must be the most dramatic scheduled flights in commercial aviation. But weather, not time rules airline punctuality. You can also drive up the Karakoram Highway.

When to go

The area is only open to foreign visitors from April to October.

Where to Stay

Gilgit Serena; pricey air-conditioning, excellent food, unbelievable views (especially of Rakaposhi) with facilities and service improving all the time. Chinar Inn (PTDC Motel). Pau Hotel, Alpine Hotel, Hunza Inn, Hunza Tourist House, Mount Baloze, Sargin Inn, Vershighoom Hotel, Golden Peak Inn, North Inn, Hotel Skyland and Jubilee. And many more — some in the process of building, some in the process of expanding. Now that the KKH and Gilgit are on the

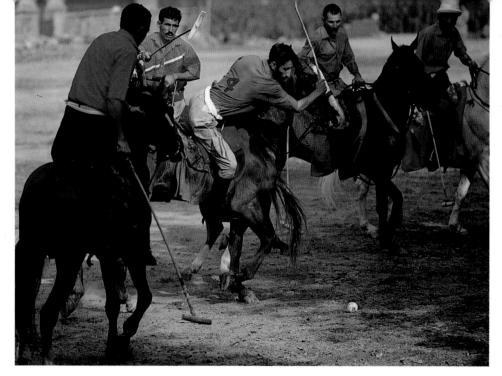

Above: Polo at Gilgit where the game has been played for more than 400 years.

Sightseeing

world tourist map advance booking is essential.

The PWD run rest houses at Nomal, Naltar, Chalt, Nagar, Singal, Gakuch, Gupis, Teru, Phandar, Yasin, and Ishkoman. Inquire through the PWD, Gilgit, or through FWO in Rawalpindi. See Listings for "Hotels".

Sightseeing

Broad and fertile, just 1,200 metres (4,000 feet) above sea level, Gilgit is glorious in spring when the apple, pear, almond, apricot, mulberry, and walnut orchards blossom. Tall plane trees, upright as guardsmen, poplars, eucalyptus, and leafy willows stand sentinel around the well-tended terraces. The little lanes and trails make easy and ideal walking and the mountain foothills are gentle at first.

The minute you leave the airfield you walk into a time-warp. Though now the most bustling bazaar on the Silk Route, dusty Gilgit still seems to hang suspended in a long forgotten limbo, despite the obvious presence of a large army and the continual stream of traffic on the other side of the river where the Karakoram Highway clings to the eastern wall of the narrow valley.

By Karakoram standards, Gilgit Valley is broad — dominated by perhaps the loveliest of all northern Pakistan's mountains. The elegant spire of 7,787-metre-high (25,550-feet) Rakaposhi hangs suspended above the terraced fields of grain and rice and the flowering apricot orchards.

Colourful cloths and beautiful Chinese silk fluttering in the breeze, fruit, spices, and the staple of the region — dried apricots — give the sprawling **bazaar** that stretches kilometres down the main street a vivid Technicolor aspect.

In these improbable emporiums, Chinese goods — crockery, cutlery, electronic products— range alongside beautifully crafted local handicrafts, shawls, woollens, baskets, batiks, even old-fashioned ski-boots. At least 350 different vernaculars and local dialects ring through the constant hubbub of the bazaar.

The greetings carved on the tall cliffs on the east wall of the valley, to catch the Aga Khan's eye when he flew in on a visit in the early 1980s, still proclaim Gilgit's joy at playing host to the leader of the world's Ismailis.

It's on the **polo ground** that some of the most exciting polo tournaments in the world are fought with heated, passionate, and ever valiant enthusiasm. The major event is staged in November to mark Independence Day and

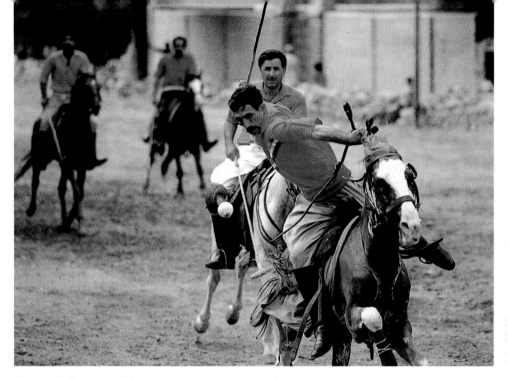

Above: Gilgit was the birthplace of the sport of kings.

there are also matches in March, but you may find exhibition and practice matches taking place at other times of the year.

Nearby a **stone memorial** honours the many brave men who died in the early struggle against Indian-held Kashmir.

Near Gilgit one of the longest **suspension bridges** in Asia — a trembling, graceful 198-metre-wide (650-feet) structure of wood and steel cable anchored only by its support towers in the cliffs — crosses the **Hunza river.** It leads on to the Gilgit suspension bridge that crosses the **Gilgit river** into the town centre.

Crossing it also is the constant stream of life of far northern Pakistan. An old man nearby from Sinkiang, China, watches shish kebabs sizzle over his charcoal fire. Chinese dumplings steam in old saucepans and everywhere there are blue-eyed Hunzakuts.

Just a few kilometres west of the town, at **Kargah Nullah** ten kilometres (six miles) along the **Punial Road,** is a stunning three-metre-high (ten-feet) **image of Buddha** carved on a cliff face about fifty metres (160 feet) above a small path by a stream to the left of the road. Some 400 metres (1,300 feet) upstream are the remains of three *stupas*, excavated in 1934.

Lakes and rivers in the valley teem with

plump and tender trout. The **Gilgit hatchery** is based near one of the valley's small hydroelectric projects on the floor of a narrow and precipitous ravine just a few kilometres north of the town.

There are many delightful easy walks you can take along the Gilgit valley, through the maize and vegetable fields and the orchards of apple, mulberry, walnut and apricot trees, to the foothills and the grazing lands beyond.

West of Gilgit the region offers unbridled adventure. The 225-kilometre (140-mile) long trail through **Punial, Gakuch,** and **Gupis** to **Yasin** in the north and the **Shandur Pass** in the west is rough going at its best.

Forty kilometres (25 miles) north of Gilgit, along the Gilgit river, Punial, once a feudal kingdom of twelve villages and 17,000 people, became part of Pakistan in 1972. Filled with orchards and small terraced fields, to its citizens it's "the place where heaven and earth meet".

The capital, **Sher Qila** — "Lion's Fort" — earned its name because it was unconquerable.

From Punial the track continues through **Singal**, sixteen kilometres (ten miles) beyond Sher Qila, Gakuch, and Gupis, to the 3,734-metre-high (12,250-feet) Shandur Pass which connects Gilgit with Chitral.

Phandar Lake, about halfway between Gilgit and the top of the Pass, is idyllic with a good **rest house** on a ridge overlooking the flat, meandering river on one side — azure waters of the trout-filled lake on the other.

Encircled by its cluster of ice peaks, its fields shaded by stands of chinar trees and willows of deepest green, another valley, **Yasin,** remains one of the most remote of the valleys in the Gilgit area, lying at the foot of the Hindu Kush range, slightly north of the road from Punial.

The gem-like tarns and glacial streams of the 3,000-metre-high (10,000-feet) **Naltar Valley,** perhaps Gilgit's loveliest alpine valley, in the shadow of graceful Rakaposhi, offer not only hardy anglers joy, but trekkers and ski enthusiasts, too.

Dotted with sparse clumps of pine, the Pakistan Armed Forces have installed two lifts on the valley's steep-sided walls to make it one of the few ski resorts in northern Pakistan.

Trekkers can walk up the valley to **Naltar Lake** and then over 4,800-metre-high (15,750-feet) **Shani Pass.** There's also a rugged trekking trail over the 4,217-metre-high (13,836-feet) **Naltar Pass** to Pakhor.

Fishing

There are many delightful places to fish in the lakes and rivers of Gilgit. Permits are issued by the Fisheries Department, Gilgit. Carry your own tackle.

The most favoured spots for trout are **Kargah,** sixteen kilometres (ten miles) from Gilgit, **Singal** in Punial, fifty-six kilometres (35 miles) from Gilgit, and **Phandar Lake,** 117 kilometres (73 miles) from Gilgit, on the Shandur Pass road.

The Road To Shangri-La

To reach Hunza, take the road south out of Gilgit and rejoin the **Karakoram Highway,** then left across the stone and concrete **Chinese bridge** over the **Gilgit River.**

Some two kilometres (one mile) from the bridge you pass through the hamlet of **Dainyor** by the Pakistan Broadcasting Company's **radio transmitter.** On a rock inside the compound are fifth-century **inscriptions** that outline the history of Gilgit's Tibetan kings.

Not far beyond, right, is the **cemetery** beneath Rakaposhi where the Chinese killed during the building of the Highway lie buried.

It's a quiet and tranquil, tree-shaded place.

Some sixteen to twenty kilometres (10-12 miles) from Gilgit, along the east bank of the **Hunza River,** there's another **memorial,** left, to the Pakistan Army men who died building the KKH and "chose to make the Karakoram their permanent abode". The tribute reads, "There shall be in their rich dust, a richer dust concealed."

The first sizable settlement, some thirty-two kilometres (20 miles) from Gilgit, is **Nomal.** Across the river you can make out the old 4WD track to Hunza that President Ayub Khan drove along in the 1960s — the only southern egress for the Hunzakuts before the Highway was built. Much of it has been swept away.

Nomal stood on the west bank but since the Highway was built most villagers have moved — not surprisingly since there's no bridge — across the river into the mainstream of the east bank.

Nomal prospers as a busy little trading centre — with vendors on either side of the highway offering luscious apples, grapes, and other fruits. Another merchant sells the bark of the paper tree that Marco Polo used to send home messages. Marks on the bark form the Arabic calligraphic inscription for "Allah the Merciful". No wonder the bark is valued highly in this region.

From Nomal, the highway runs through bleak but dramatic gorges, some as long as eight kilometres (five miles), without sign of life.

Sheer-sided, the road is carved literally out of the cliff wall and it's easy to perceive the terror of the old "Silk Route", for in summer when the river is in spate it's impossible to walk along the river bed and in winter the high passes to the north of Hunza are blocked by snow.

Then, on a handsome plateau, at a bend on the river where two gorges from the outliers of the **Hindu Kush** meet the gorge of the Hunza river, stands **Chalt** and its old fortress.

The farthest outpost of the Maharajah of Kashmir's little empire and, ultimately, of the British who provided his regime with defence, it is sixty-one kilometres (38 miles) from Gilgit.

With its near neighbours **Chaprot** and **Nilt,** nine kilometres (six miles) further on, Chalt was the scene of what E. F. Knight described as "one of the most brilliant little campaigns in military history" — the battle fought when

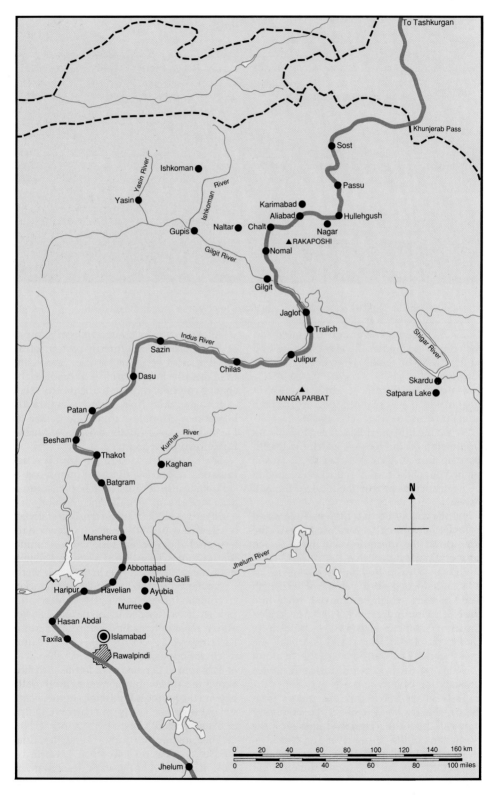

To Tashkurgan

Khunjerab Pass

Sost

Passu

Ishkoman

Yasin River

Yasin

Ishkoman River

Karimabad
Aliabad
Hullehgush
Chalt
Nagar
Naltar
▲ RAKAPOSHI

Gupis

Gilgit River

Nomal

Gilgit

Jaglot

Tralich

Shigar River

Indus River

Sazin

Julipur

Dasu

Chilas

Skardu
Satpara Lake ●

Patan

NANGA PARBAT ▲

Besham

Thakot

Kunhar River

Batgram

Kaghan

Manshera

N

Abbottabad
Nathia Galli
Havelian
Ayubia
Haripur
Murree

Jhelum River

Hasan Abdal

Taxila
⊙ Islamabad
Rawalpindi

0   20   40   60   80   100   120   140   160 km
0   20   40   60   80   100 miles

Jhelum

Above: KKH cuts through the narrow valleys that divide the greatest mountains on earth.

Colonel Algernon Durand mounted an expedition to subdue the slave-trading and raiding of the rival Hunza and Nagar kingdoms.

Fought in the most difficult terrain imaginable, it was a month-long-epic of high adventure and courage on both sides.

When the British artillery failed to make an impression on the fortress walls, the British blew up the main gate. But when the defenders rushed out of the fort, the attackers rushed in — neglecting to pursue them down the Nilt ravine.

By the following day they had reformed behind a network of prepared defences on the far side of the precipitous ravine — much more difficult to attack than the fortress — and the advance was halted for three long weeks.

It ended when a British force of 100 British and Gurkhas, which had moved down into the Nilt ravine under cover of darkness, scaled the sheer 300-metre-high (1,000-feet) precipice under the fortifications and stormed the breastworks. One outcome was the award of the Victoria Cross to two British officers for outstanding valour.

Sixty-seven kilometres (42 miles) from Gilgit, the Highway crosses the boundary between the former **Hunza** kingdom on the north bank of the Hunza river and **Nagar** on the south bank. The Highway runs through Nagar territory for eighteen kilometres (11 miles) and then crosses over to Hunza.

All along you catch intermittent glimpses of Rakaposhi, southernmost bastion of the Karakoram, a series of snow-covered cliffs, triangles, precipices, cornices, and ridges, that change colour according to the time of day.

It's on this first stretch, eighty-two kilometres (51 miles) from Gilgit, that the Highway passes an idyllic spot labelled simply **Rakaposhi Viewpoint.**

Each day truckloads of trippers and busloads of tourists disgorge themselves to sip soft drinks and tea under parasols and gaze straight up — a distance of more than 6,000 metres (20,000 feet) — the almost vertical southern face of Rakaposhi, its peak wreathed in ever-changing cloud formations — surely, for those who can aspire to no greater heights, the loveliest mountain vista in the whole world.

Not long after this the road crosses over the river again into the start of the **Hunza valley** proper. It emerges suddenly around a bend after a seemingly endless series of daunting, barren gorges.

On the opposite side of the river the village of **Minapin** is perched on a fertile shelf high above the river. Six kilometres (four miles) beyond the bridge is **Dudimal,** another Nagar village, set precariously on a narrow shoulder of the sheer high cliffs.

Then, just around the next bend, the Hunza landscape opens up before you — warm and glorious contrast to the stark desolation that has preceded it.

Above: Ismaili mosque at Altit village, Hunza Valley.

Hunza: The Real Shangri-La

For Himalayan mountaineer Eric Shipton **Hunza** was "the ultimate manifestation of mountain grandeur" — the most spectacular country he had ever seen. Few would argue. It inspired James Hilton to write his modern fable, *Lost Horizons,* set in a land of peace and plenty where people never aged.

There's some truth to the myth. Scientists discovered that, free from social stress and succoured by a monotonous diet of apricots and low intake of animal fat, the Hunzakuts did enjoy longevity.

Fruit remains the staple and in summer, to conserve fuel and precious cereals, cooking is forbidden.

In winter the people eat flour made from apricot kernels, drink brandy distilled from mulberries, and wines from the grapes that grow everywhere, smothering the poplars and roofs.

This unvarying diet of fruit and the mineral-rich waters of its rivers — which tastes like a sludge of porridge and gravel — certainly seems to work. Many centenarians still work their fields in Hunza.

Dominating all is the massive yet somehow slender, soaring profile of Rakaposhi, its snows a gleaming kaleidoscope of changing colours throughout the day as the sun shifts across the horizon and filters through the billowing clouds that boil and fret around its sceptred crown.

For a thousand years the 30,000 citizens were the lieges of the Mirs of Hunza, whose successor even today still retains many of his traditional powers. The Mirs long believed themselves the equals of the great invading forces.

They had an overwhelming conceit about their importance and the size of their empires which they rated only slightly smaller than China. The Mirs ruled until 1974 when Hunza became part of Pakistan.

For the locals little has changed — yet. The opening of the Karakoram Highway at the end of the 1970s ended their millenniums of isolation and now another avalanche, that of tourists, threatens their captivating castled kingdom, perhaps even more than the thundering rocks that powder the mountain slopes in their passing fury.

As the season changes so do the colours, from springtime green to high summer yellow to autumn gold and winter grey and white.

The alluvial fans of the side rivers have been transformed by staircases of tiny terraced fields reaching almost to the snowline, each enclosed by a high dry stone wall. In one glance you can see a massive glacier and the tiny irrigation canals that feed its waters to the fields.

These little towns, with their flat-topped houses and tiny fields, their orchards with ant-like figures working their ox-teams so far beneath The Roof of the World, give perspective to the majestic and infinite scale of matchless nature.

Long ago, the capital was at **Baltit** at the head of the lovely side valley of **Ultar,** beneath the tail of the Ultar Glacier that streams down from **Bojoahaghur Dunasir** 7,315 metres (24,000 feet) high.

One of its subsidiary peaks, a slender granite obelisk that stretches 600 metres (2,000 feet), is known as **Princess Bubuli's** throne. The soughing of the wind that whines and screams around it during the fury of a storm is said to be her mournful cry of despair at being imprisoned so long.

For the princess, says local folklore, was married to a Tibetan warlord who returned home to fight a war, leaving his wife seated on top of the peak with a cockerel and a bag of millet. As he rode away he instructed her to give the cockerel one grain a year "and when the grain is done I shall return".

But since he also told the poor princess he would return "yesterday and tomorrow, when donkeys grow horns, when millstones sprout beards, and rivers flow uphill" no wonder she remains, her lament echoing in the lonely vastness around the peak.

Petrol

In **Aliabad** only.

Where to stay

Village Hotel, Rakaposhi View Hotel, Hilltop Hotel, Rainbow Hotel, Silver Jubilee Hotel, Diran Peak Inn, Mountain View Hotel — all in Karimabad.

Rakaposhi Serena Hotel (under construction

Opposite: Fruit drying in the sun on flat roofs of Altit Village, Hunza.

Above: Young Hunzakuts sort summer bounty of apricots for drying.

1989), Prince Hotel, Deluxe Hotel, Dumani View Hotel, PTDC Motels — all in Aliabad. There are others. See Listings for "Hotels."

Sightseeing

Set 2,400 metres (8,000 feet) above sea level, a tapestry of stone-walled terraced fields the size of tennis courts, sublime in their springtime beauty, surrounds the towns of **Aliabad,** now the capital, and **Karimabad,** the former capital, each of which itself climbs up the valley's steep slopes in a series of terraces.

From Karimabad, with its **souvenir shop, post office,** and **tea shop,** set back from Rakaposhi and the great peaks of the Karakoram framing the valley in the foreground, the panorama is magnificent.

Above Karimabad, reminiscent of much architecture found in Tibet, stands the 900-year-old whitewashed **Baltit palace** of the Hunza Mirs until 1960, when the prince moved into an elegant, new, white-roofed stone palace at Karimabad set in a staircase garden of shrubs and gracious trees. From the roof of this new princely abode, the dynasty's pennant still flutters at festivals and other annual celebrations.

From Karimabad to Baltit is about two kilometres (one mile), a steepish but fascinating walk through the old village. Directly beneath the old palace, leaning dangerously downhill, look for the **mosque,** renowned for the glory of its carved pillars and crossbeams, perched precariously on a steep slope.

Baltit palace was the inspiration of a Baltistan princess, who married a reigning Mir and imported Balti masons, carpenters, and craftsmen to build Baltit — and its sister fort at Altit — as part of her dowry.

Inside the basement there's a spiral ramp to the gloomy main hall which has a square hole in the ceiling. A wooden staircase, with banisters of poplar poles, leads through this to the central lobby where another staircase leads to an open balcony, the former reception room, which has smaller windowless rooms leading off it.

Behind the balcony there's an ornately-carved **audience pavilion** containing photographs of the Mirs and their important visitors. Nearby is a kind of **"museum"** filled with coats of mail armour, weapons, and the drums that sounded the alarm.

Even more impressive is **Altit's** 1,000-year-old fort, a three-kilometre (two-mile) jeep ride or two-kilometre (one-mile) walk from Karimabad. It stands at the edge of a sheer 300-metre-drop (1,000-feet) above the Hunza River — enough, even if you never suffered before, to make you a victim of vertigo.

The fort's **watchtower,** with carved doors and windows surmounted by a Picasso-like wooden goat with ibex horns, dates back to AD 909. Using the wooden beams in the corner for footholds, it's possible, but difficult, to climb up inside the watchtower.

On the other side of the bridge beyond Ganesh, a motorable track leads to Nagar. From the village of Nagar you can apparently walk to the **Hopar** and **Hispar** glaciers, two of the long chains of glaciers extending to Baltistan.

Back on the Karakoram Highway, on the right near **Aliabad,** as you drive towards **Ganesh,** the Pakistan Mineral Development Corporation has launched a project to exploit Hunza's mineral wealth — deposits of precious and semi-precious stones such as rubies and garnets. Two kilometres (one mile) beyond this there's a path, left, to the **ruby mines.**

Then, six kilometres (four miles) beyond Aliabad, by yet another **monument** to those who died building the road, you can explore the ancient village of Ganesh with its carved **mosque** and old **swimming pool** in which all Hunza children-of-yore took mandatory lessons. Swimming the Hunza in near spate, in fact, was a major part of their initiation rites.

Hunza was an important staging post on the Silk Route and through the centuries these travellers left ancient inscriptions, in four old scripts — Kharoshthi, Sogdian, Gupta, and Tibetan — carved on the rocks on the other side of the river near Ganesh between 3,000 and 1,500 years ago. There are also more ancient rock carvings of hunting and ibex.

Follow the highway over the **Chinese bridge,** across the river Hunza. The rocks are about 200 metres (600 yards) beyond the bridge, on the left. One scholar describes them as the "Guest Book of the Silk Route".

Among the inscriptions there's a portrait of the Kushan king Gondophernes in central Asian dress who ruled Gandhara in the first century AD.

The most remote village in this region, **Shispar,** is perched beneath the tail of the **Shispar Glacier** one of the Pamir Knot's most forbidding, parallel to that of the **Chogo Lungma Glacier.** The Shispar leads up to a daunting 5,3450-metre-high (17,550-feet) pass and trails an incredible 122 kilometres down the **Biafo Glacier,** through **Askole** in Baltistan, to the **Baltoro.**

From Ganesh the highway follows the course of the Hunza River, before swinging right along the banks of the **Khunjerab river** up to the **Chinese border.**

Only opened to foreign visitors in 1986, tourist facilities are developing rapidly along this section of the highway. In the little villages of the **Upper Hunza Valley — Passu, Shispar, Gulmit,** and **Sost** — many people have turned their houses into homely bed-and-breakfast accommodation, where backpackers and upmarket tourists all mingle happily together.

Indeed, one enterprising resident, an ex-Armed Forces officer, in the village of Gulmit has turned his farmhouse and meadowlands into a comfortable climbing and trekking hotel with self-contained chalets in the grounds for those tourists who seek something more exclusive.

Nearby, on the shores of a broad belly in the Hunza river large enough to be called a lake, he has also built a new four-star hotel, the **Silk Route Lodge.** The self-contained suites and air-conditioning are identical to those found in the Pearl Continental chain of hotels.

Gulmit, itself, also offers comfortable but less sophisticated accommodation for tourists. Between Gulmit and Passu, at the tail of the glacier of the same name and two of its smaller kin, there's a delightful little lake resort atop a small hill to the west. **Buret** has its own teahouse and boat for excursions on the jade-green waters of this tiny tarn.

Where to stay

In Gulmit, Silk Route Lodge, Marco Polo Inn, Village Hotel, Horseshoe Motel Tourist Cottage, and Greenland Hotel. In Passu, Passu Inn, Hispar Hotel, and Batura Inn. In Sost, Marco Polo Shangrila, Khunjerab View Hotel, Pamir Hotel International, and the Tourist Lodge. See Listings for "Hotels".

Sightseeing

From Buret the highway climbs the high shoulders of a series of long bends until, on the crest, a view of the **Passu Cathedral,** a mountain wall adorned with perfectly symmetrical natural Gothic columns and arches, corniches and pediments, all of unhewn rock, unfurls.

Rising incredibly high, stunning in its form and beauty, it is an exquisitely-shaped piece of natural architecture that for magnificence surpasses anything wrought by Europe's architects of the Middle Ages.

East and west of the highway, out of sight but briefly, are some of the greatest peaks of the Karakoram, revealing themselves through breaks between their smaller companion mountains — the elegant pyramid and knife edge ridge of 7,785-metre-high (25,400-feet)

Above: Palace of the Mir of Hunza, Karimabad, Hunza.

Batura Mustagh I and 7,619 metre-high (25,000-feet) Shispar.

Finally, the highway enters a broad valley and the checkpoint — police, customs and immigration — at Sost, some sixty kilometres (38 miles) from the Khunjerab Pass and some 100 kilometres (60 miles) from the Chinese border check on the other side.

On either side of Sost's one main street are many guest houses, hotels, restaurants and a brawling bus station where locals and visitors clamber desperately to board the last bus to Kashgar in China, or Gilgit in Pakistan.

Some ten kilometres (six miles) beyond Sost there's a dirt road west, forbidden still to foreigners for military reasons, that leads to the magical and unspoilt village of Misghar, once the main halt on the old Silk Route.

Untouched by the twentieth century, reached only by a dizzying single lane dirt track carved out of the cliff face, 200 metres (650 feet) above a sheer drop, Misghar slumbers on in its limbo of yesteryear.

The dancing crystal clear waters from a gushing mountain spring are funnelled off along its little lanes and byways providing a never ending source of irrigation for its terraced grain fields.

Back on the highway, the road begins to climb steeply, some 1,800 metres (6,000 feet) in under fifty kilometres (30 miles), to the Khunjerab Pass, passing a final petrol station at the signboard that announces Khunjerab National Park — perhaps the most rugged and inaccessible nature sanctuary in the world.

Notable for its vivid-red marmosets, which frequently scurry across the highway in front of approaching vehicles, it's tangled and impenetrable landscape consists of foaming rivers, narrow ravines, and craggy peaks.

Finally, at a natural crossroads where three valleys meet, the Highway suddenly leaps upward towards the north-west in a series of severe hairpin bends for thirty kilometres (18 miles), finally to emerge onto the fragile but verdant summer grasslands of the Khunjerab Pass.

There, mounted Chinese and Pakistan border police mix in amicable friendliness as hordes of tourists decant — breathless and dizzy, unaccustomed and unacclimatized to the 4,593-metre-high (15,072-feet) altitude — to be photographed alongside them or against the obelisk that marks the Sino-Pak border.

Baltistan: On the Roof of the World

Pierced by the deepest ravines and gorges on earth, some so narrow that even in summer the sun is visible for only three hours a day, blasted and pummelled by icy winds that never cease to blow, the highest land in the world rejoices in the name of "Little Tibet".

No diminutive this, though. Baltistan's 26,000 square kilometres (10,500 square miles), crowned by the majesty of K2, at 8,610 metres (28,250 feet) the world's second-highest mountain, sit at an average height of more than 4,570 metres (15,000 feet).

There is no higher land in all the world. In this once-forgotten kingdom there is nothing below 2,133 metres (7,000 feet) — and level land at that altitude is rare and surprising.

Bleak granite cliffs, almost sheer, rise from one-and-a-half to six kilometres (one-four miles) high on every side. These jagged barren spurs, devoid of any vegetation, are broken beneath by expanses of rocky alpine desert. And from the great glaciers above, vast reserves of water filter slowly away during summer to nourish the Indus watershed.

The Siachen, Baltoro, and other glaciers of the Karakoram form the largest and longest in the world outside the polar region.

From their spectacular birthplace in Concordia, at the base of the K2 and the Masherbrum range, the Siachen Glacier runs for more than seventy kilometres (43 miles), the Baltoro for more than fifty-nine kilometres (37 miles), while the Batura Glacier to the north, hanging over the Karakoram Highway, streams down a similar distance from the northernmost ramparts of the Karakoram.

The new roads carved to once-isolated communities like Askole, the highest village in the region — perhaps in the world — now, however, bring tourists and poachers and hunters and this last Himalayan faunal reservoir is under threat.

Once a kingdom that held its people in bondage for a century and a half, scattered areas of the valley blossom in the summer with cherries, apricots, almonds, and pears, and the fields yield rice, maize, wheat, and fodder for the animals.

Villages of stone and timber houses with

Above: Concordia seen from the surface of the Baltoro Glacier.
Opposite: Karakoram Highway snakes beneath wind-eroded rock of the Passu Cathedral in upper Hunza.

dark and narrow stairwells riven by gloomy, unlit alleys cluster within the embrace of the fertile terraces — glittering jewels set in the tarnished silver clasp of the granite barren cliffs and soaring peaks.

Such interludes of fertility are brief and far between. Basically, Baltistan is an alpine desert — perhaps the most forbidding and fearful landscape anywhere on earth.

Lying north of Indian-held Kashmir along a stretch of the Upper Indus, Baltistan is cupped between the Karakoram mountain range and the uninhabited, desolate **Deosai Plateau** of the Himalaya.

Since time began Baltistan has remained isolated from the rest of the world. It was first mentioned in the annals of an AD 747 Chinese military expedition to aid Ladakh against a threatened invasion from Tibet.

Fascinated, the ancient Chinese geographers named it the "Tibet of the Apricots" — because of the abundance of this fruit that grew there, and still does. Long a Buddhist country, Islam was embraced in the fifteenth century and during the Mughal era it was annexed to India.

But when Aurangzeb died it soon reverted to its isolated, independent ways, only to come under a succession of local rulers — Dogras,

Sikhs, and Afghans — finally to be annexed by the kingdom of Kashmir.

At Independence in 1947, however, Baltistan chose to join Pakistan, although for many years India has consistently contended that the icy slopes of the Siachen Glacier and the heights around 7,461-metre-high (24,480-feet) Teram Kangris, a sister peak of K2, were hers.

Getting there

So formidable is the Indus gorge out of Skardu that not even the hardy Baltis ventured to cross it.

Not until October 1978, with the completion of the 170-kilometre-long (105-mile) **Shahrah-e-Skardu,** did Baltistan have any permanent access to the rest of the world.

It represents a major feat of civil engineering construction and already Skardu, long a Mecca for the high-altitude mountaineer, has become a major tourist resort as coaches, cars, and jeeps flood down the road across more than twenty bridges to the town.

In the 1980s, however, many visitors opted for the sixty-minute flight from Rawalpindi along the Indus Valley, past Nanga Parbat, banking sharply starboard to follow the Indus through one of the narrowest ravines ever flown by a civil airline.

The walls rise thousands of metres above, dwarfing the Boeing 737 jet. Nonetheless, it's best to book at least a month in advance and be prepared for disappointments. The planes only fly in clear weather and a huge backlog of passengers often builds up.

The airport is fourteen kilometres (nine miles) from Skardu and the taxi more expensive than the air fare.

Petrol

Petrol is usually available in **Skardu.** There is ordinary grade petrol at **Sasli** near the Karakoram Highway.

When to go

The best months to go to Baltistan are between April and June and in September. Beware of extreme temperatures. In summer it's extremely hot and dry, with little or no shade, but at night temperatures fall rapidly and it becomes extremely cold.

Where to Stay

Shangrila resort complex, Kachura Lake; pricey but more than reasonable in such a remote spot for the views alone, not to mention the comfort and the setting. PTDC Motel, Kachura Lake. PTDC Motel, Satpara Lake. PTDC K2 Motel, Skardu.

There are PWD rest houses in Skardu, Shigar, Khaplu, and Machlu. Inquire at PWD office, Skardu. You can also camp but there are no official campsites. See Listings for "Hotels".

Sightseeing

Leaving the plane, the most immediate impression is that of disorientation. Astonishingly, the **Skardu valley** is a pure replica of the Sahara —an area of shifting sand dunes. It is as if the Sahara had been dropped down between massive walls of rock.

Lying within this ring of 5,000-metre-high (17,000-feet) mountains the jade river Indus snakes sinuously between the ribboned dunes close beneath a massive sixty-metre-high (200-feet) island of massive rock where **Skardu** straggles along the plateau.

Above the capital stands an ancient sixteenth-century **fortress,** a network of dark corridors and recesses linked by wooden staircases. Below, the unimpressive town's tree-lined streets stretch for several kilometres, but only the **bazaar** will invite the visitor to linger.

Skardu is only eight kilometres (five miles) from **Lake Satpara,** one of the hidden pearls of Little Tibet. There's a well-preserved **Buddhist monument** on the way to Satpara, reached by crossing a small stream and climbing a rocky slope, an easy walk of about an hour.

Its emerald waters gleaming in the sun, Satpara lies at the foot of a majestic mountain. An island in its centre makes a lovely summer picnic spot.

But it is **Kachura Lake,** renamed **Shangri-la** by the owner of the **resort** that sits on its meadowlands of wild flowers and blossoming orchards, thirty-two kilometres (20 miles) downstream which perhaps has claim to be the most lovely spot in Baltistan. The lake teems with fat, sporting trout, as do many of the lakes and rivers.

South-east of Skardu, the **Khaplu Valley** winds away to Ladakh for 100 kilometres (62 miles) along perhaps the most treacherous road in Baltistan. But what views reward the effort.

The ever-changing landscapes follow the sandy valley floor, black mountains reflecting in the waters of the **Shyok River.** On the slopes little communities have carved their terraced fields and homes out of the mountainside, diverting the waters along a network of ancient irrigation aqueducts.

The local capital, distinctively Tibetan in its people and architecture, is spread out along the greenest and broadest bowl of the valley, an arena that for the non-trekker is the keypoint of the entire visit to Baltistan.

For only in **Khaplu,** so high and close together are the region's other valleys, do you catch sight of the *raison d'être* for any visit to Baltistan — its mountains.

As the morning sun slides above the eastern horizon, its rays burst in a dazzling shower of diamonds on the scintillating peak of mighty 7,820-metre-high (25,660-feet) **Masherbrum.**

Thirty-two kilometres (20 miles) north of Skardu lies the vale of **Shigar,** a landscape of gentle, smiling fields dominated by a dreamy wooden village and an ancient carved **mosque.** It is the launch pad for the incredible trek to Concordia at the base of K2.

It's only during the first few days that the

Opposite: Rakaposhi, 7,788 metres (25,550 feet) high, from old Mirs palace, Baltit, Hunza.

trail passes through populated areas. Thereafter the trekker trudges through desolate gorges and over moraines and glaciers.

From Shigar the track climbs ever higher and the valley walls close in until you reach **Dassu,** another eighty kilometres (50 miles) on, completely encircled by a range of snowcapped peaks reaching heights of more than 6,000 metres (20,000 feet).

The trek from Dassu leads up to **Paiju** and the 3,350-metre-high (11,000-feet) snout of the stupendous Baltoro Glacier, its surface riven with crevasses and pitted with corrugations that from afar look like the rutted tracks made by some monstrous vehicle.

The trek culminates in a 4,626-metre-high (15,180-feet) camp on Concordia where three gigantic glaciers meet, forming the proscenium for the most spectacular natural theatre in the world.

Within a radius of twenty-five kilometres (16 miles) stand ten of the world's thirty highest peaks including K2. Others include **Broad Peak,** 8,047 metres (26,400 feet), first climbed in 1955, and **Hidden Peak** or **Gasherbrum**, so enclosed by other peaks that it was only discovered in 1934 despite its height of 8,063 metres (26,470 feet). It was first climbed in 1958. There are three more Gasherbrum peaks, including another higher than 8,000 metres (26,250 feet).

Masherbrum, on the other side of the Baltoro Glacier, first climbed in 1960, is known as the "Doomsday" mountain because it is a killer.

K2, only 236 metres (773 feet) lower than Everest, is considered the most challenging and beautiful of all mountains. First conquered by an Italian expedition on 31 July 1954, its perils are many — avalanches, landslides, frequent and unpredictable storms, and savage winds. It has claimed more than fifty lives.

Reinhold Messner, indisputably the world's greatest mountaineer, who has climbed all fourteen peaks standing above 8,000 metres (26,250 feet) rates K2 toughest of all.

Fishing

The fishing in Skardu is excellent and the trout have a well-deserved reputation for shrewdness. The season is from April to September. Permits are issued by the **Fisheries Department,** Skardu. Take your own tackle.

The best spots are **Satpara Lake, Kachura Lake,** and the **Shyok river** in the Khaplu Valley, which has a trout hatchery.

The Punjab: Bread Basket of Pakistan

The Punjab has always tempted invaders. Five rivers tumbling down off the world's Himalayan roof flow through this vast triangular plain to pay their separate tributes to the Indus before that legendary waterway issues into the Arabian Sea. They give the province its name — Punjab means Five Waters — and ensure its proverbial, and much-prized, fertility.

With rare exceptions invaders approached via one of the northwest passages from Afghanistan and the Hindu Kush. They were the routes taken by Babur, founder of the Mughal Empire, and his ancestors Tamurlane and Genghis Khan, as well as by the earlier Greeks, Guptas, Mongols, Turks, Pathans, and the Aryans.

The Province, made up of eight Administrative Divisions and twenty-nine districts, covers 205,346 square kilometres (97,192 square miles) with a population of around sixty million.

Known as the "Cultural Capital" of Pakistan, though not the largest province, the Punjab is the most densely populated with an average of 230 persons to each square kilometre (0.386 square miles).

Hard-working, warm-hearted and sincere, the people welcome visitors with a friendly smile and ready hospitality. The poet, Allama Iqbal, who dreamt of Pakistan, was born in this province in Sialkot district and lies buried in the capital of Lahore.

Famed for the great variety of its arts and crafts — from the blue tiles of Multan to the woodwork of Chiniot — the Punjab is a land of manly games, sturdy wrestlers, *pehalwans,* robust cattle and dairy farms, folklore, romantic legends, and haunting music (See "The People", Part One).

South-west of Sutlej, the vast **Cholistan desert** of 26,000 square kilometres (10,440 square miles) covers two-thirds of the entire Bahawalpur Division.

Opposite: Performing bear and handler, Punjab Province.

The Road to Lahore: A Journey Through Time

Between Islamabad and Jhelum, the old Mughal road, the **Imperial Highway,** now the **Grand Trunk Road** from **Kabul** to **Delhi,** cuts across the weird landscape of the **Potwar Plateau** and then on to **Lahore** across the infinitely flat but ever fertile **Punjab plains** which stretch all the way to Delhi.

Geologically, despite its name, the Potwar Plateau is a basin, bounded in the west by the Indus, to the north by the **Kala Chitt** and **Margalla Hills,** and in the east and south by the meandering **Jhelum river.**

Heavily eroded by gullies, which have left strange pinnacles and pillars of earth and rock, when spring comes the Potwar takes on a brilliant mantle of yellow as fields of mustard flowers burst out on every available piece of flat land.

Millions of years ago, apes and the earliest of mankind's ancestors roamed and hunted here. More hominid fossils have been found in and around the exposed fossil beds of the **Soan gorge** than anywhere else in the world, together with those of giraffe, rhinoceros, gazelle, and crocodile.

One hundred thousand and more years ago, Stone-Age man lived in fairly large numbers along the banks of the **Soan River,** and left behind hundreds of manmade stone tools that still lie in the open.

In the 1970s a British archaeological team uncovered the remains of a 30,000-year-old house near **Riwat,** just off the Grand Trunk Road.

Daunting and forbidding, the landscape served for millenniums as a no-man's land where few lingered. The successive waves of invaders from the west and north-west never stayed long on the Potwar but marched on south to lusher pastures, leaving the few who did live in the region to themselves.

Just two kilometres (one mile) south of the junction with the Islamabad road you can see, to the right, on a long ridge of black rock the remains of one small **Ghakkar Fort,** at Riwat.

Built in the sixteenth century to stem the advance of Sher Shah, it's little more than 200 metres (650 feet) square, but the walls and gates, and a **mausoleum** and **mosque** inside, are in excellent repair.

From the top of the main gate there is an excellent view of the **Salt Range** and, to the south, the **Manikyala** *stupa.* The grave of the Ghakkar chief Sarang Khan — flayed alive and stuffed with straw by Sher Shah's men — is in the centre of the fort, marked by an inscription in modern English.

One Afghan general forcibly married Sarang Khan's daughter, resulting in a prolonged war against the Afghan, in which sixteen of her eighteen brothers died, leaving only two to carry on the line.

Some six kilometres (four miles) beyond Riwat on the Lahore road and two kilometres (one mile) to the east, along a rough track, you come to the impressively-large **Manikyala** *stupa.* It is all that remains of what was once a large Buddhist religious centre with so many *stupas* and monasteries that it was thought to have been the site of **Taxila.**

The original *stupa* is thought to have been built by Ashoka in the third century BC to house original relics from the body of the Buddha, but the present one dates from between the second and fourth centuries AD.

When Hsuan Tsang visited it he described it as shedding "a miraculous light" and found many pilgrims afflicted with ailments circumambulating it in search of a cure.

It was on the same spot in 1849 that the Sikh dynasty's armies surrendered to the British after the decisive victory at Gujrat in the Second Sikh War, leaving Britain to annexe the Punjab and the NWFP.

After another sixty-four kilometres (40 miles), beyond the village of **Sohawa,** the road climbs up a ridge of small hills, outliers of the **Salt Range** to the north, crosses the summit along the railway line, and emerges into an eroded, rust-red countryside pierced by many ravines.

To the north, especially on clear days, the snowclad **Pir Panjal** mountains in Indian-held Kashmir are visible with the main Salt Range to the south-west.

Another thirty-four kilometres (21 miles) brings you to **Dina** where a right turn, over the railway and along a corrugated and rutted trail for seven kilometres (four miles), takes you to sixteenth-century **Rhotas Fort,** built by Sher Shah and one of Pakistan's most outstanding historical monuments.

Fork left where the track divides at a wide, sandy river bed and continue to the far bank. Even though there's always water, even in dry weather, the sand is quite firm so long as you keep to the normal crossing point.

The trail then climbs to rough, stony ground, past a **mausoleum**, through the **east gate**. There's a **village** inside and you'll probably find somebody, perhaps the village school headmaster, to guide you around.

In a 4WD vehicle you can follow the bumpy track through the village to a right turn half way up the main street onto a track that leads through the fort to the **west gate**, where the most interesting ruins are situated.

You need to be fit and patient. The fort — its perimeter covers more than five kilometres (three miles) — is as large as a medium-sized town; the interior terrain is rugged, the ruins tricky and precipitous. You'll need at least three hours to see the most interesting parts.

If time is limited concentrate on the north-west portion, including the **Sohal Gate, Man Singh's palace,** and the **execution tower**.

In most sections the walls are wide enough even for those who suffer from vertigo but the drops are sheer and, overlooking the river, frightening. There are many gates and numerous posterns, but it's the massive battlements that impress.

Awe inspiring

The Sohal Gate and its well-preserved walls, flanked by two large U-shaped bastions, is the most photogenic of the ruins. Climb the steps, past a rather rundown **rest house,** to the ramparts where you obtain a splendid perspective of the size of the fort and the extremely large open areas within its walls — from the modern village to the long **south wall.**

If you walk along the top level of this section of the three-tiered ramparts you reach a large well where a wide stairway — 135 steps — leads down to the deep, clear water.

You can also take the path from the Sohal Gate to an L-shaped gate in the curtain wall that divides the outer fort from the inner fort. From the top of this gate you can see all that remains of **Man Singh's Palace** — two viewing pavilions at each end of the hill. The higher one to the west is climbed by a narrow flight of modern concrete steps without a handrail.

And from the top of this tower you can see the fortifications in their entirety, including the large **execution tower** on the **west wall** with its stone execution block and the hole through which the body of the victim was thrown. You can walk to this tower from the Sohal Gate but it's a dizzying experience.

From the viewing pavilion you can walk to the fort's north-west corner, where there's a small three-arched **mosque** with moulded inscriptions of Allah and faint traces of paint to the left of the **Shisha Gate,** so called because, to the right of it, stood **Harim's Hall of Mirrors** (Shisha means glass or mirror).

Seen from inside this part of the fort looks unimpressive. But walk down the steep steps on the other side to the outside and you'll get some idea of how elaborate the fortifications were. Some sixty steps lead by a steep well and through a narrow archway. From here you can walk down over the river sands and gain another perspective of the river frontage and the fortifications on the west ravine.

Inside the fort, follow the ravine to the gate in the centre of the **north wall** to see the original, hooded **galleries** from which the defenders poured boiling oil on their attackers.

Inside this gate is a vaulted **octagonal room**, similar to those in Lahore Fort, its original carvings and calligraphic mouldings still intact. There are also remains of blue ceramic tiles and more calligraphy on the outside of the gate.

The broad, curving ramp that leads down to a courtyard with arcaded sides, which may have served as stables or accommodation, is also not unlike that at Lahore.

Through this gate you can scramble down to the river and see, above the north-east corner of the fort, the **Khawas Khan Gate,** named after the Afghan general who took the daughter of the Ghakkar Chief Sarang Khan in forced marriage.

Follow the track on down to the river bank, across the side stream and turn right to a simple dam which formed an outside reservoir. Near this, on a path to the right, there's another gate flanked by tapered turrets. Then you come to the **east gate,** from where a track runs below the east walls of the fort, which may have been part of the old Imperial Highway.

At the south-east corner, just beyond the **Batiala Gate,** there's a fine view of the kilometre-long south wall, running along a natural ravine.

Sixteen kilometres (ten miles) beyond the Jhelum borders of Sher Shah's empire, Rohtas Fort took ten years to build — from 1540 to 1550 — and served as a frontier outpost from which to control the Ghakkars and prevent

Above: Superbly-worked ceramics adorn mosque at Bhong, Punjab.

the return of Humayun.

Sher Shah never lived to see it finished — and ten years after his death, his two successors defeated, Humayun took the fort without battle. Its Afghan governor fled and Humayun marched on in triumph to Delhi.

Ironically, six months later Humayun died after falling down the library steps of the Delhi citadel which Sher Shah had built (See "The Sword and The Fire," Part One).

The Mughal Emperors seldom visited Rohtas and it lost its importance as a frontier garrison when Akbar built the great fort at **Attock** on the Indus in the l580s.

Some fifteen kilometres (nine miles) west of the fort, 975-metre-high (3,200-feet) **Yogi Tilla,** the highest peak in the Salt Range, dominates the horizon. Steep and rocky, a

jeep track leads from the main south-west gate of the fort to an army firing range at the summit, effectively putting it out of bounds to visitors.

To the east of Dina, some sixteen kilometres (ten miles) off to the left from the Imperial Highway, stands **Mangla Dam,** one of the world's largest earth-filled dams staunching the flood waters of the Jhelum river. A road crosses the dam to Azad Kashmir.

It forms a large and attractive 160-square-kilometre (62-square-mile) lake that stretches beyond **Mirpur,** in Azad Kashmir, on its northern shores. There is an attractive drive to the hills near **Pir Gali** which twenty-six kilometres (16 miles) from Mirpur joins a surfaced road leading up into the hills.

Although there was an ancient city on the

Above: Detail from interior of Bhong Mosque.

east side of the river at **Jhelum,** 120 kilometres
(75 miles) from Islamabad, the present city
derives its importance from a military
cantonment the British built after the
annexation of the Punjab from the Sikhs in
1849. Today it is a small but important Pakistan
military base.

Two bridges now span the two-kilometre-
breadth (one-mile) of the Jhelum — a modern
toll bridge for motor traffic and the British-
built road and **rail bridge** that now carries
only the railway.

Just before the road bridge on the left, the
tall spire of a Gothic-style **Anglican church,**
consecrated in February 1857, forms a
prominent landmark. Within five months of
this, it served as a sanctuary for the wives and
children of the British garrison, when the
Indian uprising that broke out in **Meerut,** near
Delhi, in May, spread to the native garrison at
Jhelum in early July.

The Indian soldiers marched off towards
Lahore intent on attack but fell to the British
Movable Column commanded by John
Nicholson, which on hearing of the Mutiny
quick-marched from **Amritsar.**

Twelve kilometres (eight miles) from

Jhelum, at **Kharian,** the Grand Trunk Road
suddenly enters the flat, featureless but well-
irrigated farmlands of the Punjab plains, the
Pakistan bread basket. There's a right turn
here for **Chillianwala** and the **Rasul barrage.**

Thirty-two kilometres (20 miles) further on
the road reaches **Gujrat,** built by Akbar the
Great on the site of two earlier towns.

Traditional, nomadic pastoralists, the
Gujars were brought into the Punjab in large
numbers in the sixteenth century by Sher Shah
and Akbar to man the new garrisons built to
guard the Imperial Highway. Many of their
descendants are now migrant labourers.

During Akbar's time Gujrat, garrisoned by
Gujars, was known as Gujrat Akbarabad.
After the Mughal decline, the town was taken
by the Ghakkars who, in turn, lost it to the
Sikhs.

It was here that British fought the final and
decisive battle of the Second Sikh War. Those
who fell are buried in the town's **Shah Jahangir
cemetery.**

Eight kilometres (five miles) beyond Gujrat,
the Grand Trunk Road crosses a **toll bridge**
over the **Chenab** — second of the five rivers
from which the Punjab, "Land of the Five

Rivers", draws its name.

Wazirabad, some six kilometres (four miles) from the bridge, was founded in the seventeenth century by Wazir Khan, prime minister of Shah Jahan. In the nineteenth century, under the Sikhs, it became the headquarters of Ranjit Singh's Italian general, Avitabile. He built a new rectangular town surrounded by a wall.

Left from Wazirabad is a road to the ancient town of **Sialkot,** near the Indian border, believed by some archaeologists to have been the capital of King Menander about l60 BC.

On a hill in the town there's an **old fort** where the British took refuge during the l857 Mutiny. Those killed are buried in the **cemetery** at the foot of the hill.

The town also holds the **tomb** of Mian Abdul Hakim, a great seventeenth-century Muslim scholar, and a **mosque** dedicated to a popular saint, Hazrat Iman Ali-ul-Haq.

Sialkot is the birthplace of the Pakistan philosopher-poet Allama Iqbal, one of the triad who gave flesh to the dream of a separate Islamic nation. The town today is famous for its sports equipment, saddles, and musical instruments.

Twenty-six kilometres (16 miles) beyond Wazirabad, back on the Imperial Highway, a crossroads heralds the **Gujranwala** bypasses, one on either side of the town. Each is about fifteen kilometres (nine miles) long. The left bypass follows the canal that feeds water from the **Chenab** river above Sialkot to a spot near Multan, hundreds of kilometres distant.

The birthplace of Ranjit Singh in l780, the large **tomb** of his father still stands in Gujranwala. Chief of one of many ruling Sikh clans, by cunning, battle, or bribery, Ranjit Singh overcame them one by one until eventually his powerful empire stretched from the Sutlej to the Khyber, and north to Kashmir.

It's another sixty-seven kilometres (42 miles) from Gujranwala to Lahore which you enter by crossing a **toll bridge** over the river **Ravi.** Just before the bridge, you can see the four minarets of **Jahangir's tomb,** left, and, in the palm trees a few hundred metres away, the dome of **Asaf Khan's tomb.**

Opposite: The "Deer Tower", Hiran Minar, built by Jahanagir in 1607 in memory of his favourite antelope.

Above: Punjab woman decorating earthenware pottery.

146

The Salt Range: Survivor of an Ancient Sea

Cutting across the Punjab plains, from Jhelum City on the Grand Trunk Road westwards to **Mianwali** and **Kalabagh** on the Indus, are two low ranges of hills — unique for the span of geological history which reposes in them.

The **Salt Range** takes its name from the mines at **Khewra**, vast deposits of rock salt left behind during 100 million years as silt from the Indus filled in the vast marine depression that now forms the Indus plains and the Potwar Plateau.

Distinctively-coloured in bizarre reds, greens, greys, and browns, the tops of these desolate-looking hills are astonishingly lush and fertile with verdant fields, blossom-filled orchards, and glistening streams. Villages and towns are lined with shady banyan trees and mango groves.

In 326 BC, Alexander may well have crossed over the **Nandana pass** to the Jhelum river to prepare for his epic battle with Porus. Certainly, not many years later, the Salt Range was part of Ashoka's great Mauryan empire. At **Ketas** there are the remains of a *stupa* he is said to have built.

When Hsuan Tsang visited the district in AD 631 he found it part of the Singhapure kingdom of Kashmir and was unimpressed. "The climate is cold, the people are fierce, and value highly the quality of courage; moreover they are much given to deceit."

Only in the eighth century, however, did the Salt Range acquire any real importance. Most of the forts and temples in the region, in fact, date from the Hindu Shahi period of the eighth to tenth centuries.

During the eleventh century, the Janjua tribe, the most important ethnic group in the central Salt Range, converted to Islam under Mahmud of Ghazni, and were left free, remaining in power until the nineteenth century when they succumbed to the Sikhs.

Getting there

Three roads from the Imperial Highway, now the Grand Trunk Road, all converge on **Chakwal**, a drive of about two hours from Islamabad.

The first, along an unmarked right turn, is just after **Riwat village**, twenty-eight kilometres (18 miles) from Zero Point, Islamabad. Follow this for six kilometres (four miles). Then take the right fork to **Chakwal**. After sixty kilometres (38 miles) you turn right into the town.

The second road, past the village of **Mandra**, is forty kilometres (25 miles) from Islamabad. There's a tobacco factory just before you reach the turn off.

The third road leads off the highway seventy-one kilometres (44 miles) from Islamabad.

Where to Stay

Salt Department rest house, Khewra. Inquire at the Pakistan Mineral Development Corporation, Khewra. ICI guest house, Khewra. Inquire at the General Manager's office, ICI Pakistan Manufacturers Ltd, Khewra. There are also rest houses at Choa Saidan Shah. Inquire at the District Commissioner's Office.

Sightseeing

There's a side excursion from **Chakwal** south-west to Kallar Kahar on the north side of the Salt Range, and a temple at **Malot**. When Babur, the first of the Mughals, crossed the Salt Range in 1519 he was so impressed by Kallar Kahar he commissioned landscape artists to build a garden overlooking the lake.

Although this has fallen into ruin, trees and orchards on the south-west shore close to the **tomb** of a Muslim saint, make a pleasant picnic spot. The shallow salt lake is sanctuary for many birds.

To see the ruins of the **temple** at Malot you turn right six kilometres (four miles) before Kallar Kahar on to a 4WD track by the **Dokh Khushi Waterworks.** You drive past **Chhoi** village to the second turn on the left, which climbs up and down past many coal mines to the ancient, fortified village of Malot, one of the homes of the Janjua tribe.

You reach the temple which dates from between the eight and tenth centuries, by walking through the village. It stands on top of a huge rock outcrop on the southern escarpment of the Salt Range, with deep ravines on two sides and a sheer drop of 600 metres (2,000 feet) to the plains on the third.

East of Malot, standing in a small oasis on

Opposite: Catacomb cut over the centuries through the Khewra salt mines.

the valley bottom at **Siv Ganga,** is another **temple** of the same period, surrounded by trees. The pagoda-style storeyed roof is its best preserved feature.

The **Hindu temples** at **Ketas**, on either side of the main road from Kallar Kahar to **Choa Saidan Shah** just after a sharp right turn, are much more accessible.

Long an important Hindu pilgrimage centre, an impressive number of ruins remain. Every April thousands of pilgrims flock to Ketas to immerse themselves in a pool sacred to Shiva, one of the Hindu trinity.

Hindu mythology avers that when Shiva wept for the death of Sita, his wife and consort, the tears from one eye formed the pool at Ketas — and those from the other, a pool near **Ajmer** in Rajasthan.

For centuries the pool at Ketas was believed bottomless, but soundings taken in the nineteenth century showed it to be only seven metres (23 feet) deep.

The oldest temples from the Hindu Shahi period have been replastered and frequently rebuilt. You can reach the highest temple by climbing through the fort up some extremely narrow stairs to its roof — from where you can study the layout of the entire site.

It is believed that the temples were built over an earlier Buddhist and Jain site, described by Chinese pilgrims of the fifth and seventh centuries. To the east of the pool, almost impossible to define, are the ruins of a **Buddhist** *stupa* ascribed to Ashoka.

Two kilometres (one mile) north of the main road from Ketas, at **Dulmial**, there's an old **British artillery gun** of 1816.

Six kilometres (3.5 miles) beyond Ketas stands the town of Choa Saidan Shah, famous for roses and perfumes. Its Hindu origin is still evident from the ruins of its **temple** and the palm trees that line the road. Nearby, the **Dhok Tahlian Dam** has created a small and pretty **lake** with excellent fishing.

The nine kilometres (six miles) of road from Choa Saidan Shah to Khewra passes through the most spectacular part of the Salt Range. The sheer drop down the almost vertical escarpment into **Khewra** is mind boggling but the hues of the rocks should serve as an anodyne.

Atop the escarpment, **Watli Head** serves as the main source of water for the **soda ash plant** twenty kilometres (13 miles) away, carried back and forth across the steep gorge

on twelve suspension bridges that leapfrog across the ravines.

With 140 kilometres (88 miles) of tunnels, the **Khewra Salt** mine is the largest in the world and the second-largest producer of rock salt. Its seams extend the entire length of the Salt Range. Visitors travel on a small **electric train** deep beneath the hills.

Down in these subterranean depths, the rock salt becomes an exquisite mass of frosted red and pink glass — and deep inside the mine, out of transparent bricks of salt inlaid with lights, workers have built a fantastic **mosque**. There are also some magnificent stalactites in this strange but lovely nether world.

The mines have been in continuous use since the thirteenth century. In the old days salt was excavated in enormous blocks, the miners leaving supporting pillars of the same size, creating massive and lofty chambers.

The tallest — excavated during the Mughal era — is so high that guides sometimes release hot air balloons, or light flares, which reflect off the distant ceiling, to give visitors some idea of the immense scale. Other chambers, now partially inundated by crystal-clear water, have become resounding echo chambers.

The British were quick to exploit this seemingly infinite natural resource. After redeveloping the mine in 1870, renamed the **Mayo Mine,** they gave vested rights to employment in the mines to 250 families in the village — a tradition that still prevails.

At the top of the escarpment there's an old Victorian cable railway, powered by gravity, which carries limestone and gypsum quarried out of the escarpment to the cement factory at **Dandot** beneath the cliff face. You can arrange a trip on this cable railway through the cement factory manager at Khewra.

Dancing girls

From Khewra, you travel south, through **Pind Dadan Khan**, to **Nandana**. There's a road east just before Pind Dadan Khan, to **Jalalpur** and **Jhelum**. Turn on to this and after seventeen kilometres (11 miles), take the road north, through **Rawal**, to **Gharibwal** at the foot of the Salt Range.

If you turn in towards the Salt Range, immediately after a rail crossing, along an ill-defined 4WD track, you'll come to **Baghanwala** where, beside the river bed, stand the ruins of a Mughal gate, the **Shahi Darwaza** (King's door).

It was here that one royal dance girl walked a tightrope across the gorge. But when she was in the middle the king cut the rope — and as she fell the girl laid a curse on all future generations who lived there.

Later, Jahangir who often hunted there, noted that there was at least one murder each generation as a result of a feud between two village families.

The walk up the escarpment from Baghanwala to **Nandana**, alongside steep drops, dancing streams, and water mills, takes about an hour.

At the top, between the vertical cliff walls, a massive fortress of rock blocks the pass. It's believed Alexander the Great marched through Nandana on his way to meet Porus on the banks of the Jhelum.

It was here, early in the eleventh century, nursing his wounds from successive defeats by Mahmud of Ghazni, that Anandpal, the Hindu Shahi ruler re-established his capital after his flight from Hund.

From **Pind Dadan Khan,** the thirty-five kilometres (22 miles) to **Jalalpur** where the lower ridges of the Salt Range step down to the Jhelum river, present no problems.

Take the right fork over the **Rasul Barrage** across the Jhelum river to **Rasul** and continue through **Chillianwala**, and **Dinga**, to rejoin the Grand Trunk Road at **Kharian**, south of Jhelum.

There's a village near Rasul called **Mong** that may possibly be the place where Alexander's famous horse, Bucephalus, which was killed in the battle against Porus, is buried.

He personally led the funeral procession, and the horse's remains were presumably laid in a grave in one of the two cities that Alexander founded in the area after his victory, one of which he named after the horse.

It was at another village, near Rasul, **Chillianwala**, in 1848 that the Sikhs nearly defeated the British in a bloody battle. An entire cavalry regiment took flight and British casualties, including a huge number of camp followers, numbered over 2,000.

The mass grave of the British officers, surmounted by a large **stone cross** and an obelisk, can still be seen.

The Southern Punjab: Flat and Fertile

Despite its fertility, the flat Punjab is monotonous — never more so than when driving from **Lahore** or **Faisalabad** through the prosperous but rather dull landscape of the southern Punjab to **Multan** (see "The Cities," Part Three). Despite the many roads marked on the map, it's slow going.

From a distance, all look invitingly flat and easy but, in fact, turn out to have corrugations or ripples in their surface, making driving at more than forty kilometres-an-hour (25 miles) impossible.

Road conditions change rapidly so seek expert advice before choosing your route.

Many archaeological sites of the Indus Civilisation and later cultures are hidden in the sands of the vast 26,000-square-kilometre (10,000-square-mile) **Cholistan desert** that extends into the **Thar desert** of Sind.

Getting there

There are two roads to Multan, one from Islamabad and one from Lahore. From Islamabad to **Sahiwal** takes about four or five hours, but the traffic on this road, unlike the Lahore-Multan road, is fairly light.

After **Chakwal** and **Kallar Kahar** in the Salt Range, turn south across the railway line, through **Khushab** and across the **Jhelum** to the next town, **Shahour**, where you turn right off the main road to **Sargodha**.

Though a large town and major PAF fighter base, which played an historic part in two wars against India in 1965 and 1971, Sargodha has little of interest to the tourist.

From the the old town of **Sahiwal** continue along the Jhelum river south to **Jhang**. You can also continue south from Sargodha across the **Chenab river** to **Chiniot**, an attractive little town. The name is a corruption of Chandan, a king's daughter who used to hunt in men's clothing. While out hunting she saw a spot so beautiful that she ordered the town to be built there.

Today Chiniot is known for its ornate brickwork and beautifully-carved entrance gates to its houses. There's a **mosque** in the town that dates from Aurangzeb's time.

During the Mughal era its artisans, famed for the excellence of their work, helped to

Above: 16th-century Rhotas Fort, near Jhelum.

build the Taj Mahal at Agra in India and the Wazir Khan mosque in Lahore. Later, during the Sikh era, they also helped create the Golden Temple at Amritsar.

South of Chiniot lies **Faisalabad,** Pakistan's third-largest city, formerly **Lyallpur,** after Sir James Lyall, governor of the Punjab. Known as "little Manchester" because of its textile mills, it has grown rapidly in just a century and is famed as the University of Punjab's **Agriculture campus.**

Its most distinguished feature (now indescribably filthy) is the **town centre** which was laid out patriotically by Sir James Lyall in the shape of the British flag — a rectangle containing a cross and two diagonals. At the centre is a **clock tower** where eight roads meet. These eight segments form the town's main bazaars.

The next town after Faisalabad is **Jhang,** then **Kabirwala,** where the road turns right for Multan, about thirty-five kilometres (22 miles) further on.

The second choice from Lahore is west along the main road to Multan, badly corrugated, especially from Lahore to **Sahiwal,** with extremely heavy traffic. But it takes you close to the Indus civilisation city of **Harappa.** You can also visit **Pakpattan** *en route* to the south-west, and **Dipalpur,** a great centre of

religion and learning in the fourteenth century, second only to Multan in size and importance.

Pakpattan is another old town identified with one of the tribes who fought Alexander the Great and used to be the principal ferry over the **Sutlej.** The name means "ferry of the pure". It houses the **mausoleum of Baba Farid Gunj Shakar,** who died in 1270.

Belonging to the Chishtia order of dervishes, he was a great scholar and an accomplished poet who wrote Persian, Urdu, and Punjabi. His anniversary, held on the twenty-fifth day of the lunar month of Zilhij, attracts large crowds.

To reach Harappa turn right off the main road twenty-two kilometres (14 miles) after Sahiwal, at Harappa railway station. Drive over the level crossing and follow the road for about seven kilometres (four miles).

South-east from Multan, through **Lodhran** and across the Sutlej to **Bahawalpur,** is about ninety kilometres (60 miles).

An independent state until the creation of Pakistan in 1947, the capital of the same name, Bahawalpur, was built about 1780. A "new" palace, the **Daulat Khana** stands to the east of the town with an Italianate building, the **Nur Mahal,** completed in 1875, and an adjoining **mosque** in its grounds. It also has a **museum** that's well worth a visit. Its main feature is an

ethnographic exhibition of the people of the Cholistan desert with black and white photographs that show the use to which the desert nomads put their artefacts.

It also has exhibits of the Indus Civilisation from the many Indus city sites along the dry channel of the **Ghaggar river,** to the south of Bahawalpur. The town also boasts a small but extremely well-run **zoo.**

The most attractive bargain in the bazaars are the distinctive, embroidered Bahawalpuri slippers and shoes and the delicate locally-made filigree pottery.

There are two fascinating full day excursions from Bahawalpur, both needing a 4WD vehicle — one through the Cholistan desert to **Derawar Fort,** the other to **Lal Suhanra National Park.**

You'll need a guide to go to Derawar — and permission from the incumbent Amir of Bahawalpur to enter the fort. The drive through the fascinating, but barren desert, one of the driest places on earth with an average rainfall of less than twelve centimetres (five inches) a year, takes three to four hours.

Long ago this area was watered by the river **Ghaggar**, now called the Hakra and known in Vedic times as the Sarasvati. Along its 500 kilometres (300 miles) dry river bed are more than 400 archaeological sites, most dating back 4,500 years to the Indus Civilisation.

Camel herders

In the troughs between the scrub-covered sand dunes the desert nomads dig underground wells using camels to draw up the brackish water. During the rare, brief rains they dig shallow dams but when these dry up move out of the desert.

Their tall, round huts, with steeply-pitched thatch roofs, occupy the crest of the highest sand hills and keep out most of the sun. Wearing long, gathered skirts, their hardy women raise cattle and breed camels.

Its walls still intact, guarded by soldiers in fezes, **Derawar Fort** is in good condition but how long ago it was built is not known. The tombs of the Emirs are decorated with attractive blue-glazed tiles in colourful contrast to the bleached, ochre landscape.

Thirty kilometres (20 miles) west of Bahawalpur, you turn right off the Khaipur road and travel six kilometres (four miles) down a dirt track, right, to **Lal Suhanra National Park,** established in 1972 and famous for its birds and wildlife, including the rare chinkara gazelle and plentiful wild boar.

Asia's imperilled species of blackbuck have also been relocated in their former desert habitat. A nucleus breeding herd of thirty, first kept under guard in a fenced enclosure in a forest plantation, has thrived.

During winter migrating birds, including many species of waterfowl, settle on the park's lake.

From Bahawalpur, you can drive through **Ahmadpur** to **Uchh.** Or from Multan you can bypass Bahawalpur and take the road west across the **Chenab** to **Muzaffargarh**, then south to **Alipur** where the road crosses the confluence of the **Sutlej** and Chenab to **Uchh.**

Extremely ancient, the town's well worth visiting for its beautiful mosques and tombs. It reached its apogee in the thirteenth century when, together with Multan, it was a political, cultural, and literary centre.

Some of central Asia's most learned and eminent scholars, poets, and saints flocked to this independent kingdom but its glory was short-lived. Yet, even after it waned, it still attracted the pious and saintly.

The mausolea and mosques that survive reflect a strong central Asian theme in their architecture, decorated with superbly worked blue and white glazed tiles, similar to those in Multan. But, sadly, many of these outstanding tombs have been neglected and are in poor condition.

When Alexander marched down the Indus in 325 BC he built many towns and some experts postulate that Uchh is one of them.

By the seventh century it was part of the kingdom of a Brahmin ruler, Chach, often credited with originating the game of chess, but in the eighth century it became the northernmost outpost of the new Islamic empire established by Muhammad bin Qasim after he besieged the town for seven days in 712. It was another five centuries before the renaissance that saw it become a great religious centre.

From Uchh you return to the main highway and drive south along the east bank of the Indus, over the headworks of the **Panjnad irrigation scheme,** through irrigated farmland to **Ubauro,** where you enter **Sind.**

Sixty-five kilometres (40 miles) beyond Ubauro you come to a magnificent avenue of ancient trees just before entering **Rohri**, where you cross the Indus to **Sukkur** on the west bank.

154

Moenjodaro-Harappa: A Cradle of Civilization

Moenjodaro, meaning "Mound of the Dead", is the most outstanding of the cities of the Indus Civilization which flourished 5,000 years ago. It is an essential stop for anyone remotely interested in the ancient history of the subcontinent (see "The Sword and The Fire", Part One). The excavated city lies between the main Karachi-Sukkur highway and the Indus River.

Getting there

PIA fly scheduled services to Moenjodaro or you can travel by road. Inquire at the PTDC office in Karachi.

Where to stay

Moenjodaro Tourist Inn on the excavated site near the museum. Book well in advance.

Sightseeing

The most prominent remains are those of the **Buddhist** *stupa* built on the highest point 2,000 years after the fall of the Indus Civilisation, on top of the ruins of the ancient acropolis, or fortified citadel, that crowned the fifteen-metre-high (50-feet) artificial hill.

West of the *stupa* are the 4,000-year-old ruins of the city's administrative and religious buildings — the **public bath, state granary, palace,** and **assembly hall.**

Now restored with new brick, the great **bath,** more than two metres (seven feet) deep, sealed with a bitumen lining, was probably used for ritual bathing. Broad steps at either end led down to the water.

Around it was a cloister and on three sides a series of small rooms, possibly private baths for the priests. In one of these is a well. Remark the neatly arched and brick-lined drain in the base of the bath.

Beside the bath stood the great **state granary,** the equivalent of a state bank today, where wheat, barley, and sesame collected as taxes were stored. It has twenty-seven high brick platforms, in three rows of nine, separated by ventilation channels. Built on top of these were the wooden storage bins. The crumbling remains of the loading bay on the north side

are barely discernible.

To the north of the bath was the **palace,** or priests' college, with a cloistered court surrounded by rooms. About 100 metres (320 feet) to the south are the remains of the square, pillared **assembly hall,** and some of the old city fortifications.

To the east of the citadel the city was laid out in a clearly-defined grid, almost like a chessboard, with the wide main streets intersecting each other at right angles.

These divided the city into twelve separate precincts: narrower side streets off each of the main roads were lined with urban homes between high, forbidding walls.

Every so often, steps lead up to a front door, but there are no windows. Inside is the shell of an amazingly sophisticated house, each with about ten different-sized rooms, leading off a central courtyard. Most houses had two storeys. Stairs led up to the second storey and you can still see holes in the walls that held the wooden beams supporting the second floor.

Windows were small and high, protected by a wooden or stone grill that looked on to the courtyard. There were separate toilets and each house had a bathroom with a well-made brick floor and elaborate drainage systems. Most also had a brick-lined well.

Moenjodaro also had what may have been the world's first municipal or metropolitan rubbish disposal service. Many houses had rubbish bins which were emptied by the city's dustmen.

Other municipal workers tended to the covered drains that ran down the centre of each street, carefully graded so that the waste liquids flowed out of the city into the Indus, with well-placed manholes through which blockages could be cleared.

Sentry boxes at regular intervals along the streets gave shelter to the civic police force.

This basic town plan was followed by all the other Indus Civilization cities that have been excavated, the dominant features being a raised citadel to the west and the street grid plan beneath this.

In addition, throughout the Empire, there was a standardised system for building materials and other products and for weights and measures.

Opposite top: Ornate mausoleum at Uchh Sharif.

Opposite: Bahawalpur goldsmiths.

Above: Two thousand-year-old stupa dominates 5,000-year-old ruins of the Indus Civilization, Moenjodaro.

Walk through the wealthier estates in the "DK area" and you come out onto Moenjodaro's main street, "Street One", which was the city shopping centre. Each trade or industry — jewellers, metal workers, potters, and millers — had its own precinct.

About 300 metres (1,000 feet) south along the main street are more excavations where the houses were smaller. There are two rows of workers' quarters in the north-west corner — sixteen small identical single-storeyed cottages in all, with two small rooms, all sharing a nearby well, with a narrow lane on one side and a street on the other.

Four thousand years ago, when the Indus ran beneath the city walls, a one-and-a-half-kilometre-long (one-mile) embankment staunched its flood waters. Now, after millenniums of changing course, the river runs five kilometres (three miles) to the east of the ruins.

The Indus and its tributaries joined together this far-flung trading Empire. The other ancient city, Harappa, is 550 kilometres (350 miles) away on the banks of the Ravi. There was also another city, yet to be excavated, on the now dry river Ghaggar near Derawar Fort in the Cholistan desert.

Many other smaller cities were scattered up and down the banks of these rivers, between which flat-bottomed barges, similar to those in use today, plied.

Some time spent in the Moenjodaro museum will help you understand better this complex federation of city states, giving a broader vision of what the ancient city looked like and the background to its cultural and economic basis.

Women's dress

Two large murals depict the city with its ten-metre-high (30-feet) outer walls, parapets, and square watch towers. The walls narrowed at the top to form walkways for the soldiers.

Down by the river, boats unloaded cotton and grain into the same two-wheeled ox-carts used today, to carry grain up to the city granary. Nearby, priests milled around the great bath and the palace, while in the distance stretched the flat-roofed houses of this

156

prosperous city.

Women wore short skirts, dressed their hair in high and sophisticated coiffures and adorned themselves with jewellery — hair pins, earrings, and many strings of necklaces made of carnelian, agate, faience, ivory, cowrie shells, and gold.

The priests wore a robe thrown over one shoulder, like a Buddhist monk today, with their hair either short, or gathered into a bun held in place by a headband.

Crude clay representations of mother goddesses show the common people's devotion to this near universal deity, but there are very few clues regarding the state religion.

The statue of the priest-king, now on display in the **National Museum,** Karachi, indicates that Moenjodaro was ruled by a religious elite, and the many bathrooms imply ritual bathing.

There's a stunning **bronze** of a pretty dancing girl — the original is in Delhi — and many small **terracotta figurines** which, though crude and undeniably phallic, indicate a sense of humour.

None of the pottery in the museum is of outstanding beauty but it reflects efficient mass production.

Sadly, the ruins may not survive much longer. Years of irrigation without adequate drainage has led to a rise in the water table and the bricks of this ancient civilization now crumble at the touch.

Since this water table is just a few metres beneath the surface, the city's earliest remains are already lost for ever many metres beneath.

Harappa

Harappa was discovered in the mid-nineteenth century by railway engineers building the Lahore-Multan track — as a convenient quarry.

They had no idea they were destroying the remains of an ancient civilization contemporaneous with Babylon, Ur, and the Egyptian pyramids.

Although there is a good **museum**, walking around the ruins is an exercise in confusion. Originally, the city stretched roughly one kilometre (half-a-mile) to the east of its citadel, but almost everything has been erased.

Really all that's survived the ravages of time and railway contractors is the area between the citadel and the old bed of the Ravi, which has since moved eight kilometres (five miles) eastward.

Top: Stealite seal of Harappa, twin city of Moenjodaro, which flourished 5,000 years ago.

Above: Copies of terracotta figurines found in the ruins of Moenjodaro.

Three groups of buildings can be seen. Those nearest the citadel form a **workers' suburb** similar to the one at Moenjodaro — a double row of cottages, with seven, not eight as at Moenjodaro, in each row. Again they are separated by a narrow lane and surrounded by a compound wall.

Each house had three rooms and a tiny courtyard. To the north are eighteen circular brickwork surfaces belonging to the mill where grain was hand-pounded in the central hole.

Beyond these, beside the old river bed, are two rows of six brick platforms — all that remains of the great **state granary.** Separated by a wide central passageway, triangular ventilation ducts ran between the platforms which supported the wood and mud storage bins.

Above: Well — uncovered in 1987 — has cast new light on ancient Moenjodaro.

Imperial Highway: The Grand Trunk Road to Peshawar

History stretches all the way along the **Shahi Highway** — the processional mall of Mughal Emperors from the vale of Peshawar to Delhi for centuries — and so does contemporary Pakistan with its teeming towns and villages and the powerhouse of the Tarbela dam.

Sightseeing

Take the road west from **Zero Point,** Islamabad, for fourteen kilometres (nine miles) to the dual carriageway **Grand Trunk Road.**

Then another fourteen kilometres on it climbs a low cutting in a gentle range of hills, the **Margalla Pass,** the ancient route between the subcontinent and central Asia.

For the first of the Mughals, Babur the Great, who knew it as the Sangjaki Pass, the name of a nearby village, it was the gateway for his plundering invasions of the subcontinent. In his own chronicles, Jahangir noted that the name Margalla meant "a place to plunder caravans".

To the left you can see part of the original sixteenth-century cobblestoned Imperial Highway, believed to have been built by Sher Shah Suri, the Afghan ruler who, for a short while, deposed Babur's son, Humayun. (He also built Rhotas Fort).

Also on the left, is a slender granite **monument**, built in 1868 "by friends, British and Native" in honour of an Irish-born general, John Nicholson. He was so venerated by both British and Indian for his courage that after his death a religious cult, Nikal Seyn or Nikalsingh, sprang up in India.

Enlisting in the Bengal Infantry as a sixteen-year-old cadet, Nicholson spent his entire, but brief, adult life on the subcontinent, being posted to Rawalpindi as political officer after the First Sikh War in 1846, not long after Henry Lawrence became the British viceroy in Lahore.

One of the group of young men, including Abbott, instructed by Lawrence to advise the Sikhs in the Punjab and the NWFP, who found themselves cut off behind the Sikh lines when the Second Sikh War broke out in 1848, Nicholson evaded capture and then enlisted local warrior tribes to fight a guerilla war.

At one stage he duped the Sikh garrison at Attock into surrendering, delaying the advance of General Chattar Singh's forces on their way to help the Sikh army in the Punjab.

At the Margalla Pass, on the spot where the monument stands, Nicholson and his allies attacked the old tower that guarded the pass but failed to capture it. Nonetheless, his tenacity and courage that day earned the admiration of his adversaries.

Less than ten years later Nicholson was mortally wounded during the Indian Mutiny in the assault on Kashmir Gate. He was just thirty-four.

An **inscribed plaque** narrating his heroism — together with another added after Independence to commemorate the Muslim soldier who shot him — has long vanished, but a **memorial drinking fountain** nearby remains. There's also a small **temple** not far away.

Just one-and-a-half kilometres (one mile) beyond the pass, turn right for **Taxila** and drive for three kilometres (two miles) to the **museum** (see "Taxila-Gandhara: The Golden Civilization"). Modern Taxila stands alongside the Grand Trunk Road two kilometres (1.2 miles) beyond this turning.

A diversion, left, just before you cross the bridge into the town, leads down a rough track to the prehistoric mound of **Sarai Khola.** The walk from the bridge is no more than half-a-kilometre.

Though there's little to see, excavations have established that the Neolithic settlement on this spot existed around 3,000 BC and yielded stone and flint tools.

A subsequent settlement, dating from around 1,500 BC, produced female and bull terracotta figurines, shards of pottery, clay and paste beads, and copper pins. About fifty skeletons — all laid neatly east to west — were uncovered in an ancient grave.

Soon after leaving modern Taxila, there's a turn right for **Abbottabad**, then the road bypasses the industrial town of **Wah Cantonment,** centre of Pakistan's armaments industry and ordnance factories, the minarets of its modern **mosque**, in classic Mughal form, clearly visible.

At the end of the bypass, forty-three kilometres (27 miles) from Islamabad there's a **bridge** over a small stream. Turn left just before the bridge, and follow the track for about one kilometre (half-a-mile) to Wah's sixteenth-century **Mughal Garden.** This was the gentle oasis, where Akbar and his retinue paused to rest and refresh themselves in tranquil surroundings. Its **pool**, two **pavilions**, and **bath house** are now in ruins.

Mughal resort

Where once fountains played, cypress trees cast their shade over the dry stream bed and parakeets flutter and perch above. Legend has it that on their journey to Kashmir this was a favourite resort, not only of Akbar, but also Jahangir.

On a hill above the garden, there's an incredible romanesque nineteenth-century **house** given in gratitude by its British owners to the family of the man who carried the dying General Nicholson back to camp after he was wounded in Delhi.

Five kilometres (three miles) further on along the Imperial Highway, the next town is **Hasan Abdal,** a place of pilgrimage every April for Sikhs from India who come to celebrate the Baisakh festival. It has been venerated for centuries for its holy waters and its Sikh temple, **Panja Sahib Gurduwara.**

Take the right fork off the lane from the Imperial Highway, past a line of shops and a walled enclosure, to the domed archway at the end of the road, then left again. The temple is dedicated to the founder of the Sikh faith, Guru Nanak.

Founded some time early in the nineteenth century, the well-preserved temple stands in the middle of a stone tank full of fish. On a rock, opposite the steps down to the water, there's an image of a **handprint** said to have been left there by Guru Nanak.

Near the Sikh temple, next to the tomb of a Mughal courtier, is another tank filled with hundreds of huge, mahseer fish — ancestors of those that Jahangir used to catch, placing precious pearls in their mouths before throwing them back.

From here follow a paved path through some gardens to a walled garden with domed corner towers. It contains the **tomb** of a saint but which one nobody can say — it's the last resting place of either the mystic **Lala Rukh** or the even more mystical Muslim saint, Hasan Abdal.

An hour's walk away, on the hill above the Sikh temple, there's also a shrine to the Muslim saint, **Baba Wali,** and splendid views of the surrounding landscape.

Beyond Hasan Abdal, the Imperial Highway crosses the **Harro river,** an Indus tributary,

Above: Motor rickshaws serve commuters all over Pakistan.

and cuts through weird and deeply-eroded landscape, scarred and scoured by the clay diggings of local brickmakers and studded with countless standing pillars of earth.

Eventually the road hits **Lawrencepur,** named after Sir Henry Lawrence the first British viceroy in Lahore, now famous for the textile mills that produce some of the finest worsted suiting in the world.

Soon after this, about sixty-five kilometres (41 miles) from Islamabad, there's a right turn to **Tarbela Dam** which continues for twenty-nine kilometres (18 miles) to a **checkpoint**.

Just before this, there's a road west along the shores of **Tarbela Lake** to **Sirkot** in the **Gandghar hills** and down to the main Hasan Abdal-Haripur road near Haripur, twenty-nine kilometres (l8 miles) away, that gives magnificent views of this massive, manmade lake.

To visit the dam itself take the road, left, by the checkpoint which climbs for fifteen kilometres (nine miles) to the top of what was once the world's largest earth-filled dam with the two biggest spillways in the world.

Tarbela is at its most dramatic between July and September when the Indus is in spate from snowmelt and monsoon and millions of

litres a second thunder over the main spillway.

More than three times larger than Egypt's Aswan Dam on the Nile, the dam stretches almost three kilometres (l.7 miles) at the top with a base about 600 metres (2,000 feet) thick.

The road crosses the top of the spillway to a road, left, that climbs a small hill to a guest house on top where there is a splendid view of the dam — and also a large-scale concrete model.

Eight kilometres (five miles) from the dam is **Topi**, where James Abbott and his Pathan allies fought a bitter battle against the Sikh confederacy.

Take the right turn beyond Topi for the fifteen kilometre-drive (nine-mile) to **Swabi**, where the women wear attractive white charders with a red leopard's-paw pattern.

To return to the Grand Trunk Road, take the unmarked right fork near the barrier through the hamlet of **Hazro** where, in the third century BC, Alexander the Great crossed the river from Hund.

He was followed, over the same crossing more than 1300 years later, in 1008, by Mahmud of Ghazni, marching to battle against the Hindu ruler of Gandhara to win a stunning victory on the plains of Hazro.

But when Akbar built **Attock Fort,** further

downstream, the crossing lost its strategic importance and later battles took place away from the Indus, to the south.

Still remembered is the rout of one of the biggest Muslim armies of all time in 1739 by the Persian King Nadir Shah who had just captured and sacked Peshawar. Nadir defeated an army of 400,000 men under Muhammad Shah, successor to Aurangzeb, before marching on to Delhi.

At the Indus, he commandeered and built a fleet of boats to ferry across his troops and artillery and confront the Mughal force whom he overwhelmed despite the fact that he was greatly outnumbered.

Attock is some twenty-seven kilometres (17 miles) westward along the Imperial Highway from Lawrencepur. It overlooks the confluence of the **Kabul river** and the Indus, at the point where the broad, fast-moving waters enter the Indus's final gorge, running south 160 kilometres (100 miles) to **Kalabagh** to emerge at last on to the Punjab plains.

There's a **guest house** on an **island** in midstream where you can also camp and those in search of river running adventure can white water down the gorge from Attock to Kalabagh.

Akbar's massive **fort**, with a circumference of about two-and-a-half kilometres (1.5 miles), dates from the late sixteenth century when, because of trouble at Kabul, Akbar established a base here and set up a colony of rivermen to man the ferries. Their **village** stands on the river bank below the fort.

When the British came they strengthened the fort and made the town the district headquarters and cantonment. It's still a strategic military installation for the Pakistan army and visitors cannot enter it or take photographs.

During the dry season the Mughals crossed the river over a bridge of boats, which the British later anchored to piers on either side. Not long after this British engineers unsuccessfully attempted to bore a tunnel under the river.

After this failed, they built a **road and rail bridge** in 1883 that served until the end of the 1970s when a **new bridge** was finished near the fort that saves precious minutes on the journey to Peshawar.

When the Sikhs took Peshawar, Ranjit Singh built another fort on the other side of the river at **Khairabad,** but it has since disappeared.

The trunk road runs past the main entrance to the fort, the **Lahore Gate,** and some **Hindu temples.** On the right, in spring and early summer the **Tourist Inn's** attractive gardens are ablaze with colour.

The road then dips down to the narrow neck of the gorge, over the old road-rail bridge — where flash floods and snowmelt and monsoon rains often raise the river's height as much as thirty metres (100 feet) — and doubles back along the Kabul river to **Nowshera.**

Under the British this became an important cantonment town, a base for the troops fighting in the Khyber Pass and patrolling all along the North-west Frontier. It's also the place where Ranjit Singh's army inflicted a massive defeat on the Afghans in 1823.

There's a fine new **toll bridge** at the far end of the town where the road enters the thickly populated, verdant **Vale of Peshawar** for the final forty-three-kilometre-drive (27 miles) to the ancient city.

Taxila-Gandhara: The Golden Civilization

It's impossible to take in all of **Taxila** in a day. But whatever you do start with the **museum** before undertaking the Grand Tour. You'll need stout shoes. Leather permitting, if possible also try to take in **Sirkap**, the second city of Taxila, the beautiful Buddhist **monastery** of **Jaulian**, and, subject more to health and energy than leather, **Dharmarajika** — one of the largest Buddhist *stupas* in Pakistan.

Getting there

See "Imperial Highway: The Road to Peshawar".

Where to stay

There are two rest houses at Taxila run by the Archaeological Department — one right by the museum — and the PTDC runs a guest house. See Listings for "Hotels".

Sightseeing

The on-site museum houses one of the best collections of Gandharan art in Pakistan — and therefore the world — a display of utensils, coins, weights, jewellery, and toys detailing the daily life of ancient Taxila together with a useful contour model of the whole valley showing the main archaeological sites.

The first of Taxila's cities, **Bhir Mound,** lasted from the sixth century BC to the second century BC but only a small portion at the centre has been excavated. In fact, the museum is built on top of its north-west corner so you don't have far to go to start your exploration.

From the museum gate drive across the stony football field to the excavations. It's easy to imagine what it must have been like when Alexander visited it at its apogee in 326 BC.

The wide main street twisted around flat-roofed houses made of rough stone plastered over with mud, with narrow side streets leading off between high windowless walls.

Although the doors opened onto the street, the windows faced inwards to a central courtyard where there was a soakpit for drainage and sewage.

Street drains were only for rainwater, but spaced at intervals through the city were public squares, each containing a public refuse bin. There were no wells: water was brought from the river to the east.

Dressed in calf-length linen tunics with shawls around their shoulders and wearing thick-soled leather shoes, all but the poorest people carried parasols in summer.

It is thought that the large *stupa* of **Dharmarajika** was built by Ashoka to enclose a small chamber with relics of Buddha but over the centuries it was enlarged and votive *stupas* and a monastery added.

Probably the first Buddhist *stupa* in Pakistan, it is certainly one of the largest and most impressive, dating from the third century BC to the seventh century AD.

From the main gate of the museum follow the road east for two kilometres (one mile), bearing left at the fork in the road.

The entrance to the site, dominated by the **main *stupa*** fifteen metres (50 feet) high and fifty metres (160 feet) in diameter, is in the south-west corner. Treasure hunters searching for a golden casket said to contain Buddha's relics have cut a great slice in the west side.

The original *stupa*, built by Ashoka in the third century BC, is encased in the heart of the later *stupa*, for once built a *stupa* was never destroyed. They were enlarged by building another shell around the old one.

The present outside layer, dating from the time of the great second-century AD Kushan king, Kanishka, was originally surrounded by painted and gilded statues of Buddha and carvings depicting his life.

Out of its plastered and gilded dome rose a tall mast supporting seven or more stone discs. Pilgrims and devotees walked in a clockwise direction along two processional paths, one on the ground and one upon a terrace, that circled the *stupa*.

Four flights of steps at the four cardinal points lead to the terrace. The base of the *stupa* to the left of the east staircase is the best preserved section: its band of ornamental stonework dates from the fourth to the fifth century AD.

Nearby is the base of a column that once supported a guardian lion, similar to pillars that Ashoka often set up beside important Buddhist *stupas*. There's also a whole galaxy of smaller, votive *stupas*, encircling the main *stupa*, that date from the first century BC to the fourth century AD.

A major earthquake in AD 30 damaged the older *stupas* but Buddhist tradition prevented their removal and these later *stupas* were placed around their ruins.

Another *stupa* to the south of the main one, dating from the second century AD, has a square plinth of three diminishing terraces, but no dome. In the centre of the lowest terrace, ensconced in a trefoil niche, is a **statue** of Buddha and a row of headless images of Buddha, each flanked by two devotees wearing typical Kushan dress — baggy trousers and long coat.

The late fourth or fifth century AD upper terrace was placed on these images when a row of elephants, interspersed with grotesque and lifeless Atlantes figures, was added to the second terrace.

These additions dramatically illustrate the swift decline of Gandharan sculpture.

Along the path to the north stands a **row of chapels.** The last two contain four **plaster feet** that once supported two statues of Buddha, one eleven metres (35 feet) high. On either side of the feet are the lower parts of other figures, some still with traces of red paint. Originally they were all painted and gilded.

North again, beyond the chapels, there's a **large monastery** — where the monks' cells were set around five courtyards, each with a *stupa* in the centre. It dates from the first century BC to the seventh century AD. The largest court, dating from the second to third century AD, was two storeys high and contained

Above: Gaily-coloured pottery at Taxila town.

cells for 104 monks.

Destroyed in the middle of the third century AD by the Sassanian invaders, the monastery was rebuilt in a smaller, more easily defended scale but, in turn, this was burnt and completely destroyed by the White Huns in about AD 455.

Excavations uncovered the charred and crushed remains of six decapitated victims in the small court on the right. Rebuilt again, but crudely, the monastery was finally abandoned about the seventh century AD.

Headless images

The path to the right of the giant feet enters a narrow passage on the left lined by images of **two headless Buddhas** dating from the fourth to fifth century AD, their hands resting in their laps in an attitude of meditation.

The remains of a first century BC tank in the space ahead was the monks' bathing pool. Steps lead down from the north and it retains its original lime plaster lining. In the second century AD a votive *stupa* was built over the top of the steps.

In a niche on the north face of a votive stupa to the west of the tank, sits a **statue of Buddha.** The cornice and other details are Greek in character.

Near this *stupa* are the remains of a large first century BC **building** believed to have housed a statue of the reclining Buddha. It was strengthened and enlarged after a great earthquake around AD 30, when a processional path was added so the faithful could circumambulate the Buddha.

South of this building is a **group of *stupas*** of different ages built with different techniques. A silver vase with a silver scroll and a small gold casket containing tiny fragments of bone were found in one of these together with a scroll, written in Kharoshthi, dated circa AD 78.

It says the bone of Buddha was enshrined by Urasaka to bring health to the Kushan king, his family, friends, and relations and wishes that "this right munificent gift lead to Nirvana".

South of these *stupas* again is another *stupa* with stucco plaster reliefs from the second century AD. The scene on the north side depicts

Buddha's horse, Kathaka, taking leave of his master; the one on the south side shows the "Departure of Buddha". They are the earliest Gandharan stucco reliefs found so far. All others date from the fourth to fifth century AD.

A first-century AD **apsidal temple** nearby may have had a barrel-vaulted roof, similar in shape to the "chaitya halls" excavated in the hillside at Ajanta and Ellora in India, except that the apse is octagonal and once housed an octagonal *stupa*.

Sirkap: City of the Parthians

You enter **Sirkap**, the second city of Taxila, half an hour's walk away, through the city's old **north gate**. The wide main street, almost a kilometre (half-a-mile) long, begins a little to the right of the gate.

About fifty metres (165 feet) west of the gate you can see the excavations of the city wall, showing the second-century BC **Greek wall** at the bottom, the first-century BC **Saka wall** in the middle, and the first-century AD **Parthian wall** on top.

Circling the rectangular city for five kilometres (three miles), the six-metre-thick (20-feet) wall, some six to nine metres (20-30 feet) high, spaced with tall square **bastions**, enclosed some rugged defensive hills in the south-east, the isolated, easily defended hill of the acropolis in the south-west, and the city proper.

Since there were no wells, the city obtained its water from the river along the west wall.

What you see at Sirkap are the foundations of the Parthian city built about AD 30 after the great earthquake on top of the older cities of the Bactrian Greeks and Sakas.

In the reign of the Parthian king, Gondophares, when Saint Thomas the Apostle visited it, the main street was lined with small shops with wooden platforms at the front shaded by colourful awnings.

The main street leads down from the north gate. On the left, in the first block, there's a *stupa* set in a large court with rooms facing onto it. The *stupa* is said to have contained a crystal relic from the Mauryan period.

Three blocks further on stands a large **Buddhist building,** built upon the ruins of an earlier temple after the earthquake of AD 30,

with two flights of steps leading into a spacious courtyard. The steps are flanked by monastic cells east of which are the bases of two small *stupas*. The many stucco plaster heads and other decorative objects which encircled these are on show in the museum.

In a room behind the temple compound archaeologists discovered a veritable **fortune**, a king's ransom in gold and silver, buried by the Parthians in AD 60 when the advancing armies of the Kushans were threatening Taxila.

The **earliest** *stupa* at Sirkap, a small private one dating from the first century BC, is in the next block. Little remains. The base has vanished and excavations revealed only the boldly-painted, lime-stuccoed dome lying on its side — perhaps destroyed by the earthquake.

But among the ruins of the house to which this *stupa* belonged the archaeologists uncovered another treasure — of gold jewellery, bangles, earrings, pendants, finger rings, beads, lockets — also believed to have been buried about AD 60 when the Kushans attacked the city.

A **bronze statuette** of the Egyptian child-god Harpocrates, a **silver head** of Dionysus or Silenus, and a **silver spoon** were also discovered, all on show in the museum.

Another interesting *stupa*, on a plinth of thick stone walls radiating from the centre with a double flight of seven steps from the main street, stands opposite this house.

One of Taxila's most interesting monuments, the shrine of the **Double-headed Eagle,** a first-century AD *stupa*, is ornamented with a fascinating and classic mixture of Indo-Greco decoration.

Three different styles distinguish the row of corinthian pilasters with decorated niches across the front facade. Those nearest the steps clearly draw their inspiration from the traditional Greek pediment, while the ogee arches of those in the centre bear a distinct similarity to a Bengal roof, and those on the outside reflect the inspiration of the toranas seen at Mathura south of Delhi.

Ancient motif

Atop the centre niche is the double-headed eagle, a motif adopted by the Scythians from the Babylonians and Spartans, later used on the imperial arms of Russia and Germany,

Opposite: Ancient monument in the 2,000-year-old ruins of Taxila.

Above: Ruins of Sirkap second of the Gandharan cities of Taxila.

and also in Ceylon.

An octagonal white **marble pillar,** inscribed in Aramaic and now in Taxila museum, found in the wall of the priests' quarters in this shrine is believed to have been raised in honour of Romedote, one of Ashoka's advisers when he governed Taxila on behalf of his father, Bindusara.

In the next block, left, are the ruins of a small **Jain shrine.** It has a rectangular base with five decorative pilasters on each side and, standing on the four corners of the plinth, the remains of two Persepolitan columns crowned with lions.

Southwards, past the blocks where the wealthy made their homes, is the **Royal Palace,** similar in many ways to the Assyrian palace, which caught the eye of Philostratus, a Greek visitor, in AD 44. "The men's chambers and the porticoes and the whole of the vestibule were very chaste in style," he wrote.

On the hill above the Royal Palace stands another *stupa* with a magnificent panoramic view of the entire city. Legend has it that it was built to commemorate the spot on which Kunala, the son of Ashoka, was blinded.

Kunala was so handsome that his step-mother fell in love with him. When he spurned her advances she persuaded Ashoka to banish him to Taxila and then, under Ashoka's seal, dispatched an order for his eyes to be put out for wrongdoing.

Kunala was a popular prince and Ashoka's ministers at Taxila were reluctant to obey the order, but Kunala, an obedient son, insisted that the sentence should be carried out.

When Ashoka discovered his wife's treachery she was executed.

Legend and fact however do not reconcile. Ashoka died in 232 BC before Sirkap was built and the Kunala *stupa* dates from the third to fourth century AD when Sirkap was already in ruins. Nonetheless, Kunala was a place of pilgrimage for the blind for many centuries.

West of this *stupa* are the ruins of a solid and spacious **monastery,** dating from between the third and the fourth century AD, with walls almost five metres (16 feet) high.

Monks' cells encircle the usual open courtyard with an assembly hall to the south. Among its charred remains and rubble archaeologists found iron arrowheads typical of the White Huns but no skeletons.

On the hill above Kunala to the south, stands another smaller third- to fourth-century AD **monastery,** unusual because the monks' cells surround a square hall with sloping windows instead of an open court.

The Greek **temple of Jandial,** 750 metres (one-third of a mile) from the north gate of Sirkap, was built in the mid-second century BC by the Bactrian Greeks.

The only Greek temple on the subcontinent, it was abandoned and robbed of its statues of Greek gods during the Scythian invasion about 75 BC and finally destroyed by the earthquake of AD 30.

Four sandstone Ionic columns supported the front porch. From the antechamber behind, a solid iron and timber door opened onto the sanctuary, which contained statues of various Greek gods raised on a platform at the back.

Behind the sanctuary a solid mass of masonry supported a tower estimated to have been thirteen metres (40 feet) high. The tower may have been used for fire, sun, or moon worship.

Sirsukh: City of the Kushans

The last of Taxila's three cities, **Sirsukh,** endured for four centuries and was the regional capital of the Kushans from AD 80 to AD 460.

East from Jandial a signboard marks the track where, 300 metres (980 feet) along, stands the excavated south-east corner of Sirsukh's outer city wall.

The ruins boast the best preserved *stupa* and monastery in Pakistan — and on top of every hill there are more than fifty within a ten-kilometre-radius (six-mile) of Taxila alone.

The hilltop on which **Jaulian** stands provides picturesque views over the valley. Built when Sirsukh was a flourishing city during the reign of the second-century AD king, Kanishka, the monastery was restored and redecorated at the beginning of the fifth century AD only to be plundered and burnt by the White Huns in AD 455 and buried in its own debris.

When Sir John Marshall excavated the site in 1912 he found that the heat of the fire had transformed the monastery's clay figures into terracotta, leaving these, and the lime plaster statues around the *stupas*, in excellent condition.

The entrance in the north-west corner of the complex leads into the large open rectangle of the lower *stupa* courtyard lined with alcoves that held images of Buddha.

Although the domes and tiered stone umbrellas of the *stupas* have disappeared, their bases, covered in rows of stucco plaster carvings, are extremely well preserved — with images of Buddha and Bodhisattva and their attendants sitting in niches, and rows of elephants, lions, and naked figures holding up the structure above them.

A Kharoshthi inscription on one of the *stupas* names the statues and the pilgrims who built them as offerings in the early fifth century AD.

Beyond the **lower *stupa* court** to the south is the **main *stupa* court** with its gilded dome and umbrellas rising about twenty metres (65 feet). It is surrounded by all that remains of twenty-one votive *stupas* and their richly decorated bases with plaster images of Buddha, Bodhisattva, attendants, animals, and Atlantes.

More **images of Buddha** adorn the base of the **main *stupa*,** including one of the healing Buddha with a hole in his navel, the gift of Budhamitra, who "delighted in the law". While praying to be cured supplicants placed their fingers in this navel.

Across the south face is a row of coarse-bodied fifth-century AD images of Buddha. Their sensitively modelled heads were taken to the museum for safety.

One of the votive *stupas* on the south side of the main stupa contained a relic chamber — a tall, narrow, miniature *stupa*, over one metre (three feet) high, made of hard lime plaster, painted a gaudy blue and red, and crudely decorated with garnets, lapis, ruby, amethyst, crystal, carnelian, and aquamarine. It is now on show in Taxila museum. The relics were hidden inside in a copper box.

Kharoshthi inscriptions on a votive *stupa* to the west of the main *stupa* indicate that as late as the fifth century AD Kharoshthi, the national script of Gandhara, was still in use in Taxila.

West of the this enclosure is the monastery court with copies of a group of plaster sculptures behind wooden doors to the left of the entrance. The originals in Taxila museum show Buddha meditating with a standing Buddha on either side and attendant figures behind.

The one on the left carries a fly whisk; the one on the right is the god of thunder, Vajirapani, holding a thunderbolt.

By the early fifth century AD the monastery buildings were two storeys high. Twenty-eight monks lived on each floor and clay and plaster statues depicting scenes from Buddha's life adorned the niches outside the cells. Other images were spaced along the walls. In each cell is a small sloping window and a niche for the monk's lamp.

A carved wooden verandah, supported on pillars, surrounded the central tank that caught rain water from the timber and mud roof and the verandah. The bathroom is in the corner of the tank. During the dry seasons, water was carried from the wells at the base of the hill.

West of the monastery court are the hall of assembly, kitchen, store room, refectory, stewards' room, and latrine.

The **Mohra Moradu Buddhist** *stupa* and **monastery,** dating from the second to fifth century AD, very similar to Jaulian in layout, is worth visiting for the stucco plaster sculptures around the base of the main *stupa.*

Five kilometres (three miles) from the museum, the turnoff is clearly marked on the right. At the end of the trail walk across the **aqueduct** into the glen between the hills.

Mohra Moradu's delicately-modelled and lifelike sculptures are well-preserved but the exquisitely carved heads of the Buddha have been removed to the museum for safety.

There's an interesting **plaster** *stupa,* nearly four metres (13 feet) high, inside one of the monastery cells, built in memory of the monk who once lived there.

Gandhara: The Lotus City

Long ago, the lush green Vale of Peshawar to the north-east of the city, bordered by the Swat hills, was the home of a great civilization.

Although little remains to indicate the former magnificence of **Gandhara** it's exciting nevertheless to stand on the mound where the Lotus City once flourished and imagine yourself travelling back through time to 260 BC, perhaps as a pilgrim reading the edicts of Ashoka or as a Buddhist monk at **Takht-i-Bahi.**

But much remains to be excavated. **Bala Hisar,** the earliest Lotus City at **Charsadda,** the Ashoka edicts at **Shahbaz Garha,** and the monastery of Takht-i-Bahi are an easy day excursion from either Peshawar or Islamabad.

Getting there

Twenty-eight kilometres (17 miles) north-east from **Peshawar Fort,** the road to Charsadda reaches Bala Hisar and a right turn towards a river bridge. Take the dirt track north just before the bridge for one kilometre (half-a-mile) to the two mounds of Bala Hisar.

Sightseeing

Excavated twice — by Sir John Marshall in 1902 and Sir Mortimer Wheeler in 1958 — a vertical trench in one mound cuts down through many different layers and over 2,500 years of debris.

The Bactrian Greeks who arrived from Balkh in Afghanistan to rule over Gandhara in about 180 BC, laid out the second capital of **Pushkalavati** one kilometre (half-a-mile) to the north-east of Bala Hisar at what is now **Shaikhan Dheri** under King Menander.

When the site was flooded the town was moved south-east across the river to what is now the modern village of **Rajar** which stands on the remains of almost 2,000 years of continuous settlement.

To the north the unexcavated mounds of **Mir Ziarat** and **Shahr-i-Napursan,** now covered by modern graves, also bear witness to the yet-to-be-revealed wonders of ancient Pushkalavati.

Excavation reports and maps which help an understanding of these ancient civilizations are available from the Department of Archaeology, University of Peshawar, or the Asian Study Group Library in Islamabad.

The ruins of the **Buddhist monastery** at Takht-i-Bahi lie fourteen kilometres (nine miles) north-west of **Mardan** on the **Swat road,** taking the left turn north at the crossroads in Charsadda.

Two kilometres (1.25 miles) further turn right onto a single lane tarmac road through rich farmland for twenty-two kilometres (14 miles) to the main Mardan-Swat, road where you turn left to Takht-i-Bahi, one kilometre (half-a-mile) distant.

The monastery is the most impressive and complete in Pakistan with enough remains to give a vivid impression of life as a Buddhist monk so many centuries ago.

The ruins lie some three-and-a-half kilometres (two miles) away, over the railway crossing in the centre of Takht-i-Bahi, turning left at the gate of the sugar mill, and then right down a dirt road.

Standing on the crest of a hill to the right are

Opposite: Gandharan sculptors left an enduring legacy of great art.

the ruins of a large eighth, to tenth, century **Hindu Shahi fort.** When you reach the the end of the track, the *stupas* and monastery, founded in the last century BC and abandoned in the sixth or seventh century, are straight ahead.

On the right, just before you enter the main monastery from the east is a two-storey block of four **monks' cells,** each with niches for the monk's lamp and belongings.

The **court of *stupas*** at the top of the path is surrounded on three sides by alcoves or chapels which originally had roofs and contained single plaster statues of Buddha, either sitting or standing, dedicated in memory of holy men or donated by rich pilgrims. The largest would have been ten metres (30 feet) high and all would have been gilded or painted.

In the chapels and on the pilasters between them, carved on slabs of stone and fastened to the walls, *bas relief* friezes depicted scenes from the life of Buddha.

Around the centre of the court are the remains of thirty-eight votive *stupas* and more chapels which were also covered in gilded and painted statues and reliefs showing Buddha and his life.

Steps lead north to the monastery court with monks' cells ranged along three sides. Originally there was a second-storey containing fifteen more cells.

According to Hsuan Tsang, the walls of the cells were plastered and painted different colours and the wooden door posts and lintels were decorated with carvings.

There is another set of steps south from the *stupa* court, which lead to the court of the **main stupa,** which is also surrounded on three sides by roofed alcoves or chapels that once contained statues of Buddha.

One **large stupa,** originally about ten metres (30 feet) metres high, with umbrellas protecting it, stands in the centre of the court. The square base was surmounted by a hemispherical dome decorated with gilded and painted statues of Buddha and scenes from his life.

West of the *stupa* court is **another court,** long and open with ten vaulted rooms beneath and the secluded high-walled open **assembly court** in the north-west corner.

South across the top of the underground vaults is a large **chapel** with two tiers of ornamental trefoil panels divided by pilasters that may have contained a small *stupa* to commemorate some especially rich or holy person.

Steps lead down from this chapel to the chambers below with beautiful arched Gandharan doorways. To the south are the bases of two small, elaborately decorated *stupas* uncovered in perfect condition in 1910, still coated with their red and gold paint. Little of the decoration remains today.

Along the crest of the hill overlooking the monastery are two- and three-storey civilian houses, some with rooms set around a central court. Most are two-storey with one small room set on top of the other, the staircase fashioned out of protruding slabs of stone. Lit by one small sloping window, each is entered by a low door.

From Takht-i-Bahi there's a road, right, for about one kilometre (half-a-mile) to **Sahri Bahlol,** a modern village built on top of an ancient mound that is probably 2,000 years old.

More than a century ago the British excavated the site and found a walled city and a Buddhist monastery and a great many exquisite Gandharan Buddhist sculptures, which can now be seen in the Peshawar and Lahore museums and other museums around the world.

Doubtless, many more would have survived if the British had not used semi-literate sappers in the last century to uncover these precious remains and their treasures.

Not to worry — the village folk have now established a thriving trade in reproduction masterpieces, some so fine that even experts have been duped. Take note.

North-West Frontier Province: Land of the Khyber Pass

From the beginning of time the North-West Frontier Province (NWFP) has guarded the subcontinent's borders in the west, peopled by proud and independent warrior folk who kneel to no man nor government.

In 1893, bowing to the inevitable that has confronted all potential invaders and imperialists, the British agreed to draw the Durand Line which since then has served as a border between Pakistan and Afghanistan.

In the north and west the NWFP's borders touch on — or come close to — China, the USSR, and Afghanistan, all along the mountains and highlands from the Pamirs to the rugged terrain of South Waziristan, Afghanistan.

The NWFP's barren hills and passes have seen many famous conquerors and adventurers, like Mahmud of Ghazni, Alexander the Great, Tamurlane, Emperor Babur, Nadir Shah, and Ahmad Shah Abdali.

Its snow-capped peaks and lush green valleys of unusual beauty attract tourists and mountaineers from far and wide, while its art and architecture is no less wellknown than the historic Khyber Pass.

Its climate varies from the extreme cold of Chitral in the north to the extreme heat of such places as the town of D. I. Khan.

Once the cradle of Gandhara civilization, the area is now known for its devout Muslims who jealously guard their religion and culture and the way of life which they have followed for centuries.

The NWFP was created in 1901 in place of the buffer zone that then existed. It divided the region into "settled" and "tribal" areas, the latter now administered by the Federal Government under a separate administrative system. The "settled" areas that constitute the North-West Frontier Province enjoy the same autonomy as Pakistan's other provinces.

Covering an area of 74,521 square kilometres (24,210 square miles), with a population of more than twelve million, NWFP has an average of more than 150 people to each square kilometre (0.386 square miles).

NWFP is divided into two distinct geographic zones — the north, extending from the ranges of the Hindu Kush to Peshawar, and the Derajat basin to the south.

Cold and snowy in winter with heavy rainfall and pleasant summers — except for the Peshawar basin which is extremely hot in summer — the north is rapidly becoming a major tourist resort. The dry southern zone is marked by sweltering summers, relatively cold winters, and scanty rainfall.

With its capital at Peshawar, the NWFP is made up of five administrative divisions — **Peshawar, Kohat, Hazara, Dera Ismail Khan,** and **Malakand.**

Peshawar Division is composed of Peshawar and **Mardan** districts. Kohat Division is composed of Kohat and **Karak** districts. Hazara Division is composed of **Abbottabad, Manshera,** and **Kohistan** districts. Dera Ismail Khan Division is composed of D. I. Khan and **Bannu** districts. And Malakand Division includes **Swat, Dir,** and **Chitral** districts, and the Malakand Agency.

Federally Administered Tribal Areas

Pakistan's semi-autonomous Federally Administered Tribal Areas (FATA) are made up of seven agencies — **Bajaur, Mohmand, Khyber, Orakzai, Kurram, North Waziristan,** and South Waziristan — and four **Frontier Regions** (FR) attached to the districts of Dera Ismail Khan, Bannu, Kohat, and Peshawar.

These areas, within the geographical boundaries of the North-West Frontier Province, are administered at federal level by the States and Frontier Regions Division, while the Governor of NWFP acts as the agent to the president and exercises immediate executive authority.

The FATA covers a total of 27,220 square kilometres (10,422 square miles) with a population approaching 3.5 million, an average of 128 people to each square kilometre.

The tribal belt divides the settled districts of NWFP from the international border between Pakistan and Afghanistan. The tribes enjoy a good deal of autonomy thus preserving their ageless, time-honoured way of life.

Mardan: The Imprint of Two Empires

Gateway to the magic valley of Swat, **Mardan** was established as a military town roughly two centuries ago by the British, as the original home of Pakistan's crack Frontier Force Regiment created to guide regular units in the field, collect intelligence, and keep the peace on the North-West Frontier.

A **memorial arch** in the town's centre commemorates the Regiment's proud tradition of valour which began as the Corps of Guides in 1846:

"... The annals of no army and no regiment can show a brighter record of devoted bravery than has been achieved by this small band of guides. By their deeds they have conferred undying honour not only to the regiment to which they belong, but on the whole British army."

It's a tradition of courage that inspired Charles Miller's best-selling *Khyber* and stirred the pages of M. M. Kaye's *The Far Pavilions*.

The Frontier Guides were the first British soldiers to wear khaki. The traditional brilliant red-and-blue uniforms of other British soldiers meant that they were the easiest of targets for Pathan snipers.

Sightseeing

At **Shahbaz Garha,** thirteen kilometres (eight miles) east of Mardan, on the road to Swabi, just before the turnoff to the Ambela Pass and Swat, there's a right turn along a dirt track for 400 metres (436 yards) to two rocks on a hill about 300 metres to the left.

Long ago, this spot was a strategic trading centre at the junction of three major trade routes— the main road from Afghanistan to India via Pushkalavati and Hund, the trade route from China via the Indus valley and Swat, and the more northern trade route from Afghanistan via Bajaur, Dir and Swat.

The shape of the ancient city is no longer visible but the rocks, inscribed with the **edicts of Ashoka,** constitute the oldest surviving testament of historical significance in the subcontinent. Twelve edicts on the largest rock, two on the smaller, proclaim Ashoka's shame at the terrible destruction and slaughter when he conquered Kalinga in eastern India and his redeeming pledge to henceforth conquer only by "righteousness and dharma" enhanced by love.

Another legend says that the future Buddha was born at Shahbaz Garha, in his penultimate existence, as Prince Visvantara, heir to the throne, and that the prized treasure of his kingdom was a white elephant which had the power to produce rain at will.

Out of charity the prince is said to have given the elephant to an enemy country that was suffering from drought. For this, his father's subjects banished Visvantara to exile, along with his wife and two children.

On his way, he gave away his horses and his chariot. Then he met a Brahmin who asked him to give him his children. But when they were handed over they were beaten until they bled and then put up for sale as slaves in the market-place in Shahbaz Garha.

There, their grandfather, the king, recognised them and rescued them.

When his subjects learnt of these sacrifices in the name of charity they realised that the prince was a saint and invited him back from exile. Hence, goes the belief, Visvantara's sacrifices prepared him as the Buddha in his next incarnation.

From ancient descriptions by Chinese pilgrims it was possible for a Japanese archaeological team to find these places and excavate them.

To the north off the road to **Rustam** lies **Mekha-Sanda hill.** One kilometre (half-a-mile) along the road, take the second dirt track east around the north face of the hill to the steep, rocky, thirty-minute-climb to the ruins of the Buddhist **monastery.**

In five years, from 1962 to 1967, the Japanese team uncovered the base of a main *stupa*, surrounded by about thirty votive *stupas* in a courtyard, found stone and stucco sculptures of Buddha, Bodhisattva, and Hariti (the fertility goddess), as well as pottery — bowls, pots, jars, and lamps.

The site of the monastery probably dates from AD 150, when the main *stupa* was built, to AD 450, when it was abandoned, leaving only the whispering breezes to stir fitfully through the grass overlooking the Sudana plain below.

General Cunningham identified two caves at the northern base of Mekha-Sanda hill as the separate abodes of Visvantara and his wife. As ascetics they could not live together. A reddish rock on the hill is said to mark the spot where the children were flogged.

Just a little over one kilometre (half-a-mile) away on the main road, to the west, is the *stupa* at **Chanaka-Dheri.**

You can also turn east at Shahbaz Garha for **Swabi** where Babur went rhino hunting, then south along the Attock road to **Hund,** the tenth-century capital, where the Indus spreads out across the plain between the mountains and the Attock gorge.

Traces of Hund's former glory are visible in its Buddhist, Hindu, and Muslim remains, including **Akbar**'s sixteenth-century **fort** with a modern village within its square walls, each with its own gate.

The town flourished from AD 870 to AD 1001 as capital of Gandhara under the Hindu kings. But more than a thousand years before that, Alexander the Great and his army of 50,000, crossed the Indus here, on a bridge of boats built by Alexander's commander, Hephaestion, to accept the surrender of King Ambhi of Taxila.

Hund was also an important Buddhist pilgrimage centre in the second century BC, believed to be another place where, in a previous incarnation, Buddha turned himself into a huge fish during a twelve-year famine and fed the people on his own flesh.

In AD 630, Hsuan Tsang found it still flourishing but thirteen years later, returning from India, carrying fifty irreplaceable Buddhist manuscripts, and the seeds of rare and exotic flowers, he nearly drowned — and all was lost. Hsuan Tsang himself was spared and forded the river on an elephant.

In AD 870, Kabul was taken from its Turkish Hindu Shahi rulers, who fled eastwards to set up a new capital at Hund.

Not far from Hund, some seven kilometres (four miles) distance, is **Lahur,** the fourth-century BC birthplace of Panini, the great Sanskrit grammarian who taught at Taxila university and refined the Sanskrit syntax.

From Lahur you drive to Jahangira to rejoin the Imperial Highway — right for Peshawar, left for Attock.

The Khyber Pass: Echoes of Kipling

Nothing better evokes the days of the old British Empire — and the dauntless bravery of the Pathan tribesmen who refused to fall under the domination of Victoria's men — than the **Khyber Pass,** immortalised by many great authors, story tellers, and writers, especially Nobel laureate Rudyard Kipling.

"A scrimmage in a Border Station —
A canter down some dark defile —
Two thousand pounds of education
Drops to a ten rupee jezail
The Crammer's boast, the Squadron's pride,
Shot like a rabbit in a ride."

Since ancient times the Khyber, fifty-six kilometres (35 miles) long, of which forty kilometres (25 miles) is within Pakistan, has formed a vital gateway between Asia and the subcontinent — wide enough for troops and cavalry to march through in disciplined ranks. **Landi Kotal** its highest point is only 1,067 metres (3,500 feet) above sea level.

Through the Khyber advanced the great armies of Alexander the Great, of Sabuktigin and Mahmud, of Genghis Khan and Tamurlane, of Babur and Nadir Shah.

Others would have tried but for the Afridi Pathans who challenged all who came — and extracted tributes. Their bravery has been recorded for more than 2,500 years, since Herodotus wrote of them in 500 BC.

Barely fifteen kilometres (nine miles) from Peshawar, the bazaar at **Jamrud,** which marks the southern entrance to the Pass, is thronged with Pathans — fine, aquiline faces and piercing eyes — all, inevitably, carrying arms, Kalashnikovs, automatic pistols, sub-machine guns, though some still tout the old British Lee Enfield — handling them with easy familiarity.

It was the middle of the last century when the British first arrived on the Frontier but for the next thirty years until the second Afghan War of 1878-80 they failed to gain control of the Pass. Even then their hold was fragmentary, but there did ensue between the two sides a curious respect and admiration, almost an affection, for each other's fighting qualities.

Indeed, so fiercely did the Afridi defend their land that in forty-four years the British mounted more than forty expeditions —

Above: Jamrud and the gateway to the Khyber Pass.

without success — in their attempt to subdue the Afridi and make safe the road to Kabul. The greatest expedition was in 1897 when 40,000 troops were stationed in the Pass and the area around it.

In 1893, the Durand Line created a new border between British India and Afghanistan that sliced through the middle of the Pathan homelands, leaving most of the pass in India with **Torkham** as the border post.

The British left behind a number of mementos, of which perhaps the most enduring is the road that snakes through the pass and up and down the rugged hills. On almost every rock is carved, or painted, the now faded insignia and crests of famous regiments.

The other legacy that the British left behind, long after they had conceded the Pathan their right to autonomy, is the railway built in the 1920s, at the then enormous cost of more than £2 million.

Getting there

There's still a once-a-week steam train that hauls out of Peshawar station each Friday on the three-hour journey to Landi Kotal on the border with Afghanistan — a distance of fifty-one kilometres (32 miles).

The line cuts through the rocky grandeur of the Pass, winding between gorges that are sometimes as narrow as sixty metres (200 feet), and climbs to more than 1,000 metres (3,500 feet) on snaking hairpins, looping beneath itself in a series of tunnels.

Altogether there are thirty-four tunnels, and ninety-two bridges and culverts. Pure 1920s vintage, the three coach train is alternately pulled and pushed by two British-built SG 060 oil-fired engines — one at the front, the other at the back. Two engines are needed to overcome the severe gradients and the drivers use a whistle code to keep in touch with each other.

Frequent stops to clear the line, put the train back on the track after derailment, and unload freight often make the journey much longer than scheduled.

Inevitably, it's crowded with rifle-toting Pathans who pay nothing for the journey — their price for allowing the line to be built; a deal still honoured by Pakistan Railways.

From Landi Kotal, the Khyber Pass continues another sixteen kilometres (ten miles) into Afghanistan.

Unfortunately, because of the Mujahideen war in Afghanistan, the Pass was closed to foreign visitors sometime in the 1980s, but there were hopes in 1989 that following the withdrawal of Russian forces and the establishment of a popular government in Kabul, it would soon be re-opened for tourists.

Most will drive from Peshawar west along the old Imperial Highway to Jamrud. It's about an hour's drive to cover the fifty-six kilometres (35 miles) from Peshawar to Torkham, west past the **University** and **Islamia College,** where there were many refugee camps in 1988.

Doubtless the same rules will still prevail: visitors are not allowed to remain in the pass after dusk, nor to camp or leave the main road.

Sightseeing

All visitors must check in at **Jamrud Fort,** built in 1823 of rough stonework and stucco on the site of an older fort by the Sikhs. There's a stone archway across the road, the **Bab-el-Khyber,** built in 1964.

The entrance to the pass itself — wide and flat and bounded by low stony hills, each guarded by a picket of the Khyber Rifles — gives no indication of what is to come.

Nine kilometres (six miles) on, however, you get your first glimpse of the real Khyber Pass — one that will linger long in the memory. You can pull in at the first of the many **viewpoints** to take in this landscape but remember it is forbidden to photograph military installations and bridges in the Pass.

Behind you, beneath the series of hairpin bends that you have just climbed, the road sweeps down to the rich Peshawar plain. Ahead is a range of gaunt, craggy, and dramatic mountains through which the Khyber snakes its sinuous way.

Not far beyond this, another viewpoint provides a stunning panorama of the railway line on the north wall of the Pass.

Nearby is the redbrick **Shagai Fort,** built by the British in the 1920s to command the approaches from **Tirah** and now garrisoned by the Khyber Rifles.

The road then snakes down for four kilometres (three miles) to the valley floor, past a small **green mosque,** right, and beneath the **Ali Masjid Fort,** that commands the entire length of the Pass at its narrowest point.

The British soldiers who fell in the second Afghan War lie in the fort's **cemetery** above the road that here divides into two single lane highways, one on either side of the gorge, following narrow ledges beside the dry river bed.

Now the Pass bellies out into a green and fertile valley, guarded by Pathan homesteads built as fortresses complete with high, crenellated mud walls, watchtowers at each corner, pierced with gun embrasures.

Next **Zarai,** twenty-five kilometres (16 miles) from Jamrud where, on a rise to the north above the railway, stands what's left of a second-century **Buddhist** *stupa,* it's crumbling high dome resting on a three-tiered square base. It was a rich source of some fine Gandharan art when it was excavated early in the 1900s.

Beyond the *stupa,* right, are the **regimental headquarters** of the **Khyber Rifles,** where old traditions still prevail and mess silver is proudly displayed.

Soon after this the road reaches **Landi Kotal** where the railway ends. The spur leading for fifteen kilometres (nine miles) to **Landi Khana** is no longer used.

As a result of the Mujahideen war, Landi Kotal is awash with smuggled goods, especially electronic equipment and domestic appliances and the bazaar is a veritable Aladdin's Cave of modern treasures.

From a **viewpoint** west of the town, the last touch of green before the sere plains of Afghanistan, the visitor looks out to the border post of **Torkham** over a valley of tank traps and military barricades, through which a continuous caravan of camels and donkeys plods, interspersed with what pass as taxis in these parts — vintage mammoth American cars that squeeze, on rooftop, boot, and interior, as many as twenty passengers.

Brooding on the hilltop south of Torkham is the ninth-century **Kafir Fort,** where the British and Afghans fought one of the last battles of the third Afghan War in 1919.

There's a shell-pocked **PTDC restaurant and motel** at Torkham and also what was once a picnic spot overlooking Afghanistan, now part of no-man's land, where you can observe the endless stream of people criss-crossing between the two countries, as they have done throughout the decade-long civil war in Afghanistan.

Overleaf: Young Pathan warriors guard the Khyber as did their ancestors.

The Derajat: Remote and Barren

Part of the North-West Frontier Province, **Dera Ismail Khan** is the focal point of the **Derajat** where the Indus, at last free of its mountain strongholds, meanders in broad oxbows and wide bends, its waters turning the sandy, semi-arid plains on either side into green and fertile fields.

Getting there

Take the road south from Peshawar through **Darra Adam Khel** to **Kohat**, over the **Kohat Pass.** You can also drive to Kohat from Islamabad.

Where to stay

See Listings for "Hotels".

Sightseeing

At Kohat the road leads south-west for 180 kilometres (80 miles) to **Bannu**. Well beyond Kohat the land becomes bare, the saline soil ill-suited to crop production or livestock grazing and cuts through rugged, eroded hills of crimson-ochre laced with veins of white and green.

Few people live in this wilderness as the road winds down to the dry Bannu plain, ringed in the north by the dramatic battlements of the mountains of North Waziristan, part of the Tribal Area of the NWFP, forbidden to foreign visitors.

The walled town of Bannu, with its colourful bazaar, is a real oasis. Its lush palms and mango trees provide welcome shade from the heat of the scorched broad valley.

For centuries its citizens resolutely resisted the marauding tribesmen who rode or walked down from the hills around to raid it — and even today the city gates are closed each night.

Bannu was known for some time as Edwardesabad, after Sir Herbert Edwardes, one of Lawrence's young men who was political advisor during the 1840s to the ruling Sikhs.

He forbade the Sikh army from plundering and won the confidence of the tribesmen, who presented him with a note — written quarter-of-a-century earlier by another English traveller, which they had saved as an amulet to give them protection against the British. They were confident it would work.

In as much as Edwardes then proceeded to collect land taxes from the tribesmen and cajoled them into destroying the fortress walls of their villages, it did. As a result, the Sikhs built one major **fort** that is now the **headquarters** of Pakistan's Frontier Force Regiment.

Later, when the second Sikh War broke out, the tribesmen joined Edwardes in harassing the Sikh armies. Not long after this he was appointed Commissioner at Peshawar, where Edwardes College is named after him.

Bannu's **hospital** and **school** still bear the name of the British missionary who founded them. Dr. T. L. Pennell and his assistant, who died of septicaemia while still in their forties, are buried in the **graveyard** in the hospital compound along with the British soldiers killed in the Sikh war and in tribal clashes.

There's a **narrow-gauge railway** that runs south from Bannu and the road follows it until the railway veers left through **Lakki** and east to **Kalabagh.**

There's a road junction at this point. One road continues beside the railway, while the other goes south through **Pezu** to **Dera Ismail Khan,** soon degenerating into a single track through stark and forbidding desert ringed in the south-east by the **Marwat Hills.**

The road climbs the western shoulder of these hills, beneath their highest point and down through precipitous gorges, riven by wind and age, beneath a profusion of jagged peaks, to cross the flat sandy plain to **Dera Ismail Khan.**

Centuries ago, it was an important trade gateway between Afghanistan and the Punjab for the caravans that used the **Gomal Pass,** but today it's little more than a town in limbo — a place where the bicycle rickshaw is the main means of commuter transport.

The twentieth century, however, is coming to Dera Ismail Khan. Its rundown **Sikh fort** has been restored and was used briefly in the 1980s as an annexe of **Gomal University.**

East of the town there's an attractive **promenade** on the banks of the Indus where, of an evening, the townsfolk parade up and

Opposite top: British regimental crests decorate a Khyber Pass hillside.
Opposite: Jamrud Fort guards the eastern entrance to the famed Khyber Pass.

down and where, during the day, you can watch pastoralists grazing their cattle on an **island** in midstream.

Making rafts out of their earthenware urns, the herdsmen sail over to the island to milk the cattle — returning swiftly on the full urns. It's said that as the rafts churn in the swirling currents of the Indus the milk turns to butter by the time they land.

Some little distance upstream is the *raison d'etre* for any visit to Dera Ismail Khan — a vintage Glasgow-built **paddle steamer** that runs a summer ferry service across the Indus when the river is in spate and the winter bridge of boats is dismantled.

With a length of thirty metres (100 feet), she served at Basra, in Iraq, during the First World War, before moving to Kalabagh. In 1931, when the Kalabagh bridge was completed, she sailed downstream to her new base at Dera Ismail Khan where she often becomes grounded on the sandbanks.

For those of an historical bent, west of Dera Ismail Khan on the ancient trade route to the Gomal Pass leading to Afghanistan, are many ancient archaeological sites belonging to both the prehistoric and the Indus Civilization eras.

Fascinating

Perhaps the most fascinating of these is that at **Rahman Dheri,** a low mound to the left of the road twenty-two kilometres (14 miles) along the Bannu road from Dera Ismail Khan, which dates from 3,200 BC.

It follows the classic, urban grid of the Indus Civilization in typical chessboard pattern and the remains of the ancient brick houses, pottery, shards, lapis lazuli, and stone tools are everywhere.

There are many day excursions that can be made from Dera Ismail Khan, including one in wintertime across the bridge of boats over the Indus to **Darya Khan.**

Traffic on the single-lane bridge is controlled by a code that uses drum beats. The first span is anchored on a broad island, where the road cuts through reedbeds. When it's wet, it's all too easy to get bogged down in the mud.

There's another span on the other side of the island that leads to the mudflats on the opposite shore where again, when it's wet, you have to drive with extreme care.

Another excursion is to **Kalabagh,** which means "black garden", where early nineteenth-century travellers noted that the houses, among blood-red rocks streaked with white salts, were apparently built on top of each other above the clear waters of the Indus.

On the left bank, at the point where this great river broadens out on to the plains, there's a large oasis — a profusion of verdant green bursting out of the stark, red mountains and the barren desert — vegetables, fruit trees, roses, and oleanders.

Until the British built their many barrages on the Indus, Kalabagh was the most northerly, navigable point on the river. It was served by a flotilla of steamboats, some of which were wrecked as they plied through the gorges beyond the town.

Those that remained afloat sailed beneath the **cliff** in the Indus gorge to Hund where Jalalludin of Khawarizm is said to have jumped on horseback after his defeat by Genghis Khan — and lived.

Another excursion follows the canal jeep road ninety kilometres (56 miles) north to the **Chasma Barrage,** south of **Mianwali,** alongside lush, palm-fringed fields, past some Kafir Kot forts to the delightful **lake** that backs up behind the eight-kilometre-long (five-mile) barrage.

There's a comfortable **rest house** at the barrage run by the Pakistan Water and Power Development Authority — WADPA — where you can spend the night if it is vacant.

It's thought that the **Kafir Kot** ("place of the heathens") **forts** belonged to one of the wealthy Hindu Rajput kingdoms of the eighth and tenth centuries, which dominate one of the main trade routes from the north-west, at the confluence of the Indus with the Kurram river.

The canal road passes near the hill on which the southern Kafir Kot fort stands. A few kilometres south of **Bilot,** after crossing some small headworks over the canal, you can scramble up the hillside for a fine view of the fort from the south of the hillcrest.

A long section of wall constructed of limestone blocks and studded with circular towers still stands. The fort has three main **temples,** two comprising groups of temples and shrines on the same plinth, with well preserved deep-chiselled carvings, mainly rosettes.

The northern fort is thirty-eight kilometres (24 miles) distant, reached only by a long and difficult trek around the shores of the lake. You'll need a guide.

It covers about twenty-four hectares (sixty acres) atop a cliff with deep gorges on three sides. There are four temples, some badly ruined, others intricately-carved, inside.

The walls on the north side, including a gate, rise about eight metres (25 feet) and are the most impressive, but there are dramatic views from the south-west corner of the Indus and the Punjab plains beyond.

There are more eighth- and tenth-century Hindu forts in and around the Salt Range, at **Amb**, near Sukesar, and **Kalar**, near Makhad.

Mianwali, which lies beyond the barrage, is a small town and an important air force base that has become more important with the irrigation works in the area.

From there you can take the road north-west to **Talagang** and **Chakwal**, through the spectacular section where it crosses the Salt Range near Mianwali. From Mianwali to Islamabad is about five hours driving.

Darra Adamkhel: Pakistan's Dodge City

Just forty minutes and forty kilometres (25 miles) from Peshawar, in the Pathan tribal lands across the border from Pakistan's North West Frontier Province, lies the toughest town in the world, **Darra Adamkhel,** where gun law rules.

Five thousand craftsmen have established the world's least-known arms industry — turning out thousands of lethal replicas of weapons and ammunition from the arsenals of the world.

Night and day its one main street and back alleys echo to the constant sound of gunfire as apprentices, gunsmiths, and customers test the latest cutprice replicas from both the free world and the communist bloc.

"Any Pathan feels naked without a gun," says a tall, turbanned and bearded warrior, wearing an ammunition belt and six-gun in holster and carrying a Lee Enfield rifle. "To us guns are jewellery."

And Darra Adamkhel is the Pathan Tiffany's. Every single member of its 5,000 citizens is dedicated to the manufacture and sale of an astonishing variety of guns of all makes, calibres and functions.

In the labyrinth of tiny back alleys behind the main street every recess, it seems, is an armoury — small youths, some only nine or ten, intricately boring a 7 mm. calibre through a rounded steel rod, fashioning a precision barrel with only an ancient lathe and their own innate skill.

These masterpieces of the gunsmith's art are every bit as lethal as the originals from which they are lovingly copied in minute detail — even down to the manufacturer's serial number.

Kalashnikovs, Chinese makes, even the Pakistan Army's G3, compete with pen pistols that fire .22 bullets, the British Lee Enfield .303, Webley .455, sten guns, recoilless rifles, machine guns — even howitzers, anti-aircraft guns and mortars.

Outside the open-fronted shops venerable salesmen sit before stores stuffed with an assortment of machine guns, rifles, pistols, ammunition belts, ammunition cartons, and the casts of solid metal blocks from which more pistols are fashioned. From all round comes the sound of guns popping and crackling.

"Once you've bought a gun, no shop will change it after sundown on the day you buy it," says one trader. "So the rule here is that every customer tests the gun, outside the shop, before he completes the deal."

The gun trade in Darra Adamkhel is more than a century old. British firearms were the first to be copied in abundance. The originals came, mysteriously but not surprisingly, from the Khyber Rifles and other British regiments.

It's impossible to tell just how many guns a year come out of Darra Adamkhel. There are no official records and most of the craftsmen are illiterate.

"We don't need any licence or records," said forty-four-year-old Sarfraz Khan, red beard glinting in the evening sun, "either to make the guns, sell them — or use them!"

A round of machine gun fire — sprayed into the gaunt forbidding mountains which encircle Darra's adobe and mud daub shops and houses — brought obvious satisfaction to an elderly-looking Pathan in turban and robes.

"Accidents do happen sometimes," said sixty-four-year-old shop keeper Sharba Khan as he busily oiled a replica Kalashnikov. "But not too often. These guns are not used in Darra. They're meant for the more deadly business up there — where your farm or women are threatened."

The steel in his eye more than matched that of the gleaming slender barrel.

Above: Typical gunsmith's shop in Darra Adamkhel. Craftsmen have spent their entire lives making authentic and lethal replicas of small arms.

Above: Young apprentice learns the gunsmith's art in Darra Adamkhel.

Horns blaring, a continuous stream of traffic — private buses and small vans converted into cheap commuter transport — flows by, the backfire of their exhausts blending into the continual percussion of this Pathan town.

No law men patrol its streets or the surrounding lands.

As you drive off along the valley floor towards the **Kohat Pass,** thirteen kilometres (eight miles) away the sound of gunfire fades into the distance. The world is strangely silent. But in Darra Adamkhel the deadly industry continues.

If war ever came to Darra Adamkhel, nobody would ever know . . . .

Kohat Pass offers splendid views over the surrounding countryside in all directions. The **fort** at the top is now a police station. Close by is a **memorial arch** to Eric Charles Handyside, killed by tribesmen in 1926. Ten kilometres (six miles) down the pass is **Kohat,** with a splendid British cantonment and some fine gardens.

With its French windows, the Deputy Commissioner's **residence** was originally the home of the British Resident in Kabul, Louis Cavagnari, whose assassination sparked off the second Afghan War in 1879. He was an Anglo-Frenchman whose father served as a general under Napoleon. Kohat Fort is another solid reminder of British days.

Kohat also stars in a story told in the bazaars of Darra Adamkhel which recounts the kidnapping, from **Bungalow 26** in the cantonment, of Molly Ellis, a young English girl, by Pathan tribesmen in 1923 in retaliation for some sensed injustice. She was later released unharmed, but her kidnapping became something of a *cause célèbre* in both British and Pathan circles.

Parachinar: A Haven of Peace

If you extend your excursion to two days you can carry on to **Parachinar,** at the head of the Kurram valley, close to the frontier with Afghanistan, but only with permission from the Ministry of Foreign Affairs as this is tribal territory.

Sightseeing

Take the road from Kohat west to **Thal** through scenery similar to the Swat valley, but not so lush until the eroded western heights of the **Salt Range** meet the outliers of the **Sulaiman mountains.**

During the 1919 Afghan war, Afghan troops swept through the Kurram Valley to besiege the fort at Thal, which commands the river crossing, in a long and bitter campaign.

From here the road continues along the course of the **Kurram River** through the beautiful valley, on the border with Afghanistan, green and fertile, producing crops that vary from wheat and rice to spinach and opium.

At the head of the Kurram Valley, nestling amongst apple orchards and tall plane trees called chinars, is the Turis' regional capital Parachinar with its single tall and graceful minaret.

When the weather is good, as it is almost every day in summer, school classes are held outdoors so that rural parents, many of whom are still not at all sure that education is a good thing, can come and see for themselves what it is all about.

Parachinar is ringed by a number of smaller villages whose very names, such as **Shalozan, Ziaran Qubadshekel,** summon up an image of Shangri-La.

Amid the foothills of the 4.877-metre-high (16,000-feet) "White Mountain", so-called because its summit is never free from snow, farmers practice an intense form of cultivation, using terraces and complicated irrigation channels to get the best out of every scrap of available land.

Even in high summer there is a healthy chill in the air and the people wear brown or grey rough-spun woollen caps called *bakol*, indigenous to the region which, when winter comes, can be rolled down to protect the ears and neck from frostbite.

Near the **Peiwar Kotal Pass** that leads into Afghanistan at the head of the valley beyond Parachinar stands a delightful **village** where Lord Roberts, who commanded the assault on the pass during the second Afghan War in 1878, built himself a house.

Baluchistan: Sand, Sea, and Mountains

Wild, rugged, sparsely populated mountain and desert, **Baluchistan** covers a vast portion of south-west Pakistan. Much of it is high barren plateau between 1,000 and 1,250 metres (3,000-4,000 feet) above sea level, barricaded in the west along the **Afghan border** by the **Tobakakar mountains** and in the east by the **Sulaiman range** that borders the Indus river.

In the extreme south lies the **Makran,** one of the cruellest, most inhospitable deserts in the world, which so weakened Alexander the Great when he marched through it on his way home that he died within weeks of arriving.

These great empty spaces and daunting mountains — and the nomadic character of most of the Baluchi people — make Baluchistan one of the world's greatest but least known wilderness regions, imposing and dramatic.

Covering 347,190 square kilometres (134,000 square miles), Baluchistan is the largest province of Pakistan but, with little more than five million people, the least populated — with only twelve persons to the square kilometre (0.386 square miles).

Bordered in the west and north-west by Iran and Afghanistan, in the north by the provinces of **North-West Frontier** and the **Punjab,** in the east by **Sind** and in the south by the **Arabian Sea,** Baluchistan is a land of contrasts — of lofty mountains and vast, barren deserts; of lush green valleys and sunny beaches; of verdant juniper forests and gaunt mountains.

Year round temperatures register extremes at both ends of the scale: rainfall seldom exceeds thirty-five centimetres (14 inches) and often reaches no more than seven centimetres (three inches).

Opposite: Snowdusted mountains of Baluchistan.

With the capital at **Quetta**, Baluchistan province is made up of six administrative divisions — **Quetta, Sibi, Kalat, Makran, Loralai,** and **Nasirabad**.

Quetta Division is composed of Quetta, **Pishin,** and **Chagai** districts. The Loralai Division consists of **Zhob** and Loralai districts. the Sibi Division is composed of Sibi district and the **Kohlu** and **Dera Bugti** tribal agencies. the Kalat Division is made up of Kalat, **Khuzdar, Kharian,** and **Lasbela** districts; and the Makran Division comprises **Turbat, Panjgur,** and **Gwadar** districts.

Over the centuries, the region was dominated by various rulers and Sardars (tribal chiefs) more concerned with maintaining their authority than with development. During their rule, the British also confirmed the powers and privileges of the Sardars while retaining overall control.

In 1947, the states ruled by the Sardars acceded to Pakistan and the Baluchistan States Union formed in 1952 was given the status of a fully-fledged province in 1969.

Getting there

From **Sukkur**, the main road to Baluchistan leads, via **Jacobabad** and **Sibi**, over the **Bolan Pass,** crossing the Brahui mountains, to Quetta. The road north from Karachi via **Khuzdar** is forbidden to foreigners, as is the Makran desert. But driving in Baluchistan is best avoided anyway. Unless you have the instincts of an intrepid explorer and a distinct dislike of creature comforts,take the plane or train to Quetta.

Assuming you do drive, however, your exploration begins at Jacobabad.

Where to stay

See Listings for "Hotels".

Sightseeing

Jacob's former residence still serves as the **Deputy Commissioner'**s abode and his impressive **marble tomb** dominates the town cemetery, along with those of officers of the Sind Irregular Horse. Built of stone and brick these have long crumbled into ruin but Jacob's tomb has been lovingly renovated.

Notable as a major grain centre, **Jacobabad** is also of interest since it is the site of a large

heronry. During the September-October breeding season incredible numbers of night herons and egrets stalk about the town and perch on houses and trees.

Running through the wild and desolate landscapes of the **Pat** or **Kacchi** desert, the road from Jacobabad to **Sibi** covers 173 kilometres (108 miles), the shimmering heat producing incredible mirages. In summer, the constant scorching wind often proves fatal to man and beast.

Close to Sibi the **Brahui mountains** come into view on the distant horizon. The town is notable for its old **mud fort** and the highest summer temperatures ever recorded on the subcontinent.

Its annual **horse and cattle fair,** the most colourful in south-west Pakistan, held every February, draws tribesmen from all over Baluchistan.

Occupied by Mahmud of Ghazni in 1005, it was five centuries later when Ameer Chakar Rind, who united the Baluchi tribes, defeated the ruler of the Sammah dynasty at Sibi.

The Amir's sixteenth-century **fort** still stands near the town which was briefly occupied by the British in 1841. But it was not until 1879 that they established a permanent presence in the town, where Sir Robert Sandeman negotiated with the Marri and Bugti tribesmen during his pacification of the area.

Just before the **Bolan Pass,** thirty-two kilometres (20 miles) north-west of Sibi and eight kilometres (five miles) south-west of the main road, over a dry river bed, past a **ruined** *stupa* and a **Hindu temple** on the right (now used as a mosque), is **Mehr Gahr,** an early pre-Indus Civilization archaeological site.

Excavated by a French archaeological team, there are shards everywhere, some in piles, some scattered around.

Dating from between 6,000-3,000 BC, this Neolithic settlement is the earliest so far found on the subcontinent. It depicts a remarkably well-advanced society which was among the first to domesticate the water buffalo. For 6,000 years ago this semi-desert was a wetland with many lakes and marshes.

The people roamed the now vanished grasslands hunting feral sheep and swamp deer, a species long since extinct.

Opposite top: Mohamed Ali Jinnah's summer residence at Ziarat, Baluchistan.
Opposite: Sandeman Tangi, near Ziarat, Baluchistan.

Above: Camel train prepares to enter the Bolan Pass.
Opposite: Camel train moves through the Bolan Pass to summer pastures.

Ninety-six kilometres (60 miles) long, the narrow Bolan Pass is more dramatic and spectacular than the the better known Khyber Pass to the north, with giddying views of the palm-studded valley floor.

April or October, when the nomadic camel caravans are on the move to and from the high summer pastures, are the best months to travel this way.

Many invaders saw the Bolan Pass as the gateway to the wealth of the subcontinent. Even in prehistoric times it was the most direct route from central Asia, used long before the Khyber Pass.

It remains the chief route to the subcontinent from Kandahar and Herat in Afghanistan. Passing through it from India to fight the first Afghan War in 1841, a British contingent was swept away by a sudden flash flood along the the **Bolan river.**

The British negotiated with the Khan of Kalat and in 1883 were given a permanent lease to the Bolan Pass. Four years later the whole of Baluchistan was in their hands. From the end of the pass to Quetta is not far.

Khojak Pass
The **Khojak Pass** that marks Pakistan's border with Afghanistan is only 110 kilometres (69 miles) south-west of Quetta. During the 1980s it became a vital lifeline for refugees streaming out of Afghanistan and for supplies for the Mujahideen freedom fighters.

Rugged and dramatic, there are magnificent views to the distant, sandy, troubled plains of Afghanistan.

Towards the end of the struggle, citizens of the bustling border town of **Chaman,** a thriving entrepôt at the western foot of the pass were kept awake most nights by the continuous artillery bombardment of the Mujahideen and the Afghanistan defenders in the battle for Spin Buldak, a garrison town just eight kilometres into Afghanistan from Chaman.

Before the conflict broke out in 1980 overlanders crowded along this southerly route to the subcontinent, but now the only feasible overland route from the west into Pakistan is the long 724-kilometre (450-mile) desert road from Zahidan in Iran.

It enters Baluchistan between two vast salt

Above: Baluchi youngsters.
Opposite: Shoe shop in Quetta, capital of Baluchistan.

marshes, **Hamun-e-Lora** to the north and **Hamun-e-Mashkel** to the south.

From Quetta to the Indus, apart from the Bolan Pass, there are two other routes, neither of them to be recommended for the fainthearted.

The first is through **Ziarat** and **Loralai** to **Dera Ghazi Khan.** The second is through **Zhob** to **Dera Ismail Khan,** but it is unlikely foreign visitors will be given permission to make this trip.

Standing 2,450 metres (8,200 feet) above sea level, Ziarat, 123 kilometres (76 miles) from Quetta, is a delightful hill resort, cool even in summer, and snowbound and inaccessible in the winter.

It is ringed by what are claimed to be the world's largest juniper forests — the timber is used in the manufacture of pencils and the juniper berries to flavour gin. Spring, when the hillsides are carpeted with golden foxtail lilies and cuckoos are everywhere, is the best time to visit Ziarat.

There are several reasonable hotels and a **PTDC cottage complex** which make an ideal base for a walking holiday. One of the most beautiful climbs is **Prospect Point,** six kilometres (four miles) away and 300 metres (1,000 feet)

higher, which affords delightful views into the next valley.

It's still wild and unspoilt. Tiny mouse hares scuttle along the crevices of stone walls and choughs flit from tree to tree while golden eagles soar on the thermals above. In the more remote corners of the valley you may see a markhor wild goat.

Leopard also make their lair in this valley which contains the **tomb** and **shrine** of the Afghan saint who gave his name to Ziarat.

More recently, it became famous because of its association with Mohamed Ali Jinnah, the father of Pakistan, who spent his last days in **Governor's rest house** — a tall and graceful building in a garden of incredible beauty.

Two other remote and peaceful valleys are within walking distance — one off the Quetta road, sixteen kilometres (ten miles) from Ziarat along a narrow stony track through a steep gorge. This secret valley, **Mannah,** stretches sixteen kilometres (ten miles) into the mountains.

Ablaze with apple blossom in the spring, **Chautar Valley,** thirteen kilometres (eight miles) from Ziarat, is fair and lovely. The houses in the villages, made from the bark of

the juniper trees, are quite different from the mud huts of the other villages.

Despite its name, **Loralai** — ninety-four kilometres (59 miles) from Ziarat, through attractive hamlets ringed by lovely flowering orchards against the purple-black backdrop of distant mountains — is disappointing, a flat and dusty cantonment town without interest.

Noted for the quality of its almonds and pomegranates, it was often the subject of raids by the warlike Marri tribe. From Quetta it takes about five hours to drive to Loralai.

If you continue another 200 kilometres (124 miles), just beyond the Punjab border where the "Robber Road" ends at the foot of the Sulaiman mountains, set amidst a barren and rubble-strewn landscape, stands **Fort Munro.**

The term "fort" seems incongruous. The town, with its gardens and orchards, is more like a peaceful hill resort than a military outpost. It was founded by Sir Robert Sandeman and named after Colonel Munro, who was Commissioner of the Derajat Division.

For the full-day drive to **Dera Ismail Khan,** via **Muslimbagh** and **Zhob,** (formerly **Fort Sandeman**) along the **Zhob river,** you'll need a permit, an armed escort, and a 4WD vehicle to ford the rivers.

There's a good rest house at Muslimbagh, an oasis of orchards, but Zhob is a real desert town. On one of two small hills there's a **fort** which is now an army base and on the other there's a **"castle",** the former home of Sir Robert Sandeman, and still the residence of the incumbent political agent.

By train

Even the most seasoned traveller will find driving to Baluchistan extremely tiring, but if you fly in and out of Quetta you miss much of the wilderness landscape that makes Baluchistan such an experience.

Perhaps the ideal way to enjoy Baluchistan to the full but in reasonable comfort is to fly to Quetta and return by train.

Since Quetta airport is often closed because of weather conditions, this is the best option: the train will deliver you to either Lahore, Karachi, or Rawalpindi.

The train journey from Quetta to Rawalpindi takes thirty-four hours. The station at Quetta is straight from the vintage days of steam and is a magnificent experience for railway buffs.

Top: Young Baluchi boy and donkey take home the day's catch.
Above: Baluchi camel loaded with fishing nets.
Opposite: Fisherman and their catch at Gaddani Beach, Baluchistan.

The air-conditioned sleeper is comfortable, but since there is only one coach, book well in advance.

The train winds through the mountains, using some dramatic tunnels, as it slowly climbs to the Bolan Pass.

If the prospect of two days on the train is too daunting, however, fly to **Larkana** and take the night train, which enters the Bolan Pass at dawn — the best time to see it — on the twelve-hour journey to Quetta.

Top: Tagging breeding green turtles at Sandspit, Karachi Harbour.
Above: Newly-hatched and endangered green turtle heads for the sea.

Sind: Plain and Desert

The southernmost province of Pakistan, bisected by the mighty Indus, **Sind** stretches north from the Arabian Sea, bounded in the west by the deserts of Baluchistan and in the east by the Thar desert and India.

Indeed, the province derives its name the Indus, which for centuries has fed the flat alluvial plains on either side, endowing them with lush bounty in verdant contrast to the surrounding stark and sparsely populated deserts.

Cradle of one of the world's oldest civilizations, Sind has a long and fascinating history. It witnessed the first Muslim invasion of the subcontinent and later became part of both the Mughal and the British Empires.

Apart from its eastern section, it's best enjoyed by a long leisurely drive north from Karachi to Sukkur, taking in most of the historic cities and beauty spots.

With a population of more than twenty-four million, Sind covers an area of about 150,000 square kilometres (58,000 square miles).

The climate is pleasant in winter, with temperatures ranging from 10°-30°C (50°-86°F) and hot in summer when the thermometer soars to between 25°-50°C (77°-122°F).

The capital, **Karachi** (see "Glory of the East", Part Three), is the biggest city in Pakistan and its major port. It contains the majority of the province's urban population. Administratively, the province is divided into three divisions – **Hyderabad**, **Sukkur**, and **Karachi**.

Getting there

Karachi is the country's major airport and there are domestic flights to many major places in Sind which is well served by roads and rail.

When to go

Sind is best in spring or autumn, usually comfortable in winter, but excessively hot in high summer.

Where to stay

See Listings for "Hotels" outside the various cities.

Sightseeing

The **Super Highway** runs north-east from

Above: Mosque at Sukkur, Sind.
Overleaf: Sundown over Lake Manchar.

Karachi for 164 kilometres (102 miles) across the desert to **Hyderabad** — mostly through a low limestone escarpment covered with thorny shrub.

Although there's little to see, and the traffic is fast and dangerous, the **Khadeji Falls,** two kilometres (one mile) along a fork left at a cluster of small tea shops and a rusty **PTDC** sign about fifty-five kilometres (35 miles) from Karachi, command impressive views of the desert and are impressive when in spate near the end of the monsoons.

For wildlife enthusiasts, the **Sui Gas Pumping Station,** eighty-two kilometres (51 miles) from Karachi, on the Super Highway is the starting point for the safari to **Kirthar National Park,** which covers an area of 3,087 square kilometres (l,192 square miles), is perhaps the last sanctuary for the Sind wild goat, wild sheep, chinkara, gazelle, and leopard (See "Wildlife", Part Four, and In Brief for "National Parks").

Many other mammals, birds and reptiles are found in the park. Sind ibex, which was on the verge of extinction, has been rescued and its population now numbers around 4,000.

Accommodation in the park is limited to four basic and not particularly well situated rest houses so be sure to book one in advance at the offices of the Sind Wildlife Management Board, Karachi. Alternatively, you can safely camp in the park.

But you will need to take all your food and a plentiful supply of boiled water with you as

Above: Refurbished interior of Shah Jahan's mosque, Thatta.
Opposite: Chaukundi Tombs, near Thatta.

there is nothing in the park. Remember, too, that it is a wilderness — only suitable for a 4WD vehicle.

The jeep track twists and turns over arid desert for eighty kilometres (50 miles) before reaching the park, a semi-arid rocky and mountainous sanctuary alongside the border with Baluchistan.

There are good walks and some rock climbing on the slopes and summit of 1,000-metre-high (3,281-feet) **Laoot hill** in the south, with fine views over the park.

For the hardy, with wellshod seats, tour operators offer a three-day camel trek along the old trade route to **Ranikot Fort.** A one day excursion by camel to **Sani,** however, may be enough to convince you this is not entirely what the travel brochures make it out to be.

But given enough padding, there's certainly a thrill in emulating Lawrence of Arabia in what still remains a magnificent wilderness landscape, reassuringly close to civilized comforts.

Part of the southern boundary of Kirthar

National Park is formed by the **Hub Dam,** one of Karachi's major hopes of meeting the city's incessant demand for water. But the benefits are not solely physical.

Water backing up behind the dam wall has created an extensive deep-water lake offering prospects of productive fish farming and a glittering leisure resort.

Back on the Super Highway again you cross the Indus over the **Ghulam Muhammad,** or **Kotri,** Barrage, the last of the great barrages controlling the flow of the Indus between Tarbela and the Arabian Sea, to Hyderabad. It was built in 1955.

Far more pleasant, however, is the 203-kilometre-journey (126-mile) along the **National Highway,** the old route to Hyderabad which leaves Karachi past the airport and is dotted with many historical places and beauty spots to visit.

Some twenty-seven kilometres (17 miles) from Karachi, on the left, there's an astonishing necropolis — "city of the dead" — the **Chaukundi Tombs.**

The name means four-cornered and is derived from the five-star mausolea of the wealthy which are covered by masonry domes or canopies supported by columns at each of their four corners.

The finest of these with exquisitely-carved stonework date from the sixteenth and seventeenth centuries. On the women's graves, stylised carvings representing flowers and jewellery emphasise the wealth and importance of the departed female.

The carvings on the men's graves are typically chauvinistic — weapons, horses and riders. Symbolism involving animals and people is rare in Muslim culture.

There's another fascinating archaeological site thirty-seven kilometres (22 miles) beyond Chaukundi along a right turn off the highway, on the northern bank of the Gharo Creek. **Bhambore** is at least 1,400 years old.

Divided into three distinct phases, archaeologists have found shards of first-century BC Grecian pottery, similar to those at Taxila, in the lowest, waterlogged levels of the excavations.

For almost a thousand years, the Buddhists and Hindus controlled Bhambore, but it is almost certain that this is the site of **Daibul**, where Muhammad bin Qasim launched his invasion of the subcontinent.

The floor and foundations of the eighth-century mosque, the earliest known **mosque** on the subcontinent, have survived. The quay, outside the city's south wall, half-submerged by water, was built on stone foundations with bollards where the ships moored.

Pottery and coins found in the ruins indicate that Bhambore traded with the Muslim countries to the west and as far east as China.

It was abandoned abruptly in the thirteenth century but nobody knows why or how. Only the grisly skeletons, iron arrowheads in their bones, found in the ruins and the ashes and charcoal in the houses, give a clue to its macabre collapse.

Experts postulate that the Afghan invader, Jalalludin, sacked the city and then razed it by fire.

Ancient port

In the eight centuries since, the setting has changed completely. The sea has receded and the Indus changed course. More than 2,000 years ago the sea cut at least eighty kilometres (50 miles) deeper inshore.

The **museum** at Bhambore, however, gives some idea of what the port was like and has an excellent exhibition of three distinct types of pottery — unglazed, cream-coloured, black and red, with geometric patterns of birds, animals and fish; and glazed, painted with images of animals and inscriptions.

The next place of interest on the National Highway, **Haleji Lake,** is eighty-seven kilometres (54 miles) from Karachi then west five kilometres (three miles) along a turnoff to the village of **Gujo.**

A nature reserve and bird sanctuary, the lake is one of Karachi's main reservoirs with a good **rest house** belonging to the Karachi Development Authority.

An eighteen-kilometre-long (11-mile) road circles along an artificial embankment right round the lake which is studded by three small **islands.** Less than eighteen square kilometres (seven square miles) in area, this glittering pearl in the desert is one of Asia's great bird sanctuaries with more than 100,000 birds, including seventy different species of waterfowl.

These include flamingos, pelicans, purple gallinule, pheasant-tailed jacans, herons, ducks, egrets, and rare species like palearctic swans.

Even with a powerful telescope which turns the placid white rock of **Pelican Island** into a shimmering mass of furiously mating pelicans, it's impossible for ordinary people to distinguish one bird from the other.

These migrants from the northern hemisphere, some extremely rare, congregate here, as they do at Bharatupur near Agra in India, during winter.

Early morning is the best time to observe them, but at most times you will see vast flocks of coots and many kinds of duck as well as herons, flamingos, pelicans, egrets, cormorants and kingfishers, during the course of the day (See "Bird Life," Part Four).

Back on the highway, ninety-eight kilometres (61 miles) from Karachi you come to **Makli Hill,** meaning little Mecca, to the west of the road, one of the world's greatest necropolises, reputed to contain more than a million graves, tombs, and mausolea within its fifteen-square-

Opposite: Sindhi youngster with water buffalo near Larkana.

kilometre (six-square-mile) perimeter.

If ghosts require palaces, the grandeur of their mortal dwelling places on Makli Hill should satisfy them. Though many have collapsed, some in the earthquakes that occasionally reverberate through the Sind, all these tombs — dating from the fifteenth to seventeenth centuries — testify to the faith of the Mughals in the hereafter.

Many of the stately mausolea are architectural masterpieces, lovingly preserved, many restored. They vary in size with differing degrees of grandeur.

Many are the graves of kings, queens, saints, scholars, military commanders, philosophers, and poets, probably built to their own design while they were still alive.

Some have extremely delicate stone carvings and perforated stonework; others are covered with beautiful blue or white glazed tiles.

From the entrance to the tombs there's a road left to **Hadero Lake,** about eleven kilometres (seven miles) from Thatta. Like the other lakes of Sind, it's a veritable bird sanctuary, especially favoured by pelicans and flamingos.

Five kilometres (three miles) south-west of Thatta on the Makli ridge, is the fifteenth-century **Kalankot Fort,** which belonged to the Sammahs. The ruins are easily reached from the road leading to the limestone quarries that helped to build Karachi's new steel city.

Finally, to the east, directly off the highway, you reach **Thatta,** a city with a history of 2,000 years of trade, though the evidence of it is barely visible.

Nothing in its fabric of brick-and-mud houses and untidy roads evokes its past, which echoes with the tramping feet of Alexander the Great's invading army in the third century BC.

More recently it became a Mughal resort, favoured particularly by Emperor Shah Jahan who stayed here occasionally. He bequeathed a treasure in the city's seventeenth-century **mosque,** so well-preserved it's hard to believe the elegantly pointed brickwork and delicately-laid marble mosaics have weathered three centuries.

In fact, it has been much restored in the present century, and little of the original remains. Nonetheless, bathed in the soft glow of the winter sun, the curves and geometry of its complex ceiling prove an irresistible lure to the photographer.

Almost **100 domes** cover the mosque, creating an acoustical effect that enables prayers offered in front of the mihrab to be heard in any part of the building, just as at the Grand Mosque in Cordoba, Spain.

Two hundred years ago Thatta still flourished, sustained by the flood waters of the Indus which made it one of the great ports and trading centres on the river. The river, however, shifted course, leaving Thatta high, dry, and impoverished.

Like the once "fruitful, rich and fertile countryside" around it, the town withered into arid anonymity. Many houses were deserted and Thatta's glory vanished so abruptly that one nineteenth-century English visitor thought it "ruined and deserted".

Thatta's contemporary history goes back at least 600 years. It was the seat of the more or less independent Muslim rulers of Lower Sind, the Sammahs who rebelled against Delhi from the fourteenth to the sixteenth centuries.

Portuguese fleet

In 1555 a Portuguese fleet entered the mouth of the Indus to assist the rulers of Sind in a war with their local enemies. Unfortunately, the antagonists had already patched up their differences before the Portuguese arrived and the Portuguese, in a frenzy at finding themselves out of work, burned and ransacked Thatta and the surrounding country.

It was quickly rebuilt, however, only to be invaded by Humayun, the Mughal Emperor dethroned by the Afghan Sher Shah. Later it was annexed by Humayun's son, Akbar, in 1592, and became a distant part of the Mughal Empire.

When Nadir Shah of Persia took the city in 1742, it was still flourishing. Thatta then declined, not only because the Indus had shifted its course, but also because Britain's newly developed textile industry began to export cotton "lungis" to India that were better and cheaper than the once-famous Thatta lungis.

Wherever you go in Thatta you'll see wind chutes on top of the older houses — an effective form of air-conditioning in the scorching summer weather channelling what little breeze there is into the rooms below.

Opposite: Mausoleum of Sulhal-sar-Mast near Sukkur.

Above: Ruined Kot Fort, near Sukkur.
Opposite: 18th-century mausoleum of Sind ruler, Ghulam Nabi Kalhora, Hyderabad.

From Thatta the highway runs north along the west bank of the Indus to Hyderabad. Eighteen kilometres (11 miles) beyond Thatta, unseen to the left of the road, is **Kheenjar Lake,** another of Karachi's major water supplies where the Pakistan Tourism Development Corporation runs two **resort complexes** — one a bright new vision with Scandinavian-style pitched roofs on chalets of five-star rating.

Just a few metres off the main road, visitors check in at the reception and walk up a slight rise for their first view of this tranquil sheet of water, now reflecting the lowering sun.

In the reeds, at the water's edge, a family boards a frail, lateen-sailed craft overloaded with household utensils and pushes off, tacking out into the light evening breeze.

Early each morning the fishermen gather in the night's nets, some bobbing cockleshell-like on large buoyant floats, half immersed in the icy pellucid water.

The timelessness and serenity are peaceful contrast to the city life that this manmade lake — thirty-two kilometres (20 miles) long and ten kilometres (six miles) wide, one of the largest in Asia — sustains.

There's little else to see before you reach the **Kotri Bridge** over the Indus and drive into **Hyderabad** (see "The Cities", Part Three), 203 kilometres (126 miles) from Karachi.

From Hyderabad you can drive to **Sukkur** along either bank of the Indus. The east bank road is the more sensible choice, but there are a number of places on the west bank worth visiting.

Some ninety kilometres (56 miles) north of Hyderabad, at **Sani,** you turn left and head west for twenty-one kilometres (13 miles) along a dirt road through uninhabited country to the nineteenth-century **Ranikot Fort,** built by the Talpur dynasty.

Said to be the largest fort in the world, its walls have a circumference of more than twenty-four kilometres (15 miles) and are still in good condition. Inside the fort, there are two smaller **forts.**

It's on the site of an older fort that guarded the trade route from Thatta, through the Kirthar hills to **Manchar Lake** and **Sehwan,** and thence to central Asia.

North of Sani, some twenty kilometres (12 miles) distance, stands **Amri,** one of Pakistan's most ancient archaeological sites — eight hectares (20 acres) of **mounds** that have been extensively excavated and pre-date the Indus Civilisation. Indeed, the Amri people disappeared when the Indus Civilization appeared almost 5,000 years ago.

Some kilometres north of Amri is **Sehwan**, probably the town with the longest continuous existence in Sind. Set on top of a hill, it's near the ruins of a huge **fort** said to have been founded by Alexander the Great.

Today it's known best for the shrine of **Lal Shahbaz Qalandar,** the twelfth-century *sufi*, missionary, scholar, poet, and philologist who came from Marand in Persia and belonged to the Qalanderiyah order of dervishes. He wrote several books in Persian and Arabic.

Above: Young women of the fisherfolk community which lives on Lake Manchar.

Each year a massive **festival** begins on the eighteenth day of Sha'aban, in the Muslim calendar, and pilgrims from all over Pakistan flock to Sehwan.

Huge drums and gongs beat to the mass devotional dances of the saint's followers, beginning with a slow, soft humming of verses and building up to a wild crescendo of ecstasy.

The festival is a riot of noise from a bedlam of bells, gongs, cymbals, and wind instruments, but the most exciting spectacle is the dancing dervishes, dressed in long robes, beads, bracelets and coloured headbands, who whirl faster and faster in a state of glazed trance, finally to run wildly through the mausoleum doors with a deafening scream.

West of this ancient town lie the marshes and mudflats of Manchar Lake, which, although shallow, cover a vast area and are rich in fish and birdlife.

Formed in a natural depression, the lake is fed by seasonal streams and rivers from the hills and the Indus, whose water reaches it through the **Nora outfall.**

The Mirbar fishing community on Manchar live in a fascinating colony of houseboats, using traditional fishing methods, mainly nets and long baited lines. They also net waterfowl — and stalk herons by wading up to their necks in the lake and placing stuffed egrets on their ancient guns as decoys.

The next town along the main road to Sukkur, some thirty kilometres (19 miles) from the Manchar turn off, is **Khudabad**. Briefly the capital of Sind in the eighteenth century, it's now of little importance — just a small town surrounded by dozens of old **tombs** and **mosques**.

It's followed by **Dadu**, a major trade and farm centre with a crossing over the Indus, eighty kilometres (50 miles) south of the ruins of the early Indus Civilization, **Moenjodaro** (see "Cradle of Civilization", Page 155). The excavated city, perhaps the world's first metropolitan culture, lies to the east of the road and is bordered by the Indus.

The road now leads through **Dokri**, where there's a major rice research centre, past rich, well-irrigated farmland to **Larkana**. It's a town, says a Sindhi proverb, where the rich should go because they can easily spend their money there.

Twenty-four kilometres (15 miles) further on there's a west turn to **Jacobabad** and **Baluchistan**, at **Shikarpur**, once an important

caravanserai and trading centre for goods coming from central Asia via the Bolan Pass. The present town, however, was founded as recently as the seventeenth century — in 1616 — by the Daudpotra tribe.

Akbar's birthplace

From Hyderabad, on the east bank, there's an interesting excursion to **Umarkot**, 160 kilometres (100 miles) eastwards through **Mirpur Khas,** the birthplace, in 1542, of Akbar the Great in the **Rajput fort** that dominates the town.

Fringed by rising sand hills, Umarkot stands on the edge of the great **Thar desert** which is bisected by the Pakistan-Indian border and extends through most of the Indian state of Rajasthan.

It was here that Akbar's father, Humayun, fleeing from the Afghan Sher Shah, sought refuge in Sind in 1541 and married fifteen-year-old Hamida. Months later, when he attempted to cross the Thar with his pregnant bride at the hottest time of the year, he discovered that his enemies had filled the wells with sand.

His party found sanctuary at Umarkot and an **engraved stone** marks the spot where Akbar was born. There is also a small **museum** dedicated to Akbar's life.

But, despite the help of his new allies, the Rajahs of Umarkot, Humayun failed to dislodge the ruler of Sind and had to flee. Forty years after his birth, however, Akbar returned to capture his birthplace — and sweep the whole of Sind, and later Baluchistan, into his Empire.

The national highway from Hyderabad to **Sukkur** is not easy to find — signposting in Hyderabad is bad, if non-existent — so you should ask for directions.

Once on it you drive for some time until, just before **Hala**, you reach the right turn to **Bhit Shah** with its **mausoleum of Shah Abdul Latif,** a much revered Sufi mystic and a great Sindhi poet. Born in 1689, he was also the founder of a school of music.

He is credited with producing the first great work of Sindhi literature, *Risalo*. Each year his memory is celebrated when an elaborate **cultural festival** is held at the richly-decorated and painted mausoleum during the Islamic lunar month of Saffar.

Fifty-six kilometres (35 miles) from Hyderabad, Hala is actually two towns in one — the old divided from the new by three

Top: Vendor plies her wares in Sindhi town.
Above: Sindhi street cart with device that crushes nuts for oil.

Above: Larkana potter with typical Sind pottery.

kilometres (two miles).

You enter old Hala through a blue-tiled arch. Famous for its ceramic handicrafts, especially pottery and tiles, the exterior of the town mosque is faced with blue, green and white tiles. Behind it are narrow streets where you can see the pottery and tiles being moulded, painted, and baked.

Hala is also noted for its shrine to another great Sind saint — **Makhdoom Nooh.**

Soon after Hala, the character of the landscape changes from semi-desert to fields of cotton and other crops. As it passes through small towns and villages, including **Ranipur**, long stretches of the highway are lined by graceful avenues of ancient and stately trees.

Twenty-one kilometres (13 miles) beyond Ranipur, **Kot Diji's** eighteenth-century **Talpur Fort** is in splendid repair — dominating the crest of a steep hill to the right of the road. You enter it, however, from the other side of the hill.

Here the British pitched camp in 1843 as they marched south to put down the troublesome Talpur armies at the desert fortress of **Imamgarh**. There is also an archaeologically-exciting **prehistoric site** at Kot Diji, forerunner of the Indus Civilisation which adapted and

developed many of the Kot Diji community's basic cultural elements. The people flourished around 2,800 BC.

Though the lower levels are now under water, you can still visit the citadel area on high ground where the elite lived, and the outer area where the artisans and working men made their homes.

What marks out Kot Diji is the advanced use — for that era — of mud-brick houses on stone foundations and the sophisticated, well-finished pottery.

Although different in form and technique from that of Moenjodaro, many patterns on Moenjodaro pottery clearly evolved from the distinctive Kot Diji themes of horizontal and wavy lines, loops, and simple triangular patterns.

Khaipur, twenty-two kilometres (14 miles) beyond Kot Diji, is distinguished by the fine **tombs** of the Talpur Amirs of which that of Mir Karam Ali Khan Talpur, built in 1812, square and decorated with marble fretwork and coloured tiles, is an outstanding example. The town was once the capital of a small princedom ruled by a member of the Talpur family.

Not far beyond this town is **Rohri**, where

you cross the Indus to Sukkur, once an important centre for holy men of learning. Its principle feature is a **mosque** built by one of Akbar's officers in 1583 which is decorated with porcelain tiles.

Eight kilometres (five miles) east of Rohri, on the edge of a low, limestone range, lie the ruins of the ancient city of **Aror** or **Alor**, though there is little to see.

When Alexander the Great marched down the Indus he was told that it was the "Capital of Musicians . . . the most prosperous town in all India". It was here that he and his men paused to renew their strength, fortifying and garrisoning the citadel before resuming their ill-fated journey home.

Later it was a Hindu town until captured by Muhammad bin Qasim in his great conquest of AD 712.

Then the Indus flowed directly beneath its fortress, but around the tenth century this great river changed its course — more or less to the one it still follows.

When the British, marching to do battle in the First Afghan War, arrived at the Indus they crossed on a bridge of boats just as Alexander had done.

Now the visitor crosses the **Sukkur Barrage** north of which lies a large island, bursting with fields of vegetables — one of Karachi's major market gardens.

The first barrage built to exploit the waters of the Indus, it was conceived in 1847. But it was not until 1923 that the plans were finally approved — and work was not completed until 1932. It's an ideal location, for the Indus at this point runs through a fairly narrow limestone gorge.

Boats now cluster against the **quayside** at Sukkur in the lake that formed behind the barrage. A veritable holy city, it is well-endowed with the mausolea of saints. Two on one of the islands in the Indus are notable for their exceptional blue tile work using non-traditional patterns.

Another in the city has a twenty-seven metre-high (90-feet) **tower** from which you can survey the entire town, a long stretch of the river, and the islands and the barrage.

From Sukkur you can follow the west bank of the Indus to **Dera Ghazi Khan,** through **Kashmor,** 110 kilometres (69 miles) from Shikarpur on the Sind-Punjab border. Commonly known as D G Khan, it's another newish town. The original town was destroyed

by an Indus flood in 1911 and was rebuilt fifteen kilometres (nine miles) back from the river bank.

It's noted for the quality of its rope-weaving, lacquer work, and palm-leaf products. It also has an exceptionally beautiful **shrine** whereby hangs a tale, for almost every community along the the Indus valley demonstrated its importance by establishing a *sufi* shrine.

Unfortunately, D G Khan could claim no bonafide *sufi*. So the town fathers simply elevated the town's sixteenth-century founder, Ghazi Khan, to the role of saint.

More recently, in the second half of the last century, D G Khan was associated with Sir Robert Sandeman, who was appointed to the district in 1866, before becoming the Baluchistan political agent.

North from D G Khan, 210 kilometres (130 miles) along the west bank of the Indus is **Dera Ismail Khan.** Alternatively, you can cross the Indus river, and travel for sixty kilometres (37 miles) through a narrow strip of the Thar desert, to **Muzaffargarh**.

Above: Tourist enjoys an adventure safari by camel through the deserts of Sind.

Trekking in Pakistan

Naltar-Pakhor

A ten-day trek only feasible between June and September.

FIRST DAY: Travel by jeep from **Gilgit**, following the **Hunza River** to its confluence with the **Naltar River**, where you turn west to **Naltar** — a forested hill resort with abundant wildlife and good trout fishing.

You can camp outside the village beneath the pine-forested hillside with a sublime view of **Rakaposhi** on the other side of the valley.

SECOND DAY: This is an easy and pleasant walk through thick pine forest and grass-covered slopes to **Naltar Lake** along the side of the trout-filled **Naltar River**. Walking time is between four and five hours.

THIRD DAY: A tough and challenging but not too difficult climb of several hours to **Lower Shani,** partly over the **Naltar glacier.** You can camp just above the glacier with stunning views of some of the tallest peaks in the **Hindu Kush** dominating the distant horizon.

FOURTH DAY: Two hours climbing along a steep trail brings you to **Upper Shani** at the foot of 4,724-metre-high (15,500-feet) **Naltar Pass,** a superb place to camp — beneath magnificent **Naltar Peak** and the head of the Naltar Glacier with ibex on the slopes of Upper Shani.

FIFTH DAY: From Upper Shani the trail leads over the Naltar Pass to **Koriburt** involving a strenuous climb of 915 metres (3,000 feet) over the pass and then down a rock-strewn precipitous trail to Koriburt. From the top of the pass the great peaks of Rakaposhi, **Nanga Parbat,** and **Diamani** stand out in sharp relief.

SIXTH DAY: This takes you down from Koriburt to **Pakhor** in the **Ishkoman Valley,** and the road back to Gilgit.

Naltar-Baltar

This is an extension of the Naltar-Pakhor Trek from the Sixth Day when you make a steep 900-1,000-metre-climb (3,000-3,300 feet) over the 4,755-metre-high (15,600-feet) **Dianter Pass** to a delightful meadow where you camp.

SEVENTH DAY: A long hard slog at high-altitude including some tricky sections along the **Baltar**

Glacier where you camp.

EIGHTH DAY: Continue along the glacier and the side of it to **Baltoro Camp,** an ideal spot to spend a day of rest enjoying your alpine surroundings — a truly unspoilt wilderness surrounded by some of the world's greatest glaciers and rare wildlife including ibex and bears and colourful birdlife.

NINTH-TENTH DAY: More strenuous high-altitude trekking through dramatic and rugged mountain grandeur, camping at various places.

ELEVENTH DAY: Descend to **Bar Village** and the return to Gilgit.

Barpu

FIRST DAY: By jeep from **Gilgit** along the **Hunza-Nagar Valley,** skirting the base of **Rakaposhi,** to **Nagar**—a road journey of about four hours.

SECOND DAY: From Nagar the rugged trail climbs over the **Kapel Glacier** to the lovely meadowlands at **Shishkan** — which means "Summer Pastures" — and is encircled by the Rakaposhi massif on one side and the dramatic 6,705-metre-high (22,000 feet) spire of **Ultar** on the other.

THIRD-FOURTH DAYS: Tough walking at high altitudes to 4,570-metre-high (15,000-feet) **Rushpari,** the highest point of the trek, where you camp beside **Lake Rush** which sits in an amphitheatre dominated by the magnificent 7,452 metres (24,451 feet) heights of **Malubiting,** 7,000-metre-high (23,000-feet) **Golden Peak,** and 6,095-metre-high (20,000-feet) **Mount Rush,** and many more still unknown to the outside world.

FIFTH DAY: The trail winds down through stands of forest and grassy trails to **Chokotans** above the **Barpu Glacier** where you camp in a lovely meadow.

SIXTH DAY: Now the trail winds down the glacier, rugged and dramatic, and you camp alongside it.

SEVENTH DAY: More rugged walking along the glacier with another overnight camp.

EIGHTH DAY: One more final leg to the snout of the glacier and down through forests and meadows back to Nagar for another overnight stop before the return to Gilgit.

From Nagar this trek can take anything from eight to twelve days. The best time to make it is between mid-June and mid-September.

Opposite: Trekkers study route in northern Pakistan mountains.

Batura

FIRST DAY: Drive from **Gulmit Village** to the snout of fifty-eight-kilometre-long (36-mile) **Batura Glacier** where you start the rugged climb from the 8,030-metre-high (2,4776-feet) snout of the ice-flow to **Batura** base camp.

SECOND-THIRD DAYS: Rugged climbing, all above 4,300 metres (14,000 feet), in daunting landscape with beautiful panoramas camping overnight alongside the glacier.

FOURTH DAY: Tough walking up to the base camp which is encircled by the stunning amphitheatre of the Batura massif, surpassed only by that of Concordia its neighbour and the Annapurna and Dhaulagiri massifs of Nepal, and its many dramatic peaks including three of the world's forty highest peaks.

FIFTH-SIXTH DAYS: Begin the descent, camping overnight in lovely alpine meadows.

SEVENTH DAY: Descend to the snout of the glacier for the return to Gulmit.

The best time to make this trek is between mid-June and mid-September.

Baltoro Trek

An unbelievable trek along perhaps the most dramatic and rugged of all the world's glaciers, the **Baltoro**, which runs for almost sixty kilometres (36 miles) and, fed by some thirty tributaries, covers an area of 1,220 square kilometres (470 square miles).

FIRST DAY: Leave Skardu for the kick-off point at **Dassu**, travelling by jeep and tractor through the beautiful **Shigar Valley** along the **Braldo River** to camp at **Dassu village**, 2,400 metres (8,000 feet).

SECOND DAY: Rugged walking along rock-strewn trails above the foaming river through the precipitous Braldo gorge, dominated by soaring and magnificent peaks, to **Chakpu village,** a distance of less than fifteen kilometres (nine miles) which nonetheless takes between six and eight hours to cover.

Though the trail is fairly level there's no escaping the furnace heat of summer reflecting off the rock. Nor is there any drinking water -- the river is inaccessible.

THIRD DAY: From Chakpu the trail climbs more than 600 metres (2,000 feet) to **Chongo village** along a sheer and perilous switchback trail, with many sheer drops, in relentless heat. When you reach the apex you descend to the same level at which you started. Walking time is between six and eight hours.

FOURTH DAY: This is an easier walk of roughly three hours, through enchanting terraced orchards of apricot and mulberry, to what is said to be the nation's most remote village, **Askole** with revealing glimpses of traditional Balti life. There are some interesting hot springs halfway along the trail.

FIFTH DAY: Leaving Askole the trail now begins to climb towards the Roof of the World, crossing some glaciers, into a dramatic wilderness composed of contradictory desert, foaming rivers, melting glaciers, and some of the world's highest mountains.

The climb is gradual enough to be comfortable and the tree-shaded campsite at **Korofang,** alongside the fifty-nine-kilometre-long (37-mile) **Biafo Glacier,** is pleasantly cool with crystal-clear spring water.

SIXTH DAY: An extremely strenuous climb of eight to ten hours, along steep and winding trails, crossing many rushing streams, to **Bardumal** where you camp overnight. This depends, however, if the swaying **rope suspension bridge,** is in good repair — otherwise count on another two- to three-day detour over the **Darmundu Glacier.**

SEVENTH DAY: From Bardumal you climb several hundred metres on a fairly even trail to **Paiju,** at 3,200 metres (10,500 feet), beneath the 3,530-metre-high (11,580-feet) snout of the **Baltoro Glacier.** It's an idyllic overnight camp — served by icy spring water, in a meadow filled with wild flowers.

EIGHTH DAY: From Paiju you climb up to the snout of the glacier, later crossing from one side to the other, to **Liliwa** where the campsite alongside the glacier provides superb views of **Paiju Peak** and **Trango Towers.** Altogether the climb takes about six hours.

NINTH DAY: From Liliwa it's another strenuous switchback climb to gain several hundred metres along a precipitous trail frequently crossing icemelt glacial streams, foaming and difficult torrents to cross, to **Urdukas** at almost 4,000 metres (13,000 feet).

But, located alongside the glacier, this beautiful campsite provides a breathtaking panorama of Paiju, Trango, and **Baltoro Cathedral,** gothic arches and vaults of rock weathered and shaped by ice, wind, and time.

TENTH DAY: The higher the altitude, the more tiring the trek and crossing the slippery, unstable scree and stone trail from Urdukas to Gore is tiring work lasting about eight hours. The camp is perched on a ledge above the glacier not far from its conjunction with the **Mustagh**

Glacier, and overlooking a spectacular panorama of **Mustagh Tower, Masherbrum,** and **Gasherbrum IV.**

ELEVENTH DAY: From Gore the trek winds around the base of these great mountains along the Baltoro to the threshold of the natural world's greatest amphitheatre — **Concordia** at 4,270 metres (14,000 feet), dominated by the perfect pyramid peak of K2, Broad Peak, and the Gasherbrum Group where individual glaciers flow down to meet in one gigantic glacial slide.

TWELFTH DAY: Either remain to explore this eighth wonder of the world or begin your return journey back along the same route.

Deosai Plain To Nanga Parbat Base Camp Pony Trek

FIRST DAY: Arrive in Skardu to hire ponies and porters and buy supplies and food. You can camp overnight or stay in one of the motels.

SECOND DAY: From Skardu you travel gently on horseback towards the **Deosai Plains** arriving at **Satpara** village, on the banks of **Lake Satpara,** for your overnight camp in a meadow amid alpine wild flowers.

THIRD DAY: The gentle journey continues through the rugged gorge to your next overnight camp at **Kala Pani.**

FOURTH-SIXTH DAYS: The pony trek continues alongside streams and lakes to **Gudai** at the foot of the **Astor Valley.**

SEVENTH DAY: From Gudai you ride through the meadows and pine forests of the valley to the delightful village of Astor.

EIGHTH DAY: You'll need to spend a day in the village to make final preparations at **Astor** before setting off for the arctic tundra of the Deosai Plains where, at more than 4,300 metres (14,000 feet), you will have to be self-sufficient in all your needs.

You can also use this as a base for other treks over the mountain shoulders to Gilgit and to one of the mountain's base camps.

Swat Valley-Gilgit

FIRST DAY: From Matiltan, at the foot of **Batin peak** in the **Ushu valley** you follow the course of the **Ushu river** through thick forest of cedar and pine and fir trees with many magnificent waterfalls to **Palogha,** a distance of ten kilometres (six miles).

SECOND DAY: From Palogha it is another thirteen kilometres (eight miles) climb to 2,900 metres (9,500 feet) to beautiful **Lake Mahodand** — "The Lake of Fish" — where you camp overnight.

THIRD DAY: From the lake you trek through more forests and over grassy meadows to **Doanger** — the junction of two streams at the base of huge granite walls, where you camp in delightful surroundings with distant views of the high peaks, passes, and glaciers of the Hindu Kush.

FOURTH DAY: It's a steady and tiring climb through the alpine forest, now birch, and wild flower meadows, with many enchanting side valleys branching off the Ushu valley, and finally treacherous scree to 3,800 metres (12,600 feet) and your camp at **Talus** by a beautiful mountain tarn.

FIFTH DAY: This is rugged going for many hours climbing virtually 1,000 metres (3,000 feet) to the crest of the **Kachikani Pass** where, once over it, you climb down a glacier to your camp at **Kachikani col.**

SIXTH DAY: From the col you cross extremely rugged terrain with difficult trails to your next campsite at Bashgar col.

SEVENTH DAY: On from Bashgar through barren landscapes and boulder-strewn gorges and sandy river beds to another high-altitude campsite at **Laspur.**

EIGHTH DAY: From Laspur you climb again to the magnificent **Shandur Pass** where you skirt the emerald waters of its scintillating trout-filled tarn and march on to **Langer,** a total distance of fourteen kilometres (nine miles).

NINTH DAY: Another exhilarating but lengthy trek to **Teru Village,** carries you on and down another eighteen kilometres (11 miles).

TENTH DAY: An easy and delightful walk to one of Pakistan's most beautiful alpine resorts, **Phandar lake** where you camp in a lush flower-filled meadow by its shores. You can also fish for trout in the lake if you wish.

ELEVENTH DAY: Travel on to Gilgit by road through the bewitching valleys of **Gupis** and the orchards of **Punial**

Thalley La (Masherbrum Trek)

FIRST DAY: From **Skardu** you drive to the threshold of the beautiful **Shigar Valley,** one of the gateways to the Baltoro Glacier, renowned

Overleaf: Trekkers negotiate glacial moraine in Concordia beneath K2.

for its ancient mosques and fertile apple and apricot orchards, where you camp in a gorgeous setting.

SECOND-FOURTH DAYS: The trail climbs steadily along this, perhaps the most beautiful of all Pakistan's far northern alpine valleys, through beautiful lush, green meadows with heavenly vistas of the Roof of the World, meeting cheerful Balti shepherds and their flocks, to the crest of the 4,850-metre-high (16,000-feet) **Thalley Pass** to camp at **Doghani.**

FIFTH DAY: Descend from Doghani to delightful and ancient **Khaplu village,** renowned for its scenic landscape, beautiful views, fruit orchards, and old forts. It is also a major base from which to start expeditions in the Pamir Knot to the **Siachen Glacier,** and the magnificent **Masherbrum** and **Saltoro** mountain massifs.

SIXTH-TENTH DAYS: From Khaplu you climb again steadily, and tiringly, to the **Masherbrum base camp,** camping overnight at the villages of **Kande** or **Hushe,** where you can study the traditional mountain lifestyles of the Balti people.

ELEVENTH DAY: From Hushe village you climb the **Masherbrum glacier** to the base camp at the foot of the daunting Masherbrum chain, returning to Khaplu village and camping at the same sites.

TWELFTH DAY: By road from Khaplu to Skardu.

Other Treks In Brief

One: Skardu, Khaplu, Haldi, Khani, Hushe, Charaksa Glacier, foot of K7 peak (6,935 metres) and return by the same route.

Two: Skardu, Khaplu, Haldi, Khani, Hushe, Charaksa Glacier, Trinity Glacier, foot of Trinity peak (6,800 metres), Vigne Glacier, Vigne Pass, Baltoro Glacier and return to Skardu, via trek Three, or trek in reverse order.

Three: Skardu, Khaplu, Haldi, Khani, Hushe, Ghando Gore Glacier, Ghando Gore Pass, foot of Blarchendi peak, (6,705 metres), Baltoro Glacier, and back to Skardu, or in reverse order.

Four: Skardu, Khaplu, Haldi, Khani, Hushe, Masherbrum Glacier, foot of Masherbrum peak (7,821 metres), Masherbrum Pass (5,883 metres), Yarmanundo Glacier, Baltoro Glacier and back to Skardu, via trek Three, or in reverse.

Five: Skardu, Khaplu, Haldi, Khan, Hushe, Aling Glacier, foot of double peak (6,400 metres), foot of Hunch peak (6,553 metres), foot of Mitre peak (5,944 metres) and back.

Six: Skardu, Shigar, Bauma, Harel, Thalley pass (4,877 metres), Dubla Khan or Tapsa, Tusserpo Pass (5,084 metres), Dubla Khan, Olmo, Daltir, Tari, Tassa, Mundik, Khaplu, or in reverse.

Seven: Skardu, Shigar, Khutti, Skoro, Dassu, Biano, Chopko, Askole, Skoro Pass (9,573 metres), and back to Skardu or from Askole, foot of Mango Gusar peak (6288 metres), and back to Askole for return to Skardu from either Sicoro Pass or Dassu.

Eight: Skardu, Shigar, Dassu, Askole, KoroPhon, Panmah, Panmah Glacier, Chiring Glacier, Drenmang Glacier, Nobande Sobande Glacier, Skam Pass (5,407 metres), Simgang Glacier Sim Pass (5,833 metres), Choktoi Glacier and return by the same route.

Nine: Skardu, Shigar, Dassu, Askole, Drinsang, Mango, Biafo Glacier, Hispar Pass (5,151 metres), Nagar, Karimabad, Chalt, Gilgit, or in reverse.

Ten: Skardu, Shigar, Dassu, Askole, Drinsang Mango, Biafo Glacier, Simgang Glacier, Snow Lake and back by the same route.

Eleven: Skardu, Shigar, Molto, Chutran, Arandu, Chogolugma Glacier and Glaciers. around foot of Haramosh Peak Number Two (6,217 metres), and back by the same route.

Twelve: Gilgit, Jaglot, Sassi, Shah Balut, Ishkapal Glacier, foot of Haramosh peak (7,406 metres), and back by the same route.

Thirteen: Gilgit, Jaglot, Hanochal, Sassi, Dache, Iskara, Mani Glacier, Baskai Glacier foot of Laila Peak (6,218 metres), foot of Malubiting peak (7,452 metres), Phuparash Glacier and back by the same route.

Fourteen: Gilgit, Dainyor, Bilchar, foot of Dobani peak (6,143 metres), foot of Dirani/Minapin peak (7279 metres), foot of Rakaposhi peak (7,788 metres) and back by the same route.

Fifteen: Gilgit, Dainyor, Rakaposhi peak (7,788 metres) and back by the same route.

Sixteen: Gilgit, Dainyor, Hilt, Hini, Minapin, Minapin Glacier, foot of Minapin peak (7,279 metres) and back by the same route .

Seventeen: Gilgit, Dainyor, Nilt, Hini, Karimabad, Nagar, Hopar Glacier area, trek around Hopar Glacier and back by the same route.

Eighteen: Gilgit, Dainyor, Chalt, Hini,

Karimabad, Nagar, Bultar Glacier, foot of Diran peak (7,279 metres), Barpu Glacier, Miar Glacier up to foot of Miar peak (6,824 metres), foot of Malubiting peak (7,292 metres) and back by the same route.

Nineteen: Gilgit, Nanga Parbat via Bazin Glacier, Mazeno Glacier, Diamir Glacier, Patro Glacier, Rakhiot Glacier, Braldu Glacier and Rupal Valley.

Twenty: Gilgit, Karimabad, Nagar, Hispar, Hispar Glacier, Kunyung Lake Glacier, Pumarikis Glacier, Jutmaru Glacier, Kanibasar Glacier, and back by the same route.

Twenty-one: Gilgit, Passu, Momhil Glacier, Ziarat, Malanghutti Glacier, Shimshal, Yazgil Glacier, Yakshin Garden Glacier, Khorodopin Glacier, and back by the same route.

Twenty-two: Gilgit, Nomal, Naltar, Shingo Bar, Hare Shani, Dianter Pass (4,800 metres), Dianter, Bar, back to Chalt, Dainyor, Gilgit.

Twenty-three: Gilgit, Nomal, Naltar, Shingo Bar Hare Shani, Baj Gaz Pass, Naltar Pass, Chatorkhand, Mayun, Cakuch, Sher Qila, Gilgit.

Twenty-four: Gilgit, Gupis, Jundrot, Astorodami, Teru, Barsat, Shandur Pass, (3,720 metres), Sor Laspur, Mastuji, Chitral or in reverse to Gilgit.

Twenty-five: Chitral, Birmogh Lasht, Utak Pass (4,647 metres), Bashagalian, Rambur, Bumburet and back to Chitral via Ayun or in reverse or trek in Bumburet, Bambir and Rambur Valleys.

Twenty-six: Saidu Sharif (Mingora), Kalamm, Matultan, Palogha Meadow, Kacchi Kahni Pass, Sorlas Pur, Shandur Pass (to Yasin-Gilgit) or from Sorlas Pur to Mastuj-Chitral.

Twenty-seven: Gilgit, Naltar, Naltar Lake, Shoni, Naltar Pass, Koribort, Pakhere, Gilgit.

Twenty-eight: Gilgit, Naltar, Naltar Lake Shoni, Distor Bar, Baltar, Bar village Budalas, Gilgit.

Twenty-nine: Skardu, Khaplu, Machlu, Haldi, Sino, Thang, Lasht, Summer Pasture, Base Camp K6 and return by the same route.

Thirty: Saidu Sharif, Kalam, Matiltan, Baloga, Meadow Briochwood, Kacchi Kani Pass, Bashgar Gol, Laspur Shandur Pass, Teru, Phandar, Gilgit, Naltar, Hunza, Gilgit.

Thirty-one: Skardu, Khaplu, Kande, Hushe Valley, Hushe, Gondokoro Valley, Hushe, Kande, Khaplu, Skardu.

Thirty-two: Skardu, Balaghar, Upper Thale, Barooq, Thale La, Shigar, Skardu.

Thirty-three: Chitral, Maroi, Nol, Barun, South Barun Glacier, North Barun Glacier, foot of Tirich Mir peak (7,708 metres) and back by the same route.

Thirty-four: Chitral, Lasht, Shoghor, Mogh, Hot Spring (Garam Chasma), trek along Shish gol up to Purisht and back by the same route.

Thirty-five: Gilgit, Rampur, Rupal Base Camp trek around South East Face of Nanga Parbat, trek from Rupal Base Camp to Rampur, Gilgit.

Thirty-six: Skardu, Satpara Lake, return to Skardu, Chongo, Askole, below Askole Pass, trek over Askole Pass to Askole village and return by same route.

Thirty-seven: Skardu, Chongo, Askole, Balti villages, Skoro La (Pass), Shigar Meadows, Skardu.

Thirty-eight: Gilgit, Ranikot Bridge, Tato village, Fairy meadows, Base Camp of Nanga Parbat and return.

Thirty-nine: Skardu, Satpara Lake, return to Skardu, Daghoni, Saling, Talis, Khana, Haldi, Thagas, Brokhoor, Lasht, Karmane, Kharkondus (at foot of Sherpig Glacier), trek around Glacier, Kharkondus, Saling, Daghoni, Skardu.

Forty: Skardu, Baltoro, Dassu, Chakpu, Chongo, Askole, Koro, Fang, Bardumal, Plau, Liliwa, Urdukas, Gore, Concordia, Chogolisa, and back to Skardu by the same route.

Forty-one: Gilgit, Yasin, Harpin, Hushk, Shoraling, Thui Ann Pass, Gazin, Dobar, Gar, Lasht, Sost, Ishpro, Shah Jinali, other side of Pass, Shah Gram, Istaro, Chitral.

PART THREE: THE CITIES

Opposite: Imposing entrance to Mughal rose garden, Lahore.
Above: Flagstaff House in Karachi's city centre, once owned by Jinnah and lovingly restored.

Islamabad and Rawalpindi: Twin Cities, Old and New

Islamabad with its "model city" characteristics, is not representative of Pakistan. While Pakistan is an ancient land, Islamabad is a city of the late twentieth century.

Few capitals can claim such a beautiful setting. Nestling against the backdrop of the green, picturesque, and peaceful **Margalla Hills** at the northern end of the **Potwar Plateau,** its northernmost precincts climb up on to the first gentle shoulders.

It was 1959 when the decision was taken to build the nation's new capital on this spot. The first stone was laid two years later. The city's masterplan was conceived by the Athenian architectural practice, Doxiadis Associates; but subsequently several famous town planners and architects, including Edward Durrel Stone, contributed their ideas and skills.

It says much for their combined talents that, despite the incredibly-wide main malls with their stately, tree-lined sidewalks and verdant centre-islands, Islamabad is probably the most faceless and confusing capital of its age.

For while the designers worked out their logical grids on the drawing boards they forgot that a city — especially a capital city — demands both heart and soul: Islamabad has neither.

Virtually every street and precinct looks identical to the first-time visitor; and many who visit it frequently still become hopelessly lost and confused as they endeavour to locate offices and residences. Each precinct is numbered but not sequentially.

Another confusion is that some of the main malls dividing these precincts sometimes have at least three different names.

Thus for any visitor it's essential to buy the street guide published by the Capital Development Authority (CDA).

The decision to build Islamabad was taken by Ayub Khan, President of Pakistan, an Abbottabad man who yearned for the cool hills of his ancestral homelands far north of Karachi which became the capital after Independence in 1947.

Inconveniently distant from most of the country, uncomfortably hot and humid for much of the year, the nation's commercial dynamo was dubbed unsuitable for the business of federal government.

The base of the Margalla Hills on the other hand, near **Murree** and the cool northern hills, was considered ideal. It was close to the boundary of two of Pakistan's four provinces — the Punjab and the North-West Frontier Province — and athwart the nation's main east-west axis, the **Grand Trunk Road.**

Perhaps more importantly, it would form an extension of the old military cantonment of **Rawalpindi**, strategic HQ of the country's Armed Forces.

Still incomplete, the city has developed fast. Yet, despite its many shopping precincts, to all intents and purposes it remains a dormitory — the sleepy neighbour to the scruffy but nonetheless vibrant twenty-four-hour-a-day entrepôt of Rawalpindi.

From a viewpoint on **Shakarparian Hill,** a hundred metres or so above the capital, the suburbs roll away into the dark horizon to merge with Rawalpindi. There is still no visible centre apart from the Federal Parliament, presidency and surrounding infrastructures.

Of industry nothing can be seen at all, despite the inclusion of an industrial precinct on the triangular grid laid out by Doxiadis.

Pakistan's new 1962 constitution confirmed Islamabad as the seat of Federal Government, although Dacca, in the then East Pakistan, remained the seat of the central legislature.

Nine years later, however, with the 1971 war and East Pakistan's secession to become Bangladesh, Islamabad came fully into its own as capital.

Getting there

Islamabad is 1580 kilometres (980 miles) from **Karachi**, on the Grand Trunk Road between **Peshawar** 167 kilometres (103 miles) to the west and Lahore 280 kilometres (175 miles) to the south east. Islamabad International Airport is served daily by many international and domestic flights and there are express trains from major cities throughout Pakistan to **Rawalpindi** railway station.

When to go

Though cold in winter and extremely hot from May to August, both cities can be visited at any time of the year.

Where to stay

Marriott Hotel, Aga Khan Road, as good as any other hotel of the same ilk. Islamabad Hotel,

Civic Centre, just a shade beneath its neighbour, both in quality and price. Ambassador, Khyaban-e-Suhrawardy, economic and as central as anything could be central in a city without a centre.

There are many other cheaper hotels; government and provincial guest houses; and also a campsite near the Rose and Jasmine Garden on the Murree Road. See Listings for "Hotels".

Sightseeing

The best view of Islamabad is from the **Daman-e-koh Viewpoint** on the **Margalla Hills.** There are paths, viewing points, gardens, and picnic areas. You reach it — forty-five minutes by foot or ten minutes by car — from the northern end of **7th Avenue.**

It's possibly the only place where the planner's design and intent becomes apparent. The city, with its rigidly-straight avenues and neat rows of houses, is laid out below. The **Presidential Palace** and **Legislative Assembly,** and the adjoining bureaucracy of the **Secretariat**, Islamabad's equivalent of Capitol Hill or Whitehall, dominate the view to the east, counterpoint to the sublime proportions of the **Shah Faisal Mosque** tucked against the hills in the west.

The emerald waters of **Rawal Lake** glitter in the distance and, in the haze, the dark mass of **Rawalpindi** merges on the horizon with lowering thunderclouds. On a clear day, this horizon extends far beyond Rawalpindi, out over the **Potwar Plateau,** to the ridges of the **Salt Range** beyond.

Above the viewpoint, a road leads to the crest of the first ridge, a walk of between one and two hours.

What passes for a zoological garden — insecure and inadequate — lies beneath the viewpoint, populated by repressed monkeys, one unperforming bear, deer, and some splendid birds. Even though there's no admission charge, it might be as well to give **Islamabad Zoo** a miss.

There's another spectacular panorama from a small hill in the floral and arboreal **Shakarparian Park,** which you reach by turning south at the traffic lights at **Abpara Market,** or by taking the **Shahrah-e-Islamabad,** the main dual carriageway from **Zero Point** toward Rawalpindi and turning left into the park. You then go 500 metres (550 yards) down the jasmine-lined drive to the **Institute of Folk and Traditional Heritage.**

Four or five times a year, the institute stages fresh exhibitions of handicrafts, art, or music and musical instruments from different regions of Pakistan. The institute is also a serious research centre for the study and preservation of the country's traditional arts and cultures.

Leave here and stroll through the gardens, past the museum, and, also on the right, the **Lotus Lake,** so named for the flowers that bloom on its surface during the lotus season. To the left, there's a road to **West Viewpoint** and its rose garden, at the top of a hill, overlooking Rawalpindi. **East Viewpoint,** where the sunken garden is laid out as a map of the capital, overlooks Islamabad.

The park's arboreal splendour has been much enhanced by various indigenous and exotic trees planted by visiting statesmen to commemorate their visit. As you follow the winding paths through the gardens and fountains, you'll see many of them.

Past the emblem of modern Pakistan, a **sculpture** of a star and crescent, a right turn takes you in to the park's famous **Rose and Jasmine Garden,** venue each spring of the capital's flower and rose shows.

Near the park is the capital's magnificent **Olympic Centre,** a gift of the Chinese people to Pakistan. Beyond that is **Rawal Lake,** one of Rawalpindi's main reservoirs, its banks a profusion of flowering shrubs and trees, secluded paths, picnic spots, and gardens. On the dam wall there is a **viewpoint, rest house,** and **snack bar.** There are also boats for hire and fish for catching, but you'll need a permit which is available from a hut near the dam.

Lovely in spring, when the wild tulips bloom and fruit trees blossom, the woods around the lake are an ornithological paradise, habitat of many resident and migrant species.

Islamabad Club, with a riding section (non-members can hire horses to ride around the lake or Shakarparian Park) and an attractive **golf course,** lies to the west. Those riding should hire one of the stable grooms as guide for the three-hour ride around Rawal Lake's fifteen-kilometre-perimeter (ten-mile). To walk takes about four hours.

Overleaf: Majestic Faisal Mosque in foreground, Islamabad's broad avenues spread out beyond.

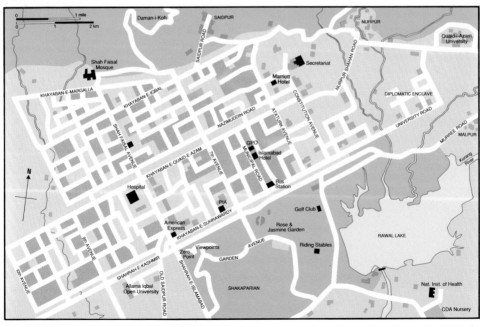

Opposite: Interior of Faisal Mosque. Above: Golden light illuminates Islamabad's Marriott Hotel.

Not far away are **Constitution Avenue** and the **Diplomatic Precinct,** each lined with embassies, displaying fascinating cultural contrasts in architectural form — from Arab Moorish and Chinese pagoda, to British concrete and red-brick Canadian. Imposingly handsome, the **Presidential Palace, Parliament Building,** and **Federal Secretariat** are distinguished by their bold, clean, white lines.

At the base of the Margalla Hills lie the campus and colleges of Islamabad's **Quaid-e-Azam university.**

But all are overshadowed by the soaring, lyrical splendour of the **Shah Faisal Mosque,** its four ninety-metre-high (270-feet) minarets thrusting towards the sky.

Turkish architect Vedat Dalokay drew his inspiration from the octagonal symmetry of the bedouin sheik's desert "tent". The massive main edifice, faced in while marble, is supported on four giant concrete girders.

Opened in 1988, three years behind schedule at a cost of US$50 million, most of it donated by Saudi Arabia, the mosque is said be the biggest in the world. It can accommodate 100,000 worshippers — 10,000 to 15,000 inside the elegant mosque, 85,000 in the courtyard.

Under the marble floor of the main courtyard, the **Islamic Research Centre** — two-stories housing **library, museum, press centre, lecture hall,** cafeteria, and the offices of the **Shariat faculty** of the Islamic University — goes about furthering knowledge and understanding of the Muslim faith.

In total contrast, at the **National Health Laboratories,** on **Lehtar Road,** near Rawal Lake, you can watch skilled handlers milk deadly snakes of their venom for research and anti-snake bite serums. Just pity the poor living prey — rabbits, mice, and guinea pigs — that scurry about in nearby cages, unaware of their grisly fate as a future cobra supper.

You need to give the directorate at least seven days notice of your visit, however.

Excursions from Islamabad

Little more than one kilometre from Islamabad on the Margalla Hills Road, the small village of **Saidpur** testifies to Pakistan's rural heritage.

Predominantly Hindu, in the days of the British Raj, its springs were venerated by villagers and pilgrims alike.

But today it's an ideal starting point for a trek along the base of the hills emerging at the eastern end of the Margalla Hills Road.

Perhaps the most interesting village within the metropolitan area, however, is **Nurpur,** four kilometres (2.5 miles) from the city centre, which contains the shrine of a seventeenth-century saint, **Syed Abdul Latif Shah,** who claimed direct descent from the Prophet Muhammad.

Despite this, religious leaders sent him into exile when he returned from a long journey through the Islamic world and he settled in Nurpur, then infamous as a "Den of Thieves", *Chourpur.*

By his grace and sanctity, however, it became known as the "Place of Light", *Nurpur.* His **shrine** stands under a shady banyan tree in the village centre and shops and kiosks in

225

the narrow lanes leading to it carry on a thriving trade with the many pilgrims who visit it.

Locks of hair, from the sick and the lame seeking a miraculous cure, hang from the branches of the banyan tree and in a small enclosure, fed with wood from a supposedly magic tree, his **eternal flame** burns day and night. Pilgrims anoint their wounds or foreheads with the ashes.

Each spring the village stages a joyous festival in honour of Syed Shah's memory — with a fairground and sideshows and pilgrims, dancing and singing for days on end, and a fairground and sideshows.

On the hillside above the village, easily seen from the top of Islamabad's Constitution Avenue, is another place of pilgrimage, the **Holy Man's cave,** with a white shrine at its base.

Leave Nurpur by the three-kilometre-long (two-mile) **Waterworks Road** to the left of the village where you then climb on foot for about forty-five minutes to the cliff face. The trail leads beneath the base of the cliff. When you reach the holy area where the priest became a hermit for twelve years in order to meditate, you should remove your shoes.

There's a large, dripping six-metre-long (20-feet) stalactite hanging down the cliff beneath the cave, the waters of which are believed to be holy. Pilgrims gather beneath it to catch a drop and drink it.

A path to the right leads over the top of the cliff and then sharply down to the cave's entrance — a tough, if brief, scramble. There is a vertical, narrow slit in the cliff face that cuts in about six metres (20 feet). It's difficult to enter and once in — shoes off — impossible to turn around.

Pilgrims decorate the banyan tree that sprouts at the mouth of the cave with written prayers and requests and hammer coins onto the tree as offerings.

If you continue up the path to the top of the hill you'll be rewarded by splendid views of the capital, Rawal Lake, and the Potwar Plateau.

Probably the best-known shrine close to the capital is that of **Golra Sharif,** some eleven kilometres (seven miles) away at the end of the road under the Margalla Hills — visited annually, it's estimated, by more than a million pilgrims.

It's dedicated to a twentieth-century mystic and religious scholar, Hazrat Mehr Ali Shah, who is said to have had powers as a miracle-maker and sang with a beautiful voice.

Even the poorest of believers can make this pilgrimage for all are given free accommodation and food for one week.

Best of all, perhaps, for residents and visitors alike, are the lovely Margalla Hills, where there are designated nature trails and walkers can observe the sanctuary's wildlife and its many fascinating bird species.

The lower slopes have been reafforested and there is thick scrub between these and the remnant pine forests that straggle along the topmost ridges of the Hills.

Walking is fairly easy, though there are many steep and stony sections and you should beware of snakes — enough reason to keep to the trails.

Many small hamlets and villages nestle in the valleys between the hills. Each has a track to the crest of the nearest ridge.

To the west, the trail starts behind the Shah Faisal Mosque and passes over a ridge into the the next valley and up to Daman-e-Koh Viewpoint.

From the zoo below, there's a three-kilometre (two-mile) circular jeep track that exits on to the viewpoint road.

From the viewpoint you can walk for between ninety minutes and two hours, via **Saidpur village** and the path by the side of the stream to the top of **Lone Tree Hill.** Another trail to this vantage point starts from the corner of **Attaturk Avenue** at the eastern end of the **Margalla Hills Road.**

Another pleasant walk, on the eastern side of the city is to follow the trail that starts at the eastern end of the Margalla Hills Road for roughly 300 metres (330 yards) and then turns left onto a **jeep track** to the old quarry. There's a nice level walk of about one kilometre (half-a-mile) into the ravine before the climb to Lone Tree Hill.

Another alternative is to stroll along the old road link between Nurpur and Saidpur, an eastward extension of the Margalla Hills Road, for about two kilometres (one mile) to a small stream.

Trekking

For serious trekkers, there's a long day's walk along the ridge from **Tret** on the **Murree Road,** with the option of an overnight stay at the **Pharila rest hut.**

Another challenging trek is to cross the

hills to **Taxila**, but the trail is not well marked and you'd be well advised to take along a guide as the scenery looks extraordinarily similar and there are few, if any, landmarks. Remember, too, that even the winter sun is energy-sapping so take along enough water to refresh yourself.

There are many more pleasant excursions to be taken from Islamabad, including one to the 914-metre-high (3,000-feet) forests at **Lehtar** and **Karor**, along the Lehtar road past Rawal Lake and the Islamabad Club.

Four kilometres (two miles) after the Murree crossroad, take the left fork past the unmistakable, mosque-like profile of the **Institute of Nuclear Sciences and Technology** at **Nilore**.

Just beyond the institute, there's a left turn to **Simly Dam** which takes you through scrubland and low brown hills clad with shrubs and succulents for about five kilometres (three miles) until you reach a right fork over a bridge which leads to the dam. From the dam to Karor is another nineteen kilometres (12 miles).

Take the road to the right of the dam to the top of the hill, where there are splendid views of the **Murree Hills** and **Murree town.** Soon after this, at a break in the trees, you come to a clearing that makes a perfect **picnic spot** — with stunning vistas of the snowclad peaks of the **Pir Panjal** mountains to the right.

Just before Karor, opposite the dispensary, a path leads down the valley on the right to a smart **Forestry Department rest house,** a good place to base yourself for walks in the forests — which are perfect for young and old as they are neither too steep nor too difficult.

Many of the trees carry scorch marks from the regular fires the villagers set to stimulate the growth of grass. The trees are also scored with deep incisions where the local folk have tapped the resin, used in the production of turpentine.

From Karor there's a new road to Murree. It's also little more than three kilometres (two miles) across a bridge over the **Soan river,** to **Lehtar.**

From the bridge there's an enjoyable five-kilometre-long (three-mile) walk to the south, through the river gorge to the ruined walls and gates of the thirteenth-century **Pharwala Fort** — strategic stronghold of the Punjabi Ghakkars, which Babur, the first of the Mughals, attacked and conquered in 1519.

The Ghakkars became trusted allies of Babur and his successors and were left to rule in peace — a trust that was rewarded when the Ghakkar chief Adam Khan aided Babur's son, Humayun, by capturing his treacherous brother, Kamran after he made a bid to take over the throne.

When the long-suffering Humayun visited Pharwala he struck out Kamran's eyes and sent him into exile in Mecca to seek atonement.

There's now a village inside the ruined walls and elders welcome visitors warmly with cups of tea and then take them on a guided tour, which includes a trip to the **gate** over the river where prisoners and enemies were executed.

There and back, the walk from the **Soan bridge** takes between four and five hours.

If you continue from the bridge you climb an uneven road to a narrow pass that leads down to the stony **Lehtar valley** and on to **Lehtar village,** forty-five kilometres (28 miles) from Islamabad, where there is another Forestry Department **rest house.**

Now the way winds through pine forest for about five kilometres (three miles), crossing a small bridge over a stream with many pleasant rock pools where you can swim or paddle. To the left is a Forestry Department **nursery.**

Later, along a ridge, you come to a scenic view of the **Jhelum river** and its valley.

There's another sixty-minute excursion to **Kahuta** from **Zero Point** past the airport on the road to Lahore and turning left about twenty kilometres (12 miles) later, soon after crossing the Soan river at the signpost inscribed **Sihala Police College.**

Then right over the **Ling river** and railway line for eleven kilometres (seven miles), past another path to Pharwala Fort and down a right-hand fork to Kahuta.

Turn left in the town centre and then bear left again at a fork in the road. After travelling about 200 metres (220 yards) through a wooded valley and over a ridge you come to the **Jhelum river** where the **Akbar bridge** leads across to **Azad Kashmir.**

There's another road straight through Kahuta to the Jhelum that crosses a bridge at **Salgran** further south. The road is surfaced but subject to subsidence.

Yet another excursion, preferably in a short-based 4WD vehicle, is the drive along the crest of the Margalla Hills in the direction of Murree. The trip takes you through cool forests, with many excellent picnic spots and splendid views. You may also see monkey, wild boar, and deer — possibly, if exceptionally lucky, leopard.

You follow the Daman-e-Koh Viewpoint road to the ridge of the hills; then turn east, keeping to the ridge route wherever the road forks until, after eight kilometres (five miles) you come to the **CDA Horticultural Department rest house** with its lovely gardens marked by paths, steps, and seats on the right, near a barrier. There are fine views to the north of the capital.

Some twenty kilometres (12 miles) along the ridge, at **Pharila**, there's another CDA rest hut to the left of the road. The road then takes some loose — and hair-raising — unguarded hairpin bends until it forks right along the Murree road.

There is another day-trip of 157 kilometres (97 miles) from **Ghora Gali** on the Murree road over the hills beyond **Taxila** to **Haripur** or **Khanpur** and back to Islamabad, through fertile valleys and forest and over verdant hills with many splendid picnic spots.

At Ghora Gali there's a dirt road, left, sixteen kilometres (ten miles) to **Lora**, where you continue another six kilometres (four miles) to **Gambir**. The road then winds twenty-six kilometres (16 miles) through forest and down a valley to a T-junction where you turn left for Khanpur twenty-nine kilometres (18 miles) on, in the Taxila valley.

There's a shorter, six-kilometre-long (four-mile) drive, however, along the right turn to Haripur that joins the **Abbottabad-Hasan Abdal** road five kilometres (three miles) to the north of the town, at a tree bearing the small blue sign, "Chatri Dam".

Pleasant winter excursions can also be made from Islamabad, including one to **Fatehjang** and **Campbellpur**, named after Sir Colin Campbell, the Scottish general who led the relief of Lucknow during the Indian Mutiny. It was formerly called **Hamalpur**, in honour of a Syed saint buried there.

Take the Grand Trunk Road to Peshawar and after seventeen kilometres (ten miles), just before a level crossing, turn left for Fatehjang, forty-six kilometres (29 miles) from Islamabad. From there you drive to the centre of **Kohat** where you negotiate a roundabout to the Campbellpur road.

Fork left over the railway and through a range of low hills to some pleasant open farmland ringed by hills. There's little of interest at Campbellpur, which is eighty kilometres (50 miles) from Islamabad, so don't dally but continue another five kilometres (three miles) beyond the town to a factory, where you fork right back to the Grand Trunk Road. The round trip totals 176 kilometres (110 miles).

However, a much longer alternative along the road south-west out of Campbellpur over the **Harro river** runs from **Nathiagali** towards its nearby confluence with the Indus and up into the **Kala Chitta Hills.**

These constitute the western extremity of the Margalla range and the dramatic rocks and crags provide fine views south over the plains and towards **Attock** in the north.

These hills are the last barrier to the rampaging flow of the Indus which, not far north, veers westward to find its way ultimately to the Arabian Sea.

After Campbellpur, turn right to **Nara**, where you can walk six kilometres (four miles) across the fields to the last of the Indus gorges — spectacular enough to be worth the effort.

From Nara take the road through **Basal** to the **Kohat-Fatehjang** road and turn left for Islamabad. The total distance is 240 kilometres (150 miles).

At Fatehjang, on the way back, you can make a side excursion to **Tanaza Dam** and its artificial lake with a terrace, picnic benches, a leaky punt and fishing, by turning south along the **Khaur road.**

Travel along this road for about sixteen kilometres (ten miles) with an isolated ridge to your left and then follow a dirt track, left, opposite a signboard on the right marking another lake. After about eight kilometres (five miles), travelling along the north side of this ridge, past a government farm, you turn right to the dam.

Misriot Dam, eleven kilometres (seven miles) south of Rawalpindi on the **Dhamial road,** is another winter picnic spot that's only about half an hour's drive from Rawalpindi's **Pearl Continental Hotel.**

Turn left on to the **Chatri Road** at the end of **Tameezuddin (church) Road** and then follow the Fauji Cereal signs along the left fork for **Dhamial.** The dam, about five kilometres (three miles) beyond Dhamial, on the right, has shady gardens with paved paths and steps up to the top of the dam where there are rowing boats for hire.

Rawalpindi: The Garrison City

Believed to have been founded between the fifteenth and sixteenth centuries, **Rawalpindi** only came into eminence in the middle of the nineteenth century when the British established a large military garrison in the town.

Today the city's sole claim to distinction is as the headquarters of the Pakistan Armed Forces. The wide, well laid-out malls of the garrison area, with its well-kept lawns and flower beds contrast dramatically with the incredible untidiness, dirt, and frenetic entrepreneurial pace of the downtown sector.

Though in a state of instant collapse, 'Pindi's main thoroughfare and its bazaars reflect a vibrancy and pace completely at odds with its somnambulant modern twin, Islamabad.

History, or myth, fancies that a Ghakkar tribal chief, one Rawal — Rawalpindi means the "village of Rawal" — settled here; or that it stands on the site of a former village named after the Rawals, a group of yogis.

There's another theory that the first people to live here were a community of snake worshippers called Takkas, who are also said to have founded Taxila.

One thing is certain — the British in their haste to build a cantonment destroyed some of the only evidence available about 'Pindi's origins: ancient ruins which they razed may well have been the remains of the city of Gajipur, capital of the Bhattis.

The British demolished, too, a massive Buddhist *stupa*, that could also have cast light on the city's ancestry — to provide building material for Rawalpindi gaol.

What is definite is that the city stood astride the chosen route of the Mughal dynasty's Imperial Highway — the Shahi Road — between Kabul and Delhi and when it was built in the early sixteenth century Rawalpindi was at least on the map.

An assiduous chronicler, Jahangir the Mughal emperor, who often hunted on the Punjab plains around the town, recorded after one such sortie that he was told by the townsfolk of a giant crocodile that lived in a deep pool. This so fascinated the Mughal that he ordered his aides to throw in one sheep and a man — no doubt hoping the saurian would leave its lair and gobble them up. To his disappointment, the sheep and the man scrambled out untouched and he never did see the monster.

The Sikh leader, Milka Singh Thepuria, took Rawalpindi in 1765, soon after the Ghakkar Mukarrab Khan, had fallen. He realised at once the strategic significance of the town and made it his headquarters, fortifying and strengthening its defences.

His son succeeded him but when he died in 1814, the city and the family's large estates outside, were claimed by the Sikh leader Ranjit Singh, who ruled Punjab from Lahore.

It was on the plains near Rawalpindi in 1849 that the Sikh armies formally surrendered to the British.

Like Milka Singh Thepuria, the British, too, recognised its strategic significance and the destiny of what would become one of the largest military garrisons on the subcontinent was sealed.

At Independence, Rawalpindi became the Pakistan Army headquarters and some years later **Chaklala**, the air force base on the outskirts of the city, became the Pakistan Air Force headquarters. The city also served, for a short while, as the temporary capital when Islamabad was being built.

Getting there

Rawalpindi stands on the Grand Trunk Road between **Peshawar** -- 173 kilometres (108 miles) to the west and **Lahore**, which is 280 kilometres (175 miles) away to the south-east. It shares Islamabad international airport with its twin (the airport, in fact, is much closer to Rawalpindi) and is an important railway centre, with daily expresses arriving from all parts of the country.

Where to Stay

Pearl Continental, The Mall, at times, not all that it should be despite its elegant new exterior and remodelled interior. Shalimar Hotel, half the price and just as comfortable even if the colour scheme is a wee bit drab. Flashman's Hotel, The Mall, enough to have accommodated the Governor-General and his retinue in the style to which they must have been accustomed, now gone to seed but on the last look about to be rebuilt completely.

There are many more. See Listings for "Hotels".

Sightseeing

There are few visible landmarks in Rawalpindi's "old town" and in the labyrinth of alleys and

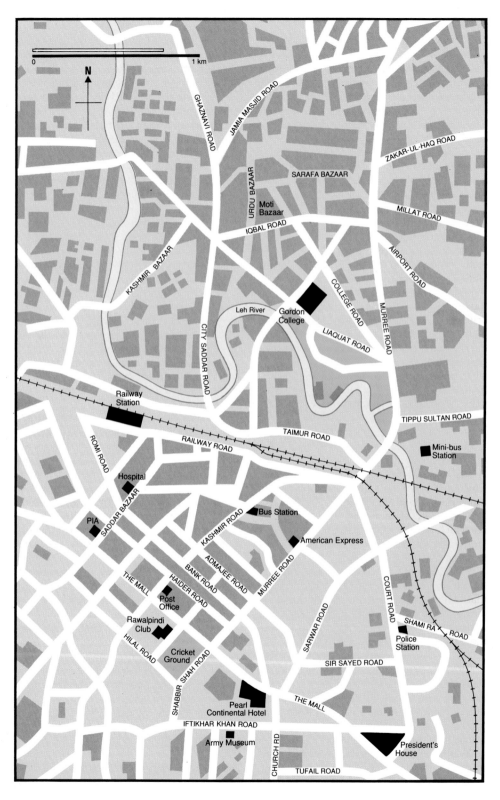

0   1 km

N

GHAZNAVI ROAD

JAMIA MASJID ROAD

ZAKAR-UL-HAQ ROAD

URDU BAZAAR

SARAFA BAZAAR

MILLAT ROAD

Moti Bazaar

IQBAL ROAD

AIRPORT ROAD

KASHMIR BAZAAR

CITY SADDAR ROAD

Leh River

Gordon College

COLLEGE ROAD

MURREE ROAD

LIAQUAT ROAD

Railway Station

TIPPU SULTAN ROAD

RAILWAY ROAD

TAIMUR ROAD

ROMI ROAD

Mini-bus Station

Hospital

SADDAR BAZAAR

PIA

KASHMIR ROAD

Bus Station

American Express

ADMAJEE ROAD

MURREE ROAD

THE MALL

BANK ROAD

HAIDER ROAD

Post Office

COURT ROAD

SHAMI RA ROAD

Rawalpindi Club

SARWAR ROAD

Police Station

HILAL ROAD

Cricket Ground

SHABBIR SHAH ROAD

SIR SAYED ROAD

Pearl Continental Hotel

THE MALL

IFTIKHAR KHAN ROAD

Army Museum

CHURCH RD

President's House

TUFAIL ROAD

230

bazaars it's easy to become hopelessly confused. The garrison area, however, is laid out in handsome style with broad, open spaces and its central feature, **The Mall,** is a distinctive and unmistakable landmark.

Immediately you cross the bridge over the **Leh River,** the divide between the old and new city, you reach the intersection of **Murree Road** with the Mall. For some, so pervading is the nostalgic ambience of the days of the British Raj, it's like entering a time warp. All that's missing is Gunga Din and Kipling's own platoon of Hussars.

The Gothic-style church on the corner of the intersection adds to the illusion. So does your first glimpse of the once-gracious **Flashman's Hotel,** colonial baroque gone to seed, on your right as you drive along the Mall.

Not far away, hidden from view, is **Rawalpindi Club,** another reminiscence of British empirical ambition with, close by, even more so, the **cricket** and **polo grounds;** and the inevitable **racecourse,** all still in use.

If the British left nothing else of worth, they left their sports: and their former bond subjects have become more skilled and adept at these than the original innovators and practitioners. Few can beat Pakistan at squash, hockey or cricket.

Nostalgia is on the rampage all the way down the Mall, taking extravagant shape, just behind the **Pearl Continental,** in **Christ Church,** the main garrison place of worship. Built in 1854 and renovated in 1879, it is all lofty vaults, dark beams, and whitewash walls, on which plaque after plaque honours the long forgotten dead who served Victoria and her successors.

They lie in the **Christian Cemetery,** off Harley Street, row upon row of gravestones that mark the unremembered and untended mortal remains of these expatriates — soldiers, officers, businessmen, women, and children; the faded, chiselled tombstone inscriptions now undecipherable.

The residential area around the church also echoes with nostalgia — houses that reflect the nineteenth-century, neo-colonial Anglo-Indian architecture that developed out of a combination of isolation from the mother country and climate.

Many of the bungalows drew their inspiration from early colonial experiences in Bengal — the word bungalow, in fact, means

"Bengal-style house". They were built with windows set high in the exterior walls, broad and shady verandahs and high-ceiling interiors — pragmatic defence against Rawalpindi's long and sweltering summers, when temperatures rise to 50°C (122°F), long before there were air-conditioners.

Stained with the patina of neglect, their better days have clearly ended, though the spacious compounds and gardens in which they stand are time-serving reminders of the gracious lives their occupants enjoyed.

It's not far from here — at the Pakistan Army's **Military Museum** — that rampant nostalgia finally busts a gut. Displayed in profusion are souvenirs and relics that reflect the subcontinent's centuries of martial history, particularly the period when the British Indian Army established the antecedents out of which the present Pakistan and Indian armies grew.

Among its coveted exhibits is the first **Victoria Cross** awarded to an Indian soldier, Subedar Khudadad Khan, for his courage on a Flanders battlefield in October 1914.

The Museum also has on display the **uniform** of Field Marshal Sir Claude Auchinleck, last British C.-in-C. in India before Independence.

South-east along the Mall stands the **State Bank of Pakistan,** the walled surroundings of the **Presidential residence** and the **city prison.**

Not far beyond is **Ayub Park,** to the left, with tree-lined avenues, golf course, walks, children's playgrounds, and artificial lakes; fine for picnics and strolling. It also houses a sports stadium.

Rawalpindi's colourful bazaars are well worth exploring but finding your way around is unbelievably difficult. The only available street map has different names to those actually on the streets.

Curios

No doubt, bazaar *aficionados* will enjoy wandering through Rawalpindi's labyrinthine network of lanes picking up souvenirs and curios. But others, in search of specific items, may find it more fun and less hassle to take along someone who knows the way — and the shop.

However, if you are determined to do it alone, turn right off **Murree Road** into **Liaquat Road** and past **Liaquat Park** on the left, where in October 1951, Liaquat Ali Khan, Pakistan's first Prime Minister, was assassinated during a Muslim League rally. The **Memorial Hall** in the park in his honour is Rawalpindi's main concert venue.

To the right there's a conspicuous mosque, and then, also on the right, is the main street **Bara Bazaar,** known to most as the "smugglers bazaar", notable for the cut price television, video, and transistor wares on offer, as well as cloth, cutlery and crockery.

The **Trunk Bazaar,** where you can buy anything from a backpack to a twelve-piece Queen Elizabeth II round-the-world set of cabin trunks, is on the right at the end of Bara Bazaar.

Off Trunk Bazaar is **Moti Bazaar** for shawls, woollens, perfumes, cosmetics, hair pieces, bracelets, beads and bangles. Close by, to the north, vendors in **Bohr Bazaar,** tout stimulants, relaxants, herbs, patent medicines, and aphrodisiacs.

From the entrance of Bara Bazaar to the roundabout, Liaquat Road is lined with **music shops** offering instruments for sale or bands for hire. Five roads meet at the roundabout, which is surrounded by garish, mammoth movie posters.

Off the roundabout, **City-Saddar Road,** first left, leads to Saddar Bazaar and back to the cantonment.

The fourth road off the dual carriageway is **Raja Bazaar Road,** 'Pindi's place for second-hand clothing. Half way down, on the right, is a wholesale vegetable market and, left, a dried fruit, nuts, and spices market — lined with conical mounds of red chillis, orange turmeric, orange and yellow lentils, and green dried peas.

Turn right at the end of Raja Bazaar into **Kalan Bazaar** — shoes and stockings on the left, cloth, chiffon scarves, hats, hair, beauty oils, and bedspreads on the right — and, left, along a narrow street lined with carved balconies, where vendors sell knives, scissors, and whips, to the **Purana Qila "old fort" Bazaar** and a small **Hindu temple.**

No trace now of the fort but plenty for the romantics: brides shop here for their wedding dresses.

If you follow Kalan Bazaar you'll find **Sarafa Bazaar,** 'Pindi's equivalent of London's Hatton Garden dealing in gold, silver and precious jewellery. You can't miss it because, on the left, there's an old-style British red post-box — Rawalpindi's first.

You'll also find shops selling copper, brass,

tin, aluminium, stainless steel kitchenware, and brass and copper antiques, where you can rummage for treasures.

When shopping in the bazaars, or even in mainstream Pakistan, bargaining and price-haggling is all part of the tradition and you can negotiate the asking price down by anything from ten to twenty-five per cent.

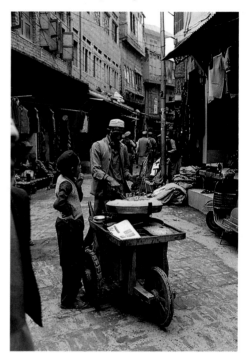

Above: Hot food vendor in the narrow streets of Peshawar's old city.

Peshawar: Fabled City of Bazaars

More than 2,500 years old, **Peshawar** can fairly claim to be not only Pakistan's oldest city but also one of the oldest in the subcontinent — a city within whose walls have echoed some of the most stirring epics of military courage and political intrigue the world has known.

Peshawar is now the capital of the North-West Frontier Province — NWFP. For many it's the most exciting city in Pakistan, perhaps more for its ancient and medieval ambience than actual monuments.

As it began, a frontier town that dominated the path from Asia to India, so it remains — its streets thronged with descendants of the proud Pathan tribesmen who, century after century, repulsed would-be conquerors and emperors through their fatalistic spirit, noble courage — and undeniable faith.

It was in the second century AD that the Kushan kings of Gandhara moved their winter capital from **Pushkalavati**, thirty kilometres (19 miles) south to Peshawar, while maintaining their summer capital at Kapisa, north of Kabul, in Afghanistan.

For more than four centuries, the Kushans ruled their enormous and prosperous empire from these two cities.

Indeed, the most magnificent Buddhist *stupa* that ever graced their empire was built in the second century at **Shah-ji-ki-Dheri,** Peshawar. Now, alas, it is the site of a utilitarian brick factory, but it remained an important pilgrimage centre for Buddhists until the seventh century.

With the decline of Buddhism, Peshawar faded in significance for close on 1,000 years, only regaining its early glory and splendour with the advent of the Mughal Empire under Babur who, in 1530, recognising its historic and strategic value, rebuilt one of its ruined forts. Akbar the Great who followed him then built the Mughal's Imperial Highway from Delhi to Kabul via Peshawar and the Khyber Pass. Peshawar's vitality and importance was assured.

When the Sikhs came to ascendancy, after the decline of the Mughal dynasty, Ranjit Singh captured Peshawar in 1818, razing a great deal of the old city and turned his woodsmen to the destruction of its many trees and gardens to provide fuel.

One of the principle targets were the city's magnificent **Shalimar gardens** and Babur's rebuilt **fort**. Indeed, in just thirty years under Sikh rule, the city's population fell by virtually half.

When the British took the city in 1849 there was no greater enthusiasm for their rule, either, for Peshawar was the headquarters from which the British attempted to bring the recalcitrant Pathan tribes of the north-west under their thumb.

Outside the old city, the British built a garrison town and today the NWFP capital is divided into three — the old city, cantonment, and a modern residential area which includes the university.

The walls of the old city, with sixteen gates, stood until the 1950s. Overlooking its maze of colourful bazaars and alleys is the impressive **Bala Hisar Fort,** built by the Sikhs in 1834.

With its tree-lined malls, imposing administration buildings, and neat parks, the cantonment area echoes loudly of the days of the British Raj. It is now used mainly by the Provincial Government.

The more modern residential area is dominated by **the university** on the **Khyber Pass road**, opposite the **Khyber Hospital**, and **Islamia College**, one kilometre (half-a-mile) beyond.

Getting there

From **Karachi** or **Islamabad**, Peshawar can be reached by air, rail, or by a choice of three roads. The most direct route from Islamabad is the Grand Trunk Road via **Attock** and **Nowshera**, a distance of 173 kilometres (108 miles).

When to go

It is easy to visit Peshawar at any time of the year.

Where to Stay

Pearl Continental, Khyber Road, formerly part of the Inter-Continental. As the Pearl it's a great improvement on the Inter — with the proud claim to the only bar in Pakistan (for non-Muslim foreigners, of course). Dean's, Islamia Road, more echoes of Empire, almost Kiplingesque in ambience, with a marvellous garden. Jan's, Islamia Road, comfortable but no garden or private parking. Green's Hotel, Shahrah-e-Pehlavi. Finally, for more of the

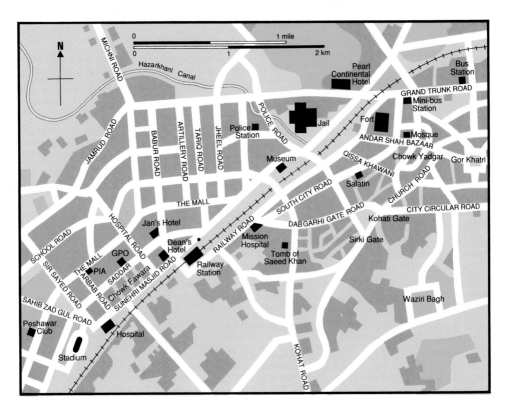

old Raj, the Peshawar Club, The Mall. Limited accommodation.

There are many more hotels in the city of varying and sometimes dubious standards and also guest and rest houses. See Listings for "Hotels".

Sightseeing

The old city shows its age. But much of its detritus is typical of cities only a century old, where western concepts of street-cleaning and refuse cleaning have long been abandoned.

But if some guide books advise you to follow your nose, they're not referring to Peshawar's more odiferous alleys and bazaars but simply using a simile for curiosity. If you do follow your fancy you won't go wrong even if you become hopelessly lost.

It's doubtful if a cartographer could bring any logical order to the city's maze of streets, overhung with "Juliet" balconies, alleys, and bazaars, but it only makes exploration the more fascinating.

Don't explore by car — the streets are inevitably crowded — but on foot or by rickshaw or tonga. Start by crossing the railway line over the **Gaol Bridge,** between the gaol

and the **Park Hotel.** Then turn left at the traffic island into **Khyber Bazaar,** a kind of medical and legal bazaar where doctors, quacks, and herbalists tout their wares, while advocates and kerbside letter writers process the endless papers of the endless litigation processes of Pakistan law.

En route you have to negotiate a "smilefield" of grinning gnashers as you pick your way through row upon row of billboards displaying flashing dentures and real-life specimens on pavements and in kiosks.

At the **traffic lights** just before the Kabul Gate **police station** you can see the remains of the old **Kabul Gate** between a section of the old city walls, while the exterior of **Lady Reading Hospital** is actually constructed from the old walls.

Beyond this spot there is a **crossroads.** Turn left and you plunge into **Qissa Khawani Bazaar,** Peshawar's fabled "Street of Story Tellers", which Sir Herbert Edwardes described as "the Piccadilly of central Asia".

Colourful fruit stalls and sweet shops jostle for space along either side of the street together with wayside barbecues selling a bewildering variety of kebabs, grilled meats, and freshly

Above: Coppersmith "Poor Honest" Ali in Peshawar's copper bazaar.

baked unleavened bread.

The central feature of the tall, narrow buildings that line the bazaar are their wooden shutters and delicately-carved wooden balconies and windows, from which hang the inevitable billboards or neon signs.

For centuries, the leaders of trade caravans and their workers gathered in this bazaar and for payment in kind or cash, would get one of the street's story tellers to recite a tale of love or daring, war or peace. Today it's more of a commercial than literary enterprise.

Turn sharp left at the end of the bazaar and you enter the **Coppersmiths' Bazaar,** where you'll find perhaps Peshawar's most famous entrepreneur, "Poor Honest" Ali, surrounded by letters from the rich and famous, such as Britain's Queen Elizabeth II and America's John Kennedy, Elizabeth Taylor, *et al.* Photographs of him with world personalities beam from every angle.

And, of course, his finely-graven and beaten brass and copperware gleam beckoningly.

Left, after the brass bazaar there's the **Peshawar Pottery** where every day except on Fridays you can watch a craftsman at his potter's wheel.

Back in the "Street of Story Tellers" you first pass through the **woollen bazaar,** stacked with blankets and shawls woven on pitlooms in Swat and Kaghan from handspun wool with vivid borders of woven tapestry; and then you come to the **bird bazaar,** followed by the **fruit bazaar** and shops selling all types of chardars.

Not far from here is the **grain bazaar** where there's a pipal tree, believed to be an offshoot of the tree under which Buddha preached.

On to **Chowk Yadgar** which has traditionally been used for political meetings, Peshawar's version of London's Hyde Park Corner, where the money changers squat on carpets, their safes behind them. Nearby is a **monument** to the Pakistan heroes who fell in the 1965 Indo-Pakistan War.

West of the square is **Andarshah Bazaar,** the **jewellery bazaar** where you can find some fine antique silver pieces, tribal jewellery, military *bric-a-brac* such as old buttons, buckles, and the regimental badges, crests and uniforms of Russian troops in Afghanistan, as well as some not-so-precious gemstones.

There's also Peshawar's last remaining Mughal mosque, the seventeenth-century **Mahabat Khan,** named after the man who twice governed Peshawar under Shah Jahan

Above: Faithful at prayer in Peshawar's Mahabat Khan mosque

and Aurangzeb.

Almost razed by the fire that raged through the Bazaar in June 1898, the mosque was saved, says a contemporary chronicle, only by the "unremitting efforts of the faithful".

During the Sikh era an Italian general serving under Ranjit Singh frequently used its twin minarets as a substitute for the gallows.

Extensively renovated this century, the mosque, nonetheless, remains a fine example of Mughal architecture with a central open courtyard and a prayer hall covered by three fluted domes.

East of the square is **Cunningham Clock Tower,** built to commemorate the diamond jubilee of Queen Victoria but named after Sir George Cunningham, the man who served as political agent in North Waziristan before becoming Governor of the NWFP from 1937 to 1948, serving a full year after Pakistan's Independence.

Nearby is the **Meena Bazaar** for women and, beyond that, a hill lined by houses built of timber and raw brick, considered safer during earthquakes than those built of baked brick. They have elaborately-carved, ornamental wooden doors and balconies.

Mughal gate

The massive **Mughal gate** at the top of the hill leads into the **Gor Khatri,** a Mughal rest house built by Shah Jahan's daughter, with rooms for travellers on all four sides of a huge central courtyard.

It occupies the spot where the second-century Buddhist shrine, the Tower of Buddha's Bowl, once stood. Later the Hindus built a shrine and later still the Mughals erected a mosque. When Ranjit Singh's army conquered Peshawar they destroyed the mosque and built a temple dedicated to Gorakhnath, which stands to the right at one end of the courtyard, beside a shrine dedicated to Nandi.

The Mughal caravanserai was used as administration offices by the Sikhs and is now occupied by a police department.

Retrace your steps to Chowk Yadgar, past a street where vendors sell holsters and bandoleers and follow **Katchery Road** to the Grand Trunk Road.

The British legacy in the subcontinent is clearly visible in Peshawar's garrison town where the British, with their distaste for the crowded, noisy bazaars and narrow alleys of the old city, worked and lived in a green haven from the heat and the dust of the inner city.

Here are the barracks, officers messes, club, churches, and bungalows, that marked the Anglo-Saxon way of life far from home.

Perhaps the most impressive of these was the Victoria Memorial Hall, built in 1905, and now the **Peshawar Museum.** Where a priceless collection of Gandharan art is displayed in the long hall, with its side galleries and raised platform at the end, British officers and soldiers once danced at grand balls with their wives and sweethearts.

There's also a fascinating exhibition illustrating, in chronological order, the life of Buddha; while, in the **Hall of Tribes,** there's an ethnological section; and finally, there's the **Muslim Gallery.**

Next to the **Peshawar Club,** on **Sir Syed Road** near the Mall, stands **St John's Church,** built between 1851 and 1860, the oldest church in Peshawar. The men of the empire and their families who died were buried in the **Christian cemetery** on **Jamrud Road,** where the inscription on one gravestone reads, perhaps somewhat unintentionally:

"Here lies
Captain Ernest Bloomfield
Accidentally shot by his orderly
March 2nd 1879
Well done, good and faithful servant"

The club, where string quartets played on the lawn in the centre of the administration buildings, still functions and its library is full of memorabilia of the days of empire.

Also on the Mall are the last remains of **Khalid Bin Walid Bagh,** once an outstanding Mughal garden, where crowds now gather under ancient trees surrounded by colourful flowers.

Karachi: "The Glory of the East"

Karachi is not yet two centuries old. It was 1839 when a British expeditionary force under Rear Admiral Maitland, aboard the seventy-four-gun flagship HMS Wellesley bombarded the crude fort on the forty-five metre-high (150-feet) bluff called Manora manned by troops of the "Char Yar" — the quadripartite of ruling Mirs of the Sind's Talpur dynasty.

They surrendered at once.

Even then "Kurrachee" was not completely unknown to the British. Forty years before, after hearing that the Talpur Mirs had sought an alliance with the French (and the Afghanistan ruler Zamah Shah) with the intention of expelling the British East India company from the subcontinent, the company had opened a factory on the banks of Layaree and had cultivated a kind of garden. It did not last long. Within a year, the Mirs closed it down, accusing the British manager, Nathan Crow, of spying out the area and analysing the strength of the dynasty's forces.

Before this, the area's history is vague. Ancient mention of a natural harbour that was possibly "Kurrachee" was made by the second century geographer Ptolemy.

Certainly the first recorded mention of "Kurrachee" — or Karachi — was made in the Tuhfat-ul-Kiram, the eighteenth-century chronicle of the Persian conqueror Nadir Shah.

A later history, an account of one of Karachi's leading nineteenth century families, the *"Memoirs of Naomal",* confirms that it was an established trading port.

The author, Seth Naomal, notes that his great-grandfather, Bhojumal, arrived there with his workers in 1729, when it was just a collection of fishing huts, to set up business and make it the seat of his trading empire. He discovered that the village, Kalachi-Jo-Goath, took its name from the head fisherman.

Early on, this trading post came under the guardianship of the Khan of Kalat and became a coveted possession over which there were many disputes.

When the Khan of Khalat finally pulled out his forces in 1795, Mir Fatah Ali Khan on behalf of himself and the three other Sind rulers who ruled Sind and Karachi, immediately marched in his troops and set about building a fortress on the **Manora** headland — a proclamation to all who desired Karachi that he would brook no opposition.

What the British had seized was no jewel to be squabbled over. With a population of around 14,000, Karachi's only value was as a trading port — developed during the forty years or so of rule by the Mirs.

But within weeks of being appointed Governor of Sind in 1843, Sir Charles Napier moved his administration to Karachi and began to put into effect the development that eventually transformed this wasteland of mudflats and mangrove swamps, fishing boats and trading dynasties into a maritime colossus of the twentieth century.

When he left he vowed that one day Karachi would be 'the glory of the East'.

Although Karachi municipality claimed nearly 191 square kilometres (77 square miles) of land, much of it was rock and sand. The town itself was spread over a densely-populated thirteen square kilometres (five square miles) in a roughly-shaped triangle which included many impressive new landmarks — **Merewether Tower, Frere Hall, the Sind Club, Holy Trinity Cathedral, St Andrew's Church, Victoria Museum, Empress Market,** and the **Municipal Offices.**

Burnes Garden had already taken shape between Elphinstone and Kutchery roads. It was here the Duke of Connaught laid the foundation stone for the Victoria Museum which, now rehoused, has become the National Museum of Pakistan.

Iron bandstand

Most impressive, perhaps, was Frere Hall, described as "Venetian-Gothic", rising forty-four metres (144 feet) high with a roof part tile, part corrugated-iron. It was built by public subscription — mostly from overseas — and housed the town's General Library and the Museum, which was later moved to the Victoria Museum.

The Hall, with its two "splendid" public rooms, was formally opened on 10 October 1865; the iron bandstands and formal gardens followed later. Now a library, it stands not far from the Sind Club, which is more imposing and less baroque.

Another landmark was the **Masonic Hall** — now the headquarters of the Sind Wildlife Management Board — the foundation stone of which was laid by Napier in 1845.

The aircraft which touched down in Karachi in 1918 was the first plane, so Karachi's biographers claim, to have landed on the subcontinent. It was on a refuelling stop *en route* to Australia from Europe. Almost at once, displaying rare foresight, the city fathers laid down a landing strip on a scrap of waste ground at **Drigh Road** where the plane landed.

In the late 1930s Sind was established as a separate province, and Karachi, in addition to the **Governor's House,** acquired an **Assembly Building** and a new **Court House.**

Karachi was the natural choice of capital at Independence — although it relinquished that distinction only twelve years later in 1959 when the federal government moved to the new city of Islamabad in the north.

In 1981 the city became so crowded, however, that it literally burst its borders. Overnight the metropolitan area was more than doubled by the authorities, from just over 700 square kilometres (285 square miles) to a massive area of more than 1,800 square kilometres (730 square miles) of concrete and shanty towns, with 7,240 kilometres of ill kept tarmac and only four square kilometres (1.6 square miles) of city parks.

Almost half a century after Mohamed Ali Jinnah's death, Karachi's population was closing on 12 million people.

The fishing township where he was born now accounts for at least eight per cent of the national population, provides jobs for twenty-four per cent of the national work force employed by large-scale industry, claims almost half of the nation's industries, and contributes one quarter of the Federal Exchequer's revenues.

One of the largest sea ports on the Indian Ocean, its docks dominate more than sixteen kilometres (ten miles) of foreshore, much of it marsh and rock reclaimed from the sea, forested with derricks and cranes.

Jinnah's birthplace, well-preserved and maintained, protected by an all-weather coat of battleship grey, floodlit at night, is the focus of Pakistan's national heritage, a shrine for those who found freedom from religious oppression and prejudice as a result of that serious young lawyer's lifelong struggle.

His 684 law books, tomes that speak eloquently of his belief in justice, are carefully preserved along with the **shirts, collars, ties, pince-nez** and the **pin-striped suits** in which he used to appear to present his cases.

Above: Mausoleum of mohamed Ali Jinnah, Karachi

A finely-carved **marble map** of Pakistan dominates this national museum — the visible embodiment of his legacy to 100 million people. Other memorabilia include the furniture which was a wedding present to his wife, his **walking stick, pipes** and a **cigarette case.**

A silver lock and key commemorate his opening of the Bengal Oil Mills in 1948 and there is an illuminated address by the Mysore State Muslim League alongside a glittering badge that denoted membership of the All-India Muslim League.

On the verandah outside, pilgrims look down on the frenzied activity which characterises downtown Karachi and, in particular, **Newnham Street,** and perhaps reflect on the contrast between the atmosphere within the walls of his birthplace and that outside.

Here, the echoes of Karachi's history are loudest amid the noise from the bazaar and the honky-tonk of traffic horns that blare night and day.

Indeed, the vital intensity of life outside Jinnah's birthplace is perhaps symbolic of the energy which freedom released and which characterises Karachi, a polyglot melting pot of cultures and trades and today the subcontinent's third largest city.

Getting there

Karachi has an international airport, a port, a railway, and is connected by the Super Highway, National Highway, and other roads to the rest of the country.

When to go

During the winter months from mid November to February when the day-time temperature is between 15°-20°C (60°-80°F). In the summer the temperature hovers around 35°-45°C (100°-115°F). In the monsoon season, during June, July and August, it is very humid, although there is little rain.

Where to Stay

Sheraton Hotel, Club Road, Avari Towers Ramada Renaissance, Fatima Jinnah Road, Pearl Continental, Dr Ziauddin Ahmed Road, refreshingly uplifted since it shed its Inter image. Mariott Hotel, Abdullah Haroon Road, service to match the comfort. Taj Mahal, Shahrah-e-Faisal Road, adequate.

Five-star hotels that justify the rating. There are many others of varying degrees of comfort and quality. See Listings for "Hotels".

Sightseeing

No traffic disturbs the ambience of the city's many old bazaars — which have survived virtually intact from before the turn of the century. Their alleys and lanes are too narrow to accommodate more than a scooter and are crowded, anyway, with shoppers browsing over an immense variety of offerings. These old bazaars are cetrally located in the heart of the old city.

Spectacularly flamboyant artists tout their skills to advertise the beauty of artificial teeth and the "skills" of the "dental practitioners" like Hu Long, who ply their trade on the kerbside in one bazaar.

The plusher the premises, the higher the dentist's price, of course. But a new plate, plus the removal of molars with cavities, is still so cheap that visitors from the western world gasp with astonishment. The job is done — often with as much skill and care as that of a western dental college graduate — for around five dollars.

Fine filigree craftsmanship is found everywhere in the **gold and silver bazaars.** Chalked notice boards display the daily price of gold by the carat, for even the most delicate and intricate work of the goldsmith's art is sold by weight.

Right and opposite: Luxurious business suite in the splendour of the Karachi Sheraton Hotel and Towers.

KEY
○ HOTELS, HOSTELS, CLUBS
● IMPORTANT BUILDINGS, COLLEGES
◆ SHOPPING CENTRES
▣ POLICE STATIONS
◇ POST OFFICES ▲ HOSPITALS
△ MOSQUES ✝ CHURCHES
▥ PARKS • CINEMAS
SCALE 0   1 MILE

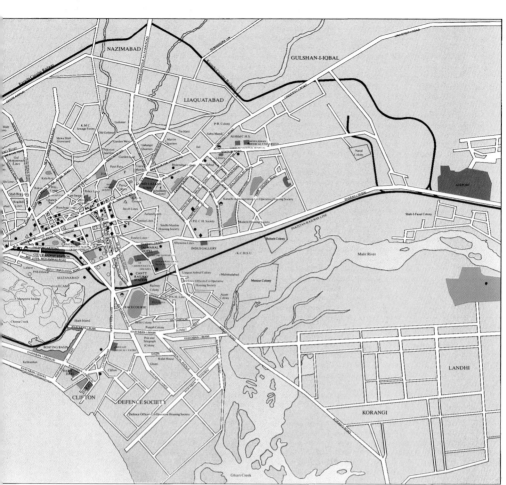

241

Fortunes in rings, pendants, bracelets and necklaces lie within a hand's breadth of the curious, the potential buyer and the light-fingered. Yet rarely is anything snatched or pocketed. Islamic Karachi puts its trust in God.

In the **fruit and spice bazaars** great heaps of polished fruit — oranges, lemons, tangerines, apples, pears, mangoes — are arranged in tidy displays. Almonds, and other nuts, some pre-shelled, and raisins are ranged alongside.

The abandoned shell of the unfinished **Hyatt Regency hotel,** in the heart of downtown Karachi, perhaps symbolises the turmoil that seems to accompany construction in the city. It looks out at three of the city's five-star hotels, none of which should be regarded as any more permanent than the skeleton which gazes upon them. The speculator and the whimsical are constantly reshaping this city.

The one place in Karachi where past, present, and future seem almost tangible, is the Sind Governor's House.

From the lush green lawns which surround it, the past has been preserved with a meticulous sense of propriety and the chronology of change from Imperial acquisition to nationhood is reflected in the portraits on the walls of the reception room.

The Governor's House was an unpremeditated gift to the yet-to-be-born nation. In style and grandeur a testament to the bravura of Empire, it was designed in 1938 and built between 1939 and 1941. Here on 11 September 1948 Jinnah died.

Architecturally, there is little else to commend Karachi except the **Quaid's Mausoleum,** which stands as enduring testimony to Jinnah's dream.

One of the most remarkable migrant enclaves is the **Dobhi Ghat,** a city within a city, which lies on the banks of the **Lyari River.** Sheets flutter like the pennants of an old world Armada of galleons.

Steam and smoke rise from the cement furnaces and boilers where the city's dirty linen is soused and boiled for hours before being flayed, with incredible vigour, against concrete flats.

Great contrast

It provides a great contrast to the old settled communities which live on the islands in **Karachi Harbour,** the oldest society in the city. At low tide these are linked to the **Manora**

Above: One of the crabbing boats that operate from the Boat Basin and take tourists and visitors crabbing in Karachi harbour.

Opposite: Over the centuries, the tide has carved out this rock arch at Prospect Point, near Karachi.

Opposite: Dhow shipyard, Karachi.

Above: Karachi carpet weaver.

Opposite: One of the many berths at Karachi Port which handles almost 20 million tons of cargo a year.

sandspit by marshland.

Population densities reach their highest on **Bhit** and **Baba** islands where the majority of Karachi's inshore fishermen live. Lanes between the stooped, overhanging wood-and-mud single, and two-storey, houses are shoulder-width.

About 5,000 people crowd together in Baba's three square kilometres (1.15 square miles) ruled by a hereditary chief. The only link with the mainland is by ferry — and the electric power which is strung across the harbour from pylon to pylon. It has two **mosques**.

Most of the island menfolk are fishermen or ferrymen. Captain Ali, whose boat like the others bears the logo and motto of one of the world's airlines, takes tourists crabbing just off the main harbour channel where rusting wrecks, top spars visible at low tide, provide an ideal habitat for crabs.

You hire these bunder boats at the Boat Basin at the end of **Mohamed Ali Jinnah Road,** across the **railway bridge,** over the **Napier Mole bridge** and along Napier Road for three kilometres (two miles).

If the moon is up it is lovely to sail further up the sheltered harbour to **Sandspit,** a ten-kilometre-long (six-mile) sandbank that protects the harbour from the open sea, which is one of only nine known marine turtle nesting grounds in the world.

Like the unique Indus Dolphin, which is blind and one of the few fresh water dolphins in the world, the marine turtle is an endangered species. Its flesh, the delight of connoisseur gourmets, makes turtle soup.

Now the beach is a turtle sanctuary. Each turtle that returns, each batch of eggs laid, is meticulously counted by dedicated officers of the Sind Wildlife Management Board's marine turtle conservation programme which is funded by the World Wildlife Fund.

To reach Sandspit by boat takes several hours, but by car from central Karachi, it only takes about thirty minutes along a metalled road that runs the full length of the spit to the lighthouse at **Manora Point** — also the site of an ancient fort.

You can also sail around the harbour. Cranes and masts dominate the wharfs lined with giant ocean-going container and cargo vessels.

The crabbing boats are part of the large registered fleet of inshore and deep-sea fishing smacks and trawlers based in Karachi. Early morning, the **fish harbour** takes on the appearance of a forest of saplings strung together by wires and pennants, thousands of boats moored alongside each other.

Close to the **Port Trust Office,** in the lee of the Napier Bridge, there is another colourful reminder of Karachi's origins. Hundreds of the high-sterned **dhows** which ply the Indian Ocean, moor here with cargoes for and from the Gulf and East African coast.

These craft, which go back more than 2,000 years, are hand-built from stem to stern, from keel to top deck. A sturdy, lofty single mast rises from the centre for the lateen sails which catch the monsoon winds that drive the dhows south and north each season.

Driving west on **II Chundrigar Road** to the corner of Napier Road, on the right is the mid nineteenth-century **Cotton Association building,** followed by the new **Habib Bank Plaza,** the tallest building in Karachi.

Further along on the left is the nineteenth-century, Greek-porticoed, **State Bank of Pakistan,** and beside it is the new State Bank building which houses the best library in Pakistan, not open to the general public.

Merewether Tower, a clock built in 1884 in memory of William Merewether, the British Commissioner of Sind from 1868 to 1877, is at the end of the road.

The forecourts of the **law courts,** close to **City Hall,** are always crowded with desks, chairs and little kiosks, huddles of advocates, petitioners, respondents, plaintiffs, and defendants. It's all grist to the mills of the myriad letter writers who prepare the reams upon reams of court pleas and plaints which daily enter the building.

From the top of the city's highest building, the thirty-three-storey, ninety-nine-metre-high (324-feet) **Habib Bank Plaza,** visitors gaze out across the city sprawl.

In the distance the graceful colonial proportions of the City Hall and some of its old contemporaries, including the 1929 **High Court of Sind** building, the 1923 **Chamber of Commerce,** the State Bank Annexe built in the same year and the splendidly regal proportions of the stately **Cotton Exchange** on which the city's fortunes were established, dance in the shimmering haze.

As the sun sets, a twinkle of distant lights marks out a wispy pleasure ground close to **Clifton Beach,** where an old **PIA 707** serves as a kiddies' playground.

Pakistan has a penchant for displaying its old aviation and armament artefacts and Karachi is no exception. On the road into the city from the Airport, old jets are mounted outside the PAF base while old naval guns stand outside the **Naval Headquarters** near **Karachi Gymkhana.**

Clifton is five kilometres (three miles) south of central Karachi along **Abdullah Haroon (Victoria) Road.**

You cross **Clifton bridge** — its parapet decorated with beautiful blue-glazed tiles — past **Bath Island,** a rich Parsee suburb, on the right until you reach **two modern monuments.** One represents the Pakistani national motto, "Unity, Faith and Discipline", and the other is a war memorial.

But apart from the small recreation area, little distinguishes Clifton, except a massive spread of faceless suburban housing.

There are magnificent sunsets from **Clifton Viewpoint,** a hill about twenty metres (65 feet) high overlooking the whole of Karachi, and there is an **amusement park, aquarium, camel,** and **horse rides** along the beach.

The funfair is halfway down the hill towards the sea with roller-coaster, ferris wheel, bumper cars, and merry-go-rounds.

Between Clifton and mainstream Karachi stands the **tomb of Abdullah Shah Ghazi,** a Muslim Saint. It's an eccentric green and white building, the sidewalk beneath it crowded with importuning beggars, dancing eunuchs, and pedlars offering roasted nuts and tea.

Inland from it, the domed roofs of the decaying **Mohattra Palace,** the house in which the Quaid's sister Fatima lived, stand out above the villas and palatial houses, on the crest of a small rise.

Like **Flagstaff House,** which Jinnah owned, it is the totem pole of the conservationists seeking to preserve the city's few remaining historic buildings. It is a magnificent and distinctive building but since Mohatarama Fatima Jinnah died in 1967 it has been left untenanted and untended and is slowly crumbling away.

Another relic is the **Bristol House Hotel,** not far from Frere Hall, in an enclave distinguished not only by the style but the age of its houses. They all belong to the same historical era as the Palace and Flagstaff House — Victorian. Today they are beautifully maintained consulate homes.

Above: Soapsville Karachi — the laundry enclave.

Grand decay

But now Bristol House's grandeur has gone, replaced by decay. Only one upper floor remains open. The higher levels, directly beneath the dangling form of a broken gargoyle, are shuttered. Birds nest in the ceiling timbers.

It was in Karachi that Sir Sultan Mohammed Shah Aga Khan III, the present Aga Khan's grandfather, was born on 2 November 1877 — just eleven months after the birth of Jinnah.

His home has long since vanished. But among the decaying ruins on the hilltop where it was built you can gaze across Karachi's sprawling suburbs, the spires of the tall Christian churches rising up in harmonic counterpart to the myriad domed mosques. Singularly distinct is the **Parsis Tower of Silence**. Some of Karachi's most illustrious citizens belong to this faith.

Christmas Day is celebrated by Christians at the old sandstone inter-denominational **church of St. Andrew's,** which was built close to the heart of downtown Karachi in 1868, with its forty-five metre-high (147 feet) spire in the Gothic style of the fourteenth century. It stands between Abdullah Haroon (Victoria) Road and Zaibun Nisa (Elphinstone) Street, near the **Empress Market.**

To the east, at the end of Shah-e-Iraq Road are **St Patrick's Roman Catholic Cathedral, school, convent** and **bishop's palace**, all built in the mid-nineteenth century. Carols are led by a joint choir from the St. Andrew's and **Holy Trinity Cathedral,** north of the **Metropole Hotel** on Abdullah Haroon (Victoria) Road.

Built as the garrison church in 1858, it has a short nave and a fifty-metre-high (165-feet) square tower. The organ is the best in Karachi.

Though rebuilt just after the turn of the century, faded sepia picture show that the original stood alone in fields, far from the bustling bazaars of Kharadar and Mithidar, a pillar of the Anglican faith.

But above all, Karachi is a city of Islam, studded with thousands of mosques of which the showpiece is the **Defence Society Mosque,** built in three years, between 1966-69, at a cost of more than four million rupees.

With an interior capacity of around 5,000 and room for another 16,500 on the lawn and the platform, it is always crowded with worshippers on Friday, the city Sabbath, who gather in the shadow of the seventy-two metre-diameter (236-feet) dome beneath the slender seventy-metre-high (230-feet) minaret.

Within this mosque and the countless others throughout the city — new ones seem to rise every week — Karachi and its citizens revitalise themselves, finding spiritual strength and tranquillity.

The **mausoleum** of Mohamed Ali Jinnah, the Quaid-e-Azam, or Father of the Nation, stands on a hill in a park at the east end of **Mohamed Ali Jinnah Road.** Faced with white marble, it has pointed Moorish arches filled with copper grills.

Inside there's a **crystal chandelier** of Chinese origin and a **silver grave railing** round the **cenotaphs** of Jinnah and other members of his family. Three times a day there is a colourful changing of the guard ceremony.

Another legacy of the British era is the large open space which lies within the walled enclosure of the headquarters of the **Karachi Racing Club,** between Clifton and the city centre.

The dirt track was laid out in 1876. More than a century later, dust still rises each week from the long rectangular course as the pounding hooves of Pakistan's finest bloodstock run through a seven- or eight-card New Year's meeting.

But for many millions, the only organised sources of recreation remain **Clifton Beach** and the century-old **Karachi Municipal Zoo,** to the west of Jinnah's mausoleum at the end of Garden Road — a forlorn remnant, little changed, of the Victorian era.

Nothing in the city so evokes the sadness of decadent Empire as this decaying relic. Now the city is planning a safari-park-style open zoo on a hundred hectare-site along University Road.

The city's only **Urdu Theatre** just manages to pay its way through a monotonous diet of cheap farce. Only a handful of people attend any other form of theatre, unlike ancient Lahore where culture is as essential to life as fresh air. Small art studios in Karachi also limp along, barely scraping a living.

Top: Caged lion Karachi Zoo.
Above: Garlanded camel on Clifton beach.

Compared with the wealth and drama of the exhibits in Lahore Museum which recount a national history extending back more than 5,000 years, the paucity of exhibits in the **National Museum** perhaps parallels Karachi's own limited history. The museum, set in a garden off **Dr Zia-ud-din Ahmed Road** is the descendant of the old Victoria and Albert Museum which was opened by the Duke of

Connaught.

It houses a well-displayed collection of Indus civilization **artefacts** from 4,500 years ago, some 1,500-year-old Gandharan **Buddhist stone sculptures,** tenth-century **Hindu sculpture** from Bangladesh, and **Muslim art objects**. But apart from these, and the **ethnological gallery,** there is little else to capture the imagination — just some illustrated manuscripts and a coins room.

A visit to the **Liaquat Memorial Library,** Pakistan's equivalent of the British Museum Library, is even more chastening — save for the kindliness and concern of the staff. All that is classical and modern of Pakistan's national literature is supposed to repose in the withered, drab shelves: but many books are not available.

Excursions From Karachi

Eighteen kilometres (11 miles) north of Karachi hot springs have created two oases at the village of **Manghopir**, where the crocodiles are regarded as sacred. They receive "sacrifices" offered in the name of the thirteenth-century holy man, Pir Mangho, to whom the village is dedicated.

According to folklore, he inadvertently brought the crocodiles with him — in the form of lice in his hair. It is said that when he cut his hair soon after his arrival hot springs began gushing out of the desert, a clump of date trees sprang up to form two oases, and the lice were transformed into crocodiles that slithered into the pool.

And there they are to this day, in a **pool** close by the **sulphur bath houses.**

Unromantic zoologists say that the crocodiles, in fact, were left behind when the **Hub river** changed course. Still, the shrine makes an interesting half-day excursion from Karachi.

For most of the well-to-do, beaches like **Butterfield Cove, Baleji, Paradise Point,** and **Sandspit** to the west of Karachi offer the most convenient and easy-to-reach resorts for day picnics and weekends out of town.

Twenty-five kilometres (16 miles) west along the coast from the Karachi sandspit, **Hawkes Bay** is the most popular beach. A gentle cove surrounded by rocky promontories with soft sands and clear water, even in winter the sun bestows a warmth not found in the city.

Ideal for bathing, wind surfing, and scuba diving, despite its close proximity to Karachi's nuclear power station, the only real hazards at Hawkes Bay are the camel attendants touting for rides and persistent snake charmers.

Picnics are lavish affairs. Keeping a wary eye on restless cobras that are clearly dissatisfied with their tenancy of a lidded basket, you can munch your way through gourmet-style buffets and then roar out to a coral head in an outboard powered dinghy to go scuba diving.

Jelly fish

Swimming is good for most of the year but there is often a swift undertow, so you should only swim in the prescribed areas.

In May and June the waters swarm with painfully-stinging jelly fish and during the July-August monsoon the sea is exceptionally rough and dangerous.

But in September-October the breakers are excellent for surfing. During winter the sea is colder, but still pleasantly warm for those used to the Atlantic. Winter is also the safest time for water sports. The clear waters in this area of the Arabian Sea are one of the best water sports areas on the Asian coast.

Baleji Beach, is even further west beyond Hawkes Bay, a succession of secluded bays with interesting rock pools, shells, and birds. The waves are dramatic, and good for body surfing, but beware of the undertow. Nearby is the nuclear power plant.

The dirt road detours around this for three kilometres to **Paradise Point,** where the waves crash through a natural arch of rock. You can snorkel here from December to March.

About twenty-five kilometres (16 miles) beyond the nuclear power plant is the first lighthouse built on this coast, at **Cape Monze.** There are some attractive, isolated coves nearby and good walks over the ridge.

After that, all that remains if you can get permission is a visit further west along the Makran coast — some forty-eight kilometres (30 miles) into Baluchistan, in fact — to perhaps the oddest spectacle within the vicinity of Karachi.

Remote and once deserted, save for a few fishing villages, **Gaddani Beach** has become one of the world's biggest ship-breaking yards. Almost daily, ocean-going giants are beached on the high tide, cut in half and then dragged forward above the high water mark by tractor and winch.

Lahore: Pearl of the Punjab

It cannot be said for certain that there was a Lahore more than fourteen centuries ago, though strong tradition claims a birth date centuries earlier.

The earliest date that science can give is the sixth century. In May 1959 archaeological "digs" under the old city revealed shards of pottery and various implements which went back that far, but nothing earlier.

Legends abound. Alexander's Bucephalus, for example, founded by the Greek military genius in 324 BC to commemorate his famous horse, has been identified as Lahore. A variant attributes the city's foundation to slaves left behind by Alexander when he turned for home.

One theory, based on local genealogical tables and the great Greek explorer-scientist Ptolemy's reference to the settlement of "Labokla" — which seems to have been one of Lahore's early names — proposes the year AD 145 as the city's birth date. But if it existed then it could only have been as a small village.

A major headache for anyone trying to trace Lahore's pedigree is the unbelievable number and variety of its names. At various times it has been called Parichhitpur, Samand Pal Nagar, Udinagar, and Loharpur.

Indeed, not until near AD 1000 did it begin to be consistently called anything like Lahore, and it rejoiced in no fewer than twenty variations of that name, from El Ahwar to Lahanur and Laharkotta.

While the city's recorded history really begins in 1021 with the arrival of another Muslim conqueror, Mahmud of Ghazni, the Lahore which he conquered was Hindu — in fact the last stronghold in the region of the Hindu Shahi kingdom.

Under Mahmud, Lahore entered upon 150 years of physical, commercial, cultural and military development. Enlarged, it became the official capital of the province and, for several years, capital of the Empire.

Though no visible trace remains, many mosques, mausolea, palaces and gardens must have been built in a city of such pre-eminence. A gap in the records leaves it unclear whether Lahore was continuously the capital thenceforth, but certainly in the reign of Khusrau Shah (1152-1160) it was, and it seems to have retained this eminence to the dynasty's end in 1186.

Then, for nearly 250 years Lahore virtually dropped out of historical sight, except for the depressing frequency with which it was attacked, entered, devastated, and abandoned.

The great Mughal dynasty — founded by Babur after his successful invasion of the Punjab — delivered Lahore from the ruin and desolation of all the preceding centuries.

More, the Mughals set the city on a pedestal so eminent and solid that two subsequent centuries of pillage and destruction could not remove the legacy of architectural and artistic splendour they bequeathed.

Under them the "Pearl of the Punjab" came into her own, became truly a queen among cities, and as the greatest of her writer sons, Abdul Fazal, claimed with pride, "the grand resort of all nations".

Today only parts of the palaces, a few graves, a mausoleum, and a couple of mosques remain — sufficient, however, to show the decline of Mughal architecture which was occurring in these later years.

Gardens, however, remain a delight in this Mughal city of Gardens. Several new ones have been added since Independence — **Jallu, Gulshan-i-Iqbal, Iqbal Park** around the **Minar-i-Pakistan, Model Town Park, Race Course Park,** and others, which deservedly attract not only town-dwellers but visitors from other cities as well. A gigantic **Lahore Park** on **Rainwind Road** is now proposed.

Sports lovers have three stadiums, including the country's biggest, **Qaddafi Stadium,** one of the arenas for the 1987 World Cup Cricket finals, and a Sports Complex in **Allama Iqbal (old Minto) Park.** A **Sports Museum** is being set up in **Olympic House.**

Lahore's annual **Horse and Cattle Show,** of course, is famous. In recent years, the show has become the premier social event of the entire Punjab, anchoring Lahore's 1,000-year-old title as capital of the five-river province.

Endowed with the country's best colleges and schools, the only **National Arts Centre,** and the most museums in the country, it's hardly surprising that this Pearl of the Punjab easily maintains its place as cultural capital of this culturally rich land.

Its museums include the oldest, the **"Lahore",** with its internationally famous exhibits, two Fine Arts Museums (**Shakir Ali** and **Chugatai Trust,** the only ones of their kind in Pakistan), the **Faqir Khana** and the

National Museum of Science.

Lahore had the distinction in December 1957 of hosting the first-ever international Islamic Colloquium and on the same occasion, in the Fort, the only international Exhibition of Islamic Arts ever held.

In 1974 the city hosted the Second Conference of Heads of Islamic States — commemorated the following year by the Summit Minar.

Getting there

Lahore International Airport, with many daily services from **Karachi**, is five kilometres (three miles) from the city centre. It is 280 kilometres (175 miles) from **Islamabad** on the Grand Trunk Road.

It is also connected to Karachi by road and rail. The Indian border is twenty-nine kilometres (18 miles) east of the city. The old Grand Trunk Road provides the only road entry into India.

When to go

It's easy to visit Lahore at any time of the year but it is extremely uncomfortable in the extreme heat that prevails between May and August.

Where to Stay

Avari Rama Renaissance, Shahrah-e-Quaid-e-Azam, The Mall, excellence personified. Pearl Continental, Shahrah-e-Quaid-e-Azam The Mall, another pearl that glistens. Faletti's Hotel, Egerton Road. More and more Jewel in the Crown nostalgia.

There are many other hotels of all prices and qualities. See Listings for "Hotels".

Sightseeing

The supreme architectural monument to Akbar is the brick **Fort** and the city wall with its twelve magnificent gateways. For all its eminence Lahore, before Akbar, was protected by massive and ancient earthworks.

These Akbar levelled, replacing and extending them with the equally massive, but even more daunting, nine-metre-high (30-feet) masonry perimeter that still glowers down on the east side of the Fort, either side of the formidable **Akbari Gate.**

The **Daulat Khan-i-Khas-o-Am, Hall of Private and Public Audience** inside the fort is almost certainly Akbar's. Although very old, enough remains, including traces of gold, to give an idea of its original glory.

The many columns, galleries, and side reception rooms — decorated with frescos and floral motifs in stucco — create an atmosphere of behind the-scenes intimacy that warms the otherwise impersonal and solemn pageantry that attended the Emperors on their way to the **Jharoka,** or **Balcony of State.**

This dignified yet relaxed-looking balcony in white marble projected from the southern side of the building, supported on brackets of red sandstone.

The flat roof above the Daulat Khan-i-Khas-i-Am, with its Mughal **watchtower,** gives a superb view of Jahangir's quadrangle below Although it bears the name of his son, this lovely area too was in fact begun by Akbar.

A curious water tank was built in the Fort at this time. Apparently its floor gave entry to a perfectly dry and beautifully furnished and equipped dining room — another example of the fascination novelties held for the tirelessly energetic mind of this ruler.

A Persian **inscription** over the north and east doors of a beautiful little **mosque** opposite Akbar's gate to the Fort records that this building, the oldest surviving dated mosque in Lahore, was constructed on the orders of Akbar's queen, Jahangir's mother, **Maryam Zamani.** It is now named after her.

It remains remarkable for its dome and its frescos, which elaborately interlace floral and geometric designs with Qur'anic inscriptions in Naskh characters. Today they are considered the finest Mughal frescos anywhere.

In the course of the first two visits he paid the city in 1662, Aurangzeb ordered construction of his supreme Lahore legacy — the **Badshahi Mosque.** He apparently told the Friday congregation at the Firoz Khan mosque he attended that they must continue to assemble for ever on that spot to recite their prayers.

Entirely constructed of brick, dressed with red limestone, and with white marble domes and ornament, the mosque forms a 170-metre (558-feet) square, elevated on a platform. Its main, eastern entry is up twenty-two formidable steps. Large tablets in Urdu and English relate the history of its building and note its official capacity of 60,000 people. Those who should know say it's actually more like 100,000.

Its exterior walls are painstakingly decorated with sculptured panels and each

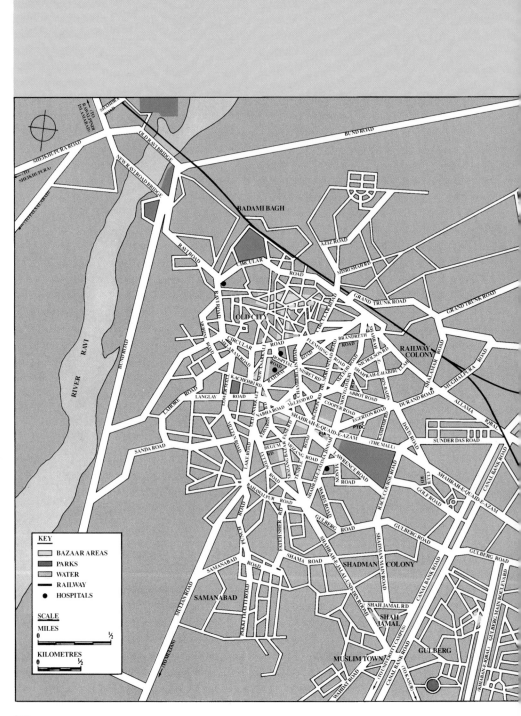

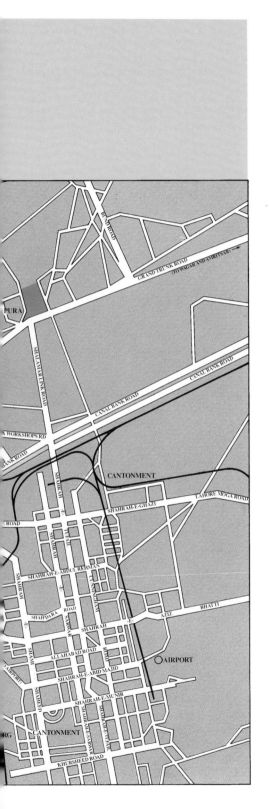

corner is marked by a square tower topped with a red sandstone turret capped with a white marble cupola.

This white-capped turret idea is repeated on a larger scale atop the fifty-three-metre-high (174-feet) **minarets** which mark the corners of the mosque. The view from the top of these is said to be very beautiful.

Sher Singh, one of Ranjit Singh's sons, used these stately towers as cannon positions for shelling the fort in 1841.

The floor of the vast **court** was originally paved in brick laid in prayer carpet, *musalla*, shapes and bordered with black stone.

The eighty cells, *hujras*, built into the walls were originally study rooms. The British demolished them in 1856. They were rebuilt to form arcades and some as toilets.

Opposite the entrance stands the **Prayer Hall,** on its twenty-five by eighty-two metre (81 by 267 feet) platform. With its red sandstone front, central archway and side arches, crenellated walls, minaret corners and magnificent white domes this hall, for all its relatively small size, is well proportioned and very fine.

Discreet white marble floral decoration relieves the otherwise unbroken red of the sandstone exterior and inside there are eight arches of massive height, so designed to carry the enormous weight of the three glorious white marble domes on the roof. There are floral motifs in relief around the walls. The Mehrab and its corner stones are faced in marble.

From the Mosque you return to the **Hazuri Bagh** of Ranjit Singh. This square garden was originally the place where Aurangzeb reviewed his troops. The other side of it is where the second major Lahore work of Aurangzeb confronts you — the **Alamgiri Gate.** The name is one of his titles and means "Conqueror of the Universe".

Aurangzeb's gate seems to share Fate's intransigence. Shortly after Aurangzeb ordered the building of the Badshahi and left, Lahore was gravely threatened and, in parts, actually damaged by encroachments of the fickle river **Ravi.**

Other Lahore monuments from Aurangzeb's time include the tiled mosque inside the **Taxila Gate,** built by one of Fidai Khan Koka's aides, Amir Abdullah Khan, who may also be responsible for another mosque which once stood in the *Nakhas Khana,* **Horse**

Market, outside what is today called the **Landa Bazaar.** Another **mosque** constructed in 1659 by the historian Mohamed Saleh Kamboh Lahori, inside the **Mochi Gate,** may also be his work.

This mosque is well-known for its exquisite and colourful glazed tiles. His house, though much altered, is also preserved inside the Mochi Gate. Lahori is himself buried in a **mausoleum** now used as a church on the **Bin Badis Road.**

Unique tomb

Also admired for the beauty of the glazed tiles on its exterior walls is another mosque inside the Mochi Gate, near **Takiya Sadhuan.** It was completed in 1671 by Afraz Khan.

Possibly from this time, though perhaps dating from the reign of Shah Jahan, is the unique **tomb** of the wife of Dara Shikoh, who died fleeing from Aurangzeb with her husband before he was executed. It is built inside a tank and is only accessible through a causeway.

Jahangir's quadrangle — begun in fact by his father — is an enchanting section of the Fort interior. Most of the area is occupied by a large garden, laid out in geometric beds around a central tank containing more than thirty fountains.

On the east and west a series of porticoed lodges in red sandstone, with richly carved columns and elaborate brackets sculpted to the forms of elephants, lions and other animals, reveals the influence which Hindu art had upon Jahangir and Akbar.

On the north side, overlooking the northern wall of the city below, is Jahangir's own sleeping chamber, known now as **Bari Khawabgah.** The frontage is a modern reconstruction but the chambers now used as a **museum,** are original. The small **pavilion** beside it today is Sikh. South is Akbar's Daulat Khana-e-Khas.

The famous **picture wall** of the fort — 745 square metres (890 square yards) of glazed surface, depicting scenes from daily life and excursions, symbols, geometrical and floral motifs — was completed by his son Shah Jahan, but this magnificent project too was begun by Jahangir.

To reach **Jahangir's mausoleum,** and those of his wife, Nur Jahan, and brother-in-law, Asaf Khan, you have to leave the city and travel five kilometres (three miles) northwest across the Ravi.

Over the water, in **Shah Dara,** Jahangir's tomb stands beyond a magnificent enclosure known as **Akbari Serai** — though, in fact, this was not Akbar's work but that of Jahangir's son, Shah Jahan.

This serai was laid out on a colossal scale for the benefit of travellers. The surrounding walls are filled with 180 porchlike arches where the user could cook, rest and sleep secure.

The corners enclose more elaborate "burjis" or pavilions. Under the British the serai became a railway depot, but today it's hard to believe. The garden breathes the wonderfully refreshing air of spacious parkland.

The serai opens onto another vast park, **Dilkusha,** once the property of Jahangir's favourite — Nur Jahan. This formidable lady was daughter of an extremely able Persian nobleman who, forced to flee his own country, found himself quickly in the service of Akbar and later became Jahangir's Prime Minister.

Nur Jahan was famous for both beauty and brains. Jahangir married her in 1611. Their fervid relationship seems to have swung perpetually between the turbulent and the torrid, but it was his will that he should be buried in the queen's Dilkusha garden and hers that his last wish should be granted.

The **monument** itself is attributed by some to Nur Jahan and by others to Shah Jahan. It is a huge, square, arcaded building in red sandstone with white marble inlay, the four corners crowned with elegant minarets, again in white marble.

Richly decorated corridors lead from each side to the central cenotaph, which is in pure white marble resting on a platform inlaid with *pietra dura*. The calligraphy on the tomb is worthy of special note.

The sides list the ninety-nine names of Allah; at the head is the Kalima in Arabic; at the foot, in Persian the name and dates of Jahangir and, above, words from the Holy Qur'an about Divine Mercy.

Opposite Jahangir's mausoleum is that of Nur Jahan's brother, **Asaf Khan,** upon whom Shah Jahan heaped honour after honour. He was father of Shah Jahan's wife, Mumtaz Mahal, whose death in childbirth inspired her husband to build the monument considered by many the most beautiful architectural creation of all time, the Taj Mahal, in Agra.

The monument to her father — in sorry dilapidation now — still commands reverence for its superb dome, set off by the simplicity of

Above: Lahore Fort's Shish Mahal — the Palace of Mirrors.
Overleaf: Badshahi mosque, built by Emperor Aurangzeb, seen from Lahore Fort.

its arcaded octagonal base.

The tomb suffered grievously, too, in the nineteenth century, being despoiled then of all its marble ornamentation. Only the **marble cenotaph** with its floral *pietra dura* inlay and the inscribed names of Allah survived intact.

Nur Jahan herself is buried a comfortable fifteen minutes walk away. Her **tomb** too was shorn of all decoration while the cenotaphs themselves — Nur Jahan's and her daughter's — disappeared.

These have since been replaced and a good amount of restoration work has been completed. Yet, despite the rose trees planted all about the garden, there is something exceptionally tragic about this despoiling.

Jahangir also loved gardens, especially those in Lahore, the **Mirza Kumran,** the **Garden of Dilamez,** and that of **Momin Ishaq Baz** — the Lover. There, with harem and nobles, he spent many festive occasions.

He also improved the road between Lahore and Agra building minarets every *kos*, a three kilometre measure (two miles) — hence known as *Kos Minars.* Wells for the benefit of travellers were dug at every third *Kos*.

One such *Kos Minar* still stands near the railway track behind the Railway Locomotive workshop, but it's in a sorry state.

The best-known relic of Jahangir's age is the so-called **tomb of Anarkali** today used as a Government Records Office.

According to legend, when Akbar saw his son, Prince Salim — the future Jahangir — smiling at one of the beautiful dancers in his harem, he suspected them of having a secret affair and had the girl built into the city wall alive.

Her name was **Anarkali** or Pomegranate Bud. The story ends, to the satisfaction of romantics, if not of historians, with her presumed lover, Jahangir, subsequently building the imposing monument which still bears her name at the site of her execution.

Inscriptions inside the tomb are now said to indicate that the tomb was actually the burial-place of Jahangir's wife Sahib-i-Jamal, who died in 1599. Historians now say there never existed a lady of Anarkali's name or character.

Inside the **Lahore Gate** is the **Mosque of Miran Sadar Jahan** (built in 1606), while on the **Shalamar Link Road** is the main **Wadda**

255

Above: Elegant 18th-century chandelier in Lahore Fort.

Mosque which, although reconstructed under Shah Jahan, was originally built by Jahangir.

Some scholars also attribute to Jahangir rather than Shah Jahan the famous **Pearl Mosque** inside Lahore Fort, together with his Daulat Khana palace.

The **Bahadur Khan** mausoleum on the **Canal Bank Road** is also, almost certainly his. Sadly, the beautiful **Idgah**, erected near the site of today's Railway Station, and the **Murtaza Khan Mosque** (1611), are both lost.

The Architect King

In all his domains no city benefited more from Shah Jahan's attention to the creative possibilities of peace than the city of his birth.

Look around at the great Mughal buildings of Lahore and study their decoration. Chances are high that you're looking at the work of Shah Jahan — or something inspired by the dynamism of his building example.

The entire northwest corner of the Fort as it is today is all his — from the marvellous court named for him and including the **Diwan-i-Khas, Lal Burj, Khawabgah,** and **Moti Masjid,** through the sadly, much despoiled, **Women's Quarters,** the **Khilwat Khana,** and into the Shah Burj itself, the **Shish Mahal** and the **Naulakha,** down the **Elephant Gateway** to the Shah Burj entrance and the famous glazed wall outside. Each demands attention.

Shah Jahan's court is smaller and conveys a totally different impression compared with the larger, adjacent, Jahangir quadrangle.

Above all, there is something friendly about the porticoes which face out onto Jahangir's fountains, while the red sandstone animals carrying the cross beams of the buildings speak inevitably to the child in everyone. By contrast, Shah Jahan's court, in purest marble, is all grace.

The superb *Diwan-i-Khas,* **Hall of Private Audience,** on the north side is an arched pavilion, pure white but for the *pietra dura* embellishment on the parapet and the floor of multi-coloured marble, arranged in geometric patterns.

A delightful **marble fountain** plays in its centre, inlaid with *pietra dura.* The ceiling, too, is of marble, while latticed marble screens of magnificent craftsmanship adorn the north side.

Opposite, on the south side of the court, lie Shah Jahan's sleeping chambers, **Khawabgah.** Originally porticoed, this five-room building retains the white marble door frames, the dadoes of the three main rooms and beautiful latticed screens, again in white marble, on the southern wall. Sikh frescos and tracery here conceal Shah Jahan's original decoration.

West of the Khawabgah lie the ruins of Shah Jahan's **Hamman,** Royal Bath. It copied the Turkish style — with hot bath, cold bath and dressing room. Most of the chequered marble flooring has gone, but evidence of the complex heating system remains.

On the north-west corner a summer pavilion — the **Lal Burj** — is two-thirds Shah Jahan; the top storey is Sikh. To judge by the gilded and painted honeycomb cornice that remains, the original decoration must have been lavish, though most of the fabric has been stripped off.

The paintings inside are Sikh. The middle storey is surrounded by a channel bearing water from a central fountain to cool the air.

West of Shah Jahan's Court are the Private Chambers, **Khilwat Khana,** where the women of the court lived, but only a ruined pavilion in the middle of the north side remains.

South is the **Paien Bagh,** Women's Garden, used as a recreation area by the women of the harem. It is planted with cypresses, fragrant shrubs and dwarf trees around a central pool.

The famous **Moti Masjid,** Pearl Mosque, stands off another tranquil garden courtyard close by. The small size and the white purity of the marble explain its name, but the building is elegant and impressively strong.

Begun by Jahangir in the last years of his reign, the work was completed in 1631 by Shah Jahan. Geometric designs, animals and people all feature in the wall: the latter are of special interest for the light they throw on the sports and amusement of the Mughal Emperors — polo, wrestling, hunting, elephant and bull fights, gladiatorial combat, and music. There is evidence too of religious belief and mythology.

Behind this remarkable wall Shah Jahan at the same time constructed a **grand entrance gate** for the **Shah Burj,** Royal Palace, and harem that it encloses, exclusively for the use of the Emperor. The originally rich decoration of this gateway has suffered with time, but some panels retain their very pretty flower mosaics.

From behind this gate fifty-eight stairs lumber up to the first court of the Shah Burj. Their six-metre-breadth (19.5-feet) and sixty-five-metre-length (213-feet) were specifically

designed to accommodate elephants, carrying members of the royal family and women of the harem.

The steps are of brick and the high walls either side are painted to look brick-like. Arrivals and departures were proclaimed by heralds stationed in the west wall galleries.

The first building seen is the **Sikh Athdara** or **Edifice of Eight Doorways** used by Ranjit Singh as a **Kachehri,** Court of Justice. It is decorated with frescos of Krishna celebrating the Spring Festival.

The second court is entirely of marble. To the north is the half-octagon Burj itself, one of the most profusely decorated monuments of the whole Mughal period. It was used as his residence by the Emperor when he stayed in Lahore.

It was here that the Treaty of Lahore which put an end to Sikh rule in the Punjab and made the territory over to the British was signed on 26 December, 1845.

In this room too, according to the Pakistan Tourism Development Corporation's handbook, the **Koh-i-Noor diamond** — now resplendent among the British crown jewels — was handed over to the British. It had belonged to the Mughal Emperors and was estimated to weigh more than 229 carats.

The large central room, richly studded with round and convex mirrors, and hence called the **Shish Mahal,** Palace of Mirrors, is decorated with *pietra dura* inlay and Sikh frescos.

It is supported, on superbly worked double columns, across five handsomely scalloped arches. The ceiling is Mughal, the walls — with their minute pieces of blue and white porcelain — Sikh.

Nine smaller rooms adjoin the central hall, all of them decorated with marquetry ceilings. The back wall — like those of the main buildings in Shah Jahan's court — is embellished with marble screening of extraordinary beauty, carved with geometrical and floral designs.

The Burj courtyard is floored with a variety of marbles and the central pool designed to give an impression of waves. The Burj itself is completed by a Belvedere overlooking the city and clearly visible from outside the fort. Unfortunately its condition is bad.

One final structure has to be mentioned — the **Bungla** or Naulakha — a marble pavilion remarkable for the purity of its stone and the intricacy of its decoration. In a single small

flower there are over 100 pieces of tiny, semi-precious stones. Most obviously, it is striking for its "Bengali-style", downward curving roof.

South of Jahangir's Quadrangle the **Diwan-i-Aam,** Hall of Public Audiences, was commissioned by Shah Jahan to replace the awnings previously used to shelter dignitaries attending the Emperor's daily appearances in the Jharoka.

Large platform

It took three years to build. The large open hall — fifty-six metres long (180 feet), eighteen metres wide (59 feet), and eleven metres high (36 feet) — stands on a larger rectangular platform, itself edged by a decorative railing in red sandstone like the forty lofty pillars which support the arches that carry the roof.

Traces of another railing, in white marble, can also be seen between the pillars at the hall's outer limits. According to travellers these balustrades separated the various ranks of dignitaries attending the audiences.

The huge platform is surrounded by the yet bigger Diwan-i-Aam quadrangle, now dedicated entirely to open gardens, but once surrounded by vaulted apartments with gateways in the middle of the east, west and south sides.

When Sikh Maharajah Ranjit Singh died his body lay in state in this hall. In the civil war which followed the fort was bombarded by cannon balls fired from the minarets of the Badshahi Mosque.

The Diwan-i-Aam roof was shattered and the hall collapsed. The building seen today is a British restoration which was used by them as a hospital.

In 1639 Shah Jahan approved a plan to bring the waters of the river Ravi from Rajpur to Lahore. Within two years the 160-kilometre-long (100-mile) Royal Canal, Shah Nahar, was completed. The Emperor then launched one of his most popular undertakings — the design and construction of the **Shalamar Gardens.**

The foundations were laid on 12 July that year and less than eighteen months later, on 31 October 1642, the Emperor paid his first state visit to the newly completed grounds.

The Shalamar Gardens — six kilometres (3.7 miles) north-east of the city on the Grand Trunk Road — embody the perfection of landscape architecture demanded by the Mughals.

Lavishly spread over three descending

Opposite: Ornate beauty of one of the mosaics in the Wazir Khan Mosque, Lahore.

Above: Lahore youngster.

Opposite: Interior of Wazir Khan mosque.

Above: Young bride.

terraces the gardens are unified by water which runs down the six-metre-wide (20-feet) central canals and their various offshoots and reservoirs, and through the countless fountains.

The highest and lowest of the three terraces are 265 metres (867 feet) square. Each is divided into quarters by water channels which, decorated with fountains in red sandstone and marble, run north-south and east-west.

In the centre of these terraces — where the channels intersect — larger pools with more fountains accentuate the cool freshness of the air.

The original name for the top terrace, **Farah Bakhsh,** Bestower of Pleasure, suggests that its gardens were planted with flowers and sweet-scented shrubs. **Faiz Bakhsh,** Bestower of Plenty, the name for the lower level, suggests this was planted with fruit-bearing trees and plants.

The higher terrace was reserved exclusively for the harem and women of the Imperial Court. A marble screen, where the red sandstone balustrade now runs, secured their privacy.

The central terrace — an oblong 265 metres (867 feet) wide but only seventy-eight metres (255 feet) long — is especially elaborate. It is divided lengthwise into three: the middle section raised and containing the great tank, over sixty metres (195 feet) across, with more than 100 fountains, four pavilions, and — one of the gardens' most splendid features — the great cascade. This large, white marble wedge carries the water down from the top terrace level to the central tank over a sculpted surface which artfully gives the impression of brilliantly cascading diamonds.

At the foot of the cascade is the Emperor's **marble throne.** Either side of the central pool are pavilions, originally of red sandstone, from which one can walk along a causeway to the platform in the middle of the great tank.

The side sections of the central terrace are dedicated to roses.

Nowadays — the opposite of the original concept — you enter the gardens at the level of the highest terrace. Initially, two great portals in the corners of the wall at the bottom end of the gardens used to be the access points and progress was upwards, so that each level was revealed — a delightful surprise — as it was reached.

Many other features — pavilions, sleeping quarters, private and public audience halls, a bath house, gateways and towers — adorn these wonderful gardens.

They are also surrounded by high walls with serrated battlements, though these could not save them from serious vandalism once the power and authority of the Emperors declined after Aurangzeb's death.

Much marble was looted for buildings in Amritsar and elsewhere. The canals and tanks were filled in and the entire garden put under the plough. Ranjit Singh was both the worst offender and, once securely in power, their preserver.

He ordered massive restoration work, re-dug the canals and tanks and plastered over the buildings from which marble had been removed.

With no solid tradition in the area it was natural that the Sikhs should imitate to a great extent the domes, arches, pillars, and vaultings used by the great Mughal architects.

Aurangzeb's Badshahi Mosque and the **Samadhi of Ranjit Singh,** built adjacent to it, illustrate this and make it possible to compare the two achievements.

Pretty in pink and bubbling with minarets, the Samadhi is one of the most eye-catching features this side of old Lahore. Together with the **Samadhi of Guru Arjan Dev** it is considered among the best Sikh monuments in the city.

The massive northern fortification wall of the fort is also Sikh — constructed by Ranjit Singh after the river had shifted northwest. The Sikhs also built numerous *havelis*, mansions, several of which deserve mention. These are the *havelis* of Kallu Bai Ahluwalia inside the **Yaki gates,** of Dhayan Singh in the **Hira Mandi** area, and of Jamadar Kushal Singh near the Fort. They are vast, and many of them today are used as Government offices.

The *haveli* **Kanwar Nau Nihal Singh** still retains beautiful frescos, though these are now at grave risk for lack of proper upkeep.

The Sikhs also constructed numerous gardens, *Baghs*, but with the exception of the **Bagh and mausoleum of Rani Gulbadan** in the **Miani area,** all have been lost.

British rule ran virtually 100 years — from 1849-1947. Consciously or unconsciously, during the first half of this rule, the British seem to have done all they could to separate Lahore from her glorious Mughal past.

Under Lord Curzon, and since, a serious effort was made by the British authorities to

Opposite: Lahore Museum, founded by Lockwood Kipling, father of Rudyard.

Above: Painting of a poem by Iqbal about a girl called Sharfun-nisa, from the book "Princes".

264

266

Opposite: Bustling Anarkali Bazaar, Lahore, named after the tragic heroine of the romance between a serving maid and one of the Mughal princes.

Above: Bustling Lahore is a city of vibrant contrasts.

Opposite: Traditional carpet weaving, Lahore.

compensate for earlier ravages through restoration of Lahore Fort, the Shalamar Gardens, Jahangir's Mausoleum, and Ali Mardan Khan's Mausoleum: the loftiest monument in the city.

He secured passage of a law for the preservation of old monuments and set up a Department of Government specifically to oversee this.

The British also made their own substantial and original contribution to Lahore's architectural heritage.

In a remarkably successful hybrid style, improbably and inelegantly, yet succinctly, described as "Mughal-Victorian", they erected numerous grand public and private buildings which, where they have been preserved, add an invaluable dimension to the city's rich architectural range and interest.

Outstanding examples border, or lie within easy reach, of the **Shahrah-i-Quaid-i-Azam** main artery (The Mall) of the city. They include the many fine colleges and schools which found Lahore's reputation as education centre of Pakistan *par excellence.*

Most notable are: **Government College** the most prestigious in the country, and of which Allama Muhammad Iqbal, founding father of Pakistan's Independence, was a distinguished alumnus; the **Foreman Christian College,** founded in 1864 in rented rooms near the **Shah Almi Gate** by an American missionary and transferred to its present campus in 1940, where it has five student hostels and its own mosque; the **Kinnaird College for Women,** and the **Islamia College,** prominent in the campaign for Independence and another institution where Iqbal was active; and **Aitcheson (Chiefs) College,** still the most expensive educational establishment in the country.

The fortlike **Railway Station** — object at the time of much discontent for the ravages its system inflicted upon venerable reaches of the ancient city — was started in 1859 under Sir John Lawrence, Chief Commissioner for the Punjab (the railway remains, incidentally, the largest landowner in the city).

Biggest Zoo

The pure Doric hall built to commemorate Lawrence's services — together with that erected in honour of the first Lieutenant-Governor, Sir Robert Montgomery (1859-1863) — now form the finest library in Pakistan, the **Quaid-i-Azam.**

267

Above: Kim's Gun, immortalized by Kipling, outside Lahore Museum.

The structures were superb and they are well-maintained. The old **Lawrence Gardens,** begun in 1860 with forty-five hectares (112 acres) of ground, and subsequently enlarged, are the biggest in the city. Adjacent is the country's biggest zoo.

In 1870 what is now the country's largest medical institution of its kind, the **King Edward Medical College,** started life, named at the time the **Mayo Hospital and Medical School,** after the British Viceroy to India assassinated in 1872.

Also named after this Lord Mayo when it was founded was today's **National College of Arts.** Its first principal was a teacher of painting and sculpture from Bombay — Lockwood Kipling, the father of Rudyard.

His charge of the Arts School was combined with responsibilities as Curator of the **Lahore Museum.** When the local market became flooded with inferior goods from Britain, **Kipling's School** became a haven for the finest Lahore craftsmen in weaving, cotton printing, wood-carving and other skills.

About the same time as the Arts School was launched, the oldest University in Pakistan opened its doors in Lahore in 1882 as the **Punjab University.** Its main buildings are now

further south but the original structure, in pure Islamic style, still stands on the Shahrah-i-Quaid-i-Azam (Mall), almost opposite the Museum.

The nucleus of Lahore Museum's outstanding collection was put together in the middle of the nineteenth century and housed in the **Wazir Khan pavilion** before it was shifted, in 1864, to what is now **Tollinton Market.** Its imposing, new, permanent home was completed in 1892 and has remained a city landmark ever since.

The coins, paintings and sculptures are outstanding. The coins — 50,000 of them going back to the sixth century BC — include the best Indo-Greek examples ever found anywhere on the subcontinent, both for inscription and impression.

The miniature paintings number about 2,000 and the most important section comes from the Punjab Hill school, with Hindu religious themes.

In the **Gandhara room** the remarkable exhibition of Greco-Buddhist art is dominated by the famous, unique, **Fasting Buddha,** regarded as one of the world's supreme artistic legacies and considered beyond value. The unlikely marriage of western (Greek) with

Asian (Buddhist) artistic tradition produced many masterpieces displayed here.

The **Muslim gallery** has fine displays of carpets, textiles, metalware, wood carvings, armour, ceramics, stone carvings, musical instruments, jewellery, manuscripts, calligraphy, and Muslim inscriptions.

In the **Donation Hall** are collections from Faqir Khana and Hifzur Rahman that are of immense value and cultural interest with chinaware and medals predominant.

Other displays of rarity and quality are the Museum's modern paintings and wood carvings, fabrics, and jewellery fashioned through the ages in the Swat Valley.

In the **Fabrics gallery,** visitors can study a wide cross section of regional fabrics, costumes, and toys; while in the **Gujranwala Gallery** superb marble sculptures, wood carvings and a Jain Temple reflect a rich and varied cultural epoch.

The **Armour Gallery** has displays of arms developed down the centuries, Sikh paintings, and British period sculptures and Sikh and African ethnological exhibits predominate the standing ethnological exhibition.

Unique in its focus, the **Freedom Movement Gallery** depicts the history of the struggle of enslaved peoples in Africa and the subcontinent to free themselves from the yoke of colonialism with particular exhibits on Tipu Sultan, Allama Iqbal, and Quaid-e-Azam, the founding father.

Outside the museum, not far away, **Zamzama,** the eighteenth-century firepiece immortalised by Kipling as **"Kim's Gun",** takes up a surprising length of space in the middle of the road.

Nearby too are the **General Post Office —** which started life in 1880 as the *Kothi Tar Ghar,* Telegraph Office, when this means of communication was introduced to the country — and the stately **High Court.**

Other notable buildings from the British period include the magnificent **Town Hall** and the **Free Masonic Lodge** — the latter preserved, thanks to the efforts of a dedicated conservationist lobby, and now being turned into a Museum for Punjab Arts and Crafts.

Of modern buildings probably the finest is **WADPA House,** headquarters of the Water and Power Development Authority, in chaste white and with the lines of a wide and lofty pagoda.

Behind is the **Punjab Assembly Hall** and,

before both, the modern **Summit Minar.** Beside that, under a marble canopy where once, in stone, Queen Victoria sat enthroned, a Qur'an lies open for reverent consultation by passers-by.

The City Arts Council's **Al-Hamra complex** is close by. In the tapering of its walls this excellent, modern, red-brick structure is reminiscent of the tomb of the famous saint Shah Rukni-i-Alam in Multan. A **Music Centre** is being added. The complex is unique in Pakistan.

The city's love of celluloid fantasy and romance is easily seen in the numerous Picture Palaces and the huge crowds that attend them, while the energy of the industry's salesmen is equally evident from a walk along their highway — **Betel Nut Street.**

In theatre, likewise, Lahore is the country's leader, not only in the Al-Hamra complex but in **Bagh-i-Jinnah** open-air stage productions and other settings which have proved popular with adult *cognoscenti* and family audiences alike.

Bazaars and market places in the Middle East and Asia are of course legendary and Lahore's — the **Kashmiri, Suha, Chhatta, Dabbi, Anarkali** or the **old city, Liberty,** and **Gulberg Main Market** further out — like those elsewhere, supply everything you could possibly, or impossibly, want from clothes to copper, brass and silverware, watches and bangles to carpets, chapatis and chai, cloth and shoes to confectionery and pills.

Before the entrance to the Badshahi Mosque, guarded by soldiers in dress uniform — red on grey — stands to one side in quiet dignity the **tomb** of one of Pakistan's founding fathers. Allama Muhammad Iqbal, scholar, poet, and statesman — was born in neighbouring Sialkot, but lived most of his life in Lahore.

In 1940, two years after his death, the Muslim League meeting in Lahore formulated its now famous demand for a separate nation for the Muslim majority regions of the subcontinent.

In Iqbal Park near Badshahi Mosque, the **Minar-i-Pakistan** — the single most outstanding modern monument in Lahore — immortalises the passage of this resolution and the date: 23 March 1940.

Excursions From Lahore

Thirty-four kilometres (21 miles) from Lahore, set in the middle of a large artificial lake, is

Jahangir's deer tower and beautiful hunting pavilion, the **Hiran Minar.**

Take the **Sheikhupura road** westwards from the toll gate on the Ravi river bridge and after two kilometres (one mile), the right fork onto the dual carriageway that runs for thirty kilometres (19 miles) across flat farmland to **Sheikhupura**.

There's a massive, red-brick square **fort** in the centre of Sheikhupura, built by Jahangir in 1619, down a side street, left, 300 metres (330 yards) past the traffic lights at the Gujranwala-Faisalabad road intersection.

Preserved by the Department of Archaeology, the fort was used by Rani Nakayan, one of Ranjit Singh's wives, as her palace in the 19th century. Her tomb is also in Sheikhupura.

Continue straight through Sheikhupura on the **Sargodha road** to the end of the dual carriageway, then, beyond a railway crossing, turn right and then left over a canal bridge, for the **Hiran Minar,** the royal antelope that features in of one the best-known stories about Jahangir. His passion for hunting dated from childhood. As a young man he spent so much time at the chase outside Lahore that his favoured hunting-ground there came to be called **Jahangirabad** (the modern **Sheikhupura**).

In the second year of his reign a royal antelope which had taken his fancy, and which he called "Mans Raj", died. The Emperor had this handsome monument raised over its remains, on which a life-size stone statue of the animal was placed.

A stone slab attached to the monument bore a Persian inscription engraved in the handwriting of Mulla Mohamed Hussain Kashmiri, famous for his calligraphy, and Jahangir ordered that no Hindu or Muslim should thenceforth hunt deer within the limits of the place.

Subsequently he ordered a **palace** to be built in Jahangirabad with a tank and tower. They stand there still — though considerably modified by the Emperor's son, Shah Jahan.

An arched causeway leads to the three-storey, white octagonal pavilion in the centre, where Jahangir sat under an elegant arcade and watched the animals. The Hiran Minar is close to the beginning of the causeway.

Twenty-nine kilometres (18 miles) south-west of Sheikhupura, **Nankana Sahib,** a pilgrimage centre, has strong links with Guru Nanak, founder of the Sikh religion, for this is where he was brought up as a child. It has **two temples** including the one where he was reputed to be born.

Among its sacred relics is a holy **cloak** embroidered with Qur'anic verses, said to have been presented to Guru Nanak by the Caliph of Baghdad.

Another excursion from Lahore leads seventy kilometres (43 miles) along the Multan road to the **Changa Manga wildlife reserve,** once the oldest irrigated plantation in the subcontinent. Established by the British in 1890, it provided fuelwood for the railway.

Steam still lives and train buffs can take a ride on the **narrow-gauge railway** through the woods hauled by a steam engine and enjoy the many species of deer that live there.

Above: Tomb of Ranjit Singh, Punjab's 18th-century Sikh ruler.

Hyderabad: City of the Present

Fourth-largest city in Pakistan, **Hyderabad** was capital of Sind between the eighteenth and nineteenth centuries. Still a bustling entrepôt, it shows no signs of decline, unlike Thatta, but there's little of any real interest and few historical monuments to testify to its former importance.

Many believe that the town of Neroon which Muhammad bin Qasim captured during his eight-century invasion of Sind is Hyderabad; others fancy it as the site of one of the cities that Alexander built along the Indus.

The present city is only 200 years old. It was built by one of the Kalhora rulers in 1786 to replace Khudabad as the capital after the Indus changed course and left Khudabad high and dry.

By the end of the eighteenth century Sind's allegiance to Afghanistan was marginal and both the British East India Company and the Sikhs were casting covetous eyes on its wealth.

In 1838, when the first Afghan War broke out, Sind became strategically important to the British as the only corridor for marching British troops to Kabul: at that time chaos reigned in the Punjab.

Without so much as a by-your-leave, the British crown annexed Sind, much to the displeasure of the Amirs of Talpur who had been faithful if not willing allies of the British.

Not surprisingly, they took to arms. The British Residency in Hyderabad was attacked by an angry mob of ordinary citizens and Sir Charles Napier, who thought that Karachi would make a good port, came to the rescue.

The final battle for Sind took place in February 1843 at Miani near Hyderabad when a Talpur army of 20,000 men faced Napier's 2,800 troops and twelve guns. Despite these inferior odds the Talpur army was overwhelmed. At least 5,000 troops were killed and Hyderabad was occupied by the British who accepted the surrender of six of the Amirs.

Battle over, triumph complete, Napier sent news of his victory to London by telegraph in a laconic, one word message in Latin —
"Peccavi" — which in English reads, "I have sinned".

Getting there

Hyderabad is 175 kilometres (108 miles) from **Karachi** on the super Highway and the older National Highway. It is 1,405 kilometres (873 miles) from **Islamabad**. It is served by train.

Where to stay

Hotel Faran and Sainjee Restaurant and Hotel. There are other hotels of varying comfort and standards, and rest houses in Hyderabad. See Listings for "Hotels".

When to go

You can visit Hyderabad at any time of the year.

Sightseeing

The battlefield at **Miani** is about ten kilometres (six miles) north of Hyderabad and some five kilometres (three miles) off the National Highway with a **memorial** to the British dead. The memorial is down a dusty narrow track in the forest and you'll need a local guide to find it.

Hyderabad's **eighteenth-century** fort was first the court of the Kalhora dynasty and then that of the Talpur Amirs. According to contemporary British descriptions it must have been splendid, but apart from the tower, main entrance, and a room in the harem, little remains to be seen.

In the 1820s Doctor James Burnes, brother of Alexander Burnes, was summoned to the fort to treat one of the Talpur rulers for an unspecified illness and described the court as "rich, splendid, but not garish".

"The walls of the audience hall were covered in paintings and its floor was bright with Persian carpets. At one end of the hall, on a large couch covered in gold-embroidered white satin, the only piece of furniture in the great room, sat a semi-circle of Mirs, wearing loose silk trousers of dark blue, long muslin shirts sashed with silk and golden and tall stove-pipe hats of velvet or brocade."

Portraits of the Amirs and their weapons are exhibited in what passes as the **Fort Museum** near the railway station.

Their stove-pipe hats are on display in Hyderabad's **Sind Provincial Museum,** near the **Polytechnic College** and opposite the **Indus Gas Office.** Indeed, this Museum is

Above: Intricately-carved timber balcony
Hyderabad.

Opposite top: Old Town, Hyderabad.

Opposite: Clock tower and archway, Hyderabad.

perhaps the only justification for a visit to Hyderabad, boasting as it does fine archaeological and ethnological collections, handsomely displayed and identified.

The only real attraction at **Shaikh Makai Fort** is the tomb of a thirteenth-century saint from Mecca, **Shaikh Makai.** Housed inside a mud fort of a much later date, his mausoleum, built in 1671, centuries after his death, attracts devotees from far and wide.

Hyderabad's main bazaar, the **Shahi Bazaar,** stretches from the **fort gate** to the **Market Tower,** and sells everything from bangles, gold and silver jewellery, Sindhi embroideries to unique hand-blocked *ajrak* prints.

Other places of possible interest in the city include the ornate **mausolea** of the Talpur and Kalhora Amirs, covering the northern part of the hill on which Hyderabad was originally built, with their blue-glazed tile work. Some have floral paintings and marble fretwork.

The Institute of Sindology at the University of Sind, on the Super Highway just before crossing the Indus, also boasts a worthwhile collection of old books, coins, and other artefacts relating to Sind.

Multan: City of the Sun God

An Urdu saying about **Multan** translated with poetic licence into English goes:

With four rare things Multan abounds,
Heat, beggars, dust and burial grounds.

Any visitor to the town, which is extremely hot in summer, will see an element of truth in this couplet. It's attributed by native tradition to a saint who, being flayed alive, called on the sun to avenge him. Multan's also extremely dusty, as the annual rainfall seldom exceeds thirteen centimetres (five inches).

But its tombs and other historic remains make it well worth visiting for an overnight stay.

For all its heat and dust, Multan has always been a rich prize for invaders. Up to 1947 it was the centre of the hides and skin trade in the subcontinent.

In Alexander's time it was probably the capital of the Malloi, a fierce tribe who shut themselves up in the fortress when he approached.

Alexander was outnumbered ten-to-one; nevertheless, in what his subjective historians described as a feat of amazing personal bravery, he scaled the battlements of the citadel and dropped almost alone into the fortress.

"He happened to land on his feet beside a fig-tree. . . . He slashed with his sword and hurled any stones that came to hand: the Indians recoiled, as his three attendants leapt down to join him, carrying the sacred shield (of Achilles)."

But the skills of the Indian archers were his undoing; his helpers were wounded and a metre-long (three-feet) arrow pierced his armour and struck him in the chest.

But when an Indian ran forward to finish him off, Alexander stabbed his attacker before he struck home. Then he collapsed, spurting blood, beneath the cover of his Trojan shield.

Eventually the walls collapsed and the Macedonians rushed in to massacre the men of Multan "down to the last woman and child". Although his wound was serious, Alexander recovered.

Hsuan Tsang, who visited Multan in AD 641 found the city agreeable and prosperous. "The greater part (of the people) sacrifice to the spirits; few believe in the law of Buddha."

He also described the temple dedicated to the sun god as magnificent and profusely decorated.

"The image of the Sun-Deva is cast in gold and ornamented with rare gems. Its divine insight is mysteriously manifested, and its spiritual powers made plain to all. Women play their music, light their torches, offer their flowers and perfumes to honour it."

The idol, broken up by Mahmud of Ghazni, was later restored and then finally destroyed by Aurangzeb in the seventeenth century.

Muhammad bin Qasim, who took Multan for the Arab Caliphate, besieged the city for more than two months in AD 712. According to one historian 6,000 warriors were put to death and their dependants taken as slaves. Not long after this, Muhammad bin Qasim was sent home to face death by execution.

Multan fell to Mahmud of Ghazni in 1005 and the Mongol, Tamurlane, in 1398. It was then taken by Nadir Shah of Persia in 1739, Ahmed Shah Durrani in 1752, and Ranjit Singh, the Sikh, in 1818.

In 1848 British forces re-enacted Alexander the Great's siege of Multan, which led indirectly to the Second Sikh War and the annexation of the Punjab by the British in 1849.

The Sikh governor Mulraj had refused to pay revenue to the Sikh Council of Regency in Lahore. Two young Britons sent to Multan as emissaries to negotiate a settlement, were murdered.

So Herbert Edwardes, the young political agent of Bannu fame, galloped to the rescue from Bahawalpur, covering the ninety kilometres (60 miles) on horseback in twenty-four hours in sweltering June.

Defeating Mulraj, he drove him into the citadel at Multan where Mulraj held out for another six months before the citadel's walls were breached. The same year the British annexed the Punjab.

Getting there

Multan 945 kilometres (587 miles) from **Karachi**, and 636 kilometres (395 miles) from **Islamabad**, is served by road and daily air and rail services.

Where to stay

Sindbad Hotel. There are other hotels of varying degrees of comfort and standards. See Listings for "Hotels".

Above: Mausoleum of Saint Ruknud-din Alam, Multan.

Sightseeing

Little remains of the **fort** today, for much of it was blown up during the siege in 1848. But inside the old enclosure is the **tomb of Rukn-ud-din,** an octagonal brick building supported by sloping towers and covered by a hemispherical dome.

The tomb is superbly decorated with dark blue, azure, turquoise and white tiles, contrasting with the deep red of the polished brick. It has intricately carved woodwork. Rukn-ud-din was a great fourteenth-century religious and political figure.

Unfortunately, the **tomb of Bahauddin Zakaria,** "the ornament of the Faith", a thirteenth-century *sufi* and spiritual leader with an extremely large following, is much neglected. It was almost completely ruined

during the siege of 1848 and only a few glazed tiles remain to decorate it.

Zakaria is regarded as the sponsor of the Suhrawardia order of dervishes in the subcontinent and credited with several miracles. His anniversary on the fifth of the lunar month of Saffar, is observed by thousands of pilgrims.

The **shrine of Shams-e-Tabriz,** the great **sufi** martyr who was murdered in 1247, is one kilometre (half-a-mile) east of the fort above the old bed of the Ravi. The tomb was rebuilt in 1780 and has a dome covered with sky-blue tiles.

Multan has some interesting handicrafts, particularly handloom weaving, pottery, and tiles which are well worth looking out for. You can see the pottery being made.

Quetta: The Fortress City

The name **Quetta** derives from the Pashtu word for fort, "kot". Lying at the head of the **Shal Valley,** encircled by rugged and daunting mountains, the Baluchistan capital commands the strategic **Bolan Pass** and the **Khojak Pass** into Afghanistan.

Quetta's recorded history begins in the eleventh century when it was captured by Mahmud of Ghazni. By the middle of the sixteenth century it was the westernmost extension of the Mughal Empire — remote and prone to attack. Indeed, the Mughals were forced to its defence on several occasions to thwart the empirical ambitions of the Persian Safavids.

During the First Afghan War the British briefly occupied the city but did not establish a permanent presence until 1876, when Sir Robert Sandeman was installed as political agent.

Devastated in 1935 by one of the greatest earthquakes yet recorded — more than 20,000 people died and the whole city was flattened — Quetta was completely rebuilt and has developed rapidly since Independence.

Set 1,680 metres (5,500 feet) above sea level, Quetta is uncomfortably hot in high summer — and bitterly cold in winter. It has an international airport and the high mountains which ring the capital form a dramatic approach through the many passes and what, for many, is a hair-raising landing. There is also a railway station.

Getting there

Quetta, 715 kilometres (444 miles) from **Karachi** and 1,489 kilometres (925 miles) from **Islamabad,** is served by regular air and rail services.

When to go

Quetta is often completely closed during the winter months. It is pleasant in April and early May and in September and October but excessively hot in the high summer.

Where to Stay

Quetta Serena, fashioned like a Baluchistan fortress, its interior is the epitome of elegance and comfort. Lourdes, Staff College Road, a touchingly quaint old faithful with a pretty garden and little else in the way of elegance but extremely friendly management and staff and adequate rooms.

There are other hotels of varying comfort and standards. See Listings for "Hotels".

Sightseeing

A frontier town and military cantonment with little grace, Quetta's busy streets and bazaars teem with fierce-looking Pathan tribesmen. More than seventy per cent of the city's population are of this origin.

During spring and summer, the colourful **bazaars** are heaped with luscious mountains of fruit — grapes, apples, and melons in particular. Handicrafts include Baluchi mirror-work embroidery, jackets, fur coats, and sandals.

The city's also renowned for a Baluchistan culinary delight — sajji, which is a charcoal-broiled leg of lamb marinaded for hours in a tangy mixture of subtle herbs and spices. Almost every food stall specialises in this delicacy. (See "Tastes of Pakistan", Part Four).

Quetta is the seat of the Baluchistan administration and **parliament** and boasts a thriving **university,** one of the subcontinent's most modern **television complexes,** and a famous and historic **military Staff College,** established in 1905 to as a result of Lord Kitchener's 1902 reorganization of the Indian Army.

The entrance is decorated by a **brass bell** salvaged from a Russian battleship. It was presented by the Japanese Imperial Navy to twenty students and two instructors who visited the battlefields in Manchuria in 1907.

Though devastated by the 1935 earthquake, the college boasts a glorious history. It was here that the cream of the British Indian Army officers were indoctrinated in the most advanced military strategies.

Its three most distinguished pre-Independence graduates were Field Marshal Sir Claude Auchinleck, Viscount Bernard Law Montgomery (whose "Desert Rats" defeated Rommel in an epic World War II battle) and Viscount William Joseph Slim, who led the 14th Army's victorious but gory battle against the Japanese in Burma during the same war.

The first two Muslim officers to attend the College during its Imperial years were K. M. Idris and Nazir Ahmed. From December 1940 to June 1941, a future President of Pakistan, a young captain, Ayub Khan, was a student.

Above: Street tailor Quetta.
Overleaf: Aerial view of mountain-encircled Quetta.

And College legend has it that during his time there, Yahya Khan, another future President, slept in the **library** at night to ensure that none of its 10,000 volumes were pilfered.

The **college museum,** housed in the bungalow once occupied by British World War II hero, Field Marshal Montgomery, is mandatory for military buffs. There's a collection of papers and photographs illustrating military life between 1905 and 1945.

One of these, written by A. P. Wavell, then a lieutenant, carries the comment by the Commandant of the time that it was a good paper but spoilt by undue emphasis on political matters which were no concern of the military.

Ironically, Wavell went on to become not only a brilliant tactician who directed much of the British war effort in the east against the Japanese, but also the penultimate Viceroy of India.

The capital also boasts a **National Museum.** It's on one of the main shopping streets, **Jinnah Road,** and has a fascinating exhibition of **antique firearms.**

Evidence of the bitter Afghan struggle between 1980 and 1989 is visible everywhere — particularly in the International Red Cross **orthopaedic treatment centre,** where refugees and Mujahideen freedom fighters undergo amputation and rehabilitation.

Nine kilometres (six miles) out of town the jade waters of **Hanna Lake** form a colourful contrast to the barren, ochre-coloured mountainsides. It's the city's main water supply and something of a weekend resort.

Before you reach the lake, there's a right turn that follows a track into the delightful **Urak valley,** rich and fertile, with vineyards and orchards of apples, peaches, plums, cherries, and apricots, clinging to the hillsides.

Above: One of Pakistan's endemic species of antelope.

Wildlife: A Vanishing Treasury of the Rare and Wonderful

Pakistan sprawling over an area nearly equal to the combined area of France, Belgium, and Britain, has a rich heritage of wildlife.

Almost all the habitats where animals flourish — snowcapped mountains, forests, plains, deserts, mighty rivers, lakes, and marine foreshore — originally supported an indigenous wildlife adapted to wide extremes of temperature, able to travel great distances in search of food and water.

Down the centuries they were joined by migrants from the Palearctic, North Africa, the Mediterranean, and Central Asia who crossed the existing land bridge and over the then lightly-forested Himalayan spurs along the west bank of the Indus.

The fauna was supplemented by thousands of waterfowl and animals, winter migrants, which travelled over the swamps and through the riverine forests left each year when the monsoon floods of the Indus ebbed.

During this century with efficient irrigation the Indus basin has become a well wooded and watered region of rich, densely populated farmland.

All but the high regions of Baluchistan and the North-West Frontier Province have been denuded of their scrub cover and the consequent loss of habitat and disturbance has led to a rapid decline of faunal reserves, aggravated until the 1970s by excessive poaching and uncontrolled hunting.

Since then the Government, guided by the Declaration of Amsterdam issued at the end of First International World Wildlife Fund Congress in 1967, has made a concerted effort to save and preserve its rapidly diminishing wildlife treasury, related to the two great zoogeographical regions of the world — the palearctic west and oriental east.

Ten of the eighteen mammalian orders are represented in Pakistan, with at least 188 described species, ranging from the world's smallest surviving mammals, the Mediterranean pigmy shrew, to the largest mammal ever known, the blue whale, and including sixty-three rodents, thirty-eight insectivores, one pholidota, three of primates, and nine aquatic mammals belonging to cetacea.

The snow leopard and the common leopard are perhaps the most endangered species in Pakistan. Shy and rarely seen, the snow leopard ranges the northern mountains above the 5,400 metres (18,000 feet) high snowline while the only remaining common leopards left are found within the protection of the national parks — perhaps just three to four in Kirthar.

The rhesus macaques and the common langur are dwindling in numbers. But following a national ban on exports of wild animals their population is expected to increase in the forested valleys of Azad Kashmir, Kaghan, and Swat where they live.

Other common but smaller predators are the foxes and jackals of the coastal plains of lower Sind and the lush green habitats of mountains more than 1,500 meters (5,000 feet) high.

Wolves occur over most of the northern uplands but have considerably decreased in recent years although two to three packs are also reported to occur in Kirthar National Park.

In their natural habitats, ibex and bharal are the main prey for the wolves in Chitral and around.

The Baluchistan bear is reported to occur in the vicinity of Ziarat, Sibi district, near Khuzdar, and possibly in Waziristan. One or two specimens were seen recently in Kirthar National Park and it is also known to occur in Chitral.

Amongst other carnivores in Pakistan are several species of smaller cats, civets, mongoose, caracal, hyaena, martens, weasels and others.

The leopard cat is more common in the hilly areas of the Punjab, NWFP and Azad Kashmir, all in hilly areas; the fishing cat near rivers in Punjab and Sind; the jungle cat in the Jhatpat area of Baluchistan, while desert cat is found in Cholistan desert, Tharparker and Kirthar. Three species of mongooses are common on plains throughout the country.

Pakistan's only wild equine, the Indian wild ass, is found near the Rann of Kutch along the edges of the Thar desert but is increasingly rare. There are three sub-species of urial — the shapu, the Baluchistan urial or gad, and the Salt Range urial in Punjab.

The markhors in Pakistan have suffered considerable persecution in the past and are

Above: Pakistan mountain bear.

now much fewer than before, while the Persian wild goat, commonly called the Sind ibex, another magnificent example of caprine beauty and agility that occupies the most difficult cliffs of the Kirthar range, is also imperilled.

The true ibex are found in the high north — in Swat, Baltistan, and Gilgit districts. And the Himalayan tahr has a limited distribution in Hunza and Nagar.

Chinkara, or Indian gazelle, possesses a much wider distribution in Pakistan, though it needs a special effort to see them.

They are found in all the peripheral, thinly inhabited districts of Sind and Punjab, whereas the goitered gazelle, rare and endangered, is restricted to the Makran and Nushki Kalat districts of Baluchistan.

In the foothills and the plains survive the last of such antelope as the nilgai, blackbuck, and both chinkara and goitered gazelle, besides hog deer, wild pig, and many medium-sized animals like the ratel, smooth-coated otter,

scaly anteater — pangolin — small Indian civet, and jungle cat.

Blackbuck can be seen in a small enclosed territory in Lal Suhanra National Park in the Cholistan Desert of Punjab. But the Nilgai, which has swiftly deteriorated in numbers, can only be seen in the Changa Manga forests of Punjab, or in eastern districts of Punjab, adjoining India.

Hog deer are also found in many parts of Punjab and Sind, whereas the barking deer is only found in the Margalla Hills, near Islamabad, and along the Jhelum valley in Punjab.

Marco Polo sheep

Musk deer though rare and endangered, like the hog deer, still survive in Swat, Dir, Kaghan, and Azad Kashmir.

In the far north, on the border with Chinese Turkistan, live the Marco Polo sheep, standing nearly 1.2 metres (four feet) high, with curved

Above: Mountain ibex in Naltar Valley.

horns up to 1.5 metres (five feet) long. In the higher mountain forests live rhesus monkey, grey langur, and a few black and red bear, musk deer, and snow leopard.

Small mammals are everywhere, including five species of shrews, four hedgehogs, and over forty rodents from the kangaroo-like jerboas of the sand dunes, to the flying squirrels of the pine forests.

Rarest mammal of all, one of the world's unique species, is the freshwater Blind Indus Dolphin, reserved to a fragile nucleus that inhabit the river in a long stretch near Sukkur, Guddu, and Taunsa Barrages on the Indus River as well as downstream of Panjnad Headworks. A 1980 census revealed that there were fewer than 340 of these strange and delightful creatures left — and a concerted conservation programme was launched.

There are many species of gerbils, sand rats, spiny mice and rats, as well as twenty-eight species of bat, ranging from giant flying foxes to tiny pigmy pipistrelles.

Of reptiles, there are three species of marine turtle (the green, hawksbill, and logger-head) specific to the sandy beaches and coves around Karachi — the green turtle and another related species. Migratory in habit, the green turtle, a huge species, has made a small strip of coast at Sandspit and Hawkes Bay one of its nine known breeding grounds.

An endangered species, the Sind Wild Life Management Board is actively involved in its protection and breeding in established hatcheries where each year thousands of eggs are hatched, the young to be released manually into the sea every year.

There are also seven species of freshwater turtle or terrapin, two tortoises, and two crocodilians. But crocodiles are on the decline. Six live in a protected but polluted and insufficient reservoir near a shrine at Manghopir, Karachi and two have been seen in Haleji lake.

In the wild, crocodiles still exist in small numbers in the Indus and its tributaries — their highest concentration being in the Nara canal and swamps along its banks, near Khaipur, Sind.

Most prominent among the 150 species of lizard in Pakistan, are four species of monitor lizard. The spiney-tailed lizard, known as the Uromastix is so common, that in all the colleges and universities, hundreds of students of zoology regularly dissect this lizard every year, and yet its population remains sizable.

There are several colourful species of agamids, geckos, blood suckers, garden lizards, skinks, sand lizards and desert-dwelling gekonids, as well as a variety of lacertids and skinks.

Despite the cold winters and dry habitat which do not favour snakes, there are more than forty-five species, including eight highly venomous land snakes, and four mildly-poisonous rear-fanged colubrids.

The dry areas and deserts of Sind and Baluchistan are home to some of the world's most deadly snakes. The Indian cobra, monocled cobra, the common krait, MacMohan's viper, Russell's viper, and the saw-scaled viper are seen with varying frequency.

The akistrodon viper is found as high as 2,400 metres (8,000 feet). The leaf-nosed viper inhabits the sand dunes of the desert, and down in the Indus delta dwell the last of the rock pythons.

The Indian boas, which are falsely said to possess two heads, the Rock python and the reticulated python, are among the largest of Pakistan's non-venomous snakes.

In addition to these species, fourteen species of marine snake, nine of them venomous, have been recorded in the waters of Pakistan's Arabian Sea.

Both the waters of the Arabian Sea and inland rivers and lakes are extremely rich in the variety of their fish species, some with unique features.

The 400 or more species of marine fish commonly found include the mackerels, tuna, hila, snappers, pomfrets, flat fish, sea-breams, eels, sardines, dhotar, threadfins, jewfishes, catfishes, carangids, mullets, and many other clupeiods, as well as shrimps, lobsters, and other crustacea.

At least twenty-eight species of shrimps and lobsters are so far known from the coast of Karachi and Makran and crabs are extremely abundant both in Pakistan's inshore and offshore waters with more than 125 species.

Within the last twenty years, two of the world's largest earth-filled dams have been built in Pakistan creating huge manmade lakes that have already become important fish breeding centres.

The most important of the 150 or more species of freshwater fish of the rivers and lakes that run through the plains of Punjab and Sind are the mahseer, rohu, singhi, thaila, singhari, khagga, and the pride of Sind, the hila which migrates up the Indus from the Arabian Sea like the salmon.

All in all, Pakistan's wildlife is a remarkable legacy, sadly diminished. It constitutes a vanishing treasury of the rare and the wonderful. But conservation laws have been enacted and national parks formed.

Wildlife Management Boards in each province now administer these sanctuaries and the laws and there is hope that in the decades ahead Pakistan will once again serve as a critical and major faunal reservoir for some of the world's rarest wildlife species, some of them unique.

Birdlife: A Feathered Fantasia

With one of the richest collections of avifauna in the world, Pakistan claims more than 600 species, of which more than 450 species are found regularly in Pakistan, although only about a third of them live there all year round. The rest are winter migrants from the palearctic and the north.

Many of these, drawn by the magnet of its manmade lakes, are migratory visitors drawn towards Pakistan from far-flung areas of the world like Northern Europe, Scandinavian North Sea, Western Siberia, Caspian Sea, Siberian Kazakastan, Tibet, Eastern Siberia, China, Japan, Manchuria, Alaska and California.

Among the most interesting are the edible game birds — including five vividly plumaged Himalayan pheasants, the Rufous turtle dove, and the snow and rock pigeons.

The desert supports three species of bustard, six species of sand grouses, coursers and pratincoles. Two francolins are found in the Indus basin, and in the drier hills are rock partridges, see-see and four species of dove.

In the wetlands there are some thirteen species of migratory duck, two wild geese, two cranes, and three storks.

In the pine and fir forests of the Himalaya live an abundance of brightly-plumaged chats, flycatchers, magpies, and jays. In winter even on the plains there are many palearctic warblers, wheatears, wagtails, pipits, and skylarks.

And although there are not so many forest and water birds like kingfishers, flycatchers, and drangoes, there are many species of birds suited to arid habitats, such as skylarks and wheatears.

And there is a remarkable array of raptors — five species of true eagle, buzzard, hawk, and falcon. In Sind twenty-two species of birds of prey have been recorded.

The pheasants are perhaps the most colourful, apart from being game birds. At least nineteen of their species including those of partridges, quails, and hill pheasants are known.

The pea fowl has now become rare in the world. Its observation being restricted to a few sightings in Tharparker (Sind) area. Western-horned tragopan, Impeyan monal pheasant, white-crested Kaleej pheasant, Chir pheasant, and Koklas pheasant are found. Partridges as well as quails are common all over Pakistan.

Persian and Northern chukors and sea partridges are added attractions of Pakistan. Several species of bitterns, storks, herons, teals, cranes, water hens, pratincoles, terns, sandgrouses, doves, cuckoos, kingfishers, bee eaters, barbets, wood peckers, larks, martins, shrikes, jays, bulbuls, thrushes, warblers, redstarts, tits, grosbeaks, finches and buntings are widely dispersed in our gardens, cultivated fields, streams, and hill slopes.

Among the resident birds of prey are the shikra, sparrow hawk, the buzzards and several species of eagles and vultures.

The houbara bustard, which attracts hundreds of falconers from Middle East countries every year, is a winter visitor to Pakistan, in the expanse of Cholistan desert, with a small number drifting southwards up to Kirthar National Park.

The Chakar, Grey, Black and See See Partridge, Western Tragopan, Koklas, Kaleej and Monal Pheasants are well-known game birds.

Opposite top: Spoonbill stork.

Opposite: Great white egret.

Opposite right: Grey heron.

Flora: The Jasmine and the Rose

Glorious in spring and summer, Pakistan has an abundance of trees, shrubs, and flowers — with more than 6,000 species of flowering plants. Depending on the climate, soil, and topography, the flora varies from tropical sea level to Arctic tundra in the high north.

Because of these extremes of temperature, Pakistan can be divided into four geophysical zones — Tropical, ever hot and winterless; Subtropical, warm summers and brief, cool winters; temperate, warm summers and pronounced winters; and Arctic, brief summers and long severe winters.

With the exception of the mountains, Pakistan's mean annual temperature exceeds 25°C (77°F) but the diurnal range appears to have no significant effect on vegetation provided tolerable limits are not over-stepped.

High diurnal ranges of temperature are found in the central Indus plains and parts of Quetta and Kalat Divisions. The highest mean annual diurnal range of 40°C (104°F) has been recorded for Kalat while in the Himalaya and Karakoram the annual diurnal range usually falls below minus 9.5°C (14°F).

With a mean annual rainfall ranging from less than fifty millimetres (19 inches) to l25 millimetres (49 inches), the variation in annual rainfall is an important factor for plant growth where the duration of the dry season determines the type of vegetation.

The vast majority of Pakistan — more than seventy per cent — is arid country. Yet few countries have such a diversity of terrain, stretching from the Arabian Sea in the west to the bleak wilderness of Tibet in Central Asia.

It produces five major botanical regions. The first group in southern and central Pakistan, on the great plains of Sind and Punjab, is an extension of the North Africa, Arabian, and Iranian deserts.

Save where water exists, either by channel or irrigation, most plants are salt and drought resistant, many with water storage tissues or other characteristics that they developed to survive in desert conditions.

Prominent among the flora are cacti, euphorbia, asclepiads, and salvadora.

The second main group, the Irano-Turanina, exists in the dry hills that extend from Iran into Baluchistan, Waziristan, Kurram, and the Khyber regions, where summers are hot and winters freezing.

Characteristic of the flora are the pencil cedar and the pine nut which are economically viable and among the extremely few arboreal species that exist. But fruit is cultivated extensively where there is water and for the botanist this region is particularly fascinating, much of its flora remaining unexplored.

The third major group is part Himalayan and part tropical — found from the plains at about 330 metres (1,000 feet) to the foothills at about 1,700 metres (5,500 feet) — in a zone that is in effect an extension of the dry Mediterranean region.

Among the most common plants are the acacias, olives, Grewias, Dodonaea, Gymnosporia, Adhatoda, Carissa, Indian coral tree, Flame of the Forest, and Mallotus which extends all the way from the Phillipines.

At around 1,000 metres (3,200 feet) the long-leaved pine, *Pinus roxburghii* (chir) is widespread and found in a number of places in pure stands. It is extensively exploited for its resin used in the manufacture of turpentine among other things.

Oaks and chestnuts

The fourth major group is Himalayan — rising from 1,700 to 3,300 metres (5,500-10,500 feet) above sea level with a great variety of plants well-suited to this temperate alpine environment.

Much of the genera is similar to that found in Europe — oaks, poplars, maples, horse-chestnuts, blue pine, yews, firs, deodars and spruces. Himalayan ivy, honeysuckle, and wild roses climb the trees.

In the forest undergrowth and open meadows there are shrubs like Berberis, Viburnum, Cotoneaster, and small flowering herbs — purple and pink geranium, Saxifrages, violets, columbines, delphiniums, primulas, gentians, anemones, and yellow buttercups.

At the edge of the tree line — at around 3,300 metres (10,500 feet) — the alpine meadows are filled with wild flowers.

One of the few trees found at this height is a species of birch, *Betula utilis*. Its white bark peels off in large sheets and since Marco Polo's time it has been used as writing material.

The fifth major group is composed of plants that flourish between 3,300 and 6,000 metres (10,800-19,700 feet), Tibetan and Central Asian

flora — such as medicinal plants like thyme, for liver and stomach complaints, Saussera, whose roots, exported to China, was used as a narcotic and as incense in temples and is now used as a perfume and insecticide; and Cordyalis, a medicinal root.

And south of Skardu, at 4,300 metres (14,000 feet) the Deosai Plains, an undulating plateau with many summer swamps where mosquitoes breed, is a unique replica of Arctic tundra with many interesting alpine and Arctic plant forms.

Most species bloom at the same time — during the brief summer of July and August — when, in addition to sedges, grasses, and dwarf willows, many plants grow in tufts and some form compact cushions.

Many exotics now flourish in Pakistan, too, especially the trees and shrubs found in the city parks of Sind and Punjab as well as herbs.

Another small botanical zone, known as the South Asian region, lies in the extreme south-east of Pakistan between latitudes 27°-28° N and includes Nagar Parker and the area of Rann of Kuch.

The flora of Nagar Parker contrasts sharply with that of the adjoining areas because of its higher rainfall and the flora is dominated by mostly Saharo-Sindian species.

Top: One of the many varieties of colourful flowers that adorn Pakistan.
Above: Fruit orchards blossom in the Hunza Valley.

Tastes of Pakistan:
A Culinary Adventure

The word curry entered the English language, we are told, in 1598. Forget you ever heard the originally Tamil word for a spicy sauce.

It has caused confusion for four centuries. Curry is curry is curry. But what is curry?

Most Pakistani (and Indian) cuisine has as much in common with what the faddish English call "curry" as Mickey Mouse has with Macbeth.

The food of Pakistan can be as subtle or as austere as it's rich historical tradition or stark geographical reality.

Cast aside all preconceptions about gritty, yellow, flour-thickened meat stews dumped over soggy rice and open the mind to a variety of dishes that encompass both the simplicity of golden baked nan bread and humble lentils and the exotic complexities of biriyani rice or Mughal dishes that stuff forcemeat inside small birds inside big birds in a cream sauce.

Forget the familiar odours of stock cubes, garlic butter and smoked bacon and enter a different world of cardamom, fenugreek, cumin, nuts and that most exotically expensive of aromatics, saffron.

The food, as anywhere else in the world, changes from province to province, town to town and is as varied as the people and their multi-coloured past.

Among ordinary Pakistanis, bread is eaten, broadly speaking, in the North and rice in the lusher South. But do not expect to find rigid conformity to this, even in the humblest roadside restaurants.

Tourists are known to have been offered beans on toast in the least likely looking hostelries.

On the frontier, Peshawar for instance, much of the traditional menu is charcoal grilled — and is the healthier for it.

Here in the Northwest, the average meal is likely to be lamb kebab and bread fashioned in some form out of the special wheat flour stonemilled for the purpose.

The bread is wonderful, varying from thin chapati, familiar in the West, to Tandoori-style nan cooked in sweat-soaked, open-fronted bakeries centred on a small clay oven dug in the floor and pushing out the most amazing aromas into the street.

It can come stuffed, usually with spiced, minced lamb — a meal in itself on a hot day. Lamb is also almost universal but marinated goat meat is difficult to tell apart. Beef is usually available only in tourist-orientated joints.

Many like their nan drenched in melted butter. Ask for it without the dressing if you don't need the extra calories.

Kebabs here come in as many forms as you can shape and flavour meat, and are grilled on barbecues or deep fried in huge "wok" like vessels often out front of the restaurant on the street.

If you suffer from a delicate stomach or simply don't feel you have enough local bugs in your system to be confident about eating anything else, deep fried food is a good bet in the caution stakes, though it won't do much for your waistline.

Still you won't be packing in routine potatoes.

Chapli kebab in the Northwest is minced meat distinctively flavoured with onion, coriander and pomegranate seeds.

Boti kebab is a more robust dish of marinated chunks of meat dressed with curd and spices.

Seekh kebab is a rich minced item, shaped sausage-fashion on a thick pepper.

Shami kebab is a plainer minced meat, "cut" with ground pulses, formed into meatballs and fried.

All kebabs share chillies and heavy garlic in common.

Dal as an accompanying dish is almost universal on the subcontinent. Spiced, fried pulse in a dozen forms from black-eyed peas through red and green lentils to bright yellow chana and giant chick pea, it can come as runny as soup or as stiff and dry as a heavy dumpling.

Tikka too is everywhere in Pakistan — meat, fish or chicken coated in a spicy red or orange yoghurt paste, grilled and eaten with nan.

In the coastal towns like Karachi, seafood can be good. Hyderabad and the wild frontier town of Quetta have a delicious marinated, delicately spiced barbecued leg of lamb or mutton, *sajji*.

In the far North, where fruit orchards flourish among the mountains, hearty lamb stews, flavoured with nuts, apricot, cardamom and cloves can be a delightful surprise.

In areas where the Mughal influences are

Above: Seafood market.

present, you will find the most exotic and richest food imaginable — providing the makings are available.

Expensive tourist restaurants and hotels will usually offer this kind of fare but beware, you may spoil your palate for life.

Consider palak gosht or gosht sabsi as it might be described — chunks of marinated, best lamb sauted in ghee (clarified butter) aromatic with ritually prepared fresh spice and then gently smothered in onion, finely chopped spinach and cream.

Kormas are casseroles cooked inside closed pans or ovens to force out the juices. In many styles, the meat is marinated and yoghurt is often an essential ingredient.

Masalas spiced

Masalas are rich but may start as comparatively uncomplicated spiced meat, fish or vegetable stew cooked atop stove or fire in ghee then highly flavoured with chillies and peppers of every hue, in pre-prepared combinations.

Keema is always minced lamb, fried with potatoes, peas or another vegetable and is a full-blooded spicy dish that requires a hearty bread or rice accompaniment because of its consistency.

Koftas are spheres of minced lamb, or sometimes vegetables, coming as small as the plastic items sliced around gold courses or in the case of the prince of the art — Nargasi Kofta — as big as a cricket ball.

Marinated spiced lamb bound with yoghurt is wrapped around hard-boiled eggs and poached in a tongue-tingling sauce that can vary from sugary sweet to vinegary, fiery hot laced with paprika.

Lunch and side dishes run through pilafs — the more or less complex pilaf rice dishes of the subcontinent — through simple stewed peas and curd cheese to humble but mouth-watering onion and tomato pickles eaten with bread.

Biriyani is a king of dishes when prepared properly over hours in a rice growing area and in good restaurants.

Meat versions are made by first poaching the chunks in a soup of coriander leaves, stock, ginger, peppers and cinnamon.

Ghee drenched rice is then charged with a subtle variation of spices, including saffron, and raisins and garlic in three or four more processes before it is combined with the meat, fried and then hermetically casseroled to complete the bewildering feast.

289

Desserts in milk areas are so many they defy description except to say that they are invariably very sweet and many serve the function of ice cream or sorbet, modifying a feeling of having dined perhaps too well to a pleasant sensation of having supped judiciously.

Pakistani food is not hamburger. If you hate very highly-peppered fare, say so when ordering. No cook in his right mind wants to serve what people simply cannot eat no matter how proud of his or her national dishes. But adjust your values about high-profile spice or stick to the international hotels offering corn flakes and meat and two veg.

Always eat highly spiced dishes with lots of plain bread or rice — an obvious balance that almost every foreigner ignores with obvious results. A runny nose, a trace of sweat on the brow and a stinging tongue are post-prandial phenomena you may come to find not only normal but will miss after a protracted stay.

Water, by the way, does not help with heavily chillied food. Turn to milk, if you must, or tea, or offset your intake with thin yoghurt side dishes combined with mint, onion, cucumber or tomato.

If you watch Pakistanis eat, water is taken on arrival in the eating house to quench thirst or after the meal to clear the palate and sweeten the breath. Rarely is water drunk while eating.

You will also notice that all eating, including the tricky business of ripping bread and shaping it into spoon-like shapes for the carriage of meat and runny sauce to mouth, is done with the right hand. A visit to the loo in any public place will explain why.

Toilet paper is not in great demand.

Unless you are a seasoned Third Worlder — and even then consider — never drink anything unbottled but proven, pure spring water.

On the road or a budget, be choosy about where you eat meat, avoid suspect, unwashed raw fruit and raw vegetables like the plague itself and never trust anybody's ice cubes. You may not protect against the runs here and there. But jaundice and hepatitis, costly, time-consuming, frustrating and debilitating, as well as sundry forms of dysentery and worse can be avoided.

Be polite and firm about it. There is no need for rudeness or embarrassment. Few foreigners have the anti-bugs to deal with all the bugs most Pakistanis have lived with since birth.

Opposite: Harvest of luscious fruit from the plains and mountain valleys adorns a Pakistan bazaar.

Above: Pakistan's equivalent of fast foods — a street vendor prepares sweet confections.

Opposite: Street snack operator fries a large form of Pakistani bread.

Sporting Pakistan

Despite the limited recreational facilities for the majority of its people, Pakistan is a sportsman's paradise — offering everything from the excitement of such popular sports as soccer, cricket, boxing, hockey, tennis, squash, horse riding, to the thrills of polo, trekking, big game fishing, fly fishing, scuba diving and mountain climbing.

Spectator sports

For many sports-lovers Pakistan is synonymous with cricket, hockey and squash. Introduced to Pakistan by the British, Pakistan sportsmen have not only excelled at these sports but given them a dimension of their own — a combination of Pakistan's ancient fighting spirit and the sublime artistry of master craftsmen.

Visitors will find both domestic and international games being played in stadiums in major towns across the country according to the season.

Yet few are aware of the many traditional sports played in Pakistan. Wrestling, horse-racing, polo, tent-pegging, *chatti*, and *kabaddi* have all been played for hundreds of years as important features of the many large and colourful festivals that occur throughout the countryside.

Cricket

Throughout Pakistan cricket is played wherever there's room enough to play and enough people to make up a team — from the back streets of Karachi to the picturesque playing fields of Ismailia College, Peshawar.

Just three years after being admitted to the International Cricket Conference, Pakistan came from behind to beat the formidable English XI and level the series in their England tour of 1954. Since then Pakistan has enjoyed victories against all major cricket-playing countries, both at home and abroad.

Hanif Mohammed, with a world-record top score of 499, is one of the most prolific run-getters in the history of the game. The 1989 captain Imran Khan is one of the most successful all-rounders of all time while moulding his side into one of the most formidable of the decade.

If Javed Miandad continues to score at his present rate, he will rewrite the record books

as a batsman. Abdul Qadir, the master spin-bowler, has not simply struck terror into the hearts of the world's top batsmen, he is one of the few players who, on more than one occasion, has against all the odds defeated the opposition on his own.

Hockey

In the last few years Pakistan dominance in hockey has waned as Australia and the European nations improved their skills and international standings.

The grace, brilliance and speed that used to thrill spectators all over the world, nevertheless, has given Pakistan a formidable international track-record in the forty-two years since Independence — Olympic gold-medallists in Rome (1960) and Mexico (1968), silver-medallists in Melbourne (1956) and Montreal (1976), bronze-medallists in Munich (1972). In addition they have won the World Cup (1971) and the Asian title (1970).

Squash

At Independence there were only ten squash courts in Pakistan and some 200 players of the game. Yet from this meagre base, one of the most phenomenal success stories in international sport has developed.

Even more remarkable is the fact that this success has been monopolised by one family — the Khans. At thirty-five years of age Hashim Khan began his remarkable record of victories which includes eight Scottish Opens and seven British Opens.

His nephew Jehangir — "Conqueror of the World" — continued the winning tradition by claiming the British Open a record nine times, the World Championship six times, and virtually every other tournament he has competed in. He played more than three years without losing a single game.

Sharing the same name, but not related, is Jansheer Khan. Already having tasted success as a teenager, Jansheer is expected, by many, to be even more successful than his illustrious namesakes.

Horse-racing

Pakistan has taken to horse racing as it has to other entertainments introduced by the British. Today Pakistan boasts of several fine racecourses, of which the Karachi Racecourse is the most famous.

Originally introduced by the Victorian

Top: Tense action in first-class Pakistan cricket match.
Above: Pakistan's world-class wrestlers.

Above: Tent pegging, an ancient and popular sport.

Garrison and now run by the Karachi Racing Club, meetings have been held regularly since 1876. Despite the fact that gambling is not allowed throughout Pakistan, the Thursday afternoon race meetings are well attended.

Tent-pegging and polo

In the lowlands, these sports are mainly confined to the rich, their employees, and personnel of the armed forces who can afford to keep a large number of horses.

But in the mountains where the sport was born they are played by everybody regardless of age, wealth, or skill.

They are not popular spectator sports and only attract support from tourists and foreign residents in addition to the families and friends of the players.

Traditional versions of these sports are played in Gilgit — in fact, polo was "invented" in Pakistan's northern areas and exported to the rest of the world by the British — at a fast and furious pace with almost no rules before large crowds of enthusiastic spectators.

Wrestling

Pakistan has a rich tradition of wrestling that goes back thousands of years. The legendary Gama was unbeaten in *kushti*, or oriental-style wrestling for nearly three decades.

His nephews, Bholo, Aslam, and Akram have carried on the tradition with successes in free-style as well as *kushti* wrestling. With the

loss of patronage by maharajahs at the time of Independence, the sport has waned and, despite government assistance, Pakistan now only make their presence felt in the Asian Games.

Lahore, Gujranwala, Sargodha, and Multan continue to produce Pakistan's top wrestlers.

Chatti and Kabaddi

The women of Pakistan have their own sport based on one of their traditional household roles — the carrying of water. A bit like an egg-and-spoon race, the *chatti* is as much a test of balance and strength as speed — with women carrying earthenware pots on their heads racing each other across a field.

Requiring both agility and strength, *Kabaddi* is a combination of chasing and wrestling. Played in the countryside, especially Punjab, in either organised tournaments or informal matches after a day's work, *kabaddi* is played between two teams of eleven men.

The rules require that one team catch an opponent who runs into their territory and for that person to wrestle free of his captor and return back to his territory within a certain time-limit — failure to do so causes his team to lose a point.

Soccer, boxing, volleyball, and rowing

As in most countries, soccer is the most popular of spectator sports, despite Pakistan's lack of international success or recognition.

What success Pakistan enjoys in boxing and weightlifting is limited to the Asian Games, as is volleyball and badminton.

Rowing in Pakistan may not be as strong as elsewhere but Pakistan oarsmen have proved their class against the best — most recently, the Peoples' Republic of China.

Participation sports

Golf has been steadily growing in popularity and several good golf courses have been established with all the pro-shop facilities for their members and visitors. In recognition of this, the Pakistan Open — staged at Lahore — has only recently been added to the Asian Circuit.

Tennis

Something of a poor second cousin to squash, the best that can be said of Pakistan tennis is that Pakistan regularly competes in the Davis Cup and not much more. For the visitor, most of the top-class hotels have a court for the enjoyment of their guests.

Hunting

Pakistan's plentiful wildlife and bird life has been diminished by over-hunting and poaching and now hunting is totally prohibited in many areas. However, enterprising operators in the Punjab lay on splendid hunting safaris in which the trophy is one of the country's plentiful supply of wild pig.

Trout fishing

For fly fishing — and Pakistan trout has some of the gamest fish in the world — the mountain rivers cascading into valleys like Hunza, Gilgit, Kaghan, Swat, and Baltistan offer memorable challenges. Permits are easy to obtain and cost little. Hire a ghillie to lead you to the best lies and bring your own tackle.

Watersports

Swimming, yachting, windsurfing, big game fishing in the Arabian Sea, skin and scuba diving are all available at Karachi.

River running

The thrills and excitement of white-water canoeing and rafting are as heart-stoppingly good as anywhere else in the world now that the following rivers of northern Pakistan have been opened to the enthusiast.

These are the: River Indus (Jaglot-Thakot), River Kunhar (Naran-Kaghan),River Swat (Behrain-Saidu Sharif), River Chitral (Dir-Butkhaila), and River Hunza (Aliabad-Gilgit).

Mountaineering and trekking

Through the ages these majestic and awesome mountains have lured nature lovers and adventurous mountaineers who have repeatedly scaled several of the major peaks rising above 6,000 metres (20,000 feet), many of which have remained unnamed and unclimbed. If you too can rise to the challenge then the treks in the sublime sanctuary of nature await you.

Since 1954 when the Karakoram range of Pakistan was opened to expeditions for climbing and more recently for trekking, the mountains and glaciers of the north have become an international playground.

Since 1975 innumerable mountaineering expeditions from foreign countries have attempted to climb the high peaks in the northern Pakistan and to trek among the lower altitude hills and valleys.

It is extremely important that each member of such expeditions be in excellent physical condition and be experienced in travel to rugged back-country places. Familiarity with camping and cross-country hiking is also important, as is a spirit of adventure and a desire for good companionship.

Mountaineering in Pakistan is the most highly skilled and demanding in the world — Nanga Parbat, for example, was first conquered in 1953 on the seventh attempt, fifty-eight years and thirty-one lives after the first.

Around fifty expeditions a year are given permission to attempt to climb some of the world's highest peaks. Most want to tackle one of Pakistan's 8,000-metre (26,250 feet) giants, among them K2, the world's second highest peak.

The majority fall within Baltistan — "Little Tibet" — where ten of the world's thirty-highest mountains stand within a twenty-five kilometre-stretch (15-mile). Now that there is an extension from the Karakoram Highway to Skardu, these are much easier to reach but there one still has to trek from Skardu, at punishingly high altitudes, for between ten and fourteen days to reach their base camp (See Listings for "Mountain" and "Trekking" regulations).

Top: Lahore's Summit Minar and marble pavilion with open Qur'an and WAPDA headquarters.
Above: Nineteenth-century clock tower, Faisalabad..
Opposite: Prime bull at Lahore's annual Horse and Cattle Show.

Above: Godwin-Austen Glacier.
Opposite: Vintage steam on a Pakistan Railways branch line.
Overleaf: Karachi, one of the subcontinent's great cities.
Following pages: Sundown over the Indus.

"Like Marco Polo – You Too Can Leave A Special Mark On The Historical Silk Road."

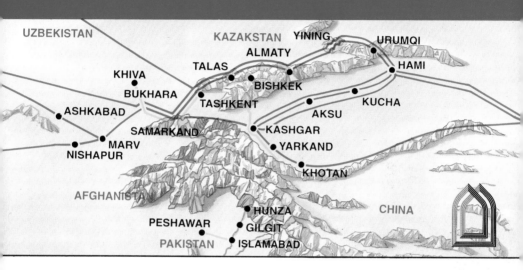

Highways that shaped history, the Silk Road were conduits for conversion as well as for commerce and conquest. This World's Longest Road has been treaded by merchants like Marco Polo, Arab traders, monks and by great warriors.

PIA provides you an opportunity to fly into Tashkent or Islamabad and wander along the ancient Silk Road's exhilarating cities of Samarkand, Bukhara, Bishkek, Kashgar, Hunza, Gilgit, Peshawar and many other cities and historical passes.

Learn of the various lifestyles, arts and cultures – explore the elegant tiled domes, exotic bazaars and centuries old architecture in the legendary, vibrant cities. Tashkent's awe-inspiring mystique in Uzbekistan and the caravanserais in Samarkand and

Bukhara. Stretching from China, view the beautiful landscapes in Kashgar. And as you enter northern Pakistan's enchanting valley of Hunza to reach Peshawar, view breathtaking scenes of the world's majestic Karakoram Range.

PIA invites you to come, see and capture all of these exciting places… as tourists. Avail our special Silk Road Tour Package. **Now you too can experience a part of history.**

For further information, please contact the nearest PIA booking office, your IATA travel agent or **PIA Tours Promotion Division** at Karachi.
Fax: 92-21-4570419
Internet: http://www.piac.com

PIA
Pakistan International
Great people to fly with

DISCOVER THE LEGACY OF
P A K I S T A N

A unique respite - rife with mesmerizing natural beauty blended with a rich cultural heritage, quaint bazaars, Mughal architecture and quiet antiquity of the Buddhist ruins - Resplendent with warm hospitality of a loving people. WAITING FOR YOU....

1965-1995
30 YEARS
WALJIS
the ultimate travel experience

TRAVEL WALJIS INC.
500, Summer Street, Suit No. 203,
Stamford CT 06901 - 1306, U.S.A.
Tel: (203) 356 0027, (800) 255-7181
Fax: (203) 348 6489

TRAVEL WALJIS PVT LTD.
Walji's Building, 10 Khayaban-e-Suhrawardy,
P.O. Box 1088, Islamabad-Pakistan.
Tel: (92-51) 270745-8 (4 lines), 270757, 270758
Fax: (92-51) 270753, 222015

PART FIVE: BUSINESS PAKISTAN

An Economic History: Fifty Turbulent Years

Pakistan's economy presents a story of almost continuous growth with only rare periods of stagnation. At independence in 1947 the major emphasis was on capital formation on one hand and the alleviation of poverty and also the elimination of social and economic inequalities on the other.

Pakistan's per capita income was estimated at US $ 440 in 1994 by World Bank, which puts it in the category of 'low income' countries. But this per capita figure, when converted at purchasing power parity (PPP), according to the methodology used by World Bank Atlas, is equivalent to US$2,010. Thus, on the basis of purchasing power comparison and the acknowledged fact that GDP per capita in Pakistan is sharply under-reported (to the extent of $ 800-1,000) Pakistan can legitimately claim a place among 'middle income' economies of the world. The World Bank affiliate IFC, has described Pakistan as one of the ten emerging capital markets in the world.

In the first decade of independence, Pakistan's resources were concentrated on the urgent problems of setting up an administrative machine and the settlement of refugees.

The small surplus of financial and organizational resources over and above the requirements of these tasks was devoted to expanding and maintaining the physical and social infrastructure.

The productive sectors were largely left to private enterprise, particularly in the manufacturing sector.

The public sector also played a positive role and was instrumental in meeting some of the basic and essential requirements of the private sector such as infrastructural facilities and long-term financing in both foreign and local currencies.

The first public sector enterprise with a commercial purpose, formed in 1950, was the Pakistan Industrial Development Corporation PIDC. Its mandate was to establish heavy engineering, fertilizer, jute, cement and chemical industries.

Competition between the two sector was healthy and many undertook joint ventures during the 1960s.

In the first half of the 1970s, however, the public sector underwent an excessive and rapid expansion that overstrained financial, management and manpower resources, resulting in an economic crisis.

Later policies have aimed at restoring private sector confidence in the market forces and encouraging the sector to play a more active role in industrial investment.

Public sector industries are being disinvested under a phased programme, which only large organizations and public utilities will survive. Pakistan ranks amongst the top seven fastest growing economies of Asia. Except for the period of the fifties and the seventies, annual gross domestic product has been growing at a rate exceeding six percent per year.

The economy has undergone marked structural changes. As a constant factor, the share of agriculture in Gross Domestic Product (GDP), declined from 53.19 percent in 1949-50 to 24.8 percent in 1995-96 while that of manufacturing has risen from 7.75 percent to 18.5 percent.

Pakistan inherited a backward agricultural economy. At independence there were only two cash crops, cotton and jute and they were exported in their raw form. Land tenure was feudal with landlords letting out cultivation to tenants without interest or right in the land and only a small share in the crops. Generally poor, these tenants were small farmers using primitive farming techniques.

But farming stagnated. Its annual growth rate up to 1960 was only 2.1 percent.

The Second Plan made a concerted effort to boost agricultural growth. As a result, agriculture achieved a growth rate of 3.8 percent surpassing the population growth rate of 2.6 percent.

This impressive achievement was the result of institutional changes, expanded use of essential inputs such as water, fertilizers, quality seeds and pesticides. Favourable weather conditions also helped the process.

Food production recorded an annual increase of 3.7 percent during the Second Plan as against 3.2 percent in the First Plan.

The rise in cash crops was more pronounced up by eleven percent a year against 4.5 percent before. Total production of principal crops registered an annual growth of 4.7 percent.

The Third Five-Year Plan (1965-70) recorded a growth rate of more than six percent. Food crops increased by 7.6 percent p.a while cash crops registered a rise of seven percent a year. Total crops production registered an increase of 9.1 percent.

In subsequent years the tempo slackened. The annual growth in the agricultural sector declined to 1.7 percent between 1970 and 1978. Unfavourable weather throughout most of this period, heavy floods in 1973, the mishap of Tarbela Dam in 1974-75, untimely and heavy rainfall in 1975-76 and scanty rains during 1976-77 were critical factors.

From 1978, however, the situation improved. Weather conditions were more favourable, Tarbela Dam began operating efficiently, and the policy of support prices for the major agricultural products and subsidies on agricultural inputs began to pay dividends.

Timely and adequate availability of essential inputs to the farmers was ensured. Procurement and support prices of some important crops such as wheat, paddy, sugarcane, and cotton were regularly increased. Subsidies on fertilizers, seeds, and the installation of tubewells were regularly rationalized.

The government also provided increased facilities on easy terms to the farmers. Small farmers were given interest-free loans and also ceilings of such loans were regularly raised.

A water management programme undertaken in irrigated zones reduced water losses caused by transition. All this resulted in the achievement of a yearly 4.4 percent growth rate in agriculture during the decade of eighties and early nineties.

During 1995-96, the agriculture sector also experienced a growth of 6.7 percent. Bumper cotton crop of 10.6 million bales was harvested in 1995-96, an income of 21.8 percent over 1994-95. Rice and wheat production also increased by 15.1 and 3.3 percent respectively. The high rates of this growth reflect both favourable weather conditions and satisfactory availability of key agricultural inputs.

By 1995-96, water availability had increased to 130.9 million acre feet from 12.4 million acre feet in 1985-86, credit disbursements from 13,685 million rupees to 17,735 million rupees in 1995-96 and fertilizer off-take from 1.5 million nutrient tonnes to 2.5 million nutrient tonnes.

These improvements were reflected in the field: land under cultivation rose from 14.69 million hectares in 1947-48 to 21.60 million hectares (estimates) in 1995-96, while the cropped area increased from 11.63 million hectares to 22.14 million hectares.

About seventy three percent of the total cropped area is under food crops, while the other remaining twenty seven percent of the total cropped area was under cash crops in 1995-96.

The total area under principal crops increased from 9.3 million hectares in 1947-48 to 17.88 million hectares in 1995-96.

Production of major crops rose from 11.4 million tonnes in 1947-48 to 71.4 million tonnes in 1994-95. Of the total production, wheat alone contributed 24.6 percent in 1995-96.

Industry

At independence Pakistan had little industrial capacity, largely a few agro-based units such as flour and rice mills and cotton ginning factories. There were no credit organizations nor were there any technical institutes or research laboratories.

In 1949 the private sector was assigned the key role for industrial development except in the field of defence and strategic industries.

To supplement the private sector initiatives, the Pakistan Industrial Development Corporation was given a mandate to establish such capital intensive or technologically complex industries that the private sector could not undertake.

The Pakistan Industrial Credit and Investment Corporation (PICIC) was established in 1958 to provide investment resources for private sector industries. Commercial banks also started to extend credit facilities to the sector.

By 1969-70, the number of cotton textile units had increased from seventy-two to 100, sugar plants from six to twenty, cement plants from six to nine, fertilizer units from one to four, vegetable ghee factories from eleven to nineteen, cigarette plants from eight to fifteen, cycle tyre and tube units from three to eighteen.

In 1972 thirty-two private sector industries were nationalized with a subsequent decline in the annual growth rate of the manufacturing sector to its lowest level 2.8 percent during the 1970-71 to 1976-77 period.

But following a categorical assurance from the new Government of 1977 that there would be no more nationalization, the country's industrial activity resumed with new vigor.

Under the 1984 Industrial Policy many industries were deregulated and industrial incentives revised. Private investment is being encouraged and new emphasis are given to the promotion of small industries.

While the small-scale sector accounts for only 32.8 percent of manufacturing output, its share in employment is 80 percent. The creation of a job in large-scale manufacturing sector costs about eighty times that of a job in small-scale manufacturing sector.

The improved atmosphere led to a 22.1 percent average yearly growth in the private manufacturing investment from 1982-83 to 1985- 86 and investment sanctions were up by eighty-three percent.

By 1995-96, Pakistan had achieved a high degree of self-sufficiency in a number of essential products such as cotton textiles, cement, vegetable ghee, sugar, fertilizers and steel.

During July-March 1995-96 production of cotton yarn increased by six percent, 1.1 million tonnes over the corresponding period of the previous year. During the 1980s, there were twenty six vegetable ghee units under the control of Ghee Corporation of Pakistan, with a production capacity of 530 thousand tonnes. Sixteen of these units were privatized in the early nineties. There are 70 sugar mills working in the country, having a 253 thousand tonnes crushing capacity per day.

At present 20 cement units (4 in public sector and 16 in private sector), having capacity of 9.9 million tonnes, are operating in the country.

At present, the total installed capacity of fertilizer is 4.143 million nutrient tonnes which is being fully utilized. Pakistan Steel, set up at a cost of 24,700 million rupees, is an integrated steel mill with a capacity of 1.1 million tonnes a year of raw steel.

The mill has a built-in potential to expand annual production capacity to 2.2 million tonnes. During 1995-96 the mill produced 674 thousand tonnes of coke, 990 thousand tonnes of pig iron, 317 thousand tonnes of billets, and 482 thousand tonnes of M.R. products and 16.2 tonnes of C.R. production.

Thirty-two downstream projects of Pakistan Steel were also proposed for implementation by the private sector. Six projects, including one for production of wire rods and baling hoops and two pipe-manufacturing plants, were in production while the remaining downstream projects were in different stages of planning and implementation.

Energy

At independence, Pakistan had extremely limited energy supplies, largely made up of low quality coal and imported oil. Hydroelectric power generation had only a very limited capacity, three percent of the total energy output.

In the early 1950s natural gas was discovered at Sui and the pattern of energy supply started to change. Thereafter, more gas fields were found and some oil discoveries were also made.

Large hydroelectric power stations were established at Warsak, Mangla and Tarbela Dams, increasing the output of hydroelectric energy many times. In 1973, a 137 MW Nuclear Power Station was also established at Karachi to join the energy supply sources.

In 1995-96, the percentage share of each component source of energy supply in the country was: gas 34.1 percent, oil 44.6 percent, coal 5.8 percent, LPG 0.46 percent, nuclear 0.33 percent and hydel 14.67 percent.

The recoverable reserves of crude oil as of 1st January 1996, are put at 230 million US barrels. The current oil production is around 58,000 barrels per day.

As on 31st January 1996, the recoverable reserves of natural gas were estimated at 21 trillion cubic feet. The production of natural gas stood at 1,806 MMCFD during July-March 1995-96, showing a 10.8 percent increase over the corresponding period of the preceding year.

Total consumption of gas during July-March 1995-96 was 12042 million cubic meter. Consumption during 1995-96 was domestic 17.3 percent commercial 2.98 percent, industrial 50.5 percent and power 30.6 percent.

Estimated production of coal in the country during 1994-95 was 2 million tonnes. The total coal resources of Pakistan are 184 billion tonnes. Of these 95 percent are located in Thar coal field in Sindh.

The total installed power generating capacity in the country increased to 12,850 MW at the end of 1995-96. Hydroelectric power constituted almost forty percent of total capacity.

The demand for power in Pakistan has been growing at the rate of nearly 10 percent per annum over the last two decades. The supply has not been able to keep pace with the demand due to paucity of development funds in the Public Sector. Load shortage of upto 2,000 MW exist in the peak load season of nearly four months in a year.

In order to overcome the power shortages, the GOP announced a policy framework incentives aimed at attracting private investment in the field of power generation in March, 1994. The policy aims at setting up private sector funded power generation projects based upon imported fuels, indigenous coal, on a fast track basis, to meet the power requirements.

At present, there are 24 power stations with a total installed generation capacity of 12,850 MW. During 1995-96, both WAPDA and KESC generated 48,223 MKWH of energy. The consumption was about 36,000 MKW: domestic 39.1 percent, commercial 4.2 percent, industrial 31.9 percent, agricultural 17.8 percent and others 7.0 percent. From 1985-86 when only 22,917 villages were electrified the number rose to 60,144 in January 1996.

After the 1973 energy crisis, Pakistan realized the importance of utilizing and developing renewable sources of energy and launched a systematic programme to tap these sources.

The first bio-gas unit was installed in 1974 to demonstrate the utility of bio-gas technology. A national programme was launched in 1980-81.

According to Eighth Five Year Plan (1993-98), most of the renewable energy in Pakistan is obtained by burning biomes (crop residue, fire wood, shrubs, cow-dung). Energy supply from other forms of renewable other than major hydels) such as solar, wind bio-gas, etc. are negligible.

The Government policy during Eighth Plan aims at continued emphasis on demonstration and utilization of these sources of energy in far flung areas where congenital sources of energy are non-available.

Located in the latitudinal range of 24° north, Pakistan has an abundance of sunshine. Pakistan has developed a practical strategy for heating, cooking, electrifying and water pumping to tap this energy.

Solar stations are being established. The Government of Pakistan has recently signed two MoU's (one of these with a US company) for the establishment of 150 MW and 100 MW capacity of solar power generation and wind turbines respectively.

Low velocity windmills are being developed in the country for water pumping to develop dairy farming and to meet limited irrigation requirements. To promote the utilization of available energy resources, a number of steps have been taken.

These include creating additional refining capacity and enhancing the energy efficiency of the National Refinery, reducing losses in the power transmission and distribution network, establishing organizations for strengthening energy planning capacity and energy conservation.

Transport and Communication

In Pakistan, roads dominate inland transport for both passengers and freight and will continue to be the most important mode of transport in future.

Out of 114.0 billion passenger Kilometres of total traffic in 1985-86 (excluding air traffic), roads carried eighty-five percent and railways fifteen percent.

Of an estimated 37.4 billion ton Kilometre freight (excluding air freight and bulk transport of coal and oil through pipeline) roads carried seventy-seven percent and rail twenty-three percent.

The existing classified road network (excluding city streets) has a total length of 205,304 Kilometres, including high type roads of 104,735 Kilometres and low type roads of 100,560 Kilometres. Special emphasis is being laid on the rehabilitation and improvement of the existing road network and construction of new roads, especially farm-to-market roads.

The railways have been unable to play a greater role because of persistent problems of old and worn-out assets, outdated machinery, and lack of operational efficiency.

Freight carried by the railways declined from eleven million tonnes in 1985-86 to 7.5 million tonnes in 1994-95. Annual passenger traffic in the late 1990s is around 65 million.

Pakistan Railways is, however, increasing its operational efficiency, reducing arrears of replacements, modernizing existing equipment, telecommunication and related signaling systems and streamlining operational techniques.

Karachi Port and Port Qasim are the two major sea ports of the country. The Karachi Port has established a record of an annual cargo handling of over 22.631 million tonnes in 1994-95. Port Qasim is situated 50 kms South-east of Karachi. At this port a cargo volume of 9.171 million tonnes was handled during 1994-95 which brings the total volume of cargo handled in both the Ports to 31,828 million tonnes.

The fleet strength of Pakistan National Shipping Corporation (PNSC) is sixteen vessels with a dead weight tonnage of 280,338. The ships ply between Pakistan and North America, the Red Sea, Mediterranean, Europe, UK and the Adriatic and Black Sea, and East and West Africa.

It is expected that PNSC will acquire 3 container ships and 2 bulk carriers shortly to meet the market demand.

The air traffic is covered by the country's national airline PIA Pakistan International Airlines, which handled passenger traffic in revenue passenger-Kilometres of 2,268 million.

Passenger capacity in available seat Kilometres is 15,848 million with a passenger load factor of 64.5 percent. Cargo capacity in available tonne a Kilometres is 2,452 million with 58.7 percent load factor.

On 31 March 1996, PIA's fleet consisted of forty seven air craft 8 Boeing 747,9 Airbus A-300-B4, 6 Airbus A-310, 2 Boeing 707 Freighter, 7 Boeing 737, 13 Fokker F-27 and 2 Twin Otter.

In March 1996 Pakistan had 13,320 post offices 2,026 of which were in urban areas, while 11,294 were in rural areas.

The number of telegraph offices and telephones was 425 and 2,255,300 respectively, while the number of public call offices was 8,172.

By March 1996, the number of licensed radio sets increased in the country increased to 421,666 from a mere 4,000 in 1947-48. Regular television services were introduced in Pakistan in early 1960s. The number of licensed TV sets rose from 74,344 in 1968-69 to 2,217,994 by March 1996, while the number of VCR sets was 126,246.

With twenty one broadcasting stations and thirty-nine short-wave and medium-wave transmitters with a total radiating power of 3433 KW, Pakistan Broadcasting Corporation (Radio Pakistan) is providing more than 350 hours of daily programmes. Islamabad Broadcasting House is the country's biggest and most powerful station with a 100 KW transmitter.

With its five main programme-originating centres, sixteen rebroadcast centres, three super high-frequency links, five translator centres and one low-power transmitter, Pakistan Television (PTV) is now televising round the clock T.V. programmes. Besides regular programmes, PTV is also televising educational programmes on another channel PTV2. The PTV began beaming its programmes through satellite from January 1996 increasing its network to 38 countries.

Trade

Pakistan inherited a crisis-ridden trade and commerce sector at independence.

The share of trade and commerce in the national income was only nine percent in 1948 compared to nineteen percent in India.

By the end of 1952 sterling balances and foreign exchange reserves had fallen steeply and all commodities and goods were brought under import licensing.

It was about this time that Pakistan saw the introduction of trade policies which aimed at boosting exports and encouraging import substitution industries.

The momentum was also sustained by taking several institutional steps including the introduction of Export Credit.

With the Guarantee Scheme and Export Market Development Fund and the establishment of the Trading Corporation of Pakistan, opening trade offices in a number of foreign countries, exports increased from 542.4 million rupees in 1948-49 to 3,371.4 million rupees in 1971-72, while imports increased from 1,176.8 million rupees to 3,495.4 million rupees during the same period.

In May 1972 the rupee was devalued to the extent of 131 percent. This provided windfall profits to exporters and caused losses to importers. The devaluation restricted imports and helped increase exports initially. Thereafter, imports started increasing at a much faster rate than exports and by 1976-77 rose to 23,012 million rupees, while exports increased from 8,551 million rupees in 1972-73 to 11,294 million rupees in 1976-77.

The overall balance of payments deficit increased from 131 million dollars in 1972-73 to 1,051 million dollars in 1976-77, the year in which the foreign exchange reserves also declined by 252 million dollars. The post-77 Government adopted a firm policy of boosting exports and encouraging the establishment and expansion of import substitution industries.

The policy was given a new impetus by the elected government. Consequently, export earnings were 29,280 million rupees in 1980-81 and further rose to 49,592 million rupees in 1985-86.

Current import-export policies are geared towards increasing agricultural and industrial production, expanding employment opportunities and promotion of exports.

Exports during 1995-96 rose to Rs.290,973 million ($8.6 billion). The export target set for the year 1996-97 is $10 billion.

To back up high growth in the industrial sector, liberal imports of machinery, spare parts, agricultural inputs, and industrial raw materials have been allowed on a concessionary tariff framework.

Edible oil, POL, fertilizers tea, chemicals, drugs and medicines, machinery and transport equipment remain the main items of import. The import bill rose from 23,012 million rupees in 1976-77 to 89,778 million rupees in 1994-95 and further to 392,800 million rupees ($11.67 billion) in 1995-96. Import bill is projected to rise to $12 billion in 1996-97.

Efforts are however, being made to contain imports through enhancement of domestic production in the fields of oil, energy, fertilizers, food grains and engineering goods.

Pakistan is a regular recipient of aid from the World Bank and the World Bank sponsored Aid-to-Pakistan Consortium comprising the developed countries. The IMF also provides aid as a balance of payments support under various arrangements. Pakistan has achieved, in recent years, a good growth rate of over six percent. Throughout the 1980s, Pakistan's economy displayed strength in maintaining a sustained increase in per capita income and living standards without undue strain. Meanwhile, the country's economy has undergone radical structural changes. Islamisation of the economy is going on at a rapid pace.

The interest-free banking, Zakat and Usher system, introduced in Pakistan in recent years, are not only working satisfactorily in the country but are also being keenly observed in the world.

The IMF conducted a survey of the interest-free banking system in mid-1980s. Similarly, Zakat and Usher systems are being considered at various international forums.

With a per capita income of 16,623 rupees in 1995-96, the distribution of income in Pakistan is now better than in many countries, rich and poor, of the world.

Government and Economy

Entrepreneurial, modern in its approach to the twenty-first century, Pakistan actively encourages foreign investment to set up industrial undertakings.

Private investment both local and foreign is promoted and guided into priority sectors to achieve national economic objectives under each Five Year Economic Development Plan.

These lay down the targets needed for each type of industry during each Plan period.

Preference is given to foreign private investment in industries which are capital intensive, involve sophisticated technology, or break new grounds in industrial promotion not previously experienced in Pakistan.

To attract and encourage foreign investment and technology an essential contributor to rapid industrialization, the government has provided statutory safeguards to protect the rights and property of foreign investors.

The Private Investment (Promotion and Protection) Act of 1976 allows investors to repatriate at any time their initial investment, together with the undistributed profits and any capital gains that accrue, in the currency of the country from which the investment originated — provided the industrial undertaking has been approved by the Pakistan Government.

An agreement between Pakistan and the United States of America guarantees that the rights, title, assets, and interests of any American company in Pakistan can be transferred to the US Government if a payment is made in US dollars, so long as the project has been approved by the Pakistan Government.

The Treaty of Friendship and Commerce with the US Government gives protection and privileges, more importantly in respect of security, movement, conduct of business, ownership, and fair compensation, in the event of nationalization, to nationals and companies of each country in the other country by according the status of national and or most-favoured nation.

Under the Protection of Rights in Industrial Property Ordinance, no industrial property can be compulsorily acquired without authority of law which provides for adequate compensation within a reasonable time.

The quantum of compensation can be challenged in a court of law.

Remittance of company dividends or branch profits out of current earnings from approved investments or payment of royalties, technical fees and interest on foreign loans under approved agreements is allowed freely to non-residents subject to applicable withholding taxes.

Where to begin

Pakistan has a liberal de-regulated and attractive environment for investment. The investors do not have to seek prior approval of the Government for setting up an industry in any field, place and size except for arms and ammunition, high explosives, radioactive substances, security printing, currency and mint. Alcohol; except industrial alcohol is banned.

The promoters of a new company are required to obtain the consent of the Controller of Capital Issues under the Capital Issues (Continuance of Control) Act, 1947. The consent shall be issued by the Controller after obtaining approval of the concerned Ministries, namely Ministry of Finance (for a banking company), Ministry of Commerce (for an Insurance Company), Ministry of Finance/Corporate Laws Authority (for an Investment Company).

Business in Pakistan may be conducted through a private or public limited company (whether listed or otherwise) or a branch.

Company registration

A public limited company may offer shares to the public. It should have a minimum of seven shareholders with no limit on the maximum number. No restrictions are imposed on the transfer of its fully paid shares. The minimum number of directors required is seven.

The provisions of the fourth and fifth schedules of the Companies Ordinance of 1984 apply to all companies and non-listed companies which prescribe the form and the contents of the statutory accounts of such companies listed on the Pakistan Stock Exchange.

To incorporate a company, apply to the Registrar of Joint Stock Companies, enclosing a copy of the Memorandum and Articles of Association and evidence of payment of the required stamp duty. After the necessary formalities are completed, the Registrar will issue a Certificate of Incorporation.

Foreign companies incorporated outside Pakistan can operate through a branch registered under section 451 of the Companies Ordinance 1984. To obtain registration, various documents (Memorandum and Articles of Association; address of principal office, list of directors, name of the person authorized to receive notices, etc.) must be filed with the Registrar of Companies.

Various agencies provide facilities for equity, long, medium, and short-term financing to companies in Pakistan through local equity participation in a foreign controlled company by private investors, companies, public subscription or institutional finance.

Agencies that provide institutional finance include the Pak-Kuwait Investment Company Ltd. (PKIC); Pak-Libya Holding Company Ltd. (PLHC) Bankers Equity Ltd. (BEL); National Investment Trust (NIT); Investment Corporation of Pakistan (ICP); and Pakistan Industrial Credit and Investment Corporation (PICIC).

Debenture financing is also practiced with repayment periods of up to ten years.

Among the agencies that provide medium-term loans in both foreign and local currencies are the Industrial Development Bank of Pakistan (IDBP) Pakistan Industrial Credit and Investment Corporation (PICIC) National Development Finance Corporation (NDFC); and Bankers Equity Limited (BEL).

The State Bank of Pakistan guarantees exchange risks on approved foreign currency industrial loans on payment of premium for exchange risk. Such loans are generally given for financing of plant and machinery. Loans for financing locally fabricated machinery are also provided by the same organizations at concessionary rates of interest.

Pakistan has a liberal foreign exchange regime with no restrictions for holding foreign exchange, transacting, bringing in or taking out of the country. There is no restriction on repatriation of capital gains and profits. Foreign and Pakistan nationals can invest in shares quoted on the Stock Exchanges against foreign exchange on a repatriable basis. Foreign controlled manufacturing companies which export 50 percent or more of their production can borrow for working capital from domestic credit institutions without any limit and without any permission from the State Bank of Pakistan (the Central Bank) regardless of the local content in the equity. Other foreign controlled manufacturing companies can now obtain loans equal to their equity without prior permission of the State Bank.

Foreign controlled manufacturing companies can borrow for investment purposes from banks, development financing institutions (DFI) and other financial institutions or by issuing participation Term Certificates etc., without any limit and prior approval of the State Bank of Pakistan.

In 1985, Pakistan introduced a new banking system based on Islamic principles whereby interest 'RIBA' was eliminated from the banking system in working capital financing.

Finances for working capital may be provided either on the basis of Musharika or mark-up.

It's the kind of arrangement where the banks and trade and industrial organizations participate in ventures on a profit and loss sharing basis. Profits are shared in a pre-agreed proportion based on actual utilization of a bank's funds calculated on the basis of daily products and the client's investment.

Before sharing the final profits, a certain portion is given to the client by way of management fees for achieving the projected profits. If these projected profits are exceeded, a higher fee may be paid in recognition of managerial excellence, thereby restricting a bank's return to the pre-negotiated rate.

The trading business may be financed by the purchase of goods by the bank and their sale to clients at an appropriate mark-up on a deferred payment basis.

In addition, manufacturing industries may be financed by the bank purchasing manufactured goods with a buy-back agreement at a marked up price.

A new concept of financing based on profit sharing has been introduced in Pakistan called 'Modaraba'.

This financing enables a management company to control and manage the business of a Modaraba Company with a minimum of ten percent equity participation.

For this, the management company is entitled to remuneration based on an agreed percentage (not exceeding ten percent) of annual profits. The business can be for a specific or multi-purpose and for a limited or unlimited period.

Income is free of tax if ninety percent of its profits are distributed in cash or stock. The flotation and management are regulated through the Modaraba Companies and Modaraba (Flotation and Control) Ordinance, 1980 and Modaraba Companies and Modaraba Rules, 1981.

Participation Term Certificates (PTC)

Instead of interest, the holders of PTC share in the profits or loss of the business at a pre-determined rate. The rate of profit and loss sharing and principal redemption period is subject to mutual agreement of the company issuing PTCs and prospective subscribes.

As with debenture interest, payments of profits to PTC holders are deductible as a business expense for tax purposes.

In view of the strategic location of Pakistan in relation to the Middle East and Central Asian Republics, a Custom Free Export Processing Zone has been established in Karachi in order to attract foreign investment, increase exports of manufactured goods, and facilitate the introduction of new technologies and modern concepts of management and marketing.

Proposals for setting up projects in this Zone should be submitted to the Export Processing Zone Authority (EPZA) Karachi, for approval. All investments and payments within the Zone are in foreign convertible currencies. The companies established may be 100 percent foreign owned or with Pakistani collaboration in the form of non-repatriable investment (NRI).

Imports of machinery, components, spare parts and raw materials for industrial concerns in the Zone, as well as imported items destined for re-export, are freely allowed in the Zone. These items are exempted from all federal and provincial taxes and duties.

Exports from the Zone are completely free from Exchange Controls and duties. Exporters are free to export merchandise overseas without any obligation to repatriate their earnings back to Pakistan.

Free employment of expatriate is allowed with exemption of salary income tax for five years.

The principal statute governing income-tax is the Income Tax Ordinance 1979. Assessments are made in the government fiscal year (July-June) and tax is payable on assessed income during the financial year, which normally comprises twelve months ending on 30 June or 31 December. The liability to tax varies according to the residential status of the tax payer.

Corporate Tax: Residential Status

A company is regarded as resident in Pakistan if it is incorporated in Pakistan or the control and management of its affairs is situated wholly in Pakistan during the 'income year'.

Residents are liable to be taxed on total world income, regardless of where it accrues or arises or is received, whereas non- residents are not liable to be taxed on income which arises outside Pakistan unless it is deemed to accrue or arise in Pakistan or is received or deemed to be received in Pakistan.

Broadly speaking, taxable income from business is determined after deducting such expenditure as rent, repairs, insurance, bad debts, depreciation, etc.

All expenditure, other than that of a capital or personal nature, is generally admissible as a deduction, provided it is expended wholly and exclusively for the purposes of the business. Brokerage, commission, ,interest and salaries paid to non- residents will not be admissible deductions unless taxes from such payments, if applicable, have been with held or paid in Pakistan.

Operating losses can be carried forward against the profits of the succeeding six years of the same business which incurred the losses. Unabsorbed depreciation can be carried forward indefinitely. No carry-back of losses is permitted.

Tax Depreciation

Initial depreciation allowance is available — in the year of erection or installation, or in the year the asset is first used or in the year it commences, whichever is later — on plant and machinery of new industrial undertakings (forty percent), residential buildings for industrial labor (twenty-five percent), other buildings (ten percent), other machinery and equipment (twenty-five percent) and certain types of motor vehicles (twenty-five percent), all of which should not have previously been used in Pakistan.

On ships registered in Pakistan the rate allowed ranges between 5 and 20 percent.

Normal tax depreciation allowances are given generally on the reducing balance method at the prescribed rates ranging from five-thirty percent and 100 percent on below ground installations of undertaking engaged in exploration and production of petroleum.

Multiple shift allowance is also provided at fifty percent of normal depreciation on machinery and equipment, proportionate to the number of days worked in a year of 300 days, for double shift working and at 100 percent for triple shift working.

As leasing is one of the accepted modes of interest-free financing, provisions have recently been introduced whereby depreciation is also allowable to scheduled banks, financial institutions, and approved leasing companies on building and machinery or plant given on lease (other than ships and motor vehicles not plying for hire).

For building it is necessary that the leased building is used by the lessee for purposes of his business or profession. Initial depreciation is allowed at ten percent on building and at forty percent on plant and machinery. Normal depreciation is allowable at the aforementioned applicable rates.

The Finance Ordinance 1979 introduced the concept of Fees of Technical Services which provides inter-alia that such income should be deemed to accrue or arise in Pakistan (no matter where the services are rendered) if the information, services etc. for which the technical fees were paid are utilized for the purpose of business carried on by the payer in Pakistan or for the purpose of earning any income from any source in Pakistan.

Fees for technical services has been defined to mean any consideration (including any lump sum consideration) for the rendering of any managerial, technical, or consultancy services (including the provision of the services of technical or other personnel), but does not include consideration for any construction, assembly or like project undertaken by the recipient or consideration which would be income of the recipient chargeable under the head 'Salary'.

Capital Gains and Losses

Capital gains from sale of shares of a public company were exempt from tax up to 30 June, 1988. Capital gains on fixed assets (other than immovable property) which are eligible for depreciation allowance are chargeable to tax as normal business income either in the year of sale or, if there are other similar assets, over the life of such assets (pool basis).

Capital gains on immovable property, which were previously subject to provincial tax are now exempt from tax. Capital losses can be offset only against capital gains. Unabsorbed capital losses can be carried forward for adjustment against capital gains in the succeeding six years.

Tax on the dividends received by a public company from a Pakistan company is payable at the rate of 5 percent and at the rate of 15 percent in case dividends are received by a foreign company. Inter-corporate dividends declared or distributed by power generation companies is subjected to reduced rate of tax i.e., 7.5 percent. Other companies are taxed at the rate of 20 percent. Dividends paid to all non-company shareholders by the companies are subject to with holding tax of 10 percent which is treated as a full and final discharge of tax liability in respect of this source of income.

For tax purposes an expatriate is normally liable to pay income tax as if he is in Pakistan for more than 182 days in an income year.

A resident is taxed on his world income but expatriates are exempt from Pakistan tax on income arising outside Pakistan even when resident, provided they have not been resident for nine out of ten years preceding the income year.

The same applies if they have not during the seven years preceding that year been in Pakistan for an aggregate period of more than two years and provided the income is not derived from a business controlled in or a professional set-up in Pakistan and is not brought into or received in Pakistan during such income year.

Salaries which are subject to tax have been very broadly defined to include wages, annuities, pensions, gratuities, fees, commissions, perquisites, payments in lieu of salaries and wages arising from employment and compensation for loss of employment.

Irrespective of the place where salary is paid and notwithstanding the residential status, so long as it relates to services rendered in Pakistan, it is taxable in Pakistan.

Any special allowances or benefits specifically granted to meet expenses, wholly and necessarily incurred in the performance of the duties of an office or employment of profit, are not included in the expatriate's taxable income.

No tax is payable on remuneration received by an employee of a foreign enterprise for services rendered in Pakistan if the employer is not engaged in any trade or business in Pakistan, provided his stay in Pakistan does not exceed ninety days in the income year and the remuneration is not deducted from income of the employer chargeable to Pakistan tax.

Non-resident individuals are taxed at thirty percent of their total income or pay tax on their total Pakistan income as if it were the total income of a Pakistan resident, whichever of these two yield the higher amount of tax.

A non-resident can also opt for assessment at the average rate of tax calculated with reference to his total world income.

A resident individual pays tax at the graduated scale (slab rates ranging from ten to thirty five percent) on total income after deduction of a standard allowance of 50,000 rupees.

Tax Incentives

On this basis the effective rate of tax on total income ranges from twelve to twenty five percent of say, 200,000 to 500,000 rupees.

Under the Ordinance, the Federal Government has the power to make an exemption, reduction in rate or other modification in respect of tax. The following are some of the major tax incentives.

A Tax Holiday to new industrial undertakings in the field of electronics would be available for a period of 10 years. Five years Income Tax Holiday is admissible to industrial undertakings engaged in food processing, manufacture of toys, which are established between 1st July 1994 and 30th June 1997. Flat rate of income tax for non-residents has been reduced from 30 percent to 20 percent.

Income tax on dividends or shares of company set up for power generation have been reduced to 7.5 percent of the amount of such dividends.

Tax credit at fifteen percent of the cost of machinery installed for modernization, balancing, replacement and in certain cases extension of existing industrial units, allowed to Pakistani companies where machinery is installed up to June 1988. Tax credit up to thirty percent is admissible to a company in respect of amounts invested in the acquisition of share capital or a company which sets up an industrial undertaking in specified underdeveloped areas.

Rebate is allowed to all commercial and industrial exporters at the rate of fifty-five percent of the tax attributable to income from export of goods manufactured in Pakistan.

Salary income of foreign technicians is exempt from tax for a period of three years from the date of arrival in Pakistan subject to approval of their contract of service by the Commissioner of Income Tax. No 'tax on tax' is to be levied for a further period of five years if tax is paid by the employer.

The face value of bonus shares or the amount of any bonus declared, issued or paid by a company to its shareholders with a view of increasing its paid up capital is exempt in the hands of shareholders.

The following incentives would be available to the industrial units set up in the EPZ:

- complete exemption from all federal, provincial and municipal taxes; any foreign exchange control and insurance regulations as applicable in Pakistan;
- tax holiday upto the year 2000 AD, thereafter 25 percent in perpetuity;
- income accruing outside Pakistan is exempted from tax;
- the losses, if any, on an undertaking set up in the Zone may be carried forward indefinitely;
- import of equipment machinery and materials (including components, spare parts and packing material) for enterprises set up in the Zone;
- is exempted from all federal and provincial taxes and duties including customs, excise, sales tax and municipal taxes;
- 'One Window' service and simplified procedures import permits and export authorizations are also issued by the Export Processing Zone Authority (EPZA) itself;
- usual import/export restrictions enforced in Pakistan are not applicable to the zone;
- export of goods from the Zone are exempted from all duties;
- all goods and material entering into the Zone from the tariff area are considered to be exports from Pakistan, hence they are entitled to all the facilities and concessions allowed on exports to other countries.
- off-shore banking and insurance facilities are available in the Zone;
- full repatriation of capital, profits and dividends is allowed to the foreign investors and non-resident Pakistanis;
- resident Pakistanis are allowed to invest up to 100 percent in joint ventures in the Zone;
- exemption from the labour laws applicable in the country;
- there is no minimum investment required;
- free employment of expatriates with exemption of salary income tax for five years from the date of arrival in Pakistan;
- international distribution centres are allowed to be established;
- constructed warehouse buildings are available on temporary rental basis;
- duty free import of up to three vehicles is allowed proportionate to the capital investment.

Subject to the provisions of the Internal Revenue Code, taxes payable by US residents in respect of income from sources in Pakistan is allowed as a credit against US taxes payable in respect of that income.

US corporations, having no permanent establishment (viz. a branch, a place of business or factory, etc.) in Pakistan, which are public companies, and own shares carrying more than fifty percent of the voting power in a Pakistani company engaged in an industrial undertaking, are allowed a rebate of 6.25 percent against the super-tax payable by them on dividend income (15-6.25).

Royalty income (not exceeding a fair and reasonable consideration) of a US resident is exempt provided the person receiving it does not have a permanent establishment in Pakistan.

United States enterprises are not subject to Pakistan taxes in respect of their 'industrial or commercial profits' unless they are engaged in trade or business in Pakistan through a 'permanent establishment' situated in Pakistan.

Income derived by an individual who is a resident of the United States, in respect of personal or professional services performed within Pakistan, in any financial year (year commencing 1 July and ending 30 June next) is exempt from Pakistan tax if the said income is taxable in the United States, if the individual's stay in Pakistan does not exceed 183 days in that year and if the services are performed for or on behalf of a resident of the United States.

Export Brief

The **Pakistan Export Promotion Bureau** is charged with developing markets for Pakistan goods overseas. With vast resources of men and material Pakistan can supply goods to buyer's specifications to any part of the world.

Cheap labour costs and skilled manpower give the products an edge in quality and price. A well-developed air and sea network guarantees shipments to most parts of the world without too much delay.

Pakistan embassies abroad provide guidance to the buyers on sources of import, quality control, mode of shipments etc.

Quality Control

Both the Government and business sectors ensure that only goods manufactured according to international standards and gradations are exported from Pakistan.

In pursuance of this policy the Pakistan Standard Institute has laid down minimum standards for a number of manufactured goods and agricultural products.

Commercial Courts

Pakistan has established a system of commercial courts to deal with complaints in respect of quality against Pakistani exports.

Severe punishments are awarded to the defaulting exporters and overseas buyers are compensated from a special fund.

In case of complaints, buyers of Pakistani goods are advised to approach the Export Promotion Bureau with quality survey reports and other documentary proof.

The Government of Pakistan has appointed two overseas pre-shipment Inspection companies (viz. CONTECNA and SGS) to ensure correct valuation of commercial transactions against prevailing export market price in the country of supply for payment of customs duty purposes.

Display Centres

Pakistan's Export Promotion Bureau has established display centres at Karachi, Lahore, Islamabad, Peshawar, Faisalabad, Quetta, Sialkot, Hyderabad, Gujranwala, Sargodha, Abbottabad, Larkana, Swat, Mirpur and Multan where most export items are on show.

Leather and carpets

Every year Pakistan holds a leather show at Karachi and a carpet exhibition at Lahore in the first and last week of February respectively. New products and designs are put on display.

Wholesalers, retailers and consumers from all over the world attend these fairs. Visits to these exhibitions are helpful in locating the hitherto hard-to-find suppliers who can give quality goods at competitive prices.

Commerce, Trade and Industry Associations

Pakistan Chambers of Commerce and Industry and trade associations provide assistance, detailed information about their members, e.g., complete postal address, location, cable address, telephone, fax and telex number, bankers name and items of specialization, to foreign importers. For Chambers of Trade and trade associations (see listings).

Trade Directory

The Export Promotion Bureau has published a directory of all registered Pakistan exporters. Copies are available from Pakistan diplomatic missions abroad.

Buyers wishing to purchase from a new exporter should seek verification from the Export Promotion Bureau or the relevant trade association through Pakistan trade offices abroad.

Shipment

Regular shipping facilities are available from Karachi to Saudi Arabia and Gulf ports. In addition to the Pakistan National Shipping Corporation and Pan Islamic Shipping Company several foreign shipping companies such as Maersk Lines, Sinchio Lines, Merzario Lines, Y.S.Lines, American President Lines and Lloyd Triestino Lines have regular cargo sailings from Karachi.

Pakistan International Airlines, Saudia, Gulf Airlines and Emirates also operate from Karachi, Lahore and Islamabad to Middle East countries. Adequate cargo space is available on these Airlines for imports from Pakistan. Apart from cargo flights, PIA also operates special Combi flights to Saudi Arabia and the Gulf.

Restricted Export Commodities

The following items can only be exported through Pakistan's public sector agencies.

Petroleum and petroleum products, except mineral turpentine when it is to accompany and form part of paints and varnishes exported; coke; rock salt when exported under table salt, except for border trade; sodium hydroxide (caustic soda).

Special Procedure Commodities

The export of precious and semi-precious stonnes and gold jewellery (including gold jewellery embedded with indigenous or imported precious or semi-precious stonnes) is governed by the special procedure notified by the Export Promotion Bureau. Goods consigned to India can be exported only by public sector agencies in accordance with the procedure prescribed for regulating trade under the India-Pakistan Trade Protocol of 30 November, 1974.

The export of cinematography films produced in Pakistan by the private sector is subject to the production of a 'No Objection' certificate from the Culture, Tourism and Youth Affairs Division, Islamabad.

The export of pre-recorded audio-cassettes is subject to a certificate of 'No Objection' from the Ministry of Information and Broadcasting. The export of used copper and brass utensils is subject to confirmation from the Department of Archaeology and Museums that such goods do not fall within the definition of 'antiques' and that the items have been duly checked and authenticated by the Department.

The export of exotic, captive-bred birds (guineafowl, turkey, domesticated exotic pigeons, java sparrows, zebra finches, white finches, domestic ducks, domestic geese, budgerigars, cockaterils love birds, crows, house sparrows, Japanese quails, white quails, day-old ducklings, Bengal finches, serens finches, gimple finches) and domesticated rabbits is subject to clearance by the National Council of Conservation of Wildlife (NCCW) at Islamabad and provincial wildlife departments at other exit points. The export consignments must be accompanied by a quarantine certificate and caging by the animal/plant Quarantine Departments.

The export of endemic birds is subject to clearance by the National Council of Conservation of Wildlife at Islamabad and provincial wildlife departments at other exit points.

Export consignments of rose-ringed parakeet Psittacula krameri have to be covered by the Convention on International Trade in Endangered Species of Wild Fauna and Flora (CITES) and export certificate issued by the National Council of Conservation of Wildlife. The Pakistan Agricultural Research Council, Islamabad and the Commonwealth Institute of Biological Control, Rawalpindi, however, are exempted from the requirement to produce a CITES certificate in respect of export of specimens of plants and animals, including insects for scientific purpose.

The export of fillies/mares is subject to clearance by a committee comprising representatives of the Remount, Veterinary and Farms GHQ, the Livestock Division of the Jockey Club of Pakistan, and the Horse Breeders' Association.

Horses other than fillies and mares registered with Jockey Club of Pakistan can be exported through an identification certificate issued by the Jockey Club and with an export permit from the Chief Controller of Imports and Exports.

The export of cotton/blended yarn having cotton content of 50 percent or above is subject to the provisions of Schedule IV and a certificate from the Pakistan Textile Mills Association, specifying the quantity of yarn to be exported.

Consignments for countries where quantitative restrictions have been imposed shall be exported under export visas issued by the Export Promotion Bureau.

Certificates issued by the Association within the first week of every month to manufacturers of cotton yarn and exporters of cotton yarn with past performance to their credit are non-transferable and must be registered within the second week of the month at the pre-shipment stage with the Export Promotion Bureau.

If the certificate holder fails to ship the consignment within two months, the Export Promotion Bureau auction cargo to registered exporters. Each month's unallocated export quota reverts to the Export Promotion Bureau for auction.

All export contracts have to be registered with State Bank of Pakistan and exports are allowed only against registered contracts.

PART SIX: FACTS AT YOUR FINGERTIPS

Visa and Immigration Regulations

As per the law of the land, a visitor must be in possession of a valid passport issued by his government along with sufficient currency to cover expenses during his stay in Pakistan. The facility of entry without visa is not available in the case of a foreigner who intends to take up employment with or without remuneration, in Pakistan.

The Visa regulations are:

Genuine tourists, except nationals of countries indicated below, shall be given landing permits/transit visas for 3 days (72 hours), free of charge by immigration staff at entry points/airports provided they possess return air ticket, yellow fever vaccination certificate and sufficient foreign exchange. The landing permit/transit visa is extendable up to one month from the nearest visa office.

A single journey entry visa is valid for a stay of three months and can be utilized within six months from the date of its issue. Multiple journey visas are also valid for 3 months stay at a time. Foreigners entering one province of Pakistan do not have to obtain visa for entering the other province.

However, no visa is required by a bonafide tourist for sightseeing and recreation for a period not exceeding 30 days except the nationals of Afghanistan, Bangladesh, India, South Africa and the nationals of the countries not recognized by Pakistan. Such foreign tourists are not granted entry visa or extension of stay for more than 30 days. They must obtain visa before coming.

Foreign tourists, other than nationals of Afghanistan, India and countries not recognized by Pakistan, are exempt from the requirement of police registration provided their stay in Pakistan does not exceed 30 days. Those entering Pakistan through regular checkposts are not required to obtain road permits if tourist stamps are affixed on their passports. Entry visa and police registration are two different things. Therefore, those intending to stay in Pakistan for more than 30 days should get themselves registered with the nearest Foreigners' Registration Office in addition to obtaining a visa where necessary.

Departure Tax

Departing visitors must pay an airport tax of Rs. 250 economy Rs. 600 for club and class, Rs. 600 first class. Infants under two are free.

International flights

Pakistan is well served by International flights from all around the world to international airports at Karachi, Lahore, Islamabad, and Peshawar. The flying time to Karachi International Airport from New York is almost eighteen hours; from Tokyo eleven hours; from London eight hours; from Hong Kong six hours; from Jeddah almost four hours and from Abu Dhabi 100 minutes (one hour and forty minutes).

Airports

Including the four international airports, Pakistan's Civil Aviation Authority manages and maintains thirty-eight airports. New terminals are made at Karachi, Lahore and Islamabad. Other major airports are at Quetta (Baluchistan) Faisalabad, and Multan (Punjab), Hyderabad, Sukkur, Nawabshah and Moenjodaro (Sind). Gilgit (northern Area), Peshawar, Saidu Sharif and Chitral (NWFP).

Around a million passengers a year fly to Pakistan.

Customs

Visitors may import duty-free handbags and travel goods, metalwork, including trophies and prizes bestowed upon them, personal jewellery worth no more than 1,000 rupees, watch and travelling clock, personal toilet requisites including electric shaver in use, spectacles and other physical aids, cigarette lighter, two fountain pens, one penknife, and similar objects, women's hair drier, camera and five rolls of film, binoculars, tape recorder, portable typewriter, invalid chair, perambulator or go-cart and toys in reasonable quantity, if in use of an accompanying child, games or sporting requisites in actual use including sporting firearms and cartridges in reasonable quantity (subject to the production of an arms licence issued by a competent authority), 200 cigarettes or fifty cigars or half a pound of manufactured tobacco or an assortment of cigarettes, cigars, and manufactured tobacco not exceeding half a pound in weight, perfume and toilet waters up to half a pint, foodstuffs including confectionery, and non alcoholic drinks up to a value of 100 rupees.

Motor vehicles

Tourists may import free of duty a motor vehicle under a 'Carnet de passage en Douane' for a period of up to three months, provided they pledge before the Customs Officer at the place of entry that they will not transfer in any manner the ownership of the vehicle during their stay.

If the tourist is unable to re-export the vehicle in the time allowed, they may apply for an extension to the Central Board of Revenues before the expiration of the initial period.

For the purpose of this regulation, the term motor vehicle refers to any motor car, motorcycle, van, microbus, or bus.

Liquor

Visitors are not allowed to carry liquor into the country. Those who declare it at Customs will be given a receipt and can reclaim it on their departure.

Non-Muslim foreign guests in hotels authorized to sell liquor against permit can purchase it for consumption in their rooms on production of their passport.

Non-resident non-Muslim foreign visitors wishing to buy liquor from authorized hotels or distributors must obtain a permit from the prohibition office of the Excise and Taxation Department of the respective area and province in which they are staying.

Currency

The official currency is the rupee. Coins of various value are issued up to one rupee. The notes have denominations of one, two, five, ten, fifty, 100, 500 and 1000 rupees. the rupee is no more pegged to the US Dollar and hard currency exchange rates are published daily by the State Bank.

Exchange control rules are strictly enforced by the State Bank where the Chief Controller of Imports and Exports issues licences and permits, as well as implementing import-export policies.

Foreign capital investment requires approval, and transfer of capital is restricted.

Trade between Pakistan and Israel is illegal.

Currency regulations

Visitors can bring in or take out of the country the sum of 100 Pakistan rupees.

Visitors can take out any Foreign Exchange which they bring into the country less the amount encashed by an authorized dealer or money changer in Pakistan for expenses in Pakistan.

Encashment of Foreign Exchange from anybody other than a bank or authorized money changer is an offence under the Foreign Exchange Regulation Act, 1947.

Reconversion banks at exit points are authorized to reconvert upto 500 rupees of a traveller's unspent rupee balance resulting from the original conversion into local currency.

To convert larger amounts you must apply to an office of the State Bank of Pakistan.

Banks

The State Bank of Pakistan is the Central Bank. Domestic commercial banks include Allied Bank, Habib Bank Ltd, Habib Bank AG Zurich, Muslim Commercial Bank, National Bank, United Bank, Union Bank, Prime Commercial Bank, Bolan Bank, Askari Commercial Bank, Soneri Bank, Bank Al-Habib, Indus Bank, Metropolitan Bank, the Bank of Punjab, Schon Bank and cooperative banks. There are fifteen principal foreign banks including City Bank, Bank of America, Chase Manhattan Algemeine Bank, Nederland N.V., American Express, Grindlays and a number of development finance organizations.

Normal bank hours are from 9.00 am-1.00 pm Monday-Friday; and 9.00-11.00 am Saturday.

Hotels also change currency. Do not deal with street money changers.

Language

The national language is Urdu, and the official language English. Major regional languages include Punjabi, Pashtu, Sindhi and Baluchi. And there are a dazzling variety of dialects and sub-dialects.

Outside major centres, Urdu is only spoken by educated people. The only widely understood foreign language is English which is spoken by most educated people.

Religion

Pakistan is an official Islamic state but there is freedom of worship. Minority faiths include Christians, Hindus, Buddhists, and Parsis.

Muslims celebrate Friday a holy day and most offices close at 12 pm for prayers.

Government

Pakistan is an Islamic federal republic covering 796,095 square kilometres (307,760 square miles) with a population of more than 130 million. It is a member of the United Nations Organization and governed by a democratically elected Parliament that sits in Islamabad, the federal capital.

The country is divided into four autonomous provinces: Punjab, Sind, NorthWest Frontier Province, and Baluchistan, each with their own democratically elected parliamentary assembly.

Lahore is the capital of Punjab Karachi the capital of Sind; Peshawar the capital of the North-Western Frontier Province and Quetta the capital of Baluchistan.

In addition, the Gilgit region in the north constitutes a Federally Administered Tribal Area governed from Gilgit.

Azad Jammu and Kashmir "Free Kashmir" is an independent state within Pakistan, governed from Muzaffarabad.

Time

Pakistan Standard Time is five hours ahead of Greenwich Mean Time.

Tipping

Service charges are added in many restaurants and hotels. Use your discretion.

Communications

Pakistan has a sophisticated national and international communications network including satellite receiving and transmitting ground stations.

Country-wide postal, telegraphic and telephone facilities are available. There are about 13,350 post offices, nearly 26,000 letter boxes, more than 500 telegraph offices, eleven telex exchanges with more than 10,000 telex connections, nearly 500 international telex circuits and ten gentex exchanges.

The postal authority runs many special services to meet international demands for immediate delivery. "Datapost" links all major cities of Pakistan with UK, the Netherlands, Turkey, UAE, Japan, New Zealand, Oman, Sweden, Greece, Qatar, Norway, France, Kuwait, USA, Bangladesh, and Egypt.

UMS — Urgent Mail Service connects fifty-seven major centres within Pakistan and LPS — Local Packet and Parcel Service — the latest small delivery service provides economical same day delivery within Peshawar, Rawalpindi, Islamabad, Gujranwala, Sialkot, Lahore, Faisalabad, Multan, Sukkur, Rohri, Hyderabad, Kotri, Quetta, and Karachi.

To meet the modern requirements of rapid communication fax/mail Service was introduced which now connects 76 key cities of the country under which messages and documents are transmitted over long distance within seconds and their delivery is expeditiously arranged at destinations.

A separate organization, known as 'Overseas Post Circle' was created for exclusive handling of overseas mail.

There are more than 225,500 telephone connections, 862 telephone exchanges, and fifteen STD subscribers Trunk Dialling stations with fifteen STD channel and fifty-four NWD Nationwide Dialling stations with over 4,000 NWD channels.

Media

Pakistan public broadcasting systems are state run or controlled. The Pakistan Television today covers 87 percent of the population through the national network of 28 high powered broadcast stations, linked with microwave to five main programme producing and transmitting centres at Lahore, Islamabad, Karachi, Peshawar and Quetta. Special regional language programme stations have also been setup. Educational and regular programmes are now being telecast 24 hours on satellite channels which can be seen in 34 countries. There is also private television network telecasting independent programmes in Karachi, Islamabad and Lahore along with retelecast of CNN and BBC programmes. For tourists however, there is sufficient amount of Western 'whodunits' as well as cartoons. Moreover all hotels now have dish antennae facility and one can watch almost all international channels.

Radio Pakistan Broadcasting Corporation, a state controlled organization, operates 21 radio stations all over Pakistan covering 75 percent of the total area and 95 percent of population on medium wave, broadcasting round the clock for a total of nearly 350 hours daily. English news bulletins are broadcast at regular intervals, but one can always supplement them with broadcasts from other countries.

On the whole the print media is privately owned. The leading metropolitan newspapers are published from more than one place. In English language, the News International is being published from Karachi, Lahore and Islamabad; Pakistan Time from Lahore and Islamabad; Frontier Post from Peshawar and Lahore and Dawn from Karachi with a weekly edition for its overseas readers. The principal morning dailies in English are the Dawn, The Nation, Pakistan Times, The Muslim, Pakistan Observer, The News International and the Frontier Post. Business Recorder is an economic and commercial daily in English from Karachi. An important regional English daily is the Baluchistan Times, Quetta. The evening papers in English are the Star, Leader, Daily News, Parliament, Today News and Independent all from Karachi. International news coverage is inadequate though.

There are many Urdu language newspapers and magazines and many more publications in various regional languages.

Energy

Mains electricity is supplied throughout Pakistan on the 220-240 volts 50/60 cycles AC system. The supply is subject to frequent power failures. Pakistan is developing alternative energy systems such as nuclear power. Substantive deposits of natural gas beneath the country's deserts are also being exploited.

Driving

Drivers require a valid national or international driving licence. Driving is on the left as in Britain.

Car hire

Car hire facilities are available at all international airports and at most major hotels. Some car rental firms insist on a minimum age of twenty-one and many refuse to hire their vehicles to people over the age of sixty.

Yellow cabs or taxis are supposed to operate on a meter but seldom do. Negotiate the fare beforehand. At Karachi International Airport, police keep strict control on taxi operations and visitors are sometimes handed leaflets explaining the official rates, plus any surcharges. If you have difficulties consult the nearest police officer.

Medical facilities

There are modern hospitals with specialist staff in major cities, as well as private clinics. Charges are moderate. Perhaps the best of the private hospitals is the multi-million dollar Aga Khan Hospital and Medical University in Karachi where the charges reflect the quality of both staff and services.

Outside the cities, however, medical facilities are extremely thin on the ground, and even where there are hospitals or clinics they are not up to western standards. Most drugs, however, are available from the dispensaries which are found in many villages throughout the country.

For general health care avoid drinking unboiled or untreated water. Always carry purification tablets. Also be extremely cautious about eating salads and raw vegetables.

Hunting

A complete ban was imposed on the netting, hunting, poaching and export of all wild mammals and wild reptiles throughout the country including Azad Kashmir and the Northern Areas in September, 1981.

But the hunting of wild boar is encouraged throughout the country, particularly in Punjab where the species exists in abundance.

Club facilities

There are a number of good members clubs particularly in Karachi, Lahore, Quetta, Islamabad, Rawalpindi, Abbottabad, and Peshawar, which cater to a variety of tastes.

Most have facilities for golf, tennis, squash, cricket and indoor sports. There are also horse race clubs, boat club, and flying clubs.

In Brief

National Parks and Bird Sanctuaries

Pakistan has six national parks — Kirthar National Park, near Karachi; Chiltan National Park, near Quetta; Lal Suhanra National Park, near Bahawalpur; Ayubia National Park, near Muree; Chitral Gol National Park, near Chitral town; and Khunjerab National Park beyond Gilgit, on the Sino Pak border.

These national parks, located in different climatic and geographical regions, represent differrent ecosystems. The preservation of wild fauna, flora, and scenic beauty is the primary purpose of these national parks with the additional benefits of recreation, education, and research.

Kirthar National Park

The park is 152 kilometres (95 miles) from Karachi. Visitors can watch Sind ibex, urial, and chinkara from special vantage points in the hours of morning. Petrified wood and many interesting fossils have been discovered in the Kirthar mountains.

There are two visitors centres — at **Khar,** near **Hub Dam,** and at **Karchat,** near **Thano Ahmed Khan** where it is possible to stay overnight. The best time to visit is from November to January.

An added attraction is historic **Ranikot Fort —** one of the world's largest walled forts with a circumference of twenty-five kilometres (15 miles), located along the north-eastern boundary of the park.

It can be approached from the east on the National Highway detouring at Sanni. For reservations and other information, contact **Sind Wildlife Management Board,** Karachi, or the **PTDC Information Centre,** Club Road, Karachi.

Chitral Gol National Park

Chitral Gol National Park in the **North-western Frontier Province** is a high altitude scenic area with a splendid population of Kashmir markhor. If you want to see the animals, however, you need to walk.

Wolf is common but, though present in the park, snow leopard and black bear are only rarely seen. There are many bird species including pigeons and a number of splendid raptors.

Rutting stags can be witnessed in all their aggression during the December rutting season. Conducted tours are arranged by the PTDC Motel, Airport Road, Chitral.

The adjoining valleys of Rambur, Bumburet, and Birir are famous for their exotic Kalash culture. Chitral is linked by air from Peshawar. The **PTDC Motel** and the **Tirich Mir hotel** offer comfortable accommodation for visitors to the park.

Khunjerab National Park

Khunjerab National Park can be approached from Islamabad by air to **Gilgit** and then by road along the **Karakoram Highway** which passes through Khunjerab National Park. The park has gained in importance with the opening of the Pak-China border to foreigners in May 1986.

Marco Polo Sheep and Himalayan ibex can be easily seen but the park's snow leopard remains elusive.

PTDC Motels at Gilgit and Hunza offer good accommodation and conducted tours to **Khunjerab National Park** and **Khunjerab Pass.** Pakistan Tours, a subsidiary of PTDC, also arranges tours to China via Khunjerab.

Lal Suhanra National Park

Blackbuck, hog deer and nilgai can be easily seen at feeding times in semi-wild conditions in Lal

Suhanra National Park, near **Bahawalpur** in southern Punjab.

A pair of one horned Indian rhino is also present. A mixture of forest plantation, riparian, desert, and wetland ecosystems are represented in this park. Waterfowl and coarse fishing are added attractions.

It is best approached by air from either **Karachi** or **Lahore** to the historic city of Bahawalpur, and then thirty kilometres (19 miles) by road from Bahawalpur.

Accommodation is available both Bahawalpur and in the park. The **PTDC Information centre,** at **Dring Stadium** Bahawalpur will book accommodation and transport to the park.

Chiltan National Park

Seeing the grandeur of hills in Chiltan National Park is a satisfying experience. Patience and toil can be rewarding in observing the Chiltan markhor and the wolf packs.

The park can be approached by road from **Quetta** which is linked by air with **Karachi, Lahore,** and Islamabad.

Hotel accommodation is available at Quetta. The PTDC Information Centre, Muslim Hotel, Jinnah Road, Quetta will book accommodation and transport to the park.

Margalla Hills National Park

Margalla Hills National Park, on the outskirts of Islamabad, offers a panoramic view of the Potwar plateau. Monkey, cheer and kaleej pheasant are among the interesting species and the flora is fascinating.

Early morning visitors can have the satisfying experience of listening to the sonorous songs of the birds and glimpses of goral and barking deer on the high ridges.

Nearby **Rawal Lake,** visited by ducks in winter, is also popular for fishing.

The **PTDC Tourist Information Centre** at Flashman's Hotel, Rawalpindi, and at T.U, commercial Area, F-7/2, Islamabad, can help plan your visit to the park.

Ayubia National Park

Scenic beauty, monumental oak and fir trees and the koklas pheasant are fascinating. Efforts during night to spot a leopard are occasionally successful.

There is a chairlift and other recreational facilities at and around Ayubia which can be approached from Rawalpindi-Islamabad, via the **Muree Hills** where accommodation is available.

The **PTDC Tourist Information Centre,** Flashman's Hotel, The Mall, Rawalpindi will book accommodation and transport.

Zoos and Natural History Museums

Other areas of interest to tourists in this field are various city zoos, botanical gardens, and natural history museums. Zoos are located in **Karachi, Hyderabad, Bahawalpur, Lahore,** and

Islamabad, while natural history museums are located at **Islamabad** and **Karachi.**

The Natural History Museum, College Road, F-7 Markaz, Islamabad, provides good visual information on the flora and fauna of Pakistan's different ecological zones. The Zoological Survey Department also maintains a Natural History Museum at West Wharf Road, Karachi.

Jallo Recreational-cum-Zoological Park

Jallo Recreational-cum-Zoological Park near Lahore and the **Changa Manga Forest,** sixty-eight kilometres (42 miles) from Lahore, offer immense recreational facilities.

The **PTDC Tourist Information Centre,** Egerton Road, Lahore, can arrange conducted tours to these places.

Angling

You can go fishing for brown and rainbow trout in cold water streams in the uplands of the NWFP, Azad Kashmir, and the Northern Areas — and angling for the famous Mahseer in **Tarbela, Mangla** and **Hub Reservoirs,** and some of the lakes at various places in Pakistan.

Bird sanctuaries

In south-west Asia, Pakistan is one of the major winter haunts for the migratory waterfowl, a major route for birds from the Central Asia and Siberia known as the 'Indus Flyway'.

Many lakes, ponds, marshes, canals, and rivers make ideal wetland habitat for the waterfowl and offer sanctuary to a large variety of migratory species each winter.

One such spot is **Haleji Wetland Bird Sanctuary,** within easy motoring distance of **Karachi.** Others are **Zanginawar** and **Khushdil Khan Bund** in Baluchistan, **Ochali Lake** and **Chasma Barrage** in **Punjab,** and **Keenjhar Lake** in **Sind.**

Haleji Water Sanctuary

Haleji Lake Waterfowl Reserve is regarded as one of the most important wintering areas of migratory waterfowl in Eurasia. The lake is eighty-eight kilometres (55 miles) from Karachi and twenty-one kilometres (13 miles) from the historical city of **Thatta** and **Makli.**

The lake has a visitors' centre with a number of birdwatcher's hide-outs. More information from the **PTDC Information Centre,** Club Road, Karachi, which arranges conducted tours to Haleji.

Wildlife conservation organizations

1. National Council for Conservation of Wildlife Islamabad.
2. Punjab Wildlife Conservation Department, Lahore.
3. Conservator of Wildlife, NWFP, Forest Department, Peshawar.
4. Conservator of Wildlife, Sind Wildlife Management Board, Karachi.

5. Chief Conservator of Forests, Baluchistan, Quetta.
6. Director, Zoological Survey Department, Karachi.
7. World Wildlife Fund (Pakistan) Lahore, Regional offices at Karachi and Gilgit.
8. Wildlife Conservation Foundation of Pakistan, Karachi.

Major Glaciers

Pakistan's **Siachen Glacier** streams down the slopes of the world's second highest mountain, K-2, for seventy-five kilometres (46 miles). The **Hispar**, fifty-three kilometres (32 miles), joins the **Biafo** to form an ice corridor 115.87 kilometres (72 miles) long.

The **Batura Glacier** runs for more than fifty-eight kilometres (36 miles). But the most outstanding of these rivers of ice is the **Baltoro Glacier**, which runs for sixty-two kilometres (38 miles), fed by some thirty tributaries, and covers an area of 1,220 square kilometres (470 square miles).

Seen from a distance the glacier appears smooth and beautiful but in fact it is a chaotic tumbling mass of rock and ice, troughs and hillocks, and the detritus of centuries. It is a unique corner of earth.

Here, in a frozen wilderness of crag, cornices and crevasses, rise towering spires of granite, great snowy peaks with fluted icy ridges and pinnacles that pierce the sky.

Length And Location Of Major Glaciers

Siachen, Karakoram, Baltistan, 72.4 kms (45 miles);
Hispar, Karakoram, Hunza, 61.2 kms (38 miles);
Biafo, Karakoram, Shigar, 59.5 kms (37 miles);
Baltoro, Karakoram, Concordia, 59.5 kms (36 miles);
Batura, Karakoram, Hunza, 64.4 kms (40 miles);
Yengunta, Karakoram, Baltistan, 35.4 kms (22 miles);
Chiantar, Hindu Kush, Chitral. 33.8 kms (22 miles);
Tirich, Hindu Kush, Chitral, 29 kms (18 miles);
Atrak, Hindu Kush, Chitral, 29 kms (18 miles);
Karanbar, Hindu Kush, Swat, 25.5 kms (16 miles).

Major Mountains

The spectacular conjunction of the **Godwin-Austen** and **Baltoro glaciers** is called **Concordia**. This austere amphitheatre, surrounded by many mountain peaks over 7,925 metres (26,000 feet) high, is perhaps the most imposing natural landscape in the world.

Of the fourteen 8,000-metre-high (26,250 feet) mountains on earth, four are found in Concordia — K-2 at 8,611.5 metres (28,253 feet) second only to Everest, **Broad Peak** 8,046.72 metres (26,400 feet), **Gasherbrum-I** 8,068 metres (26,470 feet), and **Gasherbrum-II** 8,034.52 metres (26,360 feet).

In the **Lesser Karakoram** there are equally great peaks such as **Rakaposhi**, 7,788 metres (25,552 feet), the dominant giant of the **Hunza Valley**, its north face a fantastic, sheer 5,791.2 metres (19,000 feet) precipicce of plunging snow and ice.

And there are countless mountains of more than 7,000 metres (23,000 feet) in the Karakoram range, and hundreds of nameless summits above 6,000 metres (20,000 feet), mere points on the map.

The shapes, sizes, and colours provide such tremendous contrast that it defies description. **K2** is the indisputable monarch of the sky, massive and ugly **Mustagh Tower**, deceptively sheer **Gasherbrum II**, "the Egyptian Pyramid" that even Cheops would have preferred for a tomb, Chogolisa, and **Broad Peak** in whose eternal embrace lies Hermann Buhl, the first man to climb **Nanga Parbat**.

Baltoro Cathedrals with their great knife-edge ridges, the sky-cleaving monoliths of **Trango Towers**, and — most beautiful of all — the **Peak of Perfection**, Paiju 6,600 metres (21,654 feet), first climbed by a Pakistani expedition in 1977.

The western bastion of the Himalayan range is **Nanga Parbat**, 8,125 metres (26,660 feet), sixth-highest mountain in the world, once dreaded as the "Killer Mountain" but climbed many times by expeditions since the first disasters.

The **Hindu Kush** is also a vast mountain fastness containing hundreds of peaks, many above 7,000 metres (23,000 feet), including **Tirich Mir**, 7,708 metres (25,290 feet) which is the highest point of the range and the forty-first highest mountain in the world.

In the league of Great Mountains this is how Pakistan stands according to the Royal Geographic Society of Britain:

Peak	Altitude	Range	Rating
1. K2(Chogori)	28,250f/8,610M	Karakoram	2
2. Namga Parbat	26,660f/8,125M	Himalaya	8
3. Gasherbrum I	26,470f/8,068M	Karakoram	11
4. Broad Peak	26,400f/8.047M	Karakoram	12
5. Gasherbrum II	26,360f/8,035M	Karakoram	14
6. Gasherbrum III	26,090f/7,925M	Karakoram	15
7. Gasherbrum IV	26,000f/7,925M	Karakoram	16
8. Disteghil Sar	25,868f/7,885M	Karakoram	20
9. Khiangyang Kish	25,760f/7,852M	Karakoram	22
10. Masherbrum	25,660f/7821M	Karakoram	24
11. Rakaposhi	25,550f/7,788M	Karakoram	27
12. Batura MustaghI	25,540f/7,785M	Karakoram	28
13. Kanjut Sar	25,460f/7,760M	Karakoram	29
14. Saltoro Kangri	25,400f/7,742M	Karakoram	33
15. Peak 35	25,279f/7,705M	Karakoram	34
16. Batura MustaghII	25,361f/7,730M	Karakoram	35
17. Trivor	25,329f/7,720M	Karakoram	36
18. Tirich Mir	25,290f/7,708M	HinduKush	41

Other Mountains Above 7,300 Metres
Ostgipfel 7,691 metres 25,233 feet Hindu Kush
Westgipfel 7,487 metres 24,564 feet Hindu Kush
Saser Kangri 17,672 metres 25,170 feet Karakoram
Chogolisa SW 7,665 metres 25,148 feet Karakoram
NE-Gipfel 7,654 metres 25,110 feet Karakoram
Shispare 7,619 metres 25,000 feet Karakoram
Skyang Kangri 7,544 metres 24,750 feet Karakoram

Mamostong 7,526 metres 24,690 feet Karakoram
Saser Kangri II 7,513 metres 24,650 feet Karakoram
Saser Kangri 17,672 metres 25,170 feet Karakoram
Pumar Kish 7,492 metres 24,581 feet Karakoram
Noshaq 7,492 metres 24,581 feet Hindu Kush
K12 7,468 metres 24,503 feet Karakoram
Teram Kangri I 7,463 metres 24,490 feet Karakoram
Malubiting W,7,452 metres 24,451 feet Karakoram
Sia Kangri 7,422 metres 24,350 feet Karakoram
Cloud Peak 7,415 metres 24,330 feet Karakoram
Teram Kangri II 7,406 metres 24,300 feet Karakoram
Haramosh 7,406 metres 24,299 feet Karakoram
Istor-o-Nal 7,403 metres 24,290 feet Hindu Kush
Nordgipfel 7,373 metres 24,190 feet Hindu Kush
Mount Ghent 7,400 metres 24,280 feet Karakoram
Rimo 17,385 metres 24,230 feet Karakoram
Rimo II 7,380 metres 24,213 feet Karakoram
Teram Kangri III 7,381 metres 24,216 feet Karakoram
Sherpi Kangri 7,380 metres 24,212 feet Karakoram
Karun Kuh 7,350 metres 24,112 feet Karakoram
Momhil Sar 7,342 metres 24,090 feet Karakoram
Mount Ghent NE 7,342 metres 24,089 feet Karakoram
Saraghrar Peak 7,338 metres 24,075 feet Hindu Kush
Mount Spender 7,330 metres 24,050 feet Karakoram
Gasherbrum V 7,321 metres 24,020 feet Karakoram
Dunasir II 7,320 metres 24,015 feet Karakoram
Dunasir I 7,318 metres 24,009 feet Karakoram
Baltoro Kangri 17,312 metres 23,990 feet Karakoram
Baltoro Kangri III 7,310 metres 23,983 feet Karakoram
Baltoro Kangri II 7,300 metres 23,950 feet Karakoram

Mountain Climbing Regulations

Foreign mountaineering expeditions wishing to climb in Pakistan must apply in duplicate to the nearest Pakistan Embassy. Applications for all peaks except K2 are accepted by Pakistan embassies between 1 January and 31 October in the year before the expedition is planned. In the case of K2, the world's second highest mountain, applications must be made two years in advance.

Parties applying for permission must list at least three or four peaks that they wish to climb in order of preference — although no expedition will be given permission for more than one 8,000-metre peak (26,250 feet) except under special dispensation.

Royalty fees

The royalty fees for climbing expeditions to Pakistan major peaks in 1989 were 45,000 rupees for K2; and 35,000 rupees for other peaks more than 8,000 metres (26,250 feet); 25,000 rupees for peaks of more than 7,500 metres (24,600 feet); 20,000 rupees for peaks of more than 7,000 metres (23,000 feet); and 15,000 rupees for peaks at an altitude of between 6,000 and 7,000 metres (19,650-23,000 feet).

These royalties are payable when applying.

Where a peak of higher altitude is allocated the expedition will pay the balance within fourteen days of this advice. If this is not paid the allocation

will be automatically cancelled and the sum paid previously will not be refunded.

Where a peak of lower altitude is allocated the balance of the royalty will be refunded.

Expeditions are bound to accept these allocations as final. In the event of refusal to do so the royalty paid is forfeit.

Where it is impossible to allocate any of the preferred peaks to an expedition they will be asked to identify other peaks they might wish to climb. However, if there are none to their liking the whole of the royalty is refunded.

Joint foreign-Pakistan expeditions must also pay the specified royalty when applying for allocation of a peak but if their application is successful they will be given a refund of fifty per cent.

Apart from specific differences in pay scales and weight loads, mountain regulations are virtually identical to "Trekking Regulations."

Trekking Regulations

Trekking means travelling on foot to a maximum height of 6,000 metres (19,600 feet) for sightseeing and recreation at various natural and cultural sites in places where means of modern transport are either not available or are purposely not used.

Details of trekking tour operators are also given later in these Listings.

Cancellations

Permits can be cancelled by the government at any time without explanation. Visitors wishing to postpone or cancel a visit must notify the Tourism Division immediately

Briefing-debriefinng

Leaders of trekking parties to restricted areas must report to the Tourism Division before leaving Islamabad-Rawalpindi for their expedition. They will be briefed on what to take and advised on matters such as insurance and arrangements for special weather forecasts from Radio Pakistan.

Trekking teams should allow for a stay of between four and six days to compete this formality.

Leaders must also report on their return from the restricted areas and brief the tourism division on their experiences.

Liaison officer

Trekking parties must pay for the transport of the liaison officer from Rawalpindi-Islamabad and back. In the city the officer will use the same accommodation as the rest of the party and eat the same food.

Where accommodation is unavailable the party must pay a per diem of 300 rupees a day for accommodation and food.

The liaison officer will also share the same accommodation and food as the rest of the party when resident in such places as Gilgit, Skardu, and Chitral.

For the actual trek, the party will provide whatever rations the liaison officer prefers to eat if unable to share the same food as the party at the rate of 150 rupees a day.

The liaison officer will also be provided with a porter-cum-cook paid by the party.

In no instance should the party advance money to the liaison officer. Delegated members should accompany the officer to buy his requirements.

The liaison officer will carry his own equipment like any other member of the party.

He must be consulted on any change of route, where to camp and local customs but the party is not bound to accept his advice.

Where however the liaison officer feels strongly that the security of the party or the country is in jeopardy the leader will explain in writing his reasons for not accepting the officer's advice.

The officer is also empowered in such circumstances to notify by the quickest means possible his concern to the nearest police station and seek help to stop the party from carrying out its mission.

At the first district headquarters at which the party arrives, the officer will file a complaint detailing specifics with a copy to the Ministry of Tourism.

The liaison officer is assigned to provide all possible help for the success of the expedition but he is not empowered to accept money or conduct any financial transactions.

The liaison officer will also serve as an interpreter. His other duties include maintaining discipline among the porters, resolving any disputes that may arise between the party, porters, and locals, and to summon help in the event of accidents involving any member of the party or the porters.

He shall also inform the nearest police station about the commission of any serious crime together with a report to the Tourism Division.

Equipment

The expedition will provide the liaison officer with enough equipment for him to perform his duties without risk and also supply all necessary equipment required by the porters. This will be handed to the porters in the presence of the liaison officer before the start of the ascent.

If the equipment is found to be inferior or sub-standard the expedition will be cancelled.

The liaison officer and porters will return their equipment after the expedition if the party asks for it.

Import-export of equipment

Equipment and stores can be imported into Pakistan on a temporary basis subject to the expedition leader's signed promise to re-export it.

Consumables and medicines are exempt from customs duty and sales tax subject to the leader's undertaking that they are only for use during the expedition and that any stores remaining will be re-exported. With approval from the government however the expedition may donate any surplus to a worthy cause in Pakistan.

The expedition leader will write the undertaking in triplicate along with three copies of the expedition's inventory.

Details of equipment sent in advance should be notified to the Tourism Division beforehand.

Wages and transport

Wages for porters and hire of pack animals and transport are fixed by the government. Porters working for seven days or less will be given an advance of fifty per cent when hired and the balance on the day they are discharged.

Porters engaged for longer periods will be given an advance of fifty per cent of one week's wages when hired and paid the balance at the end of the week. Thereafter they will be paid on a weekly basis.

The expedition will provide food for each porter until they are discharged.

Where bad weather forces a halt the expedition will continue to pay and feed the porters.

Insurance

The expedition will provide insurance cover of 100,000 rupees for the liaison officer to cover death or accident and insurance cover of 50,000 rupees for each porter through a recognised Pakistani insurance company.

Medical treatment

Trekking parties of more than five people must be accompanied by a qualified doctor-surgeon. Parties of five or under must be accompanied by a person qualified in first-aid.

The liaison officer and porters are entitled to free medical treatment from the doctor.

In the event of sickness or injury to the liaison officer the expedition must inform the nearest army post or senior government official and if the officer is unable to walk assign porters to carry him to the nearest motorable point for transport to hospital.

If the officer is too sick to undertake such a journey, the expedition leader must contact the nearest army post or senior government official to summon a helicopter the cost of which will be borne by the expedition.

The decision of the doctor is final. Where the liaison officer feels that any porter is in need of evacuation he will instruct the expedition leader to arrange this.

Porters who suffer sickness or injury and subsequent hospital treatment will be paid half the daily wage until they recover.

Medical treatment in Pakistan hospitals is usually free. But where not, the expedition is responsible for meeting the cost of treatment.

Photography

Permission for aerial photography of Pakistan's northern areas must be obtained from the captain of the aircraft. It is forbidden to photograph any military installations, equipment, airports, local women, and prohibited buildings and places.

Parties accompanied by professional photographers or film makers must engage a second liaison officer to accompany the photographic team which must remain with the main party. The liaison officer must confirm that no prohibited film or photographs were taken before the film can leave Pakistan.

Photograpers who defy security restrictions can be charged under the Official Secrets Act, 1923.

Permission for photography or filming is subject to the party supplying free of cost, and freight charges, one copy/print of any film of academic or commercial interest or, as the case may be, one complete set of photographs.

Accidents

In the event of an accident or the death of an individual, the expedition leader must tell the liaison officer who will report the tragedy to the nearest police station and senior government official. If military help is needed, the liaison officer will ask the Deputy Commissioner to arrange it. Where a helicopter is summoned, the expedition will bear the cost.

The liaison officer will be responsible for obtaining death certificates.

Foreign exchange

All foreign exchange transactions will be conducted according to the prevailing foreign exchange regulations.

Security rules

Trekking parties must not indulge in any activity that may offend religious sentiments or local customs. An expedition will operate in only one area at a time. The expedition can only deviate from the specified route in an emergency and then only with the permission of the liaison officer.

Any maps issued by the government must be returned before departure when the deposit on these will be returned. Copies of any topographical data collected during trekking must be given to the liaison officer.

Any data, botanical, fossil, or other specimens — and any collections — can only be exported with the prior permission of the government. The leader must also provide a set of all such specimens to the government.

Trekking fees

The trekking fee in 1989 was 100 rupees for each individual.

Miscellaneous

The expedition members will be responsible for the safety of the liaison officer and the leader must also ensure that he is treated with courtesy.

Porters will be hired through the local administration. The maximum weight a porter can carry is twenty-five kilos (55 Ibs) and porters will only walk in any one day the distance from one traditional halt to another. The decision of the liaison officer about which is a traditional halt is final.

Porters must sign an undertaking to be of good behaviour which is deposited with a representative of local administration with one copy to the expedition leader.

Expeditions must endeavour to arrive according to their advance schedule so as to avoid pressure on local transport and accommodation in the "take off" area.

Parties are advised to make their air bookings from Rawalpindi to the Northern Areas as soon as they receive permission for their trek together with the number of persons in the party and the total weight of their cargo and the probable dates of their flights. A copy of this information must also be sent to the Tourism Division.

Flights to Northern Areas and Chitral are subject to weather conditions and PIA or their agents may be unable to give firm dates of bookings. In this event, the expedition should ask PIA or their agents to notify the officer-in-charge, Northern Areas, PIA Offices, Share-e-Quaid Azam, Rawalpindi.

Expeditions should anticipate possible delays of between two and three weeks in both Rawalpindi and the Northern Areas/Chitral in case the weather turns suddenly bad.

The alternative, subject to the KKH being open, it to travel by road from Rawalpindi and back.

Expeditions must register their members with the Foreigners Registration Officer in the Office of Senior Superintendent of Police, Rawalpindi, before their departure to the mountains and also upon their departure from Pakistan.

Expeditions from non-English speaking countries must include at least one English-speaking member in the party.

The expedition shall be responsible for clearing all rubbish, e.g., by digging a hole and burying it or burning it. The liaison officer will confirm whether this condition has been fulfilled or not when the expedition returns.

The expedition must protect natural resources, particularly forest and animal life in the area in which itis trekking and the liaison officer will also confirm whether this condition has been fulfilled or not.

The expedition must also respect the religious injunctions of the Muslim faith with particular regard to dietary prohibitions regarding pig flesh (pork) and alcohol.

In the event of a breach of these rules the expedition and its sponsors will be disqualified from trekking in Pakistan for a maximum of five years and may also face court charges for breaking the relevant law or laws.

Trekking Advisory

Any reasonably fit person can trek, but the fitter you are, the more you will enjoy it. Do as much walking and exercise as possible to prepare yourself for Pakistan's mountain trails.

Trekking is becoming more and more popular. These high altitude areas are divided into two zones. Permits are required to trek anywhere near international borders and are often refused.

The best time for trekking is between June and July when the snow has melted but the monsoons have not started. Unlike Nepal, the trekking areas are extremely remote and there is little communication or support.

You should arrange your trek through one of the trekking agencies, PTDC, or recognised tour operators, who can hire your porters, guides, and equipment and organise your food supplies. Treks are not cheap, especially the longer ones, and inexperienced trekkers will find walking in the low altitude foothills more enjoyable when you can walk from rest house to rest house and do not need to carry camping equipment.

Health experts recommend inoculations against tetanus, polio, cholera, typhoid and para-typhoid. A gamma globulin injection provides some protection against hepatitis, an endemic infection in Pakistan.

A risk that the trekker shares with the climber is that of mountain sickness — a combination of nausea, sleeplessness, headaches and potentially lethal oedemas, both cerebral and pulmonary. Sudden ascents to heights of 3,650 metres (12,000 feet) and more, without acclimatization, can lead to an accumulation of water, either on the lungs or brain. Swift descent for prompt medical treatment is the only answer (See "Mountain Sickness").

Trekking along these rough, rocky trails demands that you wear strong, comfortable boots with good soles. At low altitude, tennis shoes or running shoes cushion the feet enough.

Above the snowline

Above the snow level, boots large enough to allow one or two layers of heavy woollen or cotton — never nylon — socks, are essential. Wearing light casuals or sneakers after the day's work will help relax your feet.

For women, wrap-around skirts are preferable to slacks. Shorts offend many mountain communities. Men should wear loose fitting trousers or hiking shorts. Two light layers of clothing are better than a single thick one. If you get too hot, you can peel the top layer off.

At really high altitudes wear thermal underwear. It's best to carry too many clothes than not enough. Drip-dry fabrics are best.

However, your pack should be as small as possible, light, and easy to open. The following gear is recommended.

Two pairs of woollen or corduroy trousers or skirts; two warm sweaters; three drip-dry shirts or T-shirts; ski or thermal underwear (especially from November to February); at least half-a-dozen pairs of woollen socks; one pair of walking shoes; one pair of sandals; light casual shoes or sneakers; woollen hat; gloves or mittens; strong, warm sleeping bag with hood; a thin sheet of foam rubber for a mattress; padded anorak or parka; plastic raincoat; sunglasses and sun lotion; toilet gear; towels; medical kit; water bottle; and a light day pack.

Your medical kit should include pain killers (for high-altitude headaches); mild sleeping pills (for high-altitude insomnia); streptomycin (for diarrhoea); septram (for bacillary dysentery); tinidozole (for amoebic dysentery); throat lozenges and cough drops; ophthalmic ointment or drops; one broad spectrum antibiotic; alcohol (for massaging feet to prevent blisters); blister pads; bandages and elastic plasters; antiseptic and cotton; a good sun block; and a transparent lip salve.

In addition to these, you should carry a torch, candles, lighter, pocket knife, scissors, spare shoelaces, string, safety pins, toilet paper, and plastic bags to protect food, wrap up wet or dirty clothes, and carry your litter, plus food, tents and photographic equipment. Much of this can be bought in Pakistan.

Cooking and eating utensils are normally provided by the trekking agency and carried by the porters.

Always carry your trekking permit in a plastic bag where you can get to it easily. Lock your bag against theft or accidental loss. And make sure you have plenty of small currency for minor expenses along the way.

Boil water

Carry a good supply of high-energy food like chocolate, dried fruits, nuts, and whisky, brandy, or vodka for a warming nightcap.

Water is contaminated so do not drink from streams no matter how clear or sparkling they look. Chlorine is not effective against amoebic cysts. All water should be well boiled or treated with iodine — four drops a litre and leave for twenty minutes before drinking.

Normally the day starts with early morning tea at around six o'clock. Break camp and pack, followed by a breakfast of hot porridge and biscuits, ready to be on the trail by around seven o'clock.

Lunch is taken around noon, the cook having gone ahead to select the site and prepare the meal. By late afternoon, they day's trek is ended and camp pitched, followed by dinner. At these high altitudes, after a hard day's walking, there's little dallying over the camp fire. Though sleep is fitful and shallow, most are ready to hit the sack by eight pm.

Speed is not the essence. Pause frequently to enjoy the beauty of a particular spot, talk to the passing locals, photograph, or sip tea in one of the rustic wayside tea shops.

Walk at your own pace. Drink as much liquid as possible to combat high altitude and heat dehydration. Never wait for blisters to develop but pamper tender feet with an alcohol massage.

Mountain sickness

There are three main types. Early mountain sickness is the first, and acts as a warning. It can develop into pulmonary oedema (waterlogged lungs) or cerebral oedema (waterlogged brain). The symptoms are headache, nausea, loss of appetite, sleeplessness, fluid retention, and swelling of the body.

Mountain sickness develops slowly, manifesting itself two or three days after reaching high altitude. The cure is to climb no higher until the symptoms have disappeared.

Pulmonary oedemia is characterized, even when resting, by breathlessness and a persistent cough, accompanied by congestion of the chest. If these symptoms appear, descend at once.

Cerebral oedema is less common. Its symptoms are extreme tiredness, vomiting, severe headache, staggering when walking, abnormal speech and behaviour, drowsiness, even coma. Victims must return at once to a lower altitude and abandon all thoughts of their trek.

If left untreated mountain sickness can lead to death. It's endemic in the high north where even experienced mountaineers sometimes forget that their climb begins where other mountain ranges end. For instance, the K2 base camp is some 1,000 metres (more than 3,000 feet) higher than the summit of the Matterhorn. Above 3,000 metres (10,000 feet) the air becomes noticably thinner.

Take your time

Youth, strength, and fitness make no difference. Those who climb too high, too fast, expose themselves to the risk of acute mountain sickness.

At 4,300 metres (14,108 feet), for example, the body requires three to four litres of liquid a day. Even at low altitude try to drink at least a litre a day.

You should plan frequent rest days between the 3,700- and 4,300- metre (12,000-14,000 feet) contours, sleeping at the same altitude for at least two nights. Climb higher during the day but always descend to the same level to sleep.

Never pitch camp more than 450 metres (1,500 feet) higher in any one day, even if you feel fit enough for a climb twice that height.

If you begin to suffer early mountain sickness, go no higher until the symptoms have disappeared. If more serious symptoms appear, descend immediately to a lower elevation, Mild symptoms should clear within one and two days.

If the victim is unable to walk he should be carried down on a porter's back or by yak. No matter what the reason, never delay, even at night.

Some victims are incapable of making correct decisions and you may have to force them to go down against their will. The victim must be accompanied.

Treatment is no substitute for descent. If a doctor is available, he can treat the victim but the patient must descend.

Because of lack of radio communications and helicopters, emergency evacuations are difficult to organize. Such a rescue operation takes time and costs a great deal of money.

Some agencies maybe able to arrange helicopter rescues for its trekkers but individuals stand no chance.

A Demographic Profile

Pakistan, ninth most populous country in the world after China, India, USSR, USA, Indonesia, Brazil, Japan, and Bangladesh, has the highest rate of population growth of all nine — approximately 2.90 percent as per present estimates.

Punjab possesses more than half the total population, fifty-six percent, with an average of 354 persons to each square kilometre, followed by 207 to the square kilometre in Sindh, 228 in the NWF and only 17 — five percent of the national population-in Baluchistan which contains forty-four percent of the country's total land area.

Sex, age and marital status

In Pakistan according to 1981 census, there were 111 males to every 100 females. According to the Federal Bureau of Statistics, this ratio has decreased: in 1993 it was 104 males to 100 females. In all the developed countries — and most developing countries — females out number males. The average life expectancy of females in developed countries is about three to five years more than that of males.

The predominance of females in developed countries, therefore, is more marked in the older age groups of fifty and over. In Pakistan in 1981, except for 0-4 age group, there were more males than females in all age groups, even those of fifty and over. This demographic paradox can only be explained by the surmise that females are not so well looked after as males in Pakistan.

Age Structure

According to Federal Bureau of Statistics, in 1993, 46.1 percent of Pakistan's population was under fifteen while only 4.1 percent was 65 years and over. Therefore only half the population is in the working age group of fifteen to sixty-four, whereas in developed countries about two-thirds of the population is in the working age-group.

Marital Status (15 years and above)

Out of the total population aged over fifteen, sixty-nine percent were married, six percent widowed, and twenty-five percent unmarried. When the male-female ratio is distorted, as in Pakistan, a number of males, statistically, cannot find brides to marry, as men outnumber women by about four percent. The divorce ratio is negligible — less than 0.27 percent of those married.

Literacy

Pakistan's literacy rate increased from 21.7 percent in 1972 to 26.2 percent in 1981 — an annual rate of half percent. There were sharp differences between the literacy ratio of the male and female population. Similarly, there were sharp differences between rural and urban literacy.

Increase in the literacy rate remained slow in the following years. However, the sharp difference between male and female and between urban and rural is decreasing gradually. In 1995-96 Pakistan's literacy rate is estimated at 37.9 percent, 50 percent male and 25.3 percent female. Literacy rate for urban and rural areas is 58.3 and 28.3 percent respectively.

The number of primary schools in 1995-96, including mosque schools, was 115,744 with an enrollment of 11.5 million. The number of middle schools was 10,586 in 1995-96 with an enrollment of 3.5 million, and 10,344 high/secondary vocational schools with 1.4 million students. The number of colleges (Arts, Science and Professional) was 864 with an enrollment of 882,218 while that of universities was 24 with 71,441 students. As compared to the previous year the enrollment in these institutions improved by 1.3 percent at the primary level, 3.8 percent at middle and 5 percent at high/secondary vocational level. At college (arts, science and professional) and university levels the enrollment increased by 3.2 percent and 1.7 percent respectively.

University education has expanded considerably in the last few decades. Although no new university has been established by the public sector in the recent past, but the private sector has been encouraged to establish universities or graduate schools. So far nine universities have been given a charter by the government.

Language

Punjabi is the most commonly spoken family language, followed by Pashtu, Sindhi, Siraiki, and Urdu. The category of 'others' contains those languages and dialects of the different regions of Pakistan whose percentage is less than one.

Ability to Read the Qur'an

Pakistan is predominantly Islamic: Muslims constitute 96.7 percent of the population. The important minorities, Christians and Hindus each total 1.5 percent of the total population — or 1.9 million people.

Out of a total of 1.9 million Hindus, 1.7 million live in Sindh. Similarly out of a total of 1.9 million Christians, 1.6 million live in Punjab.

Other minorities — their aggregate only totals 0.3 percent of the total population — are Ahmadis, Parsis, Sikhs and Buddhists.

Thirty-eight percent of the Muslim population aged ten or more expressed their ability to read the Holy Qur'an. The percentage for males was 35.8 and 41.4 for females.

Migration

Migration is of three types — from one district to another in the same province, one province to another, and emigration abroad.

Internal migrant population constituted 11.8 percent of the total population, one-third of whom moved within their own province while the remainder moved from one province to another.

The number of migrants in the NWFP was five percent of the total migrant population out of whom 36.5 percent had moved within the province and the remainder came to live within the NWFP from other provinces — 20.2 percent from the Punjab, and 13.8 percent from the FATA. In the Punjab, 63.4 percent of the migrant population were found to be migrants, out of whom 42.2 percent had moved within the province, while 43.6 percent had come from India, Bangladesh, and other countries.

The migrant population of Sindh was 27.9 percent of total migrant population, 42.3 percent of whom had come from India, Bangladesh, and other countries, 22.8 percent from the Punjab, and 13.3 percent from the NWFP, while only 14.6 percent had moved within the province.

In nomadic Baluchistan only 2.7 percent of the total migrant population had moved there from other places, out of whom 44.3 percent came from within the province, 21.3 percent from the Punjab, and 11.2 percent from the NWFP.

More than 3 million Pakistanis migrated abroad during 1971-81, 82.8 percent of them from rural areas. The largest number of emigrants were from the Punjab, accounting for 43.0 percent of the total. The percentage of emigrants from the NWFP was 34.6, and from Sindh 17.6 percent. Only a small number left Baluchistan.

In recent years the manpower export to the Gulf countries has declined more than 50 percent following the increased competition from other Asian countries. However on the emigration abroad front the Government is trying to seek more job opportunities and has decided to streamline the export of manpower. The target is to send about 0.3 million labourers of various categories abroad each year.

People employed

The Labour Force Survey 1992-93 defined as employed all persons ten years of age and above who worked at least one hour and were either 'paid employed' or 'self-employed'. Based on this definition the employed labour force was estimated to 32.08 million. It has now grown up

34.92 million during 1995-96. There has been a slight increase in the number of employed persons in urban areas which is estimated at 10 million as against 9.8 million last year. The increase in rural employment, however, is more pronounced. It grew from 24.23 million in 1994-95 to 24.92 million in 1995-96.

The large proportion of employed labour force in rural areas indicates that non-wage employment, mainly comprising of self-employed and unpaid family helpers, dominates the employment scene in Pakistan. However, there is an exodus of youth from rural towards urban areas, thereby increasing pressure on already meagre social amenities in the urban areas.

Occupation

The agriculture sector continues to be the major employment generating sector absorbing 50 percent of the labour force. The trade sector absorbed 12.78 percent, while the manufacturing sector generated employment opportunities for 10.12 percent of the labour force. The sectorial distribution of employed labour force in 1995-96 was; agriculture 50.04, mining and quarrying and manufacturing 10.12, construction 6.50, wholesale and retail trade 12.78, transport 4.95, finance, community, social and personal services 14.70 and others 0.86.

Employed persons by occupation in 1995-96 estimates include: Professional workers 4.59, administrative workers 0.94, clerical workers 4.37, sales workers 11.98, services workers 4.56 agriculture workers 49.06, and production workers 24.69.

Unemployment

The Labour Force Survey 1993-95 defines unemployment as all persons 10 years of age and above who during the reference period; (a) with out work i.e. were not in paid employment or self employment (b) currently available for work i.e. were available for paid employment or self employment during the reference period and (c) seeking work i.e. had taken specific steps in a specified recent period to seek paid employment or self employment. According to this definition some 1.78 million people of the labour force were estimated as unemployed in 1995-96 compared to 1.23 million in 1994-95. The rate of open unemployment according to the Survey was 4.84 percent in 1995-96 compared to 7.74 percent in 1992-93.

The unemployment rate has fallen more rapidly in the urban areas than in the rural areas. In the urban areas it has fallen from 8.19 percent in 1990-91 to 5.88 percent in 1994-95 while in the rural areas it has fallen from 5.48 percent in 1990-91 to 4.29 percent in 1994-95. Similarly the fall in unemployment rate amongst the female population is relatively greater being 10.32 percent in 1992-93 as against 14.23 percent in the previous year. The male unemployment rate declined from 4.54 percent in 1990-91 to 4.27 percent in 1991-92 and 3.76 percent in 1992-93.

Festivals and Holidays

January

CHIEF OF AIR STAFF CHAMPIONSHIP (GOLF)
Golf Course Peshawar. (See listings for Hotel) Accommodation.

February

SIBI MELA
Traditional sports, exhibitions, concerts and PTDC stall in Industrial Exhibition.
Sibi Town is about 110 miles from Quetta on Quetta-Sukkur Highway. Accommodation: Government Rest House only.
SINA HORSE AND CATTLE SHOW
At Jacobabad, about 85 kms from Sukkur. Low class hotels at Jacobabad. Sukkur and Jacobabad are both connected by air with Karachi. (See listings for Hotels) in Sukkur.
FRONTIER AMATEUR GOLF CHAMPIONSHIP
Golf Course Peshawar. (See listings for Hotels).
JOSHAN-E-LARKANA
At Larkana, which is connected by air with Karachi. Accommodation: Mehran and Faiz Hotels, Archaeology Rest House in Moenjodaro. (See listings for Hotels) in Larkana.
NATIONAL HORSE AND CATTLE SHOW
Features camel dancing, tent-pegging, tattoo show and exhibition, at Fortress Stadium, Lahore. (See listings for Hotels).

March

FOLK FESTIVAL OF PAKISTAN
Folk Dances, artisans at work, folk products on display and for sale, folk music and many more activities. Organized by Institute of Folk Heritage, Islamabad. At Shakraparian, Islamabad. (See listings for Hotels).
JASHAN-E- SHIKARPUR
Cultural activities, exhibitions and traditional sports. At Shikarpur, about 42 kms from Sukkur. (See listings for Hotels) in Sukkur.
PAKISTAN DAY (23 March)
Commemorates 1940 decision to press for a Muslim nation independent of India. Military Parades, processions, and other activities are held in Quetta, Karachi, Lahore, Peshawar and Rawalpindi. The largest parade is held at Racecourse Ground, Rawalpindi, and includes displays of the latest planes and weapons.

April

HORSE AND CATTLE SHOW
Local games and competitions.
At Dera Ismail Khan, 340 kilometres (210 miles) from Peshawar. Linked by air. Accommodation: New Sharba Hotel and other lower class hotels.

May

MAY DAY-LABOUR DAY (1 May)
Public Holiday throughout Pakistan.
ASHURA (MUHARRAM)
Commemorating the death of Hazrat Imam Hussein, Grandson of Prophet Mohammad. Two highly emotional days of mourning with processions and public displays featuring self-flagellation. Observed throughout Pakistan.
JOSHI OR CHILIMJUSHT
Kalash spring festival with music, dancing and exchange of foods. In Chitral which is linked by air and by road with Peshawar. (See listings for Hotels) in Chitral.

July

BANK HOLIDAY (1 July)
Other offices and businesses remain open.
UTCHAL
Kalash harvest festival with singing, dancing and feasting. Celebrated throughout Kalash Valleys. (See listings for Hotels) in Chitral.
EID-MILLAD-UN-NABI
The Prophet Mohammaed's birthday. Celebrated throughout Pakistan.

August

INDEPENDENCE DAY (14 August)
Commemorates founding of Pakistan in 1947. Celebrated throughout Pakistan.

September

DEFENCE OF PAKISTAN DAY (6 September)
Commemorates the India Pakistan War of 1965 over Kashmir with processions, parades and Airforce displays at Rawalpindi, Lahore, Peshawar, Sargodha, Karachi and Quetta.
ANNIVERSARY OF QUAID-E-AZAM'S DEATH (11 September)
Observes the death of Pakistan's Founding Father with meetings and rallies which are held throughout Pakistan.
PHOOL
Chitral and Kalash festivals celebrating reaping of grapes and walnuts.
(See listings for Hotels) in Chitral.

November

IQBAL DAY
Commemoration of the birthday of the poet, Allama Iqbal. Celebrated throughout Pakistan.

December

CHOWAS
Winter festival to welcome the first snow fall in Chitral Valley. Activities restricted indoors. (See listings for Hotels) in Chitral.
BIRTHDAY OF QUAID-E-AZAM (25 December)
Celebrations also coincide with Christmas.
BANK HOLIDAY (31 December)
Other office and businesses remain open on 31 December.
Some regional festivals arranged on the occasion of Urs of the mystics are:
Shah Abdul Latif Bhittai festival
The festival is held every year to mark the Urs celebration of popular Sindh mystic Shah Abdul Latif Bhittai in the month of February.
Sehwan Sharif
Concerned district authorities holds this festival to mark the Urs celebration of Lal Shahbaz Qalandar during August-September each year.
Mela Bari Imam
Federal Ministry of Religious Affairs holds the said Mela each year to mark the Urs celebrations of Shah Abdul Latif during March/April.
OTHERS
These holidays vary each year.
SHAB-E-BARAT
A religious festival featuring fireworks and light displays which is celebrated throughout Pakistan.
EID-UL-FITR
Muslim religious festival at the end of Ramadan, the month of fasting, with cultural and social activities. Celebrated throughout Pakistan.
EID-UL-AZHA (Hajj)
The sacrifice of Ismail is commemorated with exchange of dishes, new clothes and household visits, celebrated throughout Pakistan. Also coincides with beginning of annual pilgrimage to Makkah.

Museums of Pakistan

Allama Iqbal Residence and Library
Lahore
Specializes in history

Agricultural Museum Lyallpur
Founded 1909, renowned for its botanical work.

Air Force Museum
Peshawar
Founded 1964. Mementoes and souvenirs, including vintage aircraft of what is arguably one of the world's greatest combat air forces.

Archaeological Museum
University of Karachi
Founded 1956. Noted for its archaeological work.

Archaeological Museum
Peshawar University
Founded 1966. Noted for its archaeological work and art exhibits.

Archaeological Museum Banbhore
Founded in 1960. Noted for its exhibits of Pre-Christian times and other archaeological work.

Archaeological Museum Harappa
Founded 1926. Noted for its exhibits excavated from the ruins of Moenjodaro's twin city.

Archaeological Museum Moenjodaro

Founded 1925. Noted for its exhibits from one of the earliest and greatest cradles of civilization

Armed Forces Museum Islamabad

Exhibits reflect the heritage and contemporary image of the country's armed forces.

Armoury Museum Lahore

Old fort. Founded 1928. Noted for its exhibits of firearms and weapons through the ages.

Army Museum Rawalpindi

Founded 1961. Relics and mementoes of two centuries of military history, from the East India Company's first army to the present day Pakistan Army. Includes Sir Claude Auchinleck's uniforms and the first Victoria Cross ever to be won by an Asian soldier.

Bahawalpur Museum

Founded 1974. Noted for its exhibits relating to regional art, history, and ethnology.

Bahawalpur State Museum

Founded 1948. Noted for its exhibits of archaeology, natural history, and applied arts.

Bhitshah Cultural Museum

Founded 1962. Specializes in arts and crafts.

Botanical Museum Rawalpindi

Noted for its botanical work.

Dir Museum Chakdara

Founded 1970. Specialises in regional archaeology and ethnology.

Faqir Khana Museum Lahore

Founded 1937. Noted for its work in the arts, applied arts and crafts, and history.

Folk Art Museum Islamabad

Founded 1973.

Geological Museum Quetta

Specializes in regional geology.

Hyderabad Museum

Founded 1974. Specialises in art, crafts, archaeology, and anthropology.

Industrial and Commercial Museum Lahore

Founded 1950. Specializes in industrial and commercial research.

Islamia College Museum Peshawar

Founded 1934. Specializes in zoology.

Lahore Museum

Founded 1864. Outstanding exhibits in archaeology, history, fine arts, applied arts crafts and ethnology.

Mangla Dam Museum

Founded 1967. Specializes in natural history, geography and archaeology.

Natural History Museum Lahore

Government College
Founded 1910. Noted for its natural history work.
National Museum of Pakistan
Karachi
Founded 1950. Noted for its archaeological and ethnological exhibits.

National Museum of Pakistan Islamabad

Artistic, historical, and ethnological exhibits.

Pakistan Forest Museum Abbottabad

Founded 1952. Specializes in forestry, arboreal research, and timber products.

Peshawar Museum

Founded 1907. Outstanding exhibits in archaeology, art, applied arts, and ethnology.

Quaid-e-Azam Museum

Karachi
Jinnah's birthplace and now a museum and library dedicated to the memory of Pakistan's founding father.

Science & Technology Museum

Engineering University Lahore
Founded 1969. Specializes in engineering and technology.

Shakir Ali's Lahore Residence

Founded 1975. Art gallery and history.

Sikh & Mughal Galleries Old Fort, Lahore

Founded 1964. Specializes in art and history.

Sind University Educational Museum

Hyderabad
Founded 1959. Specializes in education (arts and crafts)

Swat Museum Saidu Sharif

Founded 1959. Noted for its outstanding Buddist relics and artefacts from the Golden Age of Swat Valley and its ethnological exhibits.

Talpur House Museum

Hyderabad

Taxila Museum

Founded 1918. Noted for its priceless treasures from one of the greatest Buddhist cultures ever known to have existed.

Umar Kot Museum

Founded 1968. Specializes in regional history.

Gazetteer

Aliabad (Hunza)
Islamabad 648, Karachi 2,228, Lahore 763. Alt: 2,130 metres Pop: 47,000.

Bahawalpur
Islamabad 729, Karachi, 851, Lahore 441. Pop: 280,000.

Chitral
Islamabad 381, Karachi 1,942, Lahore 650. Alt: 1,500 metres. Pop: 78,000.

Dera Ghazi Khan
Islamabad 578, Karachi 913, Lahore 503. Pop: 159,000.

Faisalabad
Islamabad 372, Karachi 1,181, Lahore 143. Pop: 1,100,000 million.

Gilgit
Islamabad 568, Karachi 2,129, Lahore 838. Alt: 1,400 metres. Pop: 78,000.

Gujrawala
Islamabad 238, Karachi 1,286, Lahore 68. Pop: 937,000.

Gujrat
Islamabad 150, Karachi 1,430, Lahore 138. Pop: 241,000.

Hyderabad
Islamabad 1,405, Karachi 175, Lahore 1,117. Pop: 1,173,000.

Islamabad
Karachi 1,580, Lahore 288. Pop: 318,000.

Karachi
Islamabad 1,580, Lahore 1,292. Pop: 1,200,000 million.

Khunjerab
Islamabad 800, Karachi 2.380, Lahore 1,088. Alt: 5,000 metres.

Lahore
Islamabad 28. Karachi 1,292. Pop: 4,000,000 million.

Larkana
Islamabad 1,194, Karachi 486, Lahore 906. Pop: 193,000.

Mardan
Islamabad 178, Karachi 1,755, Lahore 463. Pop: 230,000.

Mingora (Swat)
Islamabad 280, Karachi 1,860, Lahore 568. Alt: 1,750 metres. Pop: 78,000.

Mirpur Khas
Islamabad 169, Karachi 1,503, Lahore 211. Pop: 180,000.

Multan
Islamabad 636, Karachi 945, Lahore 348. Pop: 1,061,000.

Peshawar
Islamabad 167, Karachi 1,728, Lahore 436. Pop: 820,000.

Quetta
Islamabad 1,489, Karachi 715, Lahore 1,207. Pop: 414,000.

Rawalpindi
Islamabad 13, Karachi 1,567, Lahore 275. Pop: 1,153,000.

Sahiwal
Islamabad 471, Karachi 1,051, Lahore 168. Pop: 219,000.

Sargodha
Islamabad 261, Karachi 1,226, Lahore 172, Pop: 422,000.

Sialkot
Islamabad 230, Karachi 1,410, Lahore 117, Pop: 438,000.

Skardu (Baltisan)
Islamabad 715, Karachi 2,295, Lahore 1,003, Alt: 2,500 metres, Pop: 41,000.

Sukkur
Islamabad 1,088, Karachu 491, Lahore 801, Pop: 277,000.

Listings

Airlines

Bahawalpur

Pakistan International Airline
Chowk Fawara
Tel: 5655

Faisalabad

Aero Asia
Block-8
New Civil Line
Tel: 627024

Gulf Air
40/3
New Civil Line
Tel: 623302

Saudi Arabian Airline
SGA Southern Travel (Pvt) Ltd
Tel: 20202/20768

Islamabad

Aero Asia
Block-12/D
Blue Area
Tel: 219341/5

Airlanka
1-A, Shaheed Plaza
Tel: 210947/891706

China Xinjiang Airlines
Blue Area
Block 32
Tel: 223447/6

Gulf Air
Blue Area
W Plaza
Tel: 210243

KLM Royal Dutch Airline
Shahid Plaza
Blue Area
Tel: 829686/5

Kuwait Airways
Shahid Plaza
Blue Area
Tel: 212194/822727

Malaysian Airlines
Blue Area
Shahid Plaza
Tel: 213382

Northwest Airlines GSA
Nazimuddin Rd
1-D, Rehmat Plaza
Tel: 812174

Pakistan International Airline
Blue Area
Tel: 825094

Philippine Airlines
Shahid Plaza
Tel: 821568

Saudi Arabian Airlines
52 Modern Plaza
Blue Area
Tel: 210168/3

Shaheen Air International
32 Buland Markaz
Blue Area
Tel: 813935

Singapore Airlines
Holiday Inn Hotel
Tel: 821555

Syrian Airlines
Hotel Marriott
Abdullah Harron Road
Tel: 812576

Karachi

Aero Asia
43-J, Block-6
PE CHS
Tel: 4545625

Aeroflot
Holiday Inn C Plaza
Shahra-e-Faisal
Tel: 529210/324

African Airlines International
15 Trade Towers
A Haroon Road
Tel: 5680962/4148

Air Canada
15-Trade Tower
Hotel Metropole
Tel: 511349/779

Air France
Hotel Marriott
Tel: 5682007/1071

Air Mauritius
Hotel Metropole
Tel: 520589

Air Tanzania
Embassy Hotel
Tel: 449238/228

Airlanka Ltd
Service Club Building
Mereweather Road
Tel: 5680382

Alia (The Royal Jordanian Airline)
Hotel Metropole
Tel: 512027/568226

Alitalia
Hotel Metropole
Tel: 511097/8

American Airlines
11-Avari Plaza
Fatima Jinnah Rd
Tel: 526567/466

Austrian Airlines
24-Hotel Metropole
Tel: 515633

Balkan Bulgarian Airlines
4-Bright Apt
Shopping Arcade
Main Clifton Rd
Tel: 515314/3

Belgian World Airline (Sabena)
3-S J Syed House
II Chundrigar Rd
Tel: 215376/219331

Bhoja Airline (PVT) Ltd
Bhoja Terrace
Shahra-e-Liaquat
Tel: 215378/219331

Biman Bangladesh Airlines
Avari Tower
Shahra-e-Faisal
Tel: 514103/510069

British Airways
PLC Marriot Hotel
Tel: 5686058/76

CAAC Civil Aviation Administration of China 25/C,
24th Street,
PECHS Block-6,
Tel: 435570

Canadian Pacific Airlines
Avari Tower
Shahra-e-Faisal
Tel: 523386

Cathay Pactfic Airways Limited
Hotel Metropole
Tel: 524218/520683

Eastem Airlines
34-Hotel Metropole
Tel: 5660153

Egypt Air
Avari Towers
Shahra-e-Faisal
Tel: 513233

Emirates Airlines
265-A, R A Lines
Sarwar Shaheed Rd
Tel: 5683377

Ethiopian Airline
Hotel Metropole
Tel: 511349/51179

Gulf Air
Kashif Centre
Shahra-e-Faisal
Tel: 5675237

Indian Airlines
Pearl Continental Hotel
Tel: 5681577/2034

Iran Air
10-Hotel Mehran
Tel: 526293/528274

Iraq Airways
Avari Plaza
Shahra-e-Faisal
Tel: 529474

Japan Airlines,
JAL Avari Plaza
Shahra-e-Faisal
Tel: 510162/1

Kenya Airways
4-Lakson Square Building
Sarwar Shaheed Rd
Tel: 5685730/520770

KLM Royal Dutch Airlines
Qasr-e-Zainab
Club Road
Tel: 5689071

Korean Air
18-Hotel Metorpole
Tel: 528182/529898

Kuwait Airways
Sheraton Hotel
Tel: 5685754

Libyan Arab Airlines
Hotel Mehran
Tel: 523577/6

Lot-Polish Airline
Hotel Metropole
Tel: 520589

Lufthansa German Airlines
Pearl Continental Hotel
Tel: 5685811/6

Malasian Airlines
Sheraton Hotel
Tel: 5682434/2338

Northwest Airlines GSA
Sharif Centre
M T Khan Road
Tel: 5611215/514

Olympic Airways
10-Hotel Metropole
Tel: 5660153

Pakistan International Airlines
Strachen Road
Tel: 5689631/40

Philippine Airlines
34-Hotel Metropole
Tel: 515851/6

Royal Nepal Airlines Corporation
Service Club Building
Tel: 526480/514421

Saudi Arabian Airlines
Al-Sehat Centre
Rafiqui Shaheed Rd
Tel: 5670166/76

Scandinavian Airlines
System SAS
Hotel Metropole
Tel: 515893

Shaheen Air
International
Avari Plaza
Shahra-e-Faisal
Tel: 5660165/9

Singapore
Airlines
Service Club Bldg
Tel: 5660330/4

Swissair
Hotel Metropole
Tel: 512066/
5682307

Syrian Arab
Airlines
6-Club Road
Tel: 5685820

Tarom-the
Romanian Air
Transport
177-2,
Fowler Lines
Shahra-e-Faisal
Tel: 7783033/9261

Thai Airways
International
Public
Company Ltd
Hotel Metropole
Tel: 5660160/3

Trans World
Airlines (TWA)
Hotel Metropole
Tel: 511779

United Airlines
14-Hotel
Metropole
Tel: 5684732/1

Yemen Airways
Hotel Metropole
Tel: 514776

Lahore
British Airways
Egerton Road
Transport House
Tel: 63011883/
6301575

Egypt Air
5-Davis Road
Tel: 6306793

Emirates Airline
Regent House
3-Imtiaz Plaza
Tel: 6360281/0

Gulf Air
25/A, Davis Rd
Tel: 6369731

Indian Airlines
Ambassador
Centre
Davis Road
Tel: 211230

Korean Air
5-Davis Road
Tel: 6303436

Kuwait Airways
15-A,-Davis Road
Tel: 6368206/7

Malaysian
Airlines
Egerton Road
Tel: 6365055

Northwest
Airlines GSA
PIA Towers
Gulberg Road
Tel: 879715

Pakistan
International
Airlines
11-E, Egerton Road
Tel: 6302556

Philippine Airlines
7-Egerton Road
Tel: 6302794

Saudi Arabian
Airlines
Indus Hotel
Tel: 6305411/4

Shaheen Air
International
Wapda House
Tel: 6360825

Singapore Airlines
WAPDA House
Tel: 6303269

Swissair
P Continental Hotel
Tel: 6362007/
6303207

Syrian Arab
Airlines
Hotel Ambassador
Tel: 6301861/5

Turkish Airlines
Imtiaz Plaza
Tel: 6303503/1029

Mirpur (A K)
Gulf Air
Sector B-2,
Part-II
Alama Iqbal Rd
Tel: 3999

Multan
Gulf Air
55-C/XILMQ Rd
Tel: 74905

Peshawar
Gulf Air
Galaxy Hotel
Khayber Bazar
Tel. 213171

Shaheen Air
International
Cantonment Plaza
Tel: 278409/671

Quetta
Pakistan
International
Airline
17-Nalli Road
Tel: 820861

Rawalpindi
British Airways
P Continental
Hotel
Tel: 566791

Gulf Air
Haider Road
Tel: 584412

Sialkot
Gulf Air
Naveed Centre
Kutchery road
Tel: 87408

PIA Domestic Booking Office

Abbottabad
Tel: 6884

Attock
Tel: 3822/3622

Badin
Al Hamra Hotel
RCD Highway Rd
Tel: 210519/573

Bahawalpur
Chowk Fawara
Tel: 4989

Bannu
Shahra-e- Quaid-e-
Azam, Cantt
Tel: 3573/3921

Chitral
Polo Ground Rd
Tel: 2863/2963

Dal Badin
United Hotel
Quaide-e-Azam
Road
Tel: 604

Dera Ghazi Khan
11-Khan Market
Quaid-e-Azam Rd
Tel: 64172/62146

Dera Ismail Khan
7-A, Aziz Bathi
Road, Cantt.
Tel: 711668/697

Indus Travel
Service
Circular Road
Tel: 3962

Faisalabad
26, New Civil
Lines
Tel: 649493/611267

Airport Road
Tel: 2841/3390/
2333

Hyderabad
430 Saddar
Tel: 782762/784228

Islamabad
99-11 Aabpara
Market
Tel: 25091-2/31

Jacobabad
Station Road
Tel: 3684/8251

Jiwani
Main Bazar
Tel: 289/389

Karachi
Avenue Centre
264 RA Line
Statchen Road
Tel: 5689631
Ext: 6629

Civic Centre
KDA Complex
Gulshan-e-Iqbal
Tel: 5842855

Clifton Travel
(PVT) Ltd
Clifton
Tel: 5871571-5 Lines

Din Air Link
(PVT) Ltd
Gulshan-e-Iqbal
Tel: 4976414/5

Karachi Aviation
(PVT) Limited
Shahra-e-Faisal
Tel: 4530648/
4543044

North Travel
(PVT) Ltd
Groumandar
Tel: 4927071-4
Lines

Pearl Continental
Hotel
Shahra-e-Azam
Tel: 5689639

Quality Travel
(PVT) Ltd
Bahadurabad
Tel: 4947572-4
Lines

Sadaf Par Avion
(PVT) Ltd
North Nazimabad
Tel: 6677440-4
Lines

Kharian
Gulf Building
GT Road
Tel: 2408/2904

Kohat
Spinzer Travel
Hangu Road
Tel: 4175/2375

Khuzdar
Tel: 2225/2580

Taimoor
Enterprises
GT Road
Tel: 2375

Lahore
Shahdin Building
Shahra-e-
Quaid-e-Azam
Tel: 53951/306951

11-E, Egerton Rd
Tel: 62705

Larkana
Station Road
Tel: 46583/44015

Mianwali
Bilu Khil Road
Tel: 2952/2024

333

Mirpur (Azad Kashmir)
Choudhry
Khawaja Associates
Main Bazar
Tel: 3214/2161

Moenjodaro
Station Road
Tel: 46583/44015

Multan
65 Abdali Road
Tel: 570131

Muzaffarabad
Chattar
Tel: 4877/3121

Nawabshah
Sakrand Road
Tel: 64615/4614

Panjgar
Bashir Building,
Saddar Bazar
Tel: 3300/2525

Parachinar
Hussainabad
Tel: 2208/2013

Pasni
Main Pasni Bazar
Tel: 501

Peshawar
33 The Mall
Contonment
Tel: 270214

Quetta
17 Halli Road
Tel: 820901

Rawalkot
Khirk Road
Tel: 3093/3246

Rawalpindi
49 Jinnah Avenue
Tel: 815041

Saidu Sharif
Faizabad Road
Tel: 711137/48

Skardu
Chashma Bazar
Tel: 2491/3325

Samundri
Moon Express
Tel: 92

Sehwan Sharif
PIA Booking Office
Tel: 620104

Sialkot
Kutchery Road
Tel: 263384/835

Sukkur
Queens Road
Tel: 25744/24548

Taxila
Overseas
Employment
Coporation
Tel: 65485/62385

Turbat
Tel: 412322/055

Zhob
10-A, Market Rd
Tel: 3366/2875/
2954

Car Hire

Islamabad
Avis Rent-a-Car
Walji's Building
10 Khayaban-e-
Suhrawardy
PO Box 1088
Tel: 270745-8
Fax: 270753/
828264
Tlx: 5836/5769

Lahore
Avis Rent-a-Car
Ali Complex,
23 Empress Road
Tel: 6316031
Fax: 6366146
Tlx: 447609

Avari Hotel
Shahra-e-Quaidi-
Azam
Tel: 6375805

Karachi
74-F, Block 6
PECHS
Tel: 4540672
Fax: 4540212

Avis Rent-a-Car
Avari Towers
Fatima Jinnah
Road
Tel: 5676323/7955

Rawalpindi
Avis Rent-a-Car
7-Rahim Plaza
Murree Road
Tel: 568879

Gilgit
Avis Rent-a-Car
Gilgit Serena
Tel: 2665/4129
Fax: 4129

Hunza A-Rent-a-
Car
Tel: 47045

Skardu
Tel: 3468

Consulates

Karachi
Afghanistan
30/2, Off:
Khayaban-e-Shamsi,
St 9, Phase-V, DHS,
Tel: 5842263
Fax: (021) 5842263

Australian Trade
Commission
Suite 3,
Federation House
Shahra-e-Firdousi,
Clifton
Tel: 5870535
Fax: (021) 5870025

Australian Trade
Commission
43/1-n, Block-6
Razi Road PECHS
Tel: 4549111/112
Fax: 4547382
Tlx: 20795 AHST PK

Bahrain
Bungalow No
25/A, Sunset
Lane, Phase-II,
Extension DHA,
Tel: 5894374-75
5894735
Fax: (021) 5894376

Bangladesh
9, Ch,
Khaliquzzaman
Road, Clifton,
Tel: 5683537/3984
Fax: (021) 5682303
Tlx: 29137
BDESH PK

Belgium
Consulate and
Trade Office
Pearl Continental
Hotel, Club Road
Tel: 5685526
Fax: (021) 5683419
Tlx: 24259

Belize
D-28, Block 6,
PECHS
Tel: 448527/
6644901
Fax: (92 21) 4536855

Bosnia and
Herzegovina
No 1 School
Road, F-8/3
Tel: 261041/03
Fax: (051) 261004

Brazil
113-A, SMCHS
Main Shahra-e-
Faisal
PO Box 7255
Tel: 4556086/89/
4550217
Fax: (021) 4555154
Tlx: 20994 AJCL PK

Cameroon
Pent House No
27, Kehkashan
Shopping Mall,
172-N, Tariq Rd,
Tel: 4534383/
4927390
Fax: (021)
4538433/4548616
Tlx: 21763 AS VCS

Canada
Beach Luxury
Hotel
Tel: 5610685
Fax: (021)
5610673/4
Tlx: 23899
AVARI PK

Chile
2/24, Al-Yousuf
Chambers,
Shahra-e-Liaquat,
GPO Box 793
Tel: 2622375
Fax: (021)
2620228/2630936
Tlx: 27500
SALEM PK

China
Plot No ST-20,
Block IV, Clifton,
Tel: 5874087/
168/819
Fax: (021) 5874226

Commercial
Section
43-6/B, Block 6
PECHS
Tel: 4530523/4/6
Fax: (021) 4530525

Comoros
36, Shrifiabad
Tel: 4933696

Czech
99-Clifton
Tel: 5873792/94
5874436
Tlx: 25690
OBZAM PK

Denmark
F-50, Feroze
Nana Road
Bath Island
Tel: 5873732
Fax: (021) 5874459
Tlx: 28038
KGROS PK

Dominica
Latif House,
50/C Block 6,
PECHS
Tel: 4559111
Tlx: 26614
AJCKR PK
Fax: (021) 4548300

Ecuador
Apt. C1, Afzal
Courts,
Kehkashan Clifton
Tel: 535218

Finland
Finlay House,
PO Box 4670
II Chundrigar Rd
Tel: 2428485
Fax: (021)
2417818/2427565
Tlx: 23674
JFKAR PK

France
12-A Mohammad
Ali Bogra Road
Bath Island
Tel: 5873797/8
Tlx: (021) 5874093/
3073

Germany F-95,
Khayaban-e-Roomi
Block 7, Clifton
Tel: 5870234
Fax: (021) 5874009
Tlx: 2772
AAKC PK

Gambia
Schon Centre,
II Chundrigar Rd,
Tel: 2630855/
6000-10
Fax: (021) 2636325
Tlx: 21386
SCON PK

Greece
Hakim Sons Building, 19 West Wharf Rd
Tel: 202015-19
Fax: (021) 2314260/2418480
Tlx: 2364 YAQIN PK

Guinee
21-B, 7th Central Street
Defence Housing Society
Tel: 540262/1602

Guyana
Ebrahim Building, West Wharf Road
Tel: 2312255/0105
Fax: (021) 2310205
Tlx: 23715
HAEGS PK

Hungary Trade Commission
No. F-27/1, Block 9, Clifton,
Tel: 5866501/2
Fax: (021) 5875293
Tlx: 2813 HUNG PH

Iceland Trade Commission
Seedat Chambers
Dr Ziauddin Ahmed Road,
Tel: 5687961/65
Fax: (021) 5687329
Tlx: 29107
DEECO PK

Iran
81, Shahrah-e-Iran, Clifton
Tel: 5874370-71
Tlx: 20231 IRAN PK
Fax: (021)-5874633

Ireland
1-AI/I, Saba Avenue Phase-V, Ext. DHA
PO Box 12419
Tel: 5876945
Fax: (021) 5842061
Tlx: 23047 EIRE PK

Italy
85-Clifton Road
Tel: 5874582
Fax: (021) 5870134
Tlx: 24412 ITAIC PK

Japan
233 EI Lines-Raja Ghazanfar Ali Khan Road,
Tel: 5681331-32
Fax: (021) 5684627
Tlx: 29064 RYOJI PK

Jordan
23-27 Reclaimed Area
Timber Road
Tel: 2851174-76
2851182
Fax: (021) 2851901
Tlx: 21019 PSL PK

Korea
51-C, Clifton
Tel: 5874638
Fax: (021) 5868732

Korea Democratic Peoples Republic
26/I, 20/2, 1st Street Gazri Street,
Phse-VDHA
Tel: 5431390
Fax: (021) 5888139
Tlx: 20812

Kuwait
St-l9 Block-IV Clifton,
Tel: 5873805/4675
Fax: (021) 5874710

Liberia
KPT Gate No 11, TPX Yard M T Khan Road,
Tel: 5686218/5547

Madagascar
H # 78, Margalla Road,
Tel: 214466
Fax: (051) 824761
Tlx: 54065
WAKII PK

Malayasia
1st Floor, Lakson Squre Building,
Tel: 23925 RIZVI PK
Fax: (021) 5684070

Maldives
Ameejee Chambers
PO Box 51
Campbell Street
Tel: 2627945
Fax: 021) 2621910
Tlx: 2692AVSNS PK

Malta
Gokal Chambers
Beach Hotel Rd,
Tel: 5610766
Fax: (021) 5610760-61
Tlx: 29158
GOKAL PK

Mexico
Lakson Square Bldg-2
Sarwar Shaheed Rd
Tel: 5689081-89/ 5681628
Fax: (021) 5683410
Tlx: 23280/06
LAKSN PK

Monaco
Gulzaman No 2 Sunnyside Road, Civil Lines,
Tel: 5684987

Morocco
B # D-19, Block-7 Kahkashan, Clifton
Tel: 535698/578122

Mozambique
105, Alamgir Rd, Bahadarabad Society,
Tel: 7731432/9171
Fax: (021) 8323
Tlx: 21503
TAWAB PK

Mayanmar (Burma)
G-18, Apartment No 3 Khoro Apartment, Main Clifton Rd
Tel: 532626
Fax: (021) 2433273
Tlx: 20257
NAVED PK

Nepal
301-302, Mehdi Towers 3rd Floor, 115A, SMHS Shahra-e-Faisal,
Tel: 4533611-4 Lines
Fax: (021) 4550041
Tlx: 23913 META PK

Netherlands
4-A, Ch Khaliquzzaman Road,
Tel: 5680670
Fax: (021) 5682696
Tlx: 21169
HOLKR PK

New Zealand
Comm. Union Building 74/I-A, Lalazar, MT Khan Road
Tel: 5611071-75/ 5611802-8
Fax: (021) 5610805/959
Tlx: 29692 NZHCP PK

Niger
204-2nd Floor, Sunset Twoer 1-D, Sunset Boulevard
Defence Housing Authority
Tel: 5882211
Fax: (021)5661165

Honorary
5 and 6
Chartered Bank Chambers
II Chundrigar Rd
Tel: 24148894
Tlx: 2032/29775
ULA PK

Oman
A-1-A, South Seaview Avenue Phase-II, DHA
Tel: 5888307
Fax: (021) 5887216
Tlx: 20954
OMAN PK

Phillipines
1/29, Kazzam Manzil Randle Rd
Tel: 7728046-48
Fax: (021) 7724908/7732965
Tlx: 20656
SPRAY PK

Poland
10/B, Lalazar MT Khan Road
Tel: 5610147/177
Fax: (021) 5610686
Tlx: 29819
DLHAN PK

Portugal
Mavani Chambers, 1st Floor Thaoomal Khushaldas Rd
PO Box 652
Tel: 219866/ 5661405

Qatar
House No 16,

Phase V,
Khayaban-e-Hafiz, Phase-II, DHA
Tel: 6862171-3
Fax: (021) 5872377
Tlx: 29362 QCK PK

Romania
245/2/H, Block 6, PECHS
Tel: 4541289/90
Fax: (021) 4549653
Tlx: 21865
ROCOM PK

Russia
8/26, Flench Street
Bleak House Rd
Tel: 5683309/ 512853
Tlx: 20687
GERFE PK

Russia Trade Representative
68, Shahrah-e-Iran, Clifton
Tel: 587415/ 5874393-94
Tlx: 28073
VTORG PK

Saudi Arabia
20/22 Khayabane-Hafiz,
Phase-V, DHA
Tel: 5841154/56
Fax: (051) 5840910
Tlx: 25473 NAJD PK

Senegal
104, Al-Farid Centre
MT Khan Road
Tel: 5686225/1853
Fax: (021) 5684506

Seychelles
4, Jinnah Cooperative Housing Society,
Tel: 454912/ 4536348
Fax: (021) 4545905/8809
Tlx: 20917 ANIS PK

Singapore
Lakson square Building # 2
Sarwar Shaheed Rd
Tel: 5685308/6419
Fax: (021) 5683410/4336
Tlx: 20206 LAKSN PK

Somalia
S/31, SITE
Maripur Road
Tel: 2561323/
2574367-8-9
Fax: (021) 2563080
Tlx: 29546 RAUF
PK

South Africa
1-5D, Link
Avenue, Phase-II,
Defence Housing
Authority,
Tel:

Spain
No 1 1st Floor
Services Club Ext
Building,
Mereweather Rd
Tel: 522333/
5680307
Fax: (021)
Tlx: 24368 AKBAR
PK

Sri Lanka Trade
Commissioner
B-49, Street 12,
Gulshan-e-Faisal,
Bath Island,
Clifton,
Tel: 5861705-06
Fax: (021) 5874779
Tlx: 23085
LANTR PK

Sri Lanka
Towellers House
WSA 30
Block-1, FB Area
Tel: 6326868/
6316767
Fax: (021) 6314884

Swaziland
PIA Building,
Strachen Road,
Tel: 5684655/4038
Fax: (021) 5687810

Sweden
5-6, Chartered
Bank Chambers
II Chundrigar Rd
Tel: 2415697/4884
Fax: (021)
2412046/5684522
Tlx: 20326/29775
ULA PK

Tanzania
6th Floor, Hotel
Sarah Building
Parr Street
Saddar,
Tel: 524195/96

Fax (92-21)
5677540
Tlx: 0091 GMDEL
PK

Thailand
F-16, Block 9
Kehkashan
Clifton,
Tel: 5874417
2581243
Fax: (021) 8574555
Tlx: 28003 THIA
PK

Tunisia
103,3rd Floor
Standard
Insurance House
II Chundrigar Rd
Tel: 2414584/6733
Fax: (021) 2419193
Tlx: 29407 SFTM
PK

Turkey
D-201, Block 5,
Kehkashan Clifton,
Tel: 5874194
Fax: (021) 5874691

Turkey
Commercial
Office
D-1, First Gizri
Lane,
Defence Housing
Authority,
Tel: 5866894
Fax: (021) 5874237
Tlx: 25120

UAE
84-Clifton
Shahra he -Iran
Tel: 5873819/20
Fax: (021) 5874387
Tlx: 2891 EMRT PK

United Kingdom
York Place
Runnymede
Lane, Clifton
Tel: 5872431/36
5874300
Fax: (021) 5874014
Tlx: 24180
UKREP PK

USA
8, Abdullah
Haroon Road,
Tel: 5685170/9
Fax: (021) 5683089

Uzbekistan
No 9, F/4/1
Hatim Alvi
Road, Clifton

Tel: 5870415
Fax: (021) 5863950
Tlx: 20292
BKKHI PK

Zambia
Pagganwala
Lodge
238 Staff Lines
Fatima Jinnah Rd
Tel: (021)
5682461/2425968
Fax: (021) 2417184
Tlx: 20650 ANJM
PK

Lahore

Austria
4-Lawrence Road
Tel: 6362625/0009
Fax: (042) 6358809
Tlx: 44580 INTER
PK

Belgium
6, Egerton Road
Tel: 6306122-23
Fax: (042) 6368699

Brazil
438-X, Phase III
LCCHS, Cant
Tel: 7354591/8777
Fax: (042) 7235100

Denmark
27, Main Gulberg
Tel: 871555/
876006
Tlx: 44439 JRA PK

France
41 Zaffar Ali
Road, Gulberg 5
Tel: 57111522
Fax: (042) 5835059

Germany
60-Main Gulberg
PO Box 3151
Tel 44710 HKL PK
Fax: (042) 5760695

Greece
71-A, Main
Gulberg
Tel: 7223810/
5712493

Hungary
49-C Ghous-ul-
Azam Road
Tel: 5756999/
757140-43
Fax: (042) 7580027
Tlx: 44520
SWEMBPK

Iran
55-Shamshad II
Tel: 75909226-29
Fax: (042) 7575650

Italy
516, 5th Floor,
Alfalah Building,
Mall Road
Tel: 6361113/
5711853
Fax: (042) 576047

Malaysia
Jinnah Rafi
Foundation
Empire Centre,
9-K, Main
Boulevard,
Gulberg,
Tel: 6368663/
5712667
Fax: (042) 368643

Netherlands
2nd Floor
Emirates Bank
Building
14-Egerton/
Kashmir Road
Tel: 6368680
Fax: (042) 6368119
Tlx: 44423 EMCO
PK

Norway
295/3, Sarwar Rd
Tel: 214186/
7356487
Fax: (042) 7230577

Spain
60, Shahrah-e-
Quaid-e-Azam
Tel: 6301196-99/
6305505
Fax: (042) 6369204
Tlx: 44382
FEROZ PK

Sweden
308 Upper Mall
Tel: 575340-07
Fax: (042) 5710624

Sri Lanka
Associated
House, 7-Egerton
Road,
Tel: 6306106/ 6108
Fax: (042) 6368742
Tlx: 44729 AEL PK

Turkey
30-Shahrah-e-
Quaid-e-Azam
Tel: 7311390/
7244181
Fax: (042) 724839

United Kingdom
Syed Babar Ali
Foundation Bldg
308, Upper Mall
Tel: 571059/
87024-42

Peshawar

Afghanistan
17-CB-Gul
Mohar Lane,
University Town
Tel: 842486
Fax: (0521) 842335

France
10, Fort Road 10
Cantt
Tel: 273177/
275838

Iran
18-111/C, Park
Avenue
University Town
Tel: 4111/41259/
42270
Tlx: 2385

USA
11 Hospital Road
Tel: 279801-3
Fax: (521) 276712

Quetta
Afghanistan
36-BE, Chaman
Housing Society
Chaman Road
Tel: 834659
Tlx: 247 AFCNQ

France
7, Regal Plaza
Circular Road
Tel: 440878

Iran
2/33, Shahra-e-
Hali
Tel: 64379
Fax: (081) 65288
Tlx: 78280

Foreign Missions

Islamabad

Afghanistan
H#8, Street 90,
G-6/3,
Tel: 217553/4
Fax: (051) 217552
Tlx: 54681 Afeid
PK

Albania
H No 231, Sector F-10,/2, Street No.18
Tel: 297030i
290740
Fax: 290750

Algeria
H # 107, St 9, Sector E-7
Tel: 210165/6

Argentina
20-Hill Road, F-6/3
GPO Box 1015
Tel: 211117
Fax: (051) 223165

Australia
Diplomatic Enclave No 2
PO Box No 1046
Tel: 214902-5
Fax: (051) 214763
Tlx: 5804
AUSEM PK

Austria
H#13, Street-I, F-6/3,
Tel: 210237
Fax: (051) 216754
Tlx: 5531 OEBOI PK

Bangladesh
H No 1, Street 5, F-6/3,
Tel: 213885
Fax: (051) 213883
Tlx: 5615 DOOT PK

Belgium
H#2, Street 10, F-6/6, 210031-32 821735
Fax: (051) 822358
Tlx: 5865 AMBEL PK

Belgium Trade Commission
House No 2, Street 10 F-6/3
Tel: 821713
Fax: (051) 214346

Brunei Darussalam
House # 16 Street No 21 F-6/2
Tel: 823038/833738
Fax: (051) 823138
Tlx: 4704 BRU PK

Brazil
180-G, (New 50) Attaturk Avenue, Sector G-6/3
PO Box 1053
Tel: 212497/210185
Fax: (051) 823034
Tlx: 5711 BRAZ PK

Canada
Diplomatic Enclave Sector G-5
PO Box 1042
Tel: 211101-03/211106
Fax: (051)211540
Tlx: 5700 DOCAN PK

China
Diplomatic Enclave, Ramna-4
Tel: 824786
Fax: (051) 821116

Czech
Street No 27 House No 49 F-6/2
PO Box 1335
Tel: 210195/221258
Fax: (051) 825327
Tlx: 5705 ZAMIN PK

Cyprus
H No 351-B, Khayaban-e-Iqbal F-7/2
PO Box 2165
Tel: 218762/214970
Fax: (021) 218729

Denmark
H# 9, St-90, Ramna 6/3,
PO Box 1118
Tel: 214210/12
Fax: (051) 823483
Tlx: 5825 AMBDK PK

Egypt
Plot Nos 38-51, UN Boulevard Diplomatic Enclave, Ramna-5/4,
Tel: 212476/210377
Fax: (051) 823453

Ethiopia
5, Sector 9,

Sector F-8/3,
Tel: (051) 856598/697

Finland
H # 11, Street-90 G-6/3,
Tel: 822136/212323
Fax: (051) 214327

France
Diplomatic Enclave, Crn Constitution Ave G-5,
Tel: 213981-3

Germany
Diplomatic Enclave, Ramna-5,
Tel: 212412
Fax: (051) 212911
Tlx: 5871 AAIBA PK

Ghana
Hill View Plaza, 76-E, 1st Floor, Jinna Avenue,
Tel: 22189/222190
Fax: (051) 222191

Greece
H # 6, Main Margalla Road, Sector F-7/3
Tel: 825186/822558
Fax: (051) 825161
Tlx: 54232 GRAM PK

Holy See
Street 5, Diplomatic Enclave, PO Box 1106
Tel: 210491
Fax: (051) 820847

Hungary House
No 12 Margalla Road, F-6/3,
PO Box 1103
Tel: 211593
Fax: (051) 825256
Tlx: 54634 HUEMB PK

Iceland
H # 28, Street 1 F-6/3,
PO Box 1104
Tel: 210023
Fax: (051) 8212245
Tlx: 5811 CSCIB PK

India
G-5, Diplomatic Enclave
Tel: 814371/75 210718
Fax: (051) 224286
Tlx: 5819 INDEM PK

Indonesia
Diplomatic Enclave, Street No 5, Remna 5/4,
Tel: 811291 (4 Lines)
Fax: (051) 213588
Tlx: 5679 INDON PK

Iran
Plot # 222-238, St 2, Sector G-5,/1, Diplomatic Enclave,
Tel: 212740/694
Fax: (051) 824839

Iraq
57, St 48, F-8/4,
Tel: 253391/93
Fax: (051) 253394

Italy
54, Khayaban-e-Margalla, F-6/3,
Tel: 210791-92/222983-84
Fax: (051) 222986
Tlx: 5861 ITALD PK

Japan
Plot Nos. 53-70 Ramna 5/4 Diplomatic Enclave 1
Tel: 219721
Fax: (051) 218073
Tlx: 5805 TAISI PK

Jordan
131, St. 14, E/7
Tel 211782/83
Fax: (051) 823207
Tlx: 5701 URDUN PK

Kazakstan
House, No. 2 Street No. 4, F-8/3,
Tel: 262924/261797
Fax: (051) 262806

Kenya
House No. 10, St 9

Sector F-7/3
PO Box 2097
Tel: 211243
Fax: (051) 212542
Tlx: 5741 KEREP PK

Korea
Block No 13, Street No 29, Diplomatic Enclave II,
Tel: 218089-91,
Fax: (051) 211407

Korea Democratic Peoples Republic
H # 9,Stl8 F-8/2
Tel: 252754

Kuwait
No l,2 & 24, Diplomatic Enclave, University Road
Tel: 212801 (4 Lines)
Fax: (051) 212809
Tlx: 5611 KW1IS PK

Lebanon
H # 6, St 27, Shalimar 6/2
Tel: 5551 ELTP PK
Fax: (051) 826410

Libya
F-8/3, 12-Margalla Road
Tel: 851974/880
Tlx: (051) 261459

Malayasia
H # 78, Margalla Road, F-6/2,
Tel: 210147/214466
Fax: (051) 824761
Tlx: 54065 WAKIL PK

Mauritius
H # 27, Street 26, Sector F-6/2
Fax: (051) 210076
Tlx: 54362 MAU PK

Morocco
H No. 6-Gomal Road, E-7210820
Tel: 210860
Fax: (051) 822743
Tlx: 5718 MORM PK

Mayanmar
(Burma)
H # 12/1, St 13,
F-7/2,
Tel: 210620/822460
Fax: (051) 221210
Tlx: 54282 MEISI
PK

Nepal
H # 11, St. 84
Attaturk Avenue
G-6/4,
Tel: 210642/
212754
Fax: (051)
009251-217875
Tlx: 54165
NEPEMB PK

Netherlands
2nd Floor, PIA
Building, Blue
Area
PO Box 1065
Tel: 214336/7
Fax: (051) 220950
Tlx: 5817 NETH PK

Nigeria
H#6,St22,
F-6/2
PO Box 1075
Tel: 212465-66
Fax: (051) 824104
Tlx: 5875 NIG PK

Norway
H#25, St 19,
Shalimar 6/4
PO Box 1336
Tel: 211223-7
Fax: (051) 223102
Tlx: 5541
NORAM PK

Oman H # 53,
Street,
48, F-8/4
PO Box: 1194
Tel: 254925
Fax: (051) 255074
Tlx: 5704 OMAN
PK

Palestine
486, Street No 9
F-10/2
PO Box 1061
Tel: 291185

Phillipines
20 - C, College
Road, F-7/2,
PO Box 1052

Tel: 212654/721/
822720
Fax: (051) 221218
Tlx: 54613
AMPHI PK

Poland
House No 8-B,
Embassy Road
F-6/4,
Tel: 212170/
826245
Fax: (051) 213626

Portugal
H # 4-A, Main
Margalla Road,
F-7/2,
Tel: 210789/213395
Fax: (051) 221416
Tlx: 5721 PORTE
PK

Russian
Federation
Ramna-4,
Khayaban
Suharawardy,
Diplomatic
Enclave
Tel: 214603-04
Fax: (051) 826552
Tlx: 54241
USSRE PK

Romania
House No 13
St 88, G-6/3
Tel: 210607/
212583

Qatar
H # 20,
Khayaban-e-
Iqbal,
Sector F-6/3,
Tel: 214635/6
Fax: (051) 820868
Tlx: 5869
QATARI PK

Saudi Arabia
House No.14
Hill Road, F-6/3
Tel: 821056/59
Tlx: 54040/33

Somalia
House No. 21,
St 56, F-6/4,
Tel: 210769/
212779
Tlx: 5609
SOMAL PK

South Africa
House No. 48
Margalla Road,
Khayaban-e-Iqbal
Sector F-8/2
Tel: 262354-56/
250318
Fax: (051)
250114/458

Spain
Street 6,
Diplomatin
Enclave Ramna 5
PO Box 1144
Tel: 211070-71/
210888
Fax: (051) 221927
Tlx: 5803 SPAIN PK

Sri Lanka
H # 315-C,
Sector F-7/2,
Khayaban-e-
Iqbal, Margalla Rd,
Tel: 211251/
214598
Fax: (051) 220710
Tlx: 5763 SLEMB PK

Sudan
House No 7
Sector No 1
G-6/3t
Tel: 212142/210183
Fax: (051) 221230
Tlx: 5617 SUDIS PK

Sweden
6-A, Agha Khan
Road, Markaz
Shalimar-66
Tel: 215544-43
Fax: (051) 825284
Tlx: 5806 SVENSK
PK

Switzerland
St 6, Dipt
Enclave, G-5/4
Tel: 211060/61
Fax: (021) 5874104
Tlx: 5815 AMSWI
PK

Syria
30-Hill Road
F-6/3,
Tel: 211303/077
Fax: (051) 216104
Tlx: 5619 SYRAM
PK

Thailand
House No 4,
St 8, F-8/3,

Tel: 859130-31/
859195
Fax: (051) 256730
Tlx: 5527 THAI PK

Tunisia
House No 221,
Street No 21, E-7
Tel: 213307/211576
Fax: (051) 221229
Tlx: 5676

Turkmenistan
House No 22-A,
F-7/1,
Nazimuddin Rd
Tel: 214913

United Kingdom
Rama-5,
Diplomatic
Enclave,
PO Box 1122
Tel: 822131-35
Fax: (051) 823439
Tlx: 54122 UKEMB
PK

Turkey
House No 58
Ataturk Avenue
G-6/3
PO Box 2183
Tel: 210939/043
Fax: (051) 221431

UAE
Diplomatic
Enclave
Plot No 122
Qaid-e-Azam
University Road
Tel: 210373/
218677-78
Fax: (051) 218672/
675

USA
Diplomatic En-
clave
Tel: 826161-79
Fax: (051) 214222
Tlx: 5864 AEISI PK

Uzbekistan
House No 6
Street No 29
F-7/1
Tel: 820779
Fax: (051) 217619

Yemen
No 16,
Street No 17
F-7/2 GPO

PO Box 1523
Tel: 821146-47
Fax: (051) 826159
Tlx: 54460 YEMID
PK

Yugoslavia
House No 14
Street 87
Sector G-6/3
PO Box 1050
Tel: 211081/210234
Fax: (051) 820965

Zambia
House No 9
Street No 62
Sector F-6/3
Embassy Road
Tel: 816795/817565
Fax: (051) 825236

Government
Adresses
Ministry of
Culture, Sports,
Youth Affairs
and Tourism
College Road
Islamabad
Tel: 820856/827051

Pakistan Tours
Limited
Head Office
Flashman's Hotel
Rawalpindi
Tel: 581480-84
Tlx: 5620 FH PK

Pakistan Tours
Limited
Faletti's Hotel
Egerton Road
Lahore
Tel: 303660
Cable: PAKTOURS

Pakistan Tours
Limited
Deans Hotel
Islamia Road
Peshawar
Tel: 72428/76481-
31

Pakistan Tours
Limited
PTDC Chinar Inn
Gilgit
Tel: 2650
Fax: 2562

Pakistan Tours
Limited
K2 Motel
Skardu
Tel: 29461/3322

Pakistan Tours Limited
PTDC District Council
Dar Bungalow Baliakot
Tel: 208

Pakistan Tours Limited
PTDC Motel Chitral
Tel: 2683

Hotels and Motels

Abbottabad (05921)

Al-Abbas Hotel
Manshera Road
Tel: 2706

Asia Hotel Eid Gah Road
Tel: 2307

Bolan Hotel
Fawwara Chowk
Tel: 2123

Gomal Hotel
The Mall
Tel: 2348

Hotel Falcon
The Mall
Tel: 4169

Hotel New Palm The Mall
Tel: 5190

Hotel Ramlina
KK Highway
Tel: 5431

New Kohsar Hotel
Jinnah Road
Tel: 2424

Royal Hotel
203, The Mall
Tel: 6493

Sarban Hotel
The Mall
Tel: 30167

Springfield
The Mall
Tel: 2334

Bahawalpur (0621)

Abaseen Hotel and Restaurant
Circular Road
Tel: 7592

Al-Hilal Hotel and Restaurant
Circular Road
Tel: 5942

Amber Hotel
Shahdin Plaza
Tel: 7322

Chamba Guest House
Stadium Road
Tel: 6624

Holiday Guest House
6/B, Abbas Road, Near Railway Station
Tel: 4556

Irum Hotel and Restaurant
Circular Road
Tel: 4730

Motel Alinas
Sarwer Shaheed Road,
Model Town A
Tel: 5560

Bhurban (051)

Pearl Continental Hotel
Murree Hill
Tel: 427082

Chitral (0533)

PTDC Motel Chitral
Tel: 2683

DI Khan (0529)

Hotel Midway and Restaurant
Indus River Bank, Cantt. Tel: 3100

Faisalabad

Al-Amin Hotel
Kotwali Road, Aminpur Bazar
Tel: 616433

Al-Jawaid Hotel
Kutchery Bazar
Tel: 27689

Al-Khayyan Hotel
Amin Bazar
Tel: 27686

Al-Qamar
Kutchery Bazar
Tel: 626261/616601

Hotel East Inn
Sheikhupura Rd
Tel: 782004-5

Hotel Midway and Restaurant P-35,
Kutchery Bazar
Tel: 615570

Khyber Hotel
Kutchery Bazar
Tel: 25380

Rays Hotel
Allama Iqbal Rd
Tel: 24006

Rex Hotel and Restaurant
Staina Road
Tel: 40699

Serena Lodges and Hotels Club Road
Tel: 30976

Gilgit (0572)

Hunza Marcopolo Inn,
Gulmit Trekking Centre
PO Gulmit Gojal Hunza
Tel: 46107

PTDC Chinar Inn Gilgit
Tel: 2650

Serena Lodges and Hotels Jutial, Gilgit
Tel: 2331

Gujranwala (0431)

Al-Ahmed Hotel and Restaurant
Wazirabad, GT Rd
Tel: 254966

CITI Top
Near Dean Plaza, GT Road
Tel: 43327

Ginza Hotel
GT Road, Gujranwala
Tel: 80514

Shelton Hotel
Gulshan-e-Iqbal, GT Road
Tel: 42001

Gujrat (04331)

Arzoo Hotel and Restaurant
GT Road, Lala Musa
Tel: 2881

Melody Inn
Railway Road
Tel: 3751

Hyderabad (0221)

Hotel City Gate
Opp: Central Jail
National Highway
Tel: 613766/611744

Hotel Faran
Saddar
Tel: 780196

Hotel Fataz
Tandi Sarak
Tel: 24425

Hotel Indus
Thandi Sarak
Tel: 782515

Hotel Star Light
Court Road
Tel: 25402

New Sainjees Motel
Thandi Sarak
Tel: 27276

New Taj Hotel
Station Road
Tel: 780592-94

Yasrab Hotel
Railway Station
Tel: 27006

Islamabad (051)

Adventure Inn
National Park Area
Tel: 212536/9

Arosa Guest House
Garden Avenue, Satellite Town
Tel: 844583/841911

Baiga (Hotel and Restaurant Bakers and sweets) 1-K Plaza, F-10 Markaz
Tel: 281127/201

Best Regency
House No 13
Kaghan Road, F-8/3,
Tel: 857874/261633

Best Western Regency Hotel
6-Is lam abad
Club Road
Tel: 218420

Capital Inn
G-8, Markaz,
Behind PIMS
Tel: 251493

Capita Lodge
Beside Rawaldam,
Club Road
Tel: 823463/818411

CITI Lodge Guest House
H# 6, Street No 56
Sector F-6/4
Tel: 225203/4

Continental House
94, Nazimuddin Road F-8/4
Tel: 852753

Dreamland Hotel
I and T Centre, G-9/4,
Tel: 858102

Dreamland Motels
Club Road
Tel: 814381

Drop Inn Guest House
21, St.88, G-6/3, Embassy Road
Tel: 826897/212157

Dwellers Guest House
House # 3 Street, 64, F-8/4,
Tel: 857445

Eastern Lounge Guest House
Jinnah Supper Market Blk-12-B.
Tel: 215025/828185

Eden Hotel
Plot # 3 A-2, F-8 Markaz
Tel: 260090

Holiday Inn Islamabad Hotel
G-6, Civic Centre
Tel: 827321

Hotel Al-Khayam
G-9, Markaz
Tel: 261021

Hotel Ambassador
Khayaban-e-Suhrwardy
Tel: 824011/4

Hotel Blue Star
1, I & T Centre
Tel: 852810

Hotel Capital
Iqbal Hall Road
CDA Store
Tel: 815099

Hotel Civic
13-West Blue
Area
Tel: 213744

Hotel Royal
International
104-E, Jinnah
Avenue
Tel: 211771/
823703

Hotel Star
G-7, Markaz,
Sitara Market
Tel: 818279

Islamabad Inn
8, Street 54,
F-7/4,
Tel: 813796

Jacaranda (PVT)
Limited
17, College Road
Tel: 223183

Jafari's Guest
House
House # 10,
Bazar Road
Tel: 213550

Jasmine House
G-8, Markaz
Tel: 252002

Kohsar House
House # 28-B
Street # 25, F-8/2
Tel: 852065

Lodging House
HNo 41, College
Road
Tel: 826146

Lord's Islamabad
11, Street 29,
F-7/1,
Tel: 216241/
213853

Luxury Guest
House
H # 1, Street #14
F-7/2
Tel: 821849

Luxury Inn
H # 2,Street No 30
7th Avenue
Tel: 812204/
813218

Margala Motel
(PVT) Ltd
1-Kashmiry
Highway
Tel: 813345/9

Marriott Hotel
Agha Khan Rd
Shalimar - 5
Tel: 826135

Palace Inn
10, Bazar Road,
G-6/4,
Tel: 811409

PTDC Motel
Markaz F-7,
Bhitai Road
Tel: 819384/
218232

Paradise Inn
House # 2 St #
79, G-6/4
Tel: 814072

Quality Inn
Hotel
G-8, Markaz,
Nori Hospital
Tel: 254574/6

Self Contained
Apartments
H # 11-A,
Street No 29
Sector F-771
Tel: 813559

Serenity Inn
119, Street 37,
F-10/1
Tel: 297492/4

Services Inn
Guest House
54-Bazar Road
G-6/4,
Tel: 811863

Shelton House
11, Kaghan Road
Tel: 856956

Sitara Hotel
G-7 Markaz,
Sitara Market
Tel: 819956

SU-Casa Guest
House
H#31, Street 20
F-7/2
Tel: 825578

The Poet
H # 35, Street 20,
F-7/2,
Tel: 213587

The President
Hotel
1-B, Blue Area
Tel: 819651/2

TM Group of
Guest Houses
H # 11, Kaghan
Road
Tel: 856428/956

Tourist Inn
9, College
Road F-7/2
Tel: 819382

VIP
Accomodators
H-18, Street 30,
Sector F-6/1
Tel: 815146

VIP House
H#13, Street #
28, Sector F-6/1
Tel: 825589/
817322

VIP House
29, Kaghan Road
Tel: 281781

VIP Place
Guest House
H # 15, Street 30
F-6/1
Tel: 817740

White House
House # 87
St 72, F-8/3,
Tel: 261369

Karachi (021)

Airport Hotel
Stargate Road
Tel: 4570145

Al-Bilal Hotel
Sohrab Katrak
Road, Saddar
Tel: 5581176

Avari Towers
Fatima Jinnah Rd
Tel: 5660100

Beach Luxury
Hotel
MT Khan Road
Tel: 5611037

Best Western
Plaza Hotel
Dr Dawood Pota

Road
Tel: 5680689/706

Chandni Hotel
Dr Dawood Pota
Road, Saddar
Tel: 511487

Chenab Hotel
Arambagh Road
Tel: 2623242/
211000

Delhi Muslim
Hotel
Aram Bagh Road
Tel: 214529/
216523

Gulf Hotel
Dr Dawood Pota
Road, Saddar
Tel: 5661239

Hill Top Hotel
Ferozabad Police
Station
Tel: 4532441/4

Holiday Inn
Crown Plaza
Tel: 5660650

Hotel
Al-Darwish
Shidi Village Rd
Tel: 7512587

Hotel Al-Dubai
Sohrab Katrak Rd
Tel: 5686489

Hotel Al-Farooq
Zainbunnisa
Street, Saddar
Tel: 5688297

Hotel Al-Kabir
231, 3-Sohrab
Katrak Road
Tel: 5683690

Hotel Al-Mairaj
Shidi Village Rd
Tel: 7512586

Hotel Al-
Maqbool
Dr Dawood Pota
Road, Saddar
Tel: 5865598

Hotel Al-Mashriq
Frere Road, Saddar
Tel: 5684025

Hotel Al-Noor
Hust Chowk,
Lea Market
Tel: 2439968/
2423152

Hotel Al-Sadaat
Near Regal
Chowk
Tel: 5688450

Hotel Al-Salatin
Dr Dawood Pota
Road, Saddar
Tel: 516362

Hotel
Ambassador
Dr Dawood Pota
Road
Tel: 514209/820

Hotel Bilal
896, C, Block 2,
Tariq Road
Tel: 432890/
446750

Hotel Bloom
Luxury
Golf Club Road
Tel: 5684491/
8584

Hotel Chilton
Mir Karamali
Talpur Road,
Saddar
Tel: 520251/9

Hotel de Paris
Mir Karamali
Talpur Road,
Saddar
Tel: 524411/2

Hotel Embassy
Shahra-e-Faisal,
Nursery
Tel: 4535461/70

Hotel Faran
Shahra-e-Faisal
Nursery
Tel: 4532478/9

Hotel Geneva
Sohrab Katrak
Road, Saddar
Tel: 5682285

Hotel Holiday
Frere Street,
Saddar
Tel: 512082

Hotel Jabees
and Restaurant
Abdullah
Haroon Road
Tel: 512015

Hotel Jhalawan
Shedi Village Rd
Tel: 741480

Hotel Karachi and Restaurant 236-Soharb Katrak Road, Saddar
Tel: 5685328

Hotel Mehran
Shahra-e-Faisal
Tel: 5660862

Hotel Metropole
Club Road
Tel: 5660153

Hotel Midway
House
Karachi Airport
Tel: 4570375

Hotel National
City Regal Radio
TV Market, Saddar
Tel: 5688042

Hotel Ocean
Near Regal
Chowk, Saddar
Tel: 5681922/53

Hotel Regency
Near Cantt
Station
Tel: 523312/
528672

Hotel Reliance
United Bakery,
Saddr
Tel: 519115

Hotel Royal City
Sarmad Road
Saddar
Tel: 5680247

Hotel Sabrina
Pakistan Chowk,
Dr Ziauddin
Ahmed Road
Tel: 2624039/
214573

Hotel Sarah
B 6 Parr Street,
Saddar
Tel: 527161

Hotel Hermain
Raja G Ali Khan Rd
Saddar
Tel: 516001/011

Hotel Shalimar
Off: Dawood
Pota Road,
Tel: 527671/
529491

Hotel Shermeen
MA Jinnah Road
Tel: 211380/
210906

Hotel Spring
Allama Iqbal Rd
Tel:449953/809

Hotel Tariq and
Restaurant
Allama Iqbal
Road, PECHS
Tel: 434321/
430367

Hotel United
Dr Dawood Pota
Road, Saddar
Tel: 515014

Hotel Zeeshan
PECHS Off
Tariq Rd
Tel: 432467/
448282

Imperial Hotel
MT Khan Road
Tel: 5681749

Karachi Sheraton
Hotel and Towers
Club Road
Tel: 5681021

Khyber Hotel
Preedy Street
Saddar
Tel: 7210359

Marriott Hotel
9-Abdullah
Haroon Road
Tel: 5680011/8

Park Hotel
(PVT) Ltd
Near Jamia Cloth
Market
Tel: 210876/9

Pearl-Continental
Hotel
Club Road
Tel: 5685021

Shah Zhob Hotel
Sabzi Mandi,
University Road
Tel: 410862/1

Lahore (042)

Adnan Hotel
Main Boulevard,
Defence
Tel: 6663142

Ali Continental
1-Mozang Road
Tel: 7351422

Amer Hotel
46, Lower Mall
Tel: 7229971

Asia Hotel
Near Railway
Station
Tel: 6366450

Avari Lahore
87, Shahra-e-
Quaid-e-Azam
Tel: 6365366

Baadees Hotel
35-Empress Road
Tel: 6365378/9

Bakhtawar Hotel
and Restaurant
11-Abbot Road
Tel: 6371898

CC Motel
105-A, Shahra-e-
Quaid-e-Azam
Tel: 311362/1

Canal View
Motel
2-Upper Mall,
Canal Bank
Tel: 877153

Central Hotel
Chowk New
Anarkali
Tel: 7353544

City Trac
Holiday Hotel
Room # 6, Naqi
Maket 75 Mall
Tel: 6303990/
2990

Clifton Hotel
Near Railway
Station
Tel: 6366743

Country
Comfort Hotel
105-A, Mall Rd
Tel: 6360346

Crystal Inn
62/3, Sher Khan
Road
Tel: 6664350/
6672394

Davis Hotel
8-Davis Road
Tel: 6302817

Executive Inn
7-A, Upper Mall,
Canal Bank
Tel: 5753257

Faletti's Hotel
3-Egerton Road
Tel: 6363955

Hotel Al-Najam
3-Lake Road,
Old Anarkali
Tel: 7359088

Hotel
Ambassador
7-Davis Road
Tel: 6301861

Hotel Bakhtawar
11, Abbot Road
Tel: 6369013

Hotel Chaman
International
Badami Bagh
Tel: 200788/
7722788

Hotel Indus
56, Shahra-e-
Quaid-e-Azam
Tel: 6302858

Hotel Kashmir
Palace (PVT) Ltd
14-Empress Road
Tel: 6136700

Hotel Liberty and
Restaurant 44
Commercial Zone
Tel: 875233/731

Hotelmen
61/1-W, LCCH
Tel: 6660097/
6674815

Hotel Menora and
Falcon Restaurant
41, Mcleod Road
Tel: 7224029

Hotel Metro
Railway Station
Tel: 6366382

Hotel Rise
Liberty Market
Gulberg-III
Tel: 870338

Hotel Services
International
Shahra-e-Quaide-
Azam
Tel: 870285

Hotel Shobra
55, Nicolson Rd
Tel: 6364962

Hotel Tezmin
Darbar Market
Tel: 7249956

Ittehad Hotel
8-Railway Station
Tel: 6363554/2

Lahore Hotel
Mcleod Road
Tel: 7235961

National Hotel
1-Abbot Road
Tel: 6363011

New Hotel
6-Montgomery Rd
Tel: 6363125

New Prince
Hotel
77 Mecload Road
Tel: 6363419

Olympic Hotel
1-Sanda Road
Tel: 7114522

Orient Hotel and
Restaurant Ltd
74-Mcleod Road
Tel: 7223907

Panache Motel
6 Abdullah
Road, Bridge
Colony
Tel: 6672814

Park Way Hotel
No. 1, Mcleod Rd
Tel: 6365908

Pearl-Continental
Hotel
Shahra-e-Quid-e-
Azam
Tel: 6360220

Prince Hotel
32-Nicholson Rd
Tel: 6663968

Rays Hotel
4-Montgomery Rd
Tel: 7223379

Regency Inn Hotel
Abid Majeed Rd
Tel: 6664514

Safari Hotel
98-C, Anand Rd
Tel: 875381

Salman
International Hotel
28, New Anarkali
Tel: 7229611

Serenity Hotel
50-B Nagi Road
Tel: 6661238

Seven Stars Motel
323 Upper Mall
Tel: 5711098

Shabistan Hotel
Mcleod Road
Tel: 6367451

Shahzadi Hotel
83 Shahzadi
Rafaquat Market
Tel: 7659011/4

Shalimar Hotel
and Restaurant
36-Liberty Market
Tel: 5758815

Shezan Hotel
and Restaurants
(PVT) Ltd
7 Dyal Singh
Mansion
Tel: 412406/
7581273

Station Hotel
1-Railway
Station Scheme
Tel: 7352171

Uganda Hotel
45-Mcleod Road
Tel: 6364393

Larkana (ON1)
Gulf Hotel
Bunder Road
Tel: 22282

Hotel Asia
Station Road
Tel: 61875

Layyah (0694)
Marjan Hotel
and Restaurant
Chowbara Road
Tel: 2698

Mianwali (0459)
Hotel Shahzad
and Munthaar
Restaurant
Shahra-e-Fazala
Tel: 2706

Mazhar Hotel
Restaurant
Opp. Flying
Coach Stand
Tel: 2541

Mingora (0536)
Hotel Marina
Behrain
Tel: 780168

Hotel Pameer
Mingora Sawat
Tel: 720205

Madyan Hotel
Madyan
Tel: 780033

Shabistan Hotel
GT Road
Tel: 710243

Mirpur (AK) (054)
Kashmir
Continental Hotel
Allama Iqbal Rd
Tel: 4303

Mirpur Khas (0231)
Hotel Abbassin
Court Road
Tel: 2153

Hotel Usmania
MA Jinnah Rd
Tel: 3184

Shezan Restaurant
and Bakers
Umerkot Road
Tel: 3261

Multan (061)
Aziz Hotel
Shershah Road
Tel: 30425

Faran Hotel and
Faran Restaurant
Kutchery Road
Tel: 41113

Firdous Hotel
Chowk Dera Adda
Tel: 33066

Hotel Al Sana
Sher Shah Road
Tel: 32501

Hotel Friends
Dera Adda Chowk
Tel: 73066

Hotel Mangol
LMQ Road
Tel: 30165

Hotel Palace
Chowk Dera
Adda
Tel: 570771/43141

Hotel Prince
Nishtar Road
Tel: 44146

Hotel Shabroze
Hassan Parwana
Road
Tel: 72296

Hotel Taj
Chowk Nawan
Tel: 31319

Hushiana Hotel
Chowk Kutchery
Tel: 43536

New Relax Hotel
Kutchery Road
Tel: 31588

Shabrose Hotel
and Restaurant
Multan Road
Tel: 4096

Shellan Guest
House
Restaurant
MDA Chowk
Tel: 572677

Shezan Residence
Kutchery Road
Tel: 512235/6

Murree (0593)
Brightlands Hotel
Imtiaz Shaheed Rd
Tel: 410270

Cecil Hotel
Mount View Rd
Tel: 410247

Grand Heights
Hotel
Hall Road
Tel: 411711

Hotel Breeze
Near Chair Lift,
Pindi Point
Tel: 411088

Hotel
Islamabad View
Imtiaz Shaheed Rd
Tel: 410795

Hotel Lalazar
Abid Shaheed Rd
Tel: 410150

Hotel Marhaba
Mall Road
Tel: 410184

Hotel Viewforth
Abid Majid Road
Tel: 411268

Kashmir Villa Hotel
Above GPO
Tel: 410408

Khyber Hotel
and Restaurant
Tel: 410182

Mall View Hotel
The Mall
Tel: 411114

Shifang Golden
Sun Hotel
Upper Jhika Gali
Tel: 411503

VIP House
22 Hall Road,
Kashmir Point
Tel: 410252

Muzaffarabad (058)
Hotel Neelam
(PVT) Ltd
Neelam Valley Rd
Tel: 4733

Nafeez Hotel and
Restaurant Eid
Ghah Road
Tel: 4487

Mawabahah (0421)
Bismilla Hotel
NMC Road
Tel: 3289

Hotel Noor-e-
Afghan
Mohni Bazar
Tel: 3289

Hotel Riaz
Station Road
Tel: 4243

Peshawar (0521)
Al-Mumtaz Hotel
GT Road
Tel: 216832

Al-Rahim Hotel
and Restaurant
LRH Hospital Rd
Tel: 213393

Amin Hotel
Amin Mansion
GT Road
Tel: 218219

Dean's Hotel
3, Islamabad Rd
Tel: 279781

Dubai Hotel
Chowk Qissa
Khani Bazar
Tel: 212100

Greens's Hotel
Saddar Road
Tel: 270184

Gulf Hotel
Cinema Road
Tel: 210107

Habib Hotel
Khyber Bazar
Tel: 210116

Hayat Hotel and
Gulf Restaurant
Farid Mansion,
GT Road
Tel: 218221/5

Hotel Galaxie
Khyber Bazar
Tel: 212174

Hotel Salateen
and Restaurant
Cinema Road
Tel: 210279

Hotel Sindbad
Near Stadium
Chowk
Tel: 275020

Hotel Spogmay
Namak Mandi
Tel: 211749

Jan's Hotel
Islamia Road,
Cantt
Tel: 276939

Khani's Hotel
Shuba Khyber
Bazar
Tel: 275625

Pearl-Continental
Hotel
Khyber Road
Tel: 276361

Rose Hotel
Shunba Khyber
Bazar
Tel: 210757

Sharjah Hotel
Dabgari Garden
Tel: 216584

Shawal Hotel
GT Road
Tel: 215397/218644

Shelton House
Old Jamrood Rd
Tel: 842087/8

VIP House
Bara Road,
University Town
Tel: 842806

Zabeel Palace
Hotel
GT Road
Tel: 218237

Quetta (081)
Al-Saleem and
Shannawaz Hotel
Tola Bam Road,

City Thana
Tel: 825073

Al-Sallah Hotel
Fatima Jinnah Rd
Tel: 62928

Al-Shams Hotel
and Restaurant
MA Jinnah Road
Tel: 74111

Al-Syed Hotel
Pani Takseem,
Cantt
Tel: 835547

Asia Hotel
Fate-ch Mohd Rd
Tel: 71581/8224216

Aslam Hotel
Quarry Road
Tel: 72035

Atif Hotel
Meezan Chowk
Tel: 62947

Azeem Hotel
Fatima Jinnah Rd
Tel: 75855

Bilal Hotel
Abdul Sttar Rd
Tel: 78061

Bomba Hotel
Abdul Sattar Rd
Tel: 79588

China Hotel
and Restaurant
Natha Sing Street
Tel: 61248

Clihon Hotel
Suraj Ganj Bazar
Tel: 75093

Darbar Hotel
Thana Road
Tel: 825049

Faran Hotel
and Restaurant
Liaquat Bazar
Tel: 70487

Geneva Hotel
and Restaurant
Munsafi Road
Tel: 822264

Ghulam
Server Hotel
Abdul Satar Rd
Tel: 827522

Green Hotel
Prince Road
Tel: 76200

Gul's Inn
Ali Bhoy Road
Tel: 821929

Hotel Abshan
Jinnah Road
Tel: 75102

Hotel Al-Abbas
Abdul Sattar Rd
Tel: 75183

Hotel Al-Marhaba
Tahir Khan Rd
Tel: 820723

Hotel Al-Muazzam
Jinnah Road,
Star Chowk
Tel: 75884

Hotel Al-Sadaat
Shahra-e-Iqbal
Tel: 61915

Hotel Al-Sadam
Munsafi Road
Tel: 62600

Hotel Bloom
Luxury
Stewart Road
Tel: 75178

Hotel Bloom Star
Stewart Road
Tel: 833351

Hotel Bolan
Student
Brewery Road
Tel: 444735

Hotel City
Baluchistan
Prince Road
Tel: 70647

Hotel Deluxe
Quarry Road
Conr. Jinnah Rd
Tel: 76908

Hotel Faran
Jinnah Road
Tel: 62749

Hotel Four
Season
Malik Plaza,
Abdul Sattar Rd
Tel: 827496

Hotel Glacier and
Grace Restaurant
Prince Road
Tel: 75130

Hotel Gulf
Munsafi Road
Tel: 822217

Hotel Haria
Masjid Road
Tel: 824364

Hotel Marina
Corner Jinnah Rd
Tel: 75109

Hotel Muslim
MA Jinnah Rd
Tel: 74930

Hotel New Grand
Behind Imdad
Cinema
Tel: 77781

Hotel line
MA Jinnah Rd
Tel: 70736

Hotel Noor
Kansi Road
Tel: 72660

Hotel Park
Jinnah Road
Tel: 61933

Hotel Saraey
Namak Musefir
Khana
Yazdan Khan Rd
Tel: 63455

Hotel Satara
Shahra-e-Liaquat
Tel: 833374

Hotel Shad Ban
Abdul Sattar Rd
Tel: 78554

Hotel Shaista
Court Road
Tel: 64955

Hotel Shalimar
and Restaurant
Abdul Sattar Rd
Tel: 73489

Hotel Shan
and Restaurant
Abdul Sattar Rd
Tel: 73489

Hotel Shees
Jinnah Road
Tel: 66839

Hotel Taran
and Restaurant
Shahra-e-Liaquat
Tel: 822506

Hotel VIP
and Restaurant
Masjid Road
Tel: 821847

Ibrahim Hotel
and Restaurant
Thana Road
Tel: 824299

Imdad Hotel
Jinnah Road
Tel: 70167/6

Insaf Hotel
Munsafi Road
Tel: 821867

Kaghan Hotel
and Al-Manzoor
Restaurant
Masjid Road
Tel: 65270

Khilji Musafer
Khana
Sirki Road
Tel: 70864/74657

Lal Kabab Hotel
Rustam Jee Lane
Jinnah Road
Tel: 835729

Lourdes Hotel
Jinnah Road
Tel: 61488

Lucky Hotel
Sirki Road
Tel: 442477

Mahmood
Tonswi Hotel
New Bus Stand
Sirki Road
Tel: 444150

Mashhadi Hotel
Kansi Road
Tel: 79842

Master Qaddoos
Musafer Khana
Sirki Road
Tel: 446567

Mir Hotel
Joint Road
Tel: 831272

Mubarak Hotel
New Bus Stand
Sirki Road
Tel: 444575

Muslim
Gulzar Hotel
Sarafa Bazaar
Tel: 821730

Muslim Hotel
and Restaurant
Near Railway
Station
Tel: 74930/71857

Nasar Ullah Hotel
Sirki Road
Tel: 446177

Naseeb Hotel
Jamal-ud-din
Afghani Road
Tel: 63676

Naveed Hotel
and Restaurant
Mission Road
Tel: 824883

New Amin Hotel
Yet Road
Corner Jinnah Rd
Tel: 82178

New Insaf Hotel
Toghi Road
Tel: 72747

New Kakar
Insaf Hotel
Circular Road
Tel: 22319

New Loudes Hotel
Staff College Road
Tel: 70168

Pakeeza Hotel
Abdul Sattar Road
Tel: 78968

Pamir Hotel
New Bus Stand
Sirki Road
Tel: 443023

Park Hotel
Shahra-e-Iqbal
Tel: 62278

Prince Hotel
Jinnah Road
Tel: 45430

Qasr-e-Gull Hotel
Suraj Gunj Bazar
Tel: 825192

Quetta Bolan Hotel
Suraj Ganj Bazar
Tel: 820525

Quetta
Serena Hotel
Shahra-e-Zarghoon
Tel: 820071

Raja Hotel
Masjid Road
Tel: 62972

Rangeen Hotel
Sarafa Bazar
Tel: 64905

Rasco Hotel
and Restaurant
Corner Churi Gali
Tel: 76997

S Agha Hotel
Masjid Road
Tel: 62785

Sariab Hotel
New Bus Stand
Sirki Road
Tel: 44022

Serena Lodges
and Hotels
Shahra-e-Zerghoon
Tel: 820079

Shawani Hotel
New Truck Stand
Sirki Road
Tel: 443997

Shees Hotel
Jinnah Road
Tel: 62497

Sitara Hotel
Shahra-e-Liaquat
Tel: 833371

Star Plus Hotel
Masjid Road
Tel: 62426

United Hotel
Masjid Road
Tel: 63792

Usmania Hotel
New Bus Stand
Sirki Road
Tel: 443118

Waghaz
Musakhail
Musafer Khana
Prince Road
Tel: 822720

**Rahim Yar Khan
(0731)**

Faran Hotel
11-Factory
Thali Road
Tel: 3309

Hotel Al-Mashriq
Railway Chowk
Tel: 72479

Kamran Hotel
Bano Bazar
Tel: 70994

Lahore Hotel
and Restaurant
Railway Chowk
Tel: 72586

New Star
Light Hotel
Shahi Road
Tel: 77642

Paradise Hotel
Bano Bazar
Tel: 72249

Paras Hotel
Shahi Road
Tel: 72588

Taj Mahal Hotel
and Restaurant
Bano Bazar
Tel: 70892

United Hotel
and Restaurant
Railway Chowk
Tel: 3241

Rawalpindi (051)

Asia Hotel
Committee Chowk
Tel: 70898/73362

Comfort Inn
189/3, Kashmir Rd
Cantt
Tel: 516165

Faisal Hotel
Murree Road
Opp. Liaquat
Garden
Tel: 73210

Falshman's Hotel
The Mall Saddar
Tel: 581489

Friends
International
Guest House
0-923/A
Gold Chamber
Murree Road
Tel: 554536

Gatmell's Motel
Airport (Jail) Road
Off The Mall
Tel: 581648/582388

Golden Grill
The Mall
Cantt.
Tel: 512842

Hotel Akbar
International
Liaquat Road
Liaquat Bagh
Tel: 532002

Hotel Al-Farooq
Murree Road
Committee Chowk
Tel: 556202

Hotel Gulnoor
Murree Road
Tel: 554110

Hotel Holiday
Iftikhar Janjua Rd
Tel: 568068/516511

Hotel Maharaja
Hotel Square
Murree Road
Tel: 70391

Hotel Marhaba
and Restaurant
118-Kashmir Road
Tel: 566022

Hotel Pakeeza
DAV College Road
Tel: 554834

Hotel Seven
Brothers
Liaquat Road
Bara Bazar
Tel: 556144

Hotel Shah Taj
Adamjee Road
Tel: 568528

Hotel Shalimar
Off The Mall
Tel: 562908

Hotel United
Hotel Square
Murree Road
Tel: 840416

Imperial Hotel
and Restaurant
Committee
Chowk,
Murree Road
Tel: 559677

Javed Hotel
Liaquat Road
Tel: 556365

Kashmirwalas
Tourist Inn
2, The Mall
Tel: 583189

Lords Hotel
379-Saidpur Rd
Tel: 414333

Moon
International
Hotel and
Restaurant
Asghar Mall
Chowk
Tel: 554936

Mushtaq Hotel
and Restaurant
Murree Road,
Committee Chowk
Tel: 553999

National City
Hotel
J-15, Murree Rd,
Liaquat Chk
Tel: 555238

New Palace Hotel
Liaquat Road
Tel: 70672

Paradise Inn Hotel
Adamjee Road
Tel: 568594/5

Pearl Continental
Hotel
The Mall
Tel: 566011

Pindi Hotel
Committee Chowk
Tel: 559305

Pine Hotel
Iftikhar Janjua Rd
Tel: 563660

Potohar Hotel
Murree Road
Tel: 556265

Prima Hotel
Hotel Square,
Committee
Chowk
Tel: 74547

Queens Hotel
Restaurants
Murree Road
Tel: 73240/50

Rawal Hotel
Hotel Square,
Murree Road
Tel: 556241/5

Rawalpindi
Popular Inn
G-261, College Rd
Tel: 72587

Sandhills Hotel
and Restaurant
Rialto Chowk,
Murree Road
Tel: 551447

Shangrila
Resort Hotels
143N-Murree Rd
Tel: 73006

Sahiwal (0441)
Modran City
Hotel
Lahore Multan Rd
Tel: 62502

Shikarpur (0761)
Sajjad Hotel
and City Top
Restaurant
Circular Road
Tel: 3645

Sialkot (04332)

Al-Shahzad Hotel
Kutchery Road
Tel: 87434

Amelia Hotel and
Restaurant Allama
Iqbal Chowk
Tel: 593415

Hotel Sarko
Aziz Shaheed Rd
Cantt.
Tel: 269714

Meryton Hotel
Wazirabad Road
Tel: 67146

Sukkur (071)
Hotel Al-Habib
Barrage Road
Tel: 84359

Hotel Forum Inn
Workshop Road
Tel: 83015

Inter Park Inn
Lab-e-Mehran
Tel: 83051

Nusrat Hotel
and Restaurant
Barrage Road
Tel: 85147

United Hotel
and Restaurant
Barrage Hotel
Tel: 83992

Sawat (0536)
Bahrain Hotel and
Restaurant Bahrain
Tel: 780534

Deluxe Hotel Main
Bazar, Bahrain
Tel: 720614

Green Hotel
Murghzar
Tel: 2008

Hotel Murghazar
Place Murghzar
Tel: 5474

Hotel Zeeshan GT
Road, Mingora
Tel: 4010

Serana Lodges
and Hotels Saidu
Shariff
Tel: 6404

Swat View Hotel
New Road
Mingora
Tel: 720886/9

Wazirabad (0437)
Faisal Hotel
(Air Contitioned)
Faisal Market
Tel: 602620

Ziarat (0833)
PTDC Motel Ziarat
Tel: 356

Tourist Information Centre

Abbottabad
Club Annexe
Jinnah Road
Tel: 34399

Bahawalpur
Stadium Market
Tel: 4657

Islamabad
Pakistan Tours
Limited PTDC
Head office H
No.170 Street # 36
Sector F-10/1
Tel: 292672-73/
294790-92
Fax: 2926381

Karachi
Shafi Chambers
Club Road
5681293
Said Tourism
1st Floor, Sea
Breeze Plaza
Tel: 7788530

Information Cell
Hotel Metropole
Tel: 56878958

Lahore
Faletti's Hotel
Egerton Road
Tel: 303660/624/
306529

Moenjodaro
PTDC Complex
Tel: 77070/40906

Multan
Saidabad Hotel
Nishtar Chowk
Bhawalpure Rd
Tel: 72294-9

Nokundi
Pak-Iran Border
(Bluchistan)

Peshawar
Dean's Hotel
Islamia Road
Tel: 276481-84/
1-279781-83

Quetta
Muslim Hotel
Jinnah Road
Tel: 825826

Rawalpindi
Flashman's Hotel
The Mall
Tel: 581480-84

Saidu Sharif
Dilsoh Hotel
Mingora
Tel: 2520

Taxila
PTDC Motel
Tel: 2344

Thatta
PTDC Hospitality
Complex Makli

Ziarat
PTDC Motel
Tel: 356

Spazio Travel
Societa Di Viaggi
and Tourism Via
Nazionale 51
Rome 00184,
Italy

World Vision
Travel Co. Ltd
3-F Akasaka
Taiyo Building
5-9 Akasaka
2-Chome
Minate-UKU
Tokyo 107, Japan

Bestway Topurs
and Safaris 202-
2678 West Broad-
way Vaconver V6K
2G3 Canada

Pakistan Tourist
Development
Corporation
Vester
Farimagsgade 3
Copenhagen 1606
Denmark

Marketing Services
(Tourism and
Travel)
High Holbom

House
52-54 High
Holborn
London WCIV
6 RL

Lan-si-Aire
Travel Inc.
Suite 508
303 Fifth Ave
New York, NY
10016

Travel Agents and Tour Operators

Abbottabad
SS Ghulam
Hussain & Sons
(PVT) Ltd
Hakimji Building
Jinnah Road
Tel: 4797

Attock
Jetair
International
23-24, Attack Plaza
Tel: 2759

Bahawalpur
Bahawalpur
Travel Agency
Noor Mahal Road
Tel: 5655

Kazmi Travels
Agency
Model Town B
Tel: 6474/4454

Milat Travels
Chowk Fawwara
Tel: 7781

PAK
International
Travels
Chowk Fawwara
Tel: 7012

Public Travel
The Mall
Tel: 3281

Time
International
Travels
12/B
Commercial Rd
Tel: 3281

Daska
Golden Air
Travels
Sambrial Road
Tel: 3502

King Travels
Sambrial Road
Tel: 2487

Malik Travels
Sambrial Road
Tel: 4228

Rana Travels
Chowk Civil
Hospital
Tel: 3809

Shalimar Travels
Sambrial Road
Tel: 3375

Faisalabad
Baig Air Travels
(PVT) Ltd
Bank Square
Tel: 615466

Bluesky Travels
(PVT) Ltd
Sargodha Road
Tel: 23231

Capri Travels
4-C, Ahmed
Mension
Tel: 625646

Dream Land
Travel Service
(PVT) Ltd
Circular Road
Tel: 25058/3

Grace Travels
(PVT) Ltd
H-04, Regency
Arcade
Tel: 611900

Makkah Travels
(PVT) Ltd
P/107, Circular Rd
Tel: 32606

Midway Air
Travels (PVT)
Limited
4-Ahmed
Mension
Tel: 53202/622737

Prince Travels
(PVT) Ltd
9-Jinnah Market
Circular Road
Tel: 28379

Royal Travels
Service (PVT)
Limited
Sargodha Road
Tel: 23938

SS Lucky Travels
Sevice (PVT) Ltd
Circular Road
Tel: 28684

Southem Travels
(PVT) Ltd
Regency Hotel
Tel: 27231/617828

Gilgit
Travel Walji's
(PVT) Ltd
Baber Road, Airport
Tel: 2665

Hunza
Travel Walji's Ltd
Tel: 47045

Gujranwala
Hejaz Travels
Urdu Bazar
Tel: 75833

Honey Travels
Khan Plaza
G T Road
Tel: 74062

Khyber
International
(PVT) Ltd
Hospital Road
Tel: 255751

Lara International
Travels oney
changer Liberty
Complex
Tel: 257069/
256069

Master Travel
Service
Trust Plaza
GT Road
Tel: 256650

Pamela Travels
Sethi Plaza
G T Road
Tel: 52226

Gujrat
Barlas Air
Travel Service
G T Road, Kharian
Tel: 2943

Jet Air Travels
Circular Road
Chowk Shah
Hussain
Tel: 26222

Sky World Travels
Kutchery Road
Tel: 26461

Haripur
Asia Travels
Khawaja Khan
Market G T Road
Tel: 4256

Kings Travels and
Tours Shoukat
Plaza, G T Road
Tel: 612232/611001

Islamabad
Aashy Travel
Service Blue Area,
Aaly Plaza
Tel: 810466

Abbas Travel
Blue Area,
Tel: 219298

Ace Travel
1-C, Blue Area
Tel: 813044

Adventure Travel
15, Wali Centre
Tel: 212490/728

Aerolina
International
(PVT) Ltd
33-Blue Area
Tel: 815540

Air International
Blue Area,
Saeed Plaza
Tel: 814022/813122

Al-Taqi Travel
(PVT) ltd
1-C, Blue Area,
Tel: 819819

American Express
Travel Service
Blue Area,
Ali Plaza
Tel: 823713

AMG Travels
Fazal-ul-Haq Road,
Blue Area
Tel: 272448

Anam Travels
Fazal-ul-Haq Road,
Blue Area
Tel: 210341/2

Atlantic & Pacific
Travels (PVT) Ltd
Blue Area, Block-51
Tel: 810269/270

Avari Travel
Agencies Ltd
Blue Area, Unit # 4
Tel: 9203198/
817656

Bagrani Travels
Blue Area,
Shalimar-6
Tel: 823687

Baig Air Travels
(PVT) Ltd
SNC Centre,
Blue Area
Tel: 318866

Baig Express
Blue Area,
Huma Plaza
Tel: 811178

Beg Express
Super Market,
Block-13
Tel: 822064

Bonds Travels
Bureau
Khayaban-e-
Suharwardy
Tel: 829673/278941

Capital Travel
Rehmat Plaza
Blue Area
Tel: 827335

Chand
International
Air Travels
Markaz F-10
Tel: 280652

Choice
International
H # 23 Street 25,
F-B/2
Tel: 261402

Cosmos Travels
Blue Area
Tel: 811214

Concordia
(PVT) Limited
West Chughtai
Plaza
West Blue Area
Tel: 823351/64

Delta Air Travels
(PVT) Ltd
Blue Area, 16-D,
Tel: 210297/278482

Eastern
Service Line
Blue Area, Block-51,
Tel: 818497

Excellency Travels
Blue Area,
Ajaib Plaza
Tel: 221601

Express Travel
International
Faza Plaza,
Blue Area
Tel: 274067/5

Falcon Group
International
Mushtaq
Mansion
Blue Area
Tel: 264487/210461

Flyhome (PVT)
Limited
Rehmat Plaza
Blue Area
Tel: 815011

Fly Domestic or
International
Fazal-e-Haq Rd
Blue Area
Tel: 220892/3

G M
International
Blue Area,
Ali Plaza
Tel: 815953

Gap Travels
Fazal-e-Haq Rd
Blue Area
Tel: 214743/046

Gerry's Travel
Agency (PVT) Ltd
Main Presidency
Road
Tel: 212525/272526

Gilani Group
of Companies
Block # 46,
Blue Area
Tel: 822126/277879

Green Fields
Travels (PVT)
Limited
Block # 5,
Blue Area,
Tel: 825800

Haseeb Express
Travel and Tour
Operators
Super Market F-6,
Tel: 214689

Hatco Travels
and Trade
Mohammadi Plaza
Blue Area,
Tel: 819378/825676

Hilal Travel
Services
Block # 25,
Blue Area
Tel: 821035/813283

Hindukush Trails
37, Street 28,
F-6/1,
Tel: 821576

Holiday Travel
Line Ltd
Agha Khan Rd
Tel: 826121

International
Travel Links
Blue Area,
Shahid Plaza
Tel: 817859

International
Travel Services
(PVT) Ltd
42-Blue Area
Tel: 811510

Karakoram Tours
Shalimar 7-2
Tel: 829120

Kayani
International
Traders
Blue Area
West Eagle Plaza
Tel: 220707/8

Kazi Enterprises
20-West,
Blue Area
Tel: 221978/210711

Keen Travels
Fazal-ul-Haq Rd
Blue Area
Tel: 276076/5

Khan Travel
4-Mohammadi
Plaza
Blue Area
Tel: 276076/5

Khyber
International
PAK (PVT) Ltd
1-A, Blue Area
Tel: 819754

Leader Air Travels
Fazal-ul-Haq Rd
Blue Area
Tel: 818685

Lords Travel
International
Block # 51,
Blue Area
Tel: 825101

Mahi
International
(PVT) Ltd
Blue Area,
Union Plaza
Tel: 817508

Marjan Services
Fazal-e-Haq Rd
Blue Area
Tel: 819572

New Arabian
Express
Block # 25,
Blue Area
Tel: 815550/
810892

Nobleman
Express
G-6 Markaz
Tel: 822933/818757

Omar Travels
(PVT) Ltd
Blue Area,
Shahid Plaza
Tel: 814885

Pak International
Travels
Blue Area,
Huma Plaza
Tel: 812240

Pak Travel
Taimur Chambers
Blue Area
Tel: 211378

Panorama
Travels and Tours
F-6, Blue Area
Tel 815266

Pasban Travel
Services
Block 1-A,
Blue Area
Tel: 814300

People's Travel
Blue Area,
Saeed Plaza
Tel: 825712/824319

Prince Travels
(PVT) Ltd
Blue Area, Saeed
Plaza
Tel: 811337

Public Travels
Quaid -e-Azam Ave
Tel: 815633/813373

Q-8 Travels
Fazal-e-Haq Rd
Blue Area
Tel: 220892/3

QUE (Travel Agents and Tour Operators) Markaz F-7, Tel: 826811/810252

Qwick Travels and Tours Operators 25, Blue Area Tel: 818332/812332

Rawat International Choughtai Plaza Blue Area Tel: 271128

Reliable Travel Super Market, F-7, Tel: 813452

Rex Travel Blue Area, Photohar Plaza Tel: 814405

Rohail Enterprises Ittihad Centre Blue Area Tel: 274644

Route International Travel Service F-6, Blue Area Tel: 214059/824058

Rowers Express (PVT) Ltd Blue Area Photohar Plaza Tel: 212571

Salman's International Block # 51, Blue Area Tel: 274173/309

Shakil Express (PVT) Ltd Khayaban-e-Suharwardy, G-6/1-1 Tel: 815691/4

Shirket-e-Maqbool (PVT) Ltd Blue Area, Shan Plaza Tel: 815919

Silk Road Tour Street-22, F-7/1 Tel: 824556

Sindbad Travel Blue Area, Aisha Plaza Tel: 9202974/ 821435

Sky Bird Travel Blue Area, Block E-30 Tel: 813079

S N Travel and Tourism Muhammadi Plaza Nazimuddin Rd Tel: 275668/215667

Speedbird Travel Blue Area, Aziz Plaza Tel: 812185

Sporteq International (PVT) Ltd Fazal-e-Haq Rd Blue Area Tel: 270665/4

Trans Pakistan Adventure Services 0,VT) Ltd Fazl-e-Haq Road Blue Area, Tel: 214796

Travel Kings (PVT) Ltd Blue Area, Whaeed Plaza Tel: 274110

Travel Services International Blue Area, Huma Plaza Tel: 813805

Travel Walji's (PVT) Ltd Blue Area Walij's Building Tel: 270745 Fax: 270753/828264

Travel Wide Services Jinnah Avenue Tel: 823318

Tourist Services Centre (PVT) Ltd F/6, Supper Market Tel: 823002

Unique Air Travels Block 8-A, Blue Area Tel: 815365/817407

United Express Zakia Aziz Plaza Blue Area Tel: 827615

United Enterprises M-5, Dossal Arcade Tel: 822860

United Travels (PVT) Ltd Buland Markaz Blue Area, Tel: 827615

Universal Travel 76-E, Jinnah Avenue Tel: 274562/1

Viking Travels Pak (PVT) Ltd (Akbar Group) Holiday Inn Hotel Tel: 217533

Voyager Private Limited Blue Area Tel: 817812/818855

Waqas Travels 44-E, Blue Area Tel: 214682/811742

Wings Air Markaz, F-10 Tel: 281543/120 Karachi

ABC Travels M A Jinnah Road Tel: 2435883/6934

Abdullah Express (PVT) Limited 17-Hotel Metropole Tel: 511238/ 5676628

ACE Travels (PVT) Ltd Lakson Square Building Sarwar Shaheed Road Tel: 5687546/58

Aero Travels Club Road Tel: 5685111/9521

Afshan Travel Services (PVT) Limited 2- Crecent Court Off: A Haroon Rd Tel: 7727370/1784

Air Guide Travels Awan — Tijarat Rd Tel: 2420850/19856

Air International Hotel Mehran Tel: 5676392

Air Travels Service Mereweather Tower Tel: 2439301/ 2440360

Air Travel Shop (PVT) Ltd Court View Bldg Tel: 5686897/74534

Air Wings Travels (PVT) Ltd Corner Chambers II Chundrigar Rd Tel: 214797/263612

Airlift Travels Rizvia Trust Building Nazimabad Tel: 624192/621976

Airpool Travels (PVT) Ltd Court Road 4-Court View Tel: 5685737/9334

Ajanee Tours Trade Tower Opp: Hotel Metorpole Tel: 5685997/58

Al Syed Travel Ltd Strechen Road Tel: 5683986

Al Falah Travels Mehboob Chambers Saddar, Tel: 513498

Al Ghaffar Travel Agency Hasrat Mohani Rd Tel: 2637011/5

Al Hassan Travel Agency Outram Road II Chundrigar Rd Tel: 2635103/0334

Al Karam Travels (PVT) Ltd Zeenat Mension II Chundrigar Rd Tel: 2415839/6264

Al Rashid Travels Shedi Village Rd Lea Market Tel: 749970/1970

Al Rehman Travels Uni Plaza Altaf Hussain Rd Tel: 2426903/18

Al Sayed Travel Service Outram Road Tel: 2634209/27

Alhamdolillah Travel Service Mangopir Road Tel: 292563

Ali Hamid Travels Liaquatabad Commercial Area-4, Tel: 4918713/ 4926740

Aly's Travel (PVT) Ltd Club Road Tel: 5686517/1447

Amar Travel Agency 4, Imperial Hotel Building M T Khan Road Tel: 5683451/5850

Ambassador Travel International (PVT) Ltd 11, Shafiq Plaza Sarwar Shaheed Road Tel: 5684518/8617

American Express Travels Service Dr Ziauddin A Road Tel: 2630263/9

Angels Travels (PVT) Ltd 12, Shafiq Plaza Sarwar Shaheed Road Tel: 5685097/8

Arkays Travels (PVT) Ltd Mereweather Rd Service Club Building Tel: 512517/9

Aroma Travel Service (PVT) Ltd Strachen Road Avenue Centre Tel: 5684085

Asad Air Travels
Frere Town Clifton
Tel: 516451/292

Atlantic Aviation
(PVT) Ltd
Lakson Squre
Building
Sarwar Shaheed Rd
Tel: 5676567/6466

Avari Travel
Agencies Ltd
11-Avari Plaza
Fatima Jinnah Rd
Tel: 5676567/6466

Bali Travels
Hussain Plaza Mir
Mohd l Baloch Rd
Tel: 7520115/37

Baloch Travels
2-Bismillah
Hotel, Lyari
Tel: 747257/75

Bangash Travel
Services
Shidi Village Rd
Al Muslim Hotel
Tel: 743515/525

Bhojani Travels
(PVT) Ltd
Kharadar
Tel: 2312521/4

Bilal Travels
North
Nazimabad
Shams Plaza, Blk-B,
Tel: 6643904/9707

Billoo Travel
Services
Adamjee
Dawood Road
Tel: 2313461/3

Bolan Express
(PVT) Ltd
Chakiawara Rd
Tel: 740238/748291

Bonds Travel
Bureau
Palace Hotel
Annexe
Dr Ziauddin A Rd
Tel: 5682325/1862

Bukhari Travel-
Tourism Services
Sheraton Hotel
Tel: 5681433/520506

Bukhara Tours
Drf Daud Pota Rd
Tel: 520351/71

Caravan Travels
(PVT) Ltd
Holiday Inn
Shahra-e-Faisal
Tel: 5681433/8746

Carewel Travels
(PVT) Ltd
Clifton Centre
Tel: 5872536/9

CITI Travels
(PVT) Ltd
Court Road
Tel: 5688228/4519

C1TILINK
Service Club
Building
Tel: 521648/523563

Classic Travels
Royal Hotel
Building
Tel: 217222/215222

Columbus Travel
Services (PVT) Ltd
New Challi
Tel: 2631142

Concord Travels
(PVT) Ltd
4-Avari Towers
Tel: 513116

Continental
Travels
Hotel Metropole
Tel: 515502/510932

Cosmos Travel
(PVT) Ltd
2-Faddo Building
M A Jinnah Road
Tel: 2415422/224

COX & KNGS
(Agents) (PVT) Ltd
M A Jinnah Road
II Chundrigar Rd
Tel: 2418205/5714

Crescent Travel
Services (PVT) Ltd
4-Trade Tower
Club Road
Tel: 5688326/521

Crown Travels
Service Club
Bldg. Extn
Mereweather Rd
Tel: 514428/421

DWYNE Travels
(PVT) Ltd
Strachen Road
Tel: 5681948

DASHT Travel
Saif Building
Chowk, Danso Rd
Tel: 747933

Data Travels
(PVT) Ltd
Court Road
Tel: 5683559/68

Deen Travel
Services (PVT) Ltd
Shahrah-e-Iraq
Tel: 5680574/2725

Eastern Travels
II Chundrigar Rd
Al-Syed House
Tel: 212280

Europa
Travels Ltd
PIDC House
Dr Ziauddin
AJ Rorad
Tel: 5681783

Escorts Travels
(PVT) Ltd
Clayton Road
Tel: 7221715/
7213312

Executive
Travels (PVT) Ltd
Lakson Square
Bldg #2
Sarwar Shaheed Rd
Tel: 519254/
5689276

Fairdeal Travels
(PVT) Ltd
Grand Hotel
II Chundrigar Rd
Tel: 213451/871

Fly Comforts
(PVT) Ltd
Holiday Inn
Shahrah-e-Faisal
Tel: 520407/8

Fly World Travels
Holiday Inn
Shahrah-e-Faisal
Tel: 522866/29

Freeway Travel
Bureau
Muljee Street,
Kharadar
Tel: 2434666/2814

Freighters
(PVT) Ltd
Kashif Centre,
Shahra-e-Faisal,
Tel: 519254/
2689276

GADIT Travels
Kharadar
Tel: 204207/
2314763

Gaylord Travels
(PVT) Ltd
57-Taj Mahal Hotel
Shahra-e-Faisal
Tel: 675520

Gerry's Travels
Agency (PVT) Ltd
25-Hotel
Metropole
Tel: 5661206/1

Golden Travel
Services
Uni Plaza
II Chundrigar Rd
Tel: 2410466/
2424327

Gulf Tour
and Travel
Corporation
14-West Wharf Rd
Tel: 201419

Gulf Travels and
Services (PVT) Ltd
Sharif Centre
M T Khan Road
Tel: 5611486/284

Gulliver's
Aviation Services
(PVT) Ltd
Block7, K C H S
Shahra-e-Faisal,
Tel: 4532057/8

Gulliver's
Travels (PVT) Ltd
Central Hotel
Building
Mereweather Rd
Tel: 5689360/3

Gulraz Travels
Dawood Pota Rd
Tel: 511711/515510

H K Travels
Service (PVT) Ltd
Mangopir Road
Tel: 295313

Hadi Travels
(PVT) Ltd
Court Road
Tel: 5688647/9117

Hama
International
(PVT) Ltd
Hotel Crown Plaza
Tel: 528319/
5675569

Hannah Travels
Mewa Shah Road
Tel: 7721846

Harrow Travels
(PVT) Ltd
33-35, Crown Plaza
Tel: 5677173/5

Haseeb Express
Travel and Tour
Operators
Mehran Hotel
Tel: 528197/8

Hasnain Travels
(PVT) Ltd
203, Panorama
Centre Saddar
Tel: 5678657/
528470

Hermain Travels
(PVT) Ltd
Shefiq Plaza
Sarwar Shaheed Rd
Tel: 5689312/6165

Highland Tours
and Travels (PVT)
Ltd PIDC House
Tel: 5689101/111

Holiday Travel
and Tours Off:
Chundrigar Road
Tel: 2636374/5

Huma Travel
Agency
Goya Mansion,
Nawab Mohabat
Khanji Road
Tel: 2436123

Ifraz Travel and
Tourism (FV1) Ltd
Jangir Park,
Saddar
Tel: 1493

Imperial Air
Services
Imperial Hotel
M T Khan Road
Tel: 552155/
551555

Indus Travels
Sea Breeze Plaza
Shahra-e-Faisal
Tel: 524442/1

Interavia
Pakistan (PVT) Ltd
P and O Plaza
II Chundrigar Rd
Tel: 226539/
2413393

JK Travels (PVT) Ltd
White House
Shahra-e-Faisal
Tel: 437426

Joli Travels
Hotel Mehran
Tel: 514837/ 511439

Khamisani Aviation and Tourism (PVT) Ltd (GSA LDT Polish Airlink and Air Mauritius)
Hotel Metropole
Tel: 5670589/ 662621
Fax: 5684398

Khllmisani Sons
6-7 Dilgusha Building
II Chundrigar Rd
Tel: 2638741-4/8-5
Fax 2639007

Khyber Express (PVT) Ltd
Lea Market
Shidi Village Rd
Tel: 7512045

Khyber International Pakistan (PVT) Ltd
18-Hotel Metropole
Tel: 528182/529896

Kings Travel
Al Ameera Centre,
Near Passport Office
Tel: 5685801/8416

Leader Travels (PVT) Ltd
17-Avenue Centre
Tel: 5684067

Mackinnons Travels
Mack Yolk Bldg
Chundrigar Road
Tel: 2419777/7727

Malik Travels Agency (PVT) Ltd
Shidi Village Rd
Tel: 7511883/7

Maniar Tours and Travels (PVT) Ltd
Hotel Marriott
Tel: 5689413/634

Manjlai Travels (PVT) Ltd
Sarwar Shaheed Rd
Tel: 5687320/22

Matchless Travels (PVT) Ltd
II Chundrigar Rd
Corner Chambers
Tel: 218175/4

Maxim's Tours and Travel (PVT) Ltd
Dr Dawood Pota Road
Tel: 514167/ 5660138

Moon Travels (PVT) Ltd
Dr Dawood Pota Road
Tel: 2312308/ 205671

Mudassir Travel and Tourism (PVT) Ltd
Shahra-e-Liaquat
Tel: 7723281/ 7735000

National Travels
Al Syed House
II Chundrigar Rd
Tel: 2631101/7001

New Arabian Express
Hotel Mehran
Shahra-e-Faisal
Tel: 5660851/8262

Noble Trave Services (PV-I) Ltd
Off: Chundrigar Road
Tel: 216462/1

Nomee Travels
G Allana Road
Tel: 201240/36

Noorani Travels New Challi Branch
M A Jinnah Road
Tel: 2621122/6224

OK Travels (PVT) Ltd
Flut Club
Tel: 7789184/7951

Orient Travels (PVT) Ltd
Saifee House
Dr Ziauddin Alimed Road
Tel: 211348/839

Overseas Travels Services (PVp Ltd
Clifton Road
Tel: 5660910/13

Pactfic Travels I
Abdullah Chamber
II Chundrigar Rd
Tel: 2634496/8

PAK Tourways
Hotel Metropole
Tel: 515809

PAK Travel Agency
Badri Building
II Chundrigar Rd
Tel: 2419678/5543

PAK Turk Enterprise
Strachen Road
Tel: 5685922

Panair (PVT) Ltd
Khayaban-e-Jami
Clifton
Tel: 573926/572032

Pardesi Travels
Merewether Tower
M A Jinnah Road
Tel: 2422441/88

Parwaz Express (PVT) Ltd
Saida Chambers
Shahra-e-Faisal
Tel: 4534381/4

Passage Travels Tours (PVT) Ltd
Sarwar Shaheed Road
Tel: 5685384/6538

Pentagon Aviation Agency
212, Hotel Metropole
Tel: 515177/62

People Express
DHA Commercial Area
Tel: 545871/544666

Pinger Travels (PVT) Ltd
Hotel Faran, Nursery
Shahra-e-Faisal
Tel: 443028/205

Pioneer Travels (PVT) Ltd
24-Taj Mahal Hotel
Tel: 5681224/31

Polani's (PVT) Ltd
Hasrat Mohani Rd
Tel: 2416201/3

Princely Travels (PVT) Ltd
Mereweather Rd
Tel: 511081/84

Princeton Travels (PVT) Ltd
Lakson Square Building
Sarwar Shaheed Rd
Tel: 515784/ 5686444

Progressive Travels
II Chundrigar Rd
Tel: 2635654/55

Qadris' (PVT) Ltd
Court Road
Tel: 524611/ 5684535

Rakaposhi Tours (PVT) Ltd
Phave-V, DHA
1st Commercial Street
Tel: 5864848/4949

Ramada Travels Services (PVT) Ltd
Club Road
Tel: 512414/47

Rehman Travels
Club Road
Tel: 5660153

Rind Travels (PVT) Ltd
Club Road
Tel: 5688237/520477

RIZCO Travels (PVT) Ltd
Kashif Centre
Shahra-e-Faisal
Tel: 529520/379

Roomi Travels (PVT) Ltd
14, Hotel Regency
Dr Dawood Pota Road
Tel: 529561/5

Roze Travels (PVT) Ltd
Ari Tower
Raja G Ali Road
Tel: 515648/543

SAAD Travels (PVT) Ltd
Hotel Mideast

Dr Waood Pota Road
Tel: 522241/529807

Safar Travels
Aiwan-e-Tijarat Road
Tel: 2417588/9741

Safeer Travels (PVT) Ltd
Shefi Court
Mereweather Rd
Tel: 5683483/63

Samina Travels
G. Allana Road
Tel: 205547/201966

Sana Travels (PVT) Ltd
State Life Building # 3
Tel: 5688137/065

Sarbaz Travels
Shidi Village Rd
Tel: 744072/74144

Shahbaz Express (PVT) Ltd
Hotel Mideast
Dr Dawood Pota Road
Tel: 528505

Shaheen International Travel Agency
Napier Road
Tel: 2414958

Shahid Travels
Altaf Hussain Rd
Tel: 2417355/6322

Shakil Air Express (PVT) Ltd
Club Road
Tel: 5864962/461

Shamsi Travel Coporation
2-Hotel Faran
Tel: 438429/448429

Shangrila Travels
1-Clifton Centre,
Tel: 571147/6

Shehzad Travels and Tours
Uni Plaza
II Chundrigar Rd
Tel: 2419754/65

Shirazi Travels (PVT) Ltd
8, Hotel Mehran
Tel: 516107

Sitara Travel Consultants (PVT) Ltd
Abdullah Haroon Road 105
Trade Tower
Tel: 5683887/4024

Skyways Travels (PVT) Ltd
High Court Road
Court View Bldg
Tel: 5681173/4955

Sohni Travels (PVT) Ltd
Sidco Avenue, R A Line
Tel: 5688189

Starlite Aviation (PVT) Ltd
262, Hotel Metropole
Tel: 517331/5

Sunley Travels
G Allana Road
Kharadar
Tel: 200641/201765

Super Travels (PVT) Ltd
Club Road, Ratio Building
Tel: 5682965

System Travels (PVT) Ltd
Shafeeq Plaza
Sarwar Shaheed Rd
Tel: 5686593/154

Tajmahal Travels (PVT) Ltd
Holiday Inn
Crown Plaza
Tel: 514819/524829

The Professionals
Shahra-e-Faisal
Tel: 524661/5

The Travel Connection (PVT) Ltd
Sarwar Shaheed Rd
Tel: 515784/5686444

The Travel Expert's
Sea Breeze Plaza
Shahra-e-Faisal
Tel: 7789182/7

Time Travels (PVT) Ltd
Ibrahim Hakim Building
II Chundrigar Rd
Tel: 212437/2633740

350

Top Travels (PVT) Ltd
Cantt Station
Tel: 522560/513165

Touchwood Travel's (PVT) Ltd
Trade Tower
Abdullah Haroon Road
Tel: 5685330/9496

Trade Wings Travel Agents
8 Marine Galleria, Clifton
Tel: 5872491/89

Tradewind Association (PVT) Ltd
33-Hotel Metropole
Tel: 5661714

Trans-Air Travels (PVT) Ltd
Marriott Hotel
Tel: 5682011/0444

Travel and Tours (PVT) Ltd
Kashif Centre
Shahra-e-Faisal
Tel: 524661/3

Travel Age
Main Clifton Rd
Tel: 534020/572957

Travel Automation (PVT) Ltd
Hotel Metropole
Tel: 511744

Travel Bureau (PVT) Ltd
18 Avari Plaza
Shahra-e-Faisal
Tel: 529288/474

Travel Centre (PVT) Ltd
Aiwan-e-Saddar Rd
Tel: 5689611/5

Travel Club (PVT) Ltd
Hmilton Court
Clifton
Tel: 587360/538164

Travel Conforts (PVT) Ltd
Lakson Square
Sarwar Shaheed Rd
Tel: 5680940/30

Travel Corporation (PVT) Ltd

Central Hotel Building
Mereweather Rd
Tel: 5686519/0424

Travel Express (PVT) Ltd
12-Service Club
Mereweather Rd
Tel: 511127/514678

Travel Inn
Strachen Road
Tel: 516943/5686901

Travel Management Consultants (PVT) Ltd
214 Hotel Metropole
Tel: 516539

Travel Masters
Off Chundrigar Rd
Tel: 219982/215038

Travel Network (PVT) Ltd
Pearl Continental Hotel
Tel: 5688552/583724

Travel Plus
Main Clifton Rd
Tel: 5869135/6

Travel Promoters (PVT) Ltd
Shefi Chambers
Mereweather Rd
Tel: 5688033/1

Travel Tips
G Allana Road
Tel: 205125/4

Travel Unlimited
2-Lakson Square-2
Sarwar Shaheed Road
Tel: 5684173

Travel Walji's (PVT) Ltd
Service Club, Mereweather Rd
Tel: 5660248/5673269
Fax: 5662563

Travel World
14-Hotel Mehran
Shahra-e-Faisal
Tel: 5676696

Travel-N-Travel
Club Road
Tel: 529486/5682672

Traveline (PVT) Ltd
Main Clifton Rd
Tel: 515387/517636

United Air Travels (PVT) Ltd
Central Club Bldg
Abdullah Haroon Road
Tel: 5686262/9664

United Travels (PVT) Ltd
Main Clifton Road
Tel: 5660246/511672

Universal Express (KARACHI) Ltd
Bundukwala Building
II Chundrigar Rd
Tel: 228592/4

Usman Air Travels (PVT) Ltd
Dr Dawood Pota Road
Tel: 518120/108

Veetan's Travel (PVT) Ltd
Kar Administration Society
Tel: 449016/4539479

Visa Travel
Shafiq Plaza
Sarwar Shaheed Rd
Tel: 5684790/96

Vision Travels (PVT) Ltd
Clifton Road
Tel: 514539/516273

Voyages International
Shafi Court
Mereweather Rd
Tel: 5683446

WCS Travels
Amber Pride
Shahra-e-Faisal
Tel: 438887/8

Welcome Travels and Tour Operators Business Record Road
Tel: 418082/420133

Western Travel Ltd
Court Road
Tel: 5683606

Winds Travels (PVT) Ltd
Hockey Club of Pakistan
Tel: 516359/69

Wonder Travel
II Chundrigar Rd
Tel: 2633047/1225

World Express (PVT) Ltd
Strachen Road
Tel: 2633047/1225

World Express (PVT) Ltd
Strachen Road
Tel: 5689471

World Vision (PVT) Ltd
Club Road
Tel: 5660145/6

World Ways Travel (PVT) Ltd
Club Road
Tel: 2633425/20

Worldlink Aviation (PVT) Ltd
34, Hotel Metropole
Tel: 513253/528241

ZEB Travels
Hasrat Mohani Rd
Tel: 2411204/7054

Lahore

A A International Travels
Mcleod Road
Tel: 7231486/7245788

Aamar International
1-Mozang Road
Tel: 7351424

Adventure N Culture
48, Shamshad Market
Tel: 5835646/7579191

Air Master (PVT) Limited
Egerton Road
5-Transport Hse
Tel: 6306209

Air Travel Concept (PVT) Ltd
5-Davis Road
Tel: 6303790/6118

Alsafa Travels
5-Davis Road
Tel: 6363937

American
Express Int'l
Travel Services
Shahra-e-Qaid-e-
Azam
Tel: 6303082/7

American
Express Travel
Service
Shahra-e-Qaid-e-
Azam
Tel: 6279230/38

Arab Int' Air
Travels (PVT) Ltd
7-Egerton Road
Tel: 6304955

Ashiana Travels
33- Queens Road
Tel: 7582524

Atlas Travels
Gulberg, Raja
Centre
Tel: 5757257/157

Benison Travel
Link Wahdat Rd
Tel: 5830183

Black Rose
Travel Ltd
8 Super Market
Tel: 410257

Bluesky
Travels Ltd
WAPDA House
Tel: 6303145

Brite Ways Travel
Shadman Main
Market
Tel: 411946

Capitol Travels
(PVT) Ltd
WAPDA House
Tel: 7356795

Citilink Travels
(PVT) Ltd
Davis Road
Tel: 6365212

Continental
Travels
Davis Road
Tel: 6364135

COX & Kings
(Agents) (PVT)
Ltd Hotel
Ambassador
Tel: 879295

Crescent Services
10, Abbot Road
Tel: 6305305

Domestic and
Overseas Travels
(PVT) Ltd
Main Boulevard
Tel: 879652/877497

East west Travels
32, Davis Road
Tel: 6364473

Eram
International
New Garden Town
Tel: 856106/
5837729

Eurasia Travels
110 Bank
Square Market
Model Town
Tel: 856106/116

Executive Ways
(PVT) Ltd
5- Davis Road
Tel: 5869345/
6363959

Faizan
International
Travels
72, Feroze Pur Rd
Tel: 7580957/
7572843

Falcon Air-
Service Ltd
3-Transport
House
Egerton Road
Tel: 6304227

Flighto Travel
Services (PVT) Ltd
Shahra-e-Qaid-e-
Azam
Tel: 325481/322617

Flights Inn
Travels
Centre Point
Main Boulevard
Tel: 5754507/
5762853

Fly Ways Travel
State Life
Building
Davis Road
Tel: 6303740

French Express
Hafeez Centre
Gulberg III
Tel: 857386/
5762831

G S A
Paramount
Aviation Ltd
Ambassador Hotel
Tel: 6302662/61

Global Express
(PVT) Ltd
Queens Road
Tel: 6302992/6463

Golden Falcon
Travel Services
(PVT) Ltd
Abbott Road
Tel: 6303566/449

Gymkhana Tours
Canal Bridge
Tel: 872481/874034

High Quality
Concept Travels
(PVT) Ltd
Hafeez Centre
Main Boulevard
Tel: 874218/19

Highland Travels
(PAK) (PVT) Ltd
YMCA Building
Shahra-e-Quaid-e-
Azam
Tel: 324178/735640

Holiday Travels
(PVT) Ltd
5-Davis Road
Tel: 6305707

International
Travel Services
(PVT) Ltd
WAPDA House
Tel: 6301814/16

Jahangir Travels
26-Empress Road
Tel: 6363250/40

Javed Aviation
Services (PVT) Ltd
Hafeez Centre
Gulberg III
Tel: 879600/
875252

Karvan Travels
(PVT) Ltd
Mozang Road
Tel: 7358670/3111

Kashif Travel
Shahra-e-Qaid-e-
Azam
Tel: 6361202/5711

Khamisani
Services (PVT) Ltd
The Mall
Tel: 6360346

Khyber
International
5-Davis Road
Tel: 6363574

Links
International
28-Empress Road
Tel: 6375841

Madni Travels
(PVT) Ltd
Shahra-e-Qaid-e-
Azam
Tel: 312512

Makdonald
Travel Agency
(PVT) Ltd
Gardee Trust Bldg
Tel: 323191

Mall View
Travels and Money
Exchanger
Naqi Arcade
Shahra-e-Qaid-e-
Azam
Tel: 6361203

Mehtab Travels
and Overseas Pro-
moters
91-Beadon Road
Tel: 6365500/400

Main Travel and
Trade (PVT) Ltd
42, Commercial
Building
Tel: 7232134/4134

Mid-East Tours
Shahra-e-Qaid-e-
Azam
Tel: 6303589/2275

Minhaaj Travel
Chuburji Centre
Tel: 7583200

Muhammadi
Travel Tours and
Cargo (PVT) Ltd
Tufail Road
Tel: 6669159

Multinational
Travels (PVT) Ltd
64-WAPDA House
Tel: 213079

Nafees Travels
(PVT) Ltd
29-Empress Road
Tel: 7226678

New Classic
Travels
7-Egerton Road
Tel: 6366155

New Travel
Team
7-E, Egerton Rd
Tel: 6305354

Nice Journey
Travels
38, Davis Road
Tel: 6368668/6457

OK Travels
79-Ferozepur Rd
Tel: 411092/
7587412

Olympic Air
Travel
The Mall
Tel: 6366971

Paragon Travels
5-Davis Road
Tel: 6304016

Prime Travel
Services (PVT) Ltd
Ambassador
Centre,
Davis Road
Tel: 6310175

Prince.Travel
Services (PVT) Ltd
5-Davis Road
Tel: 6303165/
6369420

Proficient Travel
Agencies
7-Egerton Road
Tel: 6305283

Quality Travel
Services (PVT) Ltd
5-Davis Road
Tel: 6362965/9205

Rahber Travels
Falettis Hotel
Egerton Road
Tel: 6302680/6180

Rainbow Travels
(PVT) Ltd
Tel: 6305900/4100

Raja Travels
5-Davis Road
Tel: 6369620/
6303443

Rawat
International
Queens Road
Tel: 6310923/24

Roze Travels
(PVT) Ltd
5-Davis Road
Tel: 6367067/9630

SAAD International Air Services (PVT) Ltd
Hafeez Centre Gulberg III
Tel: 874743/5762867

SAAD Travels
Hafeez Centre Gulberg III
Tel: 875707/874773

Scandia (PVT) Ltd
Transport House Egerton Road
Tel: 212315

Shalimar Tours and Travels (PVT) Ltd
29/5 Empress Rd
Tel: 6305717

Shanza Travel (PVT) Ltd
Race Course Rd
Tel: 6367437

Shimla Travels (PVT) Ltd
5-Davis Road
Tel: 6304850/796

Shozy Travels
Ferozepur Road
Tel: 7587434/9302

Skippy Travels (PVT) Ltd
9-A, Davis Road
Tel: 6303886

Sky King Travels
Al Afalah Bldg
Tel: 602710

Sky Star International,
9-Nicholson Rd
Tel: 6364733

Sky Star Travels
3-Syed Mauj Darya Road
Tel: 312987/7238178

Skyline Lahore (PVT) Ltd
WAPDA House
Tel: 6304261/62

Space Travels
25, Empress Rd
Tel: 7357269

Star Link Travel
28-Empress Rd
Tel: 6310724/26

TATA Travel's and Tours Hafeez Centre Gulberg III
Tel: 870763

The World Travel Services (PVT) Ltd
201, Asharfia Plaza Shahra-e-Qaid-e-Azam
Tel: 312141

Tradewind Associates (PVT) Ltd
7/E, Egerton Road
Tel: 6305229

Trans Global International (PVT) Ltd
WAPDA House
Tel: 6302437

Travel Crown
26, Express Road
Tel: 6303895/6369865

Travel Easy (PVT) Ltd
26, Egerton Road
Tel: 6304177

Travel Escort
35 Queens Road
Tel: 7587672

Travel Fast (PVT) Ltd
Sherpao Road Abid Majeed Rd
Tel: 37572/372

Travel Fine
7-E, Egerton Rd
Tel: 6304956

Travel Home
Egerton Road
Tel: 6303660/2771

Travel Inn
Ferozepur Road
Tel: 417485

Travel Kings (PVT) Ltd
Hotel Ambassador, Davis Road,
Tel: 6362381

Travel More (PVT) Ltd
Egerton Road Shama Plaza
Tel: 7580555

Travels Professional (PVT) Ltd
Queens Centre
Tel: 6360460

Travels Safe
Wahid Chamber
Tel: 879256

Travel Services Ltd
29-Faletti's Hotel
Tel: 6301265

Travel Track
5-Davis Road
Tel: 6305879

Travel Walji's (PVT) Ltd
23, Empress Rd Ali Complex
Tel: 6316031/45523
Fax: 6366149

Travel Window
Hafeez Centre Gulberg III
Tel: 873992

Travel Wings
7-Egerton Road
Tel: 6306933

Travel Easy Way
7-E, Egerton Rd
Tel: 6304177

Universal Travels
72, Ferozpure Rd
Tel: 7560324/7588192

VIP Travels and Tours
26-Empress Road
Tel: 6369066

Waleed Air Travels
Ravi Road
Tel: 201652

White Airways
Chouburji Centre Multan Road
Tel: 7419886

Wide Links
Hillview Acrade, Davis Road
Tel: 6369209

Zaki Travels
Nila Gumbad
Tel: 321485/7233410

Zisco Travels (PVT) Ltd
22, Nicholson Rd
Tel: 6375303/6365381

Mingora
Khyber Express (PVT) Ltd

Opp: Pameer Hotel
G T Road
Tel: 4800

MATTA International Travel Agency
Mata Chowk
Tel: 790260

Multan

Air Links (PVT) Limited
Chowk Ketchary
Tel: 43808

Air Teemer Travel Agent
LMQ Road
Tel: 40471/42070

Emas Air Services
Ketchery Road
Tel: 74359

Ghaffar Travels
1629-A, Shoping Centre
Tel: 33543/20270

Haris Travel
LMQ Road
Tel: 520036

JET Travels (PVT) Ltd
LMQ Road
Tel: 32965

Karim Travellers
46, Khan Plaza
Tel: 571135

Khan Travel Ltd
Tareen Road
Tel: 43678

Kings Air Travels
LQM Road
Tel: 51702

Multan Travels (PVT) Ltd
LMQ Road
Tel: 43192

Royal Air Travels (PVT)
LMQ Road
Tel: 72113

Safeer Travels
Kutchery Road
Tel: 512730

Shaheen Travellers (PVT) Limited
80, Abdali Road
Tel: 33004

Skyland Travels
Chowk Kutchery
Tel: 33165/34001

Skylinks Travels
Chowk Kutchery
Tel: 33165/41372

Sohail Travel Ltd
Shopping Centre #3
Tel: 33013/510343

Somi Travels (PVT) Ltd
UBL Kutchery Rd
Tel: 511383

Southern Travel (PVT) Ltd
1717-A, Kutchery Road
Tel: 40002

Star International Travels (PVT) Ltd
LMQ Road
Tel: 74036/510487

Supreme Travels (PVT) Ltd
Kutchery Road
Tel: 512036

United Travels
Khanewal Road
Tel: 524855

Peshawar
Al-Khalil Travels
Khyber Bazar
Tel: 212565

Bangash Air Services
Ramdas Road
Tel: 212458

Gandhara Travel and Tours (PVT) Ltd Saddar Road
Tel: 273832

Grand Air Net Work
Auqaf Plaza Dabgari Garden
Tel: 211055

Jani Travels
Khyber Bazar
Tel: 253993

Khyber Express (PVT) Ltd
Khyber Bazar
Tel: 252703/5

Khyber Turizam
(PVT) Ltd
5, Hazrat Shah
Plaza
Tel: 217762/219582

MIK Movers
(PVT) Ltd
Habib Medical
Complex
Tel: 220146/7

New Arabian
Express
Okaf Plaza
Tel: 220437

Orakzai Travels
Khyber Bazar
Tel: 210985

Pakistan Express
(PVT) Ltd
Fakhr-e-Alam Rd
Tel: 274631

Palmasha Travel
Agency
Shangreela Hotel
Tel: 210852

Prince
International
Travels
Peshawar
Medical Centre
Tel: 250346

Royal
International
(PVT) Ltd
Arbab Chowk
Tel: 44981/44569

Roze Travels
(PVT) Ltd
Jinnah Market
Tel: 212205

SS Travel
International and
Tour Operators
Saddar Road
Tel: 279260/275649

Sehrai Travel and
Tours Saddar Road
Tel: 272085

Shirket-e-
Maqbool (PVT) Ltd
Khyber Bazar
Tel: 212132

Southern Travels
(PVT) Ltd
Khyber Bazar
Tel: 210861

Swing Air (PVT)
Limited
Jamrud Road
Tel: 840804

Town
International
(PVT) Ltd
Jamrud Road
Tel: 41686

Trade Masters
7- Betani Arcade
Tel: 272093

Travel Walji's
(PVT) Ltd
University Road
Tel: 44225

Traveloque
(PVT) Ltd
Jamrud Road
Tel: 843262/3

United Travels
(PVT) Ltd
Saddar Road
Tel: 843262/3

United Travels
(PVT) Ltd
Saddar Road
Tel: 277101/4

Quetta
Al-Falah Travels
Circular Road
Tel: 822222

Balochistan
Tours N Travels
Shahra-e-Liaquat
Tel: 835955

Chiltan Travels
(PVT) Ltd
Tel: 448169

Quetta Travel
(PVT) Ltd
Jinnah Road
Tel: 65351

Saleem Tours and
Travels Fatima
Jinnah Road

Sky Travels
New Shabnam
Market
Tel: 820557

Speedy Travels
(PVT) Ltd
Adalat Road
Tel: 63705/65405

Rahim Yar Khan
Cholistan
Travels Town Hall
Tel: 73049/72775

Dubai Travels
Shahi Road
Tel: 76011

Murshad
International Travel
Shahi Road
Tel: 75381

Rahim Yar Khan
Travels
Shahi Road
Tel: 78556

Rohi
International
Travels
Shahi Road
Tel: 71647

Saba Travels
8-Iqbal Complex
Tel: 74248

Uni Pak Travels
Shahi Road
Tel: 78869

Rawalpindi

Aerolite Travel
Services
Jinnah Business
Centre
Tel: 418615/4

Air Fields
Travels
Bank Road
Tel: 562181

Al-Hayat Travels
The Mall Road
Tel: 564305

Al-Imran Travels
Bashir Plaza
Tel: 567661

Al-Namrah
Travels
Committee
Chowk
Tel: 501738

Al-Siddique
Corporation
(PVT) Ltd
Murree Road
Tel: 71012/18

Al-Watan Travels
Bashir Plaza
Tel: 583880

Alamgeer
Travels
Corporation
Al Abbas Market
Tel: 564973

Alvi Travels
Mobeen Plaza
Tel: 586741/583258

American
Express Travel
Related Services
Rahim Plaza
Tel: 566001

Belair Travels
31-2, The Mall
Tel: 512095/6

Bestways
6-Mall Plaza
Tel: 581679

Bluesky Travels
Limited
Al Abbas Market
Tel: 568491

Chughtai Tours
Shalimar Plazar
Tel: 581476/563710

Concordia Tours
and Trekking
Services PLC
Committee Chowk
Tel: 503495

Gill Travel Services
Murree Road
Tel: 840874

Golden Travels
Shalimar Plaza
Tel: 563677/562478

Green Field
Travels (PVT) Ltd
Pindi Club Building
Tel: 567361

Hameed Express
and Travel
Agents Lords
Hotel Building
Tel: 414666/428323

Highland Travels
(PAK) (PVT) Ltd
Haider Road
Tel: 563816

Himalaya Treks
and Tours
Murree Rad
Tel: 515371

Hunza Travel
Service
Rawalpindi
Cantt.
Tel: 564782

Khyber Express
(PVT) Ltd
Friend Hospital
Tel: 580665

Kings Way
International
Cantt. Plaza
Tel: 562277

Leader Travels
(PVT) Ltd
Pindi Club
Building
Tel: 563419

Matchless
Travels (PVT) Ltd
Pearl Continental
Hotel
Tel: 566011

Rohtas Travels
(PVT) Ltd
Canning Road
Tel: 563224/566434

Saddaran Travels
The Mall
Tel: 564151

Scan Air
International
(PVT) Ltd
8-Rahim Plaza
Tel: 581264/567735

Shakil Express
(PVT) Ltd
Haider Road
Tel: 580153

Shameen Express
Pindi Club
Building
Tel: 564480/168

Shujah
International
Bank Road
Tel: 566536

Sitara Travel
Consultants
(PVT) Ltd
Khadim Hussain
Road
Tel: 564750/566272

Sky Touch
Travels
Kashmir Road
Tel: 567599/562285

Southern Travels
(PVT) Ltd
The Mall
Tel: 510315

Style Travels
Bank Road
Tel: 584951

Super Travel
Agency
Murree Road
Tel: 844340

Tradewind
Associates (PVT)
Limited
Rawalpindi
Club Plaza
Tel: 568297/143

Travel Centre
International
Haider Road
Tel: 566165/564163

Travel House
(PVT) Ltd
Shalimar Plaza
Tel: 563332/566693

Travel Wings
(PVT) Ltd
Haider Road
Tel: 586572/3

Travel Masters
Mall Road
Tel: 563957

Travel Place
Jang Building
Tel: 70777/501101

Tourism
Development
Corporation of
Punjab Ltd
Mall Plaza,
Saddar
Tel: 565824

United Travels
(PVT) Ltd
Mobeen Plaza
Tel: 582423/580273

Universal Travel
Ciros Cinema
Building
Tel: 580445

Viking Travels
PAK Ltd
Hotel
Intercontinental
Tel: 566230

Waheed
International
Bank Road,
Saddar
Tel: 566482

World Air
Travels
Bashir Plaza
OPP: GTS
Tel: 564794/1

Sahiwal
Abid Travel
Railway Road
Tel: 2526

Royal Express
(PVT) Ltd
Sialkot
Azam Travels
Khadim Ali Rd
Tel: 582514

Bismillah Air
Travels
New Sheraz Plaza
Tel: 587709

Crossair Travels
Kutchery Road
Tel: 592374

Golden Falcon
Travel Services
(PVT) Ltd
Kutchery Road
Tel: 588030

International
Travel Services
(PVT) Ltd
Mujahid Road
Tel: 587803

National Travels
Kutchery Road
Tel: 85659

Raheel Express
Travel Services
Kutchery Road
Tel: 87248

SS Travels
Paris Road
Tel: 87381

Seven Stars
Travels
Sheraz Plaza
Tel: 586832

Skylark Ltd
Kutchery Road
Tel: 586657

Sawat
PAK Travel
Bazar Matta
Tel: 790406

355

356

All pictures taken by **Mohamed Amin** and **Duncan Willetts**
except the following:
Quaiser Khan: Pages: 21, 119, 209

Bibliography

Ali, Salim *The Book of Indian Birds*, Natural History Society, Mumbai, 1979.

Allen, Charles *Lives of the Indian Princes*, Century, London, 1984.

Amin, Willetts, Hancock, *Journey Through Pakistan* Camerapix 1982.

Amin, Willetts, Farrow, *Pakistan from Mountains to the Sea*, Camerapix 1994.

Amin, Willetts, Tetley, *The Roof of the World*, Camerapix 1989.

Amin, Quraishy, Willetts, Tetley, *Defender of Pakistan*, Camerapix 1998.

Amin, Willetts, Farrow, *Lahore*, Camerapix 1988.

Amin, Willetts, Tetley, *Karachi*, Camerapix 1986.

Amin, Willetts, Hancock, *The Beauty of Pakistan*, Camerapix 1983.

Anand, M R *The Hindu View of Art*, London, 1933.

Archer, W G *Indian Miniatures*, Victoria and Albert Museum, London, 1960.

Basham, A L *The Wonder That Was India*, Sidgwick and Jackson, London, 1954.

Chaudhari, N C *Hinduism, Chatto and Windus*, London, 1979.

Commaraswamy *The Dance of Siva*, Ananda Kentish reprint, New York/Dover, 1985.

Craven, Roy C *Indian Art: A Short History*, Thames and Hudson, London, 1976.

Davies, Philip *The Splendours of the Raj*, John Murray, London, 1984.

Monuments of India, Vol II: (Islamic, Rajput and European), Viking, London, 1989

Durrans, Brian *India — Post into Present*, BMP, London, 1982.

Gandhi, MK *My Experiments with Truth*, Penguin India reprint, New Delhi, 1982.

Grewal, Bikram *Birds of India*, The Guidebook Company, Hong Kong, 1993.

Harle, J C *The Art and Architecture of the Indian Subcontinent*, Penguin India reprint, New Delhi, 1986.

Jayakar, Pupul *The Earth Mother: An Introduction to the Ritual Art of Rural India*, Penguin India, New Delhi, 1981.

Lanoy, Richard *Speaking Tree*, Oxford University Press, New York, 1971.

Michell, George *Monuments of India, Vol 1: "Buddhist, Jain, Hindu"*, Viking, London 1989.

Mookerjee, Ajit *Arts of India*, Oxford University Press, London, 1966.

Nehru, Jawaharlal *The Discovery of India*, Oxford University Press, New Delhi, 1916.

O'Flaherty, W *Hindu Myths*, Penguin India, New Delhi 1975.

Prater, S H *The Book of Indian Animals*, Natural History Society, Mumbai, 1948.

Punja, Shobita *Museums of India*, The Guidebook Company, Hong Kong, 1990.

Monuments of India, The Guidebook Company, Hong Kong, 1994.

Randhava, M S *Indian Painting*, Vakils, Mumbai 1968.

Spear, Percival *A History of India Vol. 11*, Penguin India reprint, New Delhi, 1990.

Thapar, Romila *A History of India Vol. I*, Penguin India reprint, New Delhi, 1990.

Woodcock, Martin *Guide to the Birds of the Indian Sub-continent*, Collins, London, 1980.

Zimmer, H *Myths and Symbols in Indian Art and Civilization*, Boston, 1962.

The Art of Indian Asia, Princeton, 1955.